Waging **War**
with **Gold**

Waging War with Gold

National Security and the Finance Domain Across the Ages

Charles A. Dainoff,
Robert M. Farley, and
Geoffrey F. Williams

LYNNE
RIENNER
PUBLISHERS

BOULDER
BARNSLEY

Paperback edition published in the United States of America in 2025 by
Lynne Rienner Publishers, Inc.
1800 30th Street, Suite 314, Boulder, Colorado 80301
www.rienner.com

and in the United Kingdom in 2025 by
Lynne Rienner Publishers, Inc.
47 Church Street, Barnsley, South Yorkshire S70 2AS
www.scriptps.co.uk/rienner

© 2023 by Lynne Rienner Publishers, Inc. All rights reserved

ISBN: 979-8-89616-334-3 (pb: alk. paper)

Library of Congress Cataloging-in-Publication Data
A Cataloging-in-Publication record for the hardcover edition of
this book is available from the Library of Congress.

British Cataloguing in Publication Data
A Cataloguing in Publication record for the hardcover edition of
this book is available from the British Library.

Printed and bound in the United States of America

∞ The paper used in this publication meets the requirements
of the American National Standard for Permanence of
Paper for Printed Library Materials Z39.48-1992.

5 4 3 2 1

Contents

1	The Financial Battlespace	1
2	What Is the Finance Domain?	19
3	Financial Strategies in Antiquity	39
4	Medieval Money, Markets, and Mayhem	57
5	The Mercantilist Revolution	79
6	Pax Britannica and the Gold Standard	101
7	From the Great War to World War II	121
8	Bretton Woods and the American Century	143
9	The Digital Revolution in Financial Affairs	163
10	The Next Fifty Years of Financial Competition	185

Bibliography   201
Index   225
About the Book   249

1

The Financial Battlespace

The Wars now adays seem rather to be waged with Gold than with Iron, and unless we Pay well, we shall never be able to Punish well; and perhaps a due Disposition and Faculty to Punish and Reward, may be none of the least of our Defects; and without a due Administration of these, and a right Use of Extraordinary Persons and Means, we can never in Reason expect to do anything Great.
—John Whitlock, *Some Observations upon the Bank of England*, 1695

In 1655, King Karl X Gustav of Sweden led an invasion of the western section of Poland-Lithuania in an attempt to expand his territory. This campaign, known as the "Swedish Deluge" for its swiftness, opened up a new theater of operations in what would later be called the Second Northern War. The campaign marked the resumption of the foreign wars of the Swedish Empire following the end of Sweden's participation in the Thirty Years War in 1648. The Second Northern War would last only from 1655 to 1660, with the combatants mostly agreeing to return to the status quo ante at the end. The war settled nothing and arguably set the stage for conflicts that would engulf Europe for the rest of the century. These wars would proceed without Karl X Gustav, who died of pneumonia on February 8, 1660.[1]

The wars of the seventeenth century were bloody and costly. The expansion and professionalization of Sweden's armed forces in the early 1600s demanded additional funding.[2] Sweden had begun to systematize its tax collection apparatus in 1520, but by the mid–seventeenth century the crown was frequently forced by shortfalls to resort to more extreme fundraising measures such as selling land to the nobility or withholding payment from royal servants.[3] During the Thirty Years War the crown minted excess coins to pay its expenses, which led to devaluation of the Swedish currency in 1647. As Karl X Gustav prepared his country for another war in

1656, he realized Sweden needed more than just soldiers and weapons—what it needed most of all was a bank.[4]

On November 30, 1656, after several entreaties by the Latvian-born commissioner of the Swedish Board of Trade, Johan Palmstruch, Karl X Gustav while in the field personally leading the deluge, signed two charters creating the innovative Stockholms Banco that copied from public banks in European city-states.[5] That the launch of what would become the first modern central bank occurred on the frozen mud of an East Prussian battlefield is entirely appropriate. The Banco would loan money to the crown, and these loans would be taken from deposits of account holders rather than just from the pockets of wealthy nobles. The money from these loans could then be used by Karl X Gustav (and his successors) to finance his army to aid in Sweden's expansion.

The eleven-year path from Stockholms Banco to the Sveriges Riksbank, the world's first central bank, was short but rocky. But the relationship between the wars of seventeenth-century Europe and the development of central banking, one of the core institutions of modern finance, is clear. Sveriges Riksbank was followed twenty-six years later by the Bank of England, and during the 1700s and 1800s a tide of central banks swept across Europe. The link between central banking and war finance is additionally illustrated in the negative by the many countries that were late to create a lasting central bank, in particular the United States. Central banks are only one tool for managing and manipulating the strategic issues involved in financial operations for warmaking, what we term the *finance domain*, but they are among the most important of the technologies that states have developed to fight wars of finance. This book tracks how states have developed technologies such as central banks not simply to manage their own financial affairs, but also to influence the finances of their allies and competitors as they aggressively compete in the international system.

Finance as a Domain

Across many regions and time periods, and nearly universally for the past 200 years, it has been an existential concern for states to maintain the day-to-day ability to purchase resources rapidly and in large quantities by the issuance of highly liquid and generally accepted financial assets such as coins, notes, or bonds. The strategic vulnerability that this presents is best understood using the "domain" framework.

Military analysts increasingly think in terms of domains as distinct arenas of state competition, and consequently as an environment in which it becomes possible to measure relative state power. The most commonly cited domains include maritime, air, and land, although increasingly analysts have also begun to evaluate relative state power within the space and cyber domains. Within these domains are areas of contestation in which no state can exert legal authority, and whose existence creates systemwide problems; these spaces are generally known as "commons." Competition within and across these domains can change significantly as a result of organizational and technological advancements, even to the point of significantly changing the balance of power or even transforming the nature of hegemony itself in the international system; these advancements are known as "revolutions." In this book, we answer the question of how states use financial tools to coerce others and maximize their own security by first demonstrating that finance is a domain worthy of strategic study on its own, and that this domain undergoes revolutions in financial affairs (RFAs) in the same way that other domains undergo revolutions in military affairs (RMAs). We then review how international financial flows represent a commons, analogous to the way in which naval specialists discuss oceans and waterways. Next, we guide readers through a brief history of the development of financial systems by individual states throughout the world, in the process defining several RFAs that changed the balance of power in the international system, as well as illustrating how national security concerns have routinely guided state financial development, even as these RFAs pushed states toward new strategies and capabilities.

If we take as a given that the international system has always been anarchic and that states compete with each other to maximize either security or power, and that finance is a domain of this contestation, then we must determine how states use this domain to compete with each other. That finance is a key component of war, strategy, and international competition is not a novel or controversial claim, and dates back to the premodern or "classical" eras. For example, Herodotus made clear in *The Histories* in 430 BCE that Persian systems of finance enabled the expansion of their empire across the Levant and into the Eastern Mediterranean. Later, in *The Peloponnesian War*, Thucydides detailed the impact of finance on the conduct of the war, reporting the concerns of Spartan kings regarding the inadequacy of their monetary system in the early fourth century BCE. Ancient Greek and Roman commentators from Xenophon to Cicero discussed the demands of war on financial policy, with the latter famously declaring "the sinews of war, infinite money" in his "Fifth Philippic" against Antony in 43 BCE.[6] Further east, monetary considerations bedeviled policymakers in the Spring and Autumn Period and Warring States Period in China. Neither is this phenomenon limited to the ancient world; the relationship between the availability of money and state power has likewise preoccupied rulers from medieval to early modern Europe.[7]

Despite the fulsome and well-documented history of the relationship between money and state power, it is our contention that modern strategic analysts do not give it sufficient consideration, particularly the vulnerabilities it creates in the exigent circumstances of war. These analysts will universally agree on the importance of economics and finance, having gone so far recently as to develop the concepts of "economic" and "financial statecraft," yet the strategic community has done little to contemplate the independent effect of financial arrangements on strategic competition when discussing warfighting or diplomacy.[8] This absence is problematic not just because ignoring the finance domain gives analysts an incomplete picture of state capacities, but also because of the topic's complexity. Indeed, the use of money for international contestation involves more than the ability to transform basic economic factors into military power, to change gold into lead in a reverse alchemy that results in an improved ability to compete. For example: the role of the British navy in the nineteenth century and the American navy in the twenty-first century are understood to be critical to the warmaking ability of London and Washington, respectively. But the similar importance of the pound and the dollar are at best relatively underexamined, and arguably ignored, in many discussions of national security. Our goal in writing this book is to provide a way to more easily understand the structure of the finance domain, how international competition in this domain has affected state power and the relationships of states to one another, the impact that RFAs have had on the mechanisms of contestation, how this contestation currently works, and how it might work in the future.

Understanding the Financial Battlespace

Just as states have armies, navies, and air forces as tools of defense statecraft, they also have groups of professionals dedicated to protecting state interests in the finance domain: "gold forces," if you will. In the United States, this force is small relative to the other armed services, and its members are distributed in offices across the Department of the Treasury, the Department of Justice, and the Federal Reserve. The US gold force has been operating in some sense since 1789 and is paralleled by hundreds of similar institutions across the globe in central banks, state treasuries, and exchequers. Understanding what a gold force is and what it does is critical for understanding national security and developing a sound grand strategy.

This understanding is also critical because it is important to appreciate the breadth of the gold force's power and responsibilities. To improve this understanding, this book focuses on the state's ability to create and transmit liquid assets rapidly as a way to avoid defeat or disabling crises while in conflict with others. Other researchers have done great work in analyzing the importance of economic size broadly, fiscal and tax structure as a regular source of resources, and the use by developed states of currency as a source of general pressure and coercion. Nevertheless, it is important to draw explicit links—historically, in the present day, and looking forward—between state capacity, finance, and international competition. We believe these links have not yet been explicated in any significant way, and that the stability of the international system depends in part on state-level decision-makers understanding them.

Domain

The term *domain* has become an integral part of defense analytical thinking in the United States in the twenty-first century. Eric Heftye traces the term to the "Joint Vision 2020," a planning document published by the US Department of Defense (DOD) in June 2000 and intended to lay out a vision of US military dominance in 2020.[9] Joint Vision 2020 identifies five domains: "US forces are able to conduct prompt, sustained, and synchronized operations . . . with access to and freedom to operate in all domains—space, sea, land, air, and information."[10] *Domain* replaced the term *dimension,* which the DOD had used to characterize spheres of activity such as land, sea, and air since its founding in the late 1940s. As Heftye notes, use of the term *domain* is bound up in conceptions of US military hegemony, as the origins of the word lie in concepts of land ownership and sovereignty. Heftye gives the term some shape and form by borrowing an explanation from another doctrinal publication, the 2005 edition of the US Joint Chiefs of Staff report "Capstone Concept for Joint Operations," which defines a *domain* as "any potential operating 'space' through which the target system can be influenced—not only the domains of land, sea, air, and space, but also the virtual (information and cyber) and human (cognitive, moral, and social) domains."[11] Given this working definition, the usefulness of characterizing international finance as a domain becomes easier to grasp.

Domains require a level of strategic interaction, in that the actions of the players (usually states in this discussion) affect and anticipate those of other players. Evaluations of international power rely on comparisons across a range of military, political, and economic metrics. Especially with regard to military power, these metrics often focus on comparisons within particular domains: China's military buildup has threatened US dominance in the air and naval domains in the Western Pacific, for example.[12] While these comparisons generally involve complex calculations of military capability—for example, the Correlates of War project's Composite Index of National Capability (CINC) score[13]—they can include brute force counting of warships, assessments of the relative qualities of fighter aircraft, and analysis of the characteristics of nuclear missile silos.

Like the cyber domain mentioned above, the finance domain is a human creation; it does not exist except within a specific set of social circumstances.[14]

Unlike cyber, space, or even air, however, finance is not a *new* domain. States have acted in the finance domain for as long as substantial trade financed with liquid assets has existed, although the complexity of operations within this domain has varied over time. The effectiveness of certain kinds of operations within the finance domain depends on the overall structure of the domain and the position of the state within that domain. Even relatively weak states by conventional definitions can undertake disruptive actions—such as counterfeiting foreign currencies—and "punch above their weight" in the international system.[15] One of the most successful (if difficult to duplicate) examples is the January 1968 currency conversion implemented by the federal government of Nigeria, which effectively obliterated the liquid assets of the rebelling Biafran government.[16] In fact, certain states like Switzerland that are weak in other domains have continued to exist throughout history relying solely on their ability to manipulate the finance domain to their advantage by creating goods and services so valuable to elites in strong states that the preservation of these goods and services overrides the impulse to conquest.[17]

It is important at this point to clarify the distinction between finance as a domain and closely related areas such as economic warfare (via blockades or sanctions, for example) and materials procurement. For the purposes of this book, we define the *finance domain* as concerning in particular the managing of flows and stocks of liquid assets like money and negotiable debt in a financial commons where other states are active. Economic statecraft can include financial statecraft, but also involves the mobilizations of resources for the purposes of national security. States can mobilize resources through nonfinancial means and can prevent the mobilization of enemy resources through violence or intimidation. For example, Sparta used slave labor to mobilize agricultural and mining resources during the Peloponnesian War and used these resources to support an army consisting largely of enthusiastic citizen volunteers. The Combined Bomber Offensive of World War II sought to destroy German industrial capacity as a means of economic warfare, but did not directly damage the German system of finance.[18] Similarly, the British Royal Navy's blockade of Germany during World War I sought to deprive the German state of the basic raw materials necessary to wage war.[19] Steps short of war, such as sanctions designed to cause economic harm or to prevent the import of technologies of warfare, also fall under the category of economic statecraft.

However, while all of these examples illustrate the relationship between economics and warfare, none of them directly involve the finance domain. By contrast, the Continental System of Napoleon involved blockades and hence economic warfare, but also utilized the finance domain to gain a strategic advantage.[20] Napoleon's strategy used the Continental System to force gold outflows from Britain, which he believed would weaken the British economy.[21] The distinction here is between controlling an opponent's use of liquid assets, the sinews of war, and controlling the flow of physical resources needed for the opponent to fight and survive. Another example would be the binding by several European states of the Ottoman Empire with debt in the nineteenth century sharply limiting Constantinople's domestic and international policy latitude.[22] More recently, the United States has taken steps to limit Iran's access to international financial markets to coerce Iran into abandoning its missile and nuclear programs.[23]

Finance, Mobilization, and the State

While the efficient mobilization of financial resources is always important to warmaking entities, this mobilization becomes a domain of strategy only when there is the potential for interaction in international markets.[24] For finance to be a domain, a warmaking state needs to be dependent on financial markets in which other states are also active. Two state characteristics indicate if this is the case: first, the state's economy is substantially monetized, meaning that money and other highly liquid assets are used broadly; and, second, the state's economy is "outward facing," meaning it involves substantial international trade. These two characteristics are interrelated: without substantial international trade, there is little use for significant liquidity; and without significant liquidity, it is difficult to coordinate substantial international trade. The current complexity and interconnectedness of the global economy demands that nearly every state develop a strategy and a set of tools for competing in the finance domain, but this condition was not nearly the necessity that it is today. Although cases of true autarkic states are rare, it was possible for premodern states to survive without engaging in significant international trade. These states that did not participate in international markets, by definition, did not compete in the finance domain.

States that do compete in the finance domain to ensure their survival or establish dominance are behaving in the same way that, for example, states that build navies are competing to establish the security of their own ports or shorelines or to establish dominance in the naval commons. We further refine the concept by introducing the idea that the finance domain has undergone several RFAs throughout premodern and modern history. Before that, however, it is necessary that we discuss what happens when domains interact with one another, and when states act in ways in one domain that have an impact in another.

Domain Interactions

Domains do not exist in isolation from each other; it is possible for elements of one domain to significantly affect state behavior in another. In fact, the US Army has in recent years developed a concept termed *multi-domain battle* to characterize the domain-interactive character of modern warfare, and platforms such as aircraft carriers are specifically designed to straddle domain boundaries.[25] In addition, technological developments that open up one domain—the invention of the aircraft or the ballistic missile, to offer two examples—can have transformative effects on other domains. So it is with the development of the cyber domain, which served to extend the reach and change the tools available in the finance domain, despite the former domain preexisting the latter; international finance existed long before the invention of the computer. Just as the advent of manned flight opened the air domain while transforming the conduct of conflict in the land and maritime domains, the creation of cyberspace has changed how states compete in the finance domain.[26]

Domains are useful for categorizing spaces of conflict and can also inform institutional design. Broadly speaking, most national security apparatuses structure themselves around lines characterized by domains. For example, the uniformed military of the United States consists of the army, the air force, and the navy (the last of which includes the marine corps).[27] Each of these services focuses on a particular domain: land power, airpower, and seapower, respectively. Similar to the recent creation of the space force, some experts have argued for the creation of a "cyber force" to manage national security interests in the cyber domain.[28]

This delineation of domains among service branches has consequences for the institutional structure of the entire national security apparatus, with further downstream effects on the national security structures of other states. The identification of an organization with a domain has implications for culture, mission sets, capabilities, professional pathways, and the overall worldview of its members. Members of organizations focused on the air domain tend to view the world in terms specific to aircraft, those in the maritime domain tend not to think about solutions in terms of land competition, and so forth.[29] Furthermore, the institutionalization of domains tends to focus expectations of participants, observers, and policymakers around certain kinds of behavior; for example, members of the US Air Force expect the air force to manage aircraft and members of the US Navy expect the navy to manage boats, even though the distribution of both aircraft and boats across the services is complex and contested.

The Finance Domain—and Its Absence—from International Relations Theory

Despite its evident importance to strategic thought, finance received relatively little attention in the foundational texts of international relations.[30]

This tendency exists in historically major paradigms of realism and liberalism, while the relatively newer paradigm of constructivism as well as its close relation international political economy are better at integrating finance into their Weltanschauungen.

One of the most relevant examples (for the purposes of this book) of this absence is in the work of Edward Hallett Carr. In *The Twenty Years' Crisis, 1919–1939,* Carr laid much of the foundation for thinking about realist power politics in the modern state system and, in doing so, disaggregated different kinds of state power, demonstrating the inextricable linkages between military and economic power. Unfortunately, although Carr briefly discussed finance, he did not attempt to disaggregate financial and economic power in any sophisticated way.[31] Carr did not, for example, describe the ways in which the Triple Entente-dominated financial system attempted to constrain Germany at the end of the World War I, or the means by which Britain and the United States tried to control the access that revisionist powers had to credit.

This lack of specificity is characteristic of other foundational works of international relations. For example, in *Politics Among Nations,* Hans Morgenthau does not identify command of the international financial system as a core element of American power. When Morgenthau does mention finance, it is to echo a point Adam Smith made 175 years earlier that a financial policy, in Morgenthau's case a loan, might well be "insecure and unprofitable"[32] but should nevertheless be pursued if it enhances a state's political power. Morgenthau admittedly does get close to the idea of international finance as a domain and state financial power being a weapon to use in and of itself, but visualizes both economic and financial power as entities separate from—and subservient to—political power.

Neither is Kenneth Waltz exempt. In fact, Waltz gives no specific account of the structure of international finance in his *Theory of International Politics*, although this is not surprising as he does not discuss domestic systems of finance either.[33] We may surmise, however, that, had Waltz mentioned them, his theory would have concluded that financial institutions that grant a state competitive advantages will generally be replicated by other states in the system. However, this conclusion belies the nature of the finance domain, where the interrelationships between states structure state choice.

Waltz says nothing, for example, about the dominance of London's financial markets during the long nineteenth century, or how that dominance affected the capacity of states around the world to provide for their own defense. Similarly, he has nothing to say about how Bretton Woods structured the financial environment of the Cold War. In both cases, states could not simply choose to adopt the innovative institutions of the hegemons; they had to either operate within the constraints provided or pay the costs of going their own way.

Neorealist theory lacks any specific account of the nature of state institutions. Foundational neorealist texts have little to say about how states access the land, air, or sea domains, or whether dominance in any particular domain (land powers vs. sea powers, for example) better secures the survival or prosperity of a state. Neorealists, however, view this lack of specificity as a strength because it enables the theory to remain flexible and parsimonious and, if there is no specificity regarding the traditional strategic domains, there could hardly be an expectation of it concerning the development of financial institutions.

However, it is possible to imagine a neorealist theory of the emergence of financial institutions: as the economies of early modern Europe developed in sophistication, financial institutions likewise developed in a way that managed the distribution of capital between a state and different types of enterprises within that state. Such institutions would therefore enable said state to better mobilize its basic factor endowments of land, labor, resources, and energy. In addition, when appropriate, these institutions also mediated relations between the European pole and its colonial periphery, facilitating investment and enabling colonial powers to take advantage of the labor and resources of their colonies.

Furthermore, as is the case with military organizations, these financial institutions were not created equal; for whatever reason, some performed more effectively than others, some were more innovative, and consequently some produced benefits for their states that resulted in genuine advantages on the battlefield or in other areas of strategic competition, resulting either in increased power or hegemony. Out of a fear of falling behind, other states in the system copied these innovations and installed them within their own financial systems, which invariably involved some degree of public-private interaction.

Sadly, neorealism is ill-equipped to integrate any further theoretical refinements along this line of logic such as the development of sophisticated financial institutions in one state affecting the development of financial institutions in another; or the constellation of banks, stock exchanges, and government institutions in one state actively precluding their development in another; or, finally, the development of financial institutions in one state enabling that state to effectively control how other states fund their wars, military establishments, and other public works. One state, without launching a ship, dropping a bomb, or landing a soldier, can limit another state's ability to mobilize its basic factor endowment, and therefore its ability to maximize its own security and to compete in an anarchic international system.

The liberal challenge to realism opened space for thinking about how structural factors other than the balance of power could affect state choice: international institutions can change the payoffs of actors within the system, thereby rewarding states for seeking prosperity as well as security. However, neoliberal institutionalism largely regarded the institutionalization of international politics as a recent phenomenon, developing since the end of World War II. In addition, neoliberal institutionalism also de-emphasized the role of power in the formation and performance of international institutions, making it ill-equipped for analyzing an international financial system such as the classical gold standard. Neoliberal institutionalism can go some distance toward explaining the global impact of financial institutions in the postwar period. But because of the de-emphasis of the concept of power, it does less well at explaining how particular states can weaponize the leverage they have over different aspects of the financial system, as well as at explaining the role of finance in earlier historical periods, where international institutions were either wholly absent or had a much different character than the regimes of the Cold War. Overall, neoliberal institutionalism offers little leverage for understanding the enduring characteristics of competition in the finance domain.

Finance may also impose particularly serious problems for how liberalism and neoliberal institutionalism understand hegemonic stability. In *After Hegemony*, Robert Keohane argues that the international regimes established by North American and European states after the end of World War II should be able to sustain international cooperation even after American hegemony fades.[34] This is not contradicted by a focus on the finance domain because, of course, the economic and financial regimes established by the United States and its allies in 1945 are an immensely important part of the story of hegemony. The difference here is one of emphasis; Keohane focuses on the role that institutions play in maintaining peace and prosperity after the end of US hegemony, while a financial perspective concentrates on how such institutions further, deepen, and indeed constitute hegemony.

Constructivism and international political economy (IPE) fare better in adapting concepts of financial power to the overall idea of international contestations and the arenas in which those contestations take place, in part because these disciplines exist in reaction to the inabilities of realism and liberalism to fully explain state behavior, particularly in the late twentieth and early twenty-first centuries.[35] Two brief examples illustrate this point. First, Robert Gilpin offers not only a framework for conceptualizing the dominance of the United States in financial affairs, but also comments directly on the subject of IPE.[36] Gilpin's vision of international relations involves states engaged in a multifaceted contest with one another in which power and interest played essential roles. Hegemonic states used norms, rules, and institutions to shape the international system to their liking. We can easily fit international financial competition into this framework, as states use money not only to enhance their own capabilities, but also to place constraints on the freedom of other states. Indeed, we locate this concept within our own conception of RFAs to explain the extent to which the United States midwifed the Bretton Woods system in such a way that placed the United States at the center of the new international order.

Second, the literature on military organizations and international cooperation in general—whose major contributors include Martha Finnemore and Michael Horowitz—has focused to an extent on the importance of firm institutional foundations to the adoption and diffusion of technologies and doctrines.[37] Finnemore's book *The Purpose of Intervention,* for example, addresses these questions through the lens of the changing tendency of states to intervene militarily, but statements such as "in a society that has no central government or law enforcement, those with the means to do so enforce understandings of right and permissible conduct"[38] apply equally well to our theory of international contestation within the finance domain.

Our purpose here is to catalogue the tools that states can use to compete and influence one another within the finance domain. These tools have become more visible and arguably more powerful in the past twenty years, as the United States has wielded its financial power like a maul to enhance its hegemony. However, the existence of such tools is not limited to the twenty-first century, or to the early modern period, or to the ancients, but rather it is evident across the history of international relations.[39] We should note that although we believe the principles outlined here are universal, and we attempt to include from the broadest array of regions, cultures, and time periods, our discussion is focused on European, East Asian, and North American history for the past 800–1,000 years. There are multiple reasons for this. First, given the need to keep the scope of the discussion targeted, we focus on developments that are most critical to understanding the finance domain, which means we touch lightly or not at all on most of human history. Second, at the risk of availability bias, we found the most extensive documentation of financial developments in this period. Third, we believe that European history from roughly 1200 to 1800 is where the most dramatic development of the finance domain occurred, and the 200 years since then are crucial to understanding where we are now. We believe the finance domain has played an important role in regions and periods we do not spend time on here, and hope that further research will bring these stories to light.

Plan of the Book

The rest of the book proceeds as follows. In Chapter 2, we sketch out the central characteristics of the finance domain.

In Chapter 3, we discuss examples of systems of monetary exchange in the premodern world and review the development of finance as a strategic domain. The early empires of Mesopotamia, Egypt, and the Middle East used taxation to systematically fund their militaries by about 3,000 BCE. Steady increases in trade and taxation led to coinage, our first RFA, but taxation paid in goods and corvée labor stayed important throughout this era. By the height of the Roman Empire, a number of critical pieces of the financial domain had been developed and were in use across Eurasia, including regular systems of taxation, coins, and formalized loan contracts.

In Chapter 4, we examine the regression that occurred in Europe after the collapse of the western half of the Roman Empire. We then investigate the means through which the early Islamic polities funded their conquest of much of the Mediterranean world, and the reach of Islamic finance deep into the Eurasian continent. We look at developments in China, which by roughly the eleventh century show some of the most sophisticated monetary and financial institutions in the world. Over the next few hundred years, polities in Western Europe began to reconstruct some of the financial practices that decayed or disappeared with the fall of Rome and innovate new ones such as negotiable bills of exchange. We conclude with a discussion of two important RFAs: the development of paper currency in China and the development of public debt in Europe.

In Chapter 5, we discuss a critical RFA almost exclusively centered in Europe, when the combination of increased maritime trade, improvements in agriculture, an influx of specie from the Americas and competitive pressure in warfare triggered a substantial increase in state revenues between the early 1600s and the early 1700s. This period marks a significant leap forward in the evolution of linkages between trade, taxation, finance, and national security, as developments in economic thought and the launch of central banking—as well as a number of public-private financial schemes—demonstrated the strategic relevance of finance. Because many of these developments began with the proto-economic discussions grouped under the name mercantilism, we term this the *mercantilist RFA*.

In Chapter 6, we consider the period of the Pax Britannica, 1815 to 1914. The development of the gold standard, which was at its height from 1880 to 1914, facilitated international trade and finance, a facilitation exploited for trade in munitions and financing of warfare. However, the establishment of a gold standard did not simply increase the availability of funding for substate actors; it also had the impact of creating an international system of rules, thereby stabilizing state behavior. This system—the Pax Brittanica and the classical gold standard—ended in the destructive forces unleashed by World War I.

In Chapter 7, we cover the transformation wrought by World War I, aka the interwar period. The aftermath of the war resulted in extensive economic and social change, as the mass mobilization and high death toll of the war radically remade European politics, overturning autocratic governments in

Russia, Germany, and Austria and expanding the voting franchise elsewhere. In a development we term the *bureaucratic RFA*, the intersection of civil service professionalization, experience using monetary systems to control prewar colonies, and pressure from overvalued currencies led to more aggressive use of government controls on financial flows. In this case, countries' efforts to gain relative advantage drove an RFA, but the following competition worsened the developing depression and helped lead to world war.

Determined to learn from the chaos of 1929 to 1945, the victors in World War II attempted to create a benevolent global financial hegemony under the United States, the subject of Chapter 8. This hegemony—the *Bretton Woods RFA*—tried to adapt the best parts of the British-centered gold standard system while mitigating its weaknesses. Beyond that, it was hoped that Bretton Woods would mute the use of finance as a tool for interstate rivalry. However, shocks such as the rise of the Organization of Petroleum Exporting Countries (OPEC), the pressure of maintaining the United States' military commitments, and worldwide inflation were more than the system could easily handle. Even as governments became increasingly ready to let exchange rates and trade flows be dictated by market forces, the United States maintained its central role and Bretton Woods Institutions worked to expand trade and stabilize financial flows.

Chapter 9 concludes our history of RFAs by investigating the transformations wrought in the era of post–Cold War American hegemony. The *digital RFA* of this period is characterized by the beginning of the use of signals intelligence (SIGINT) and negotiated transparency to track financial flows outside of US financial networks and flag transactions involving enemies and competitors. After September 11, the United States put an increased emphasis on tracking terrorism financing, which led to an increased use of the Society for Worldwide Interbank Financial Telecommunication (SWIFT) system. With the Russian invasion of Ukraine, the arsenal of US digital interventions was deployed against its largest target to date, with ambiguous results.

Chapter 10 projects potential future developments in the finance domain. We evaluate six scenarios, one in which the United States remains a financial hegemon, a second in which we see a relatively orderly transition to another hegemon, three scenarios that look at the development of bipolarity in the finance domain, and a sixth that witnesses the development of a multipolar financial commons. We use the International Futures model to help generate likely paths, and to help evaluate how those paths will impact geostrategic affairs. Our argument concludes with some final thoughts on the need for policymakers and strategic analysts to carefully incorporate financial thinking into their decisionmaking. We also outline lacunae in which future research can more tightly integrate financial and strategic analysis.

Notes

1. Frost, Robert I. 2014. *The Northern Wars: War, State and Society in Northeastern Europe, 1558–1721*. London: Routledge.
2. Feld, Maury D. 1975. "Middle-Class Society and the Rise of Military Professionalism: The Dutch Arm, 1589–1609." *Armed Forces and Society* 1 (4): 419–442, at 430.
3. Hendrickson, Joshua R. 2020. "The Riksbank, Emergency Finance, Policy Experimentation, and Sweden's Reversal of Fortune." *Journal of Economic Behavior and Organization* 171: 312–332, at 314.
4. Sveriges Riksbank. 2021. *Money and Power—the History of Sveriges Riksbank*, 25–32.
5. The first charter enabled the creation of an exchange bank and the second created a loans bank. While the former is notable for the invention and circulation of paper money—at least for a few years—it is the latter charter that is of greater import for this story.
6. Cicero, Marcus. 1913. *The Orations of Marcus Tullius Cicero vol. 4*. London: G. Bell and Sons, 1913, p. 96.
7. Kakinuma, Yohei. 2014. "The Emergence and Spread of Coins in China from the Spring and Autumn Period to the Warring States Period." In *Explaining Monetary and Financial Innovation*, edited by Peter Bernholz and Roland Vaubel. Cham: Springer, 79–126.
8. See, for example Blackwill, Robert D., and Jennifer M. Harris. 2016. *War by Other Means: Geoeconomics and Statecraft*. Cambridge: Harvard University Press; Steil, Benn, and Robert E. Litan. 2006. *Financial Statecraft: The Role of Financial Markets in American Foreign Policy*. New Haven: Yale University Press.
9. Heftye, Eric. 2017. "Multi-Domain Confusion: All Domains Are Not Created Equal," Strategy Bridge, May 26; Hoffman, Frank and Davies, Michael 2013. "Joint Force 2020 and the Human Domain: Time for a New Conceptual Framework?" *Small Wars Journal*. https://smallwarsjournal.com/jrnl/art/joint-force-2020-and-the-human-domain-time-for-a-new-conceptual-framework.
10. Joint Chiefs of Staff. 2000. *Joint Vision 2020*. June. Washington, DC: US Government Printing Office, 6.
11. Joint Chiefs of Staff. 2005. *Capstone Concept for Joint Operations, Version 2.0*. Washington, DC: US Government Printing Office, 16.
12. Nye, Joseph S., Jr. 2010. *Cyber Power*. Cambridge: Harvard University Press; Alexander, Keith B. 2007. *Warfighting in Cyberspace*. Washington, DC: National Defense University Institute for Strategic Studies; Libicki, Martin C. 2012. "Cyberspace Is Not a Warfighting Domain." *I/S: A Journal of Law and Policy for the Information Society* 8 (2): 325–340; Lynn, William F., III. 2010. "Defending A New Domain—The Pentagon's Cyberstrategy." *Foreign Affairs* 89 (5): 97.
13. Singer, J. David, Stuart Bremer, and John Stuckey. 1972. "Capability Distribution, Uncertainty, and Major Power War, 1820–1965." In *Peace, War, and Numbers,* edited by Bruce Russett. Beverly Hills: Sage, 19–48. A state's CINC score is calculated using its total population, urban population, iron and steel production, energy consumption, military personnel, and military expenditure. Given the inherent problems of data collection over a now two-century period, and the change in the nature of state power since the index was first developed, we recommend using the CINC score mainly as a control variable and present it merely as an example of the ways in which state power is estimated.
14. Libicki 2012: 322.

15. Nanto, Dick K. 2008. *North Korean Counterfeiting of Currency*. Washington, DC: Congressional Research Service.

16. Kirshner, Jonathan. 1997. *Currency and Coercion: The Political Economy of International Monetary Power*. Princeton: Princeton University Press, 102–106.

17. Dainoff, Charles. 2021. *Outlaw Paradise: Why Countries Become Tax Havens*. Lanham, MD: Lexington Books.

18. Tooze, Adam. 2007. *The Wages of Destruction: The Making and Breaking of the Nazi Economy*. New York: Viking Penguin, 120–149.

19. Lambert, Nicholas A. 2012. *Planning Armageddon: British Economic Warfare and the First World War*. Cambridge: Harvard University Press.

20. Occhino, Filippo, Kim Oosterlinck, and Eugene N. White. 2007. "How Occupied France Financed Its Own Exploitation in World War II." *American Economic Review* 97 (2): 295–299; White, Eugene N. 1995. "The French Revolution and the Politics of Government Finance, 1770–1815." *Journal of Economic History* 55 (2): 227–255; Dube, Arindrajit, Ethan Kaplan, and Suresh Naidu. 2011. "Coups, Corporations, and Classified Information." *Quarterly Journal of Economics* 126 (3): 1375–1409.

21. Davis, Lance E., and Stanley L. Engerman. 2006. *Naval Blockades in Peace and War: An Economic History Since 1750*. Cambridge: Cambridge University Press, 29–33.

22. Eldem, Edhem. 2005. "Ottoman Financial Integration with Europe: Foreign Loans, the Ottoman Bank, and the Ottoman Public Debt." *European Review* 13 (3): 431; Blaisdell, Donald C. 1929. *European Financial Control in the Ottoman Empire*. New York: Columbia University Press.

23. Majd, Mariam. 2018. "The Cost of a SWIFT Kick: Estimating the Cost of Financial Sanctions on Iran." In *The Political Economy of International Finance in an Age of Inequality: Soft Currencies, Hard Landings*, edited by Gerald A. Epstein. Cheltenham: Edward Elgar: 175–193.

24. An analogy here is the importance of maritime resources and capabilities versus maritime competition: a state that used its inland waterways to move supplies and troops domestically would need ships but, if no other state's vessels accessed these waterways, they would not need to think about mobilizing resources to contest in the maritime domain.

25. See, for example, US Army Headquarters. "The Army in Multi-Domain Operations: 2028." Initial Coordination Draft v0.6h, August 7; Perkins, David G. 2017b. "Multi-Domain Battle: Driving Change to Win in the Future." *Military Review* 97 (4): 6–13; Perkins, David G. 2017a. "Multi-Domain Battle: The Advent of Twenty-First Century War." *Military Review* 97 (6): 8–13; Perkins, David G. 2017c. "Preparing for the Fight Tonight: Multi-Domain Battle and Field Manual 3-0." *Military Review* 97 (5): 6–13.

26. See below for a more complete discussion of the impact of technological developments on the conduct of international finance.

27. On December 20, 2019, President Donald Trump created a space force housed within the air force to manage the space domain. See "History." United States Space Force. Garamone, Jim. 2019. "Trump Signs Law Establishing U.S. Space Force." *DOD [United States Department of Defense] News*. https://www.defense.gov/News/News-Stories/Article/Article/2046035/trump-signs-law-establishing-us-space-force/.

28. Graham, Maj. Matt. 2016. "U.S. Cyber Force: One War Away." *Military Review* 96 (3): 111–118; Solce, Natasha. 2008. "The Battlefields of Cyberspace: The Inevitable New Military Branch—The Cyber Force." *Albany Law Journal of Science and Technology* 18 (1): 293–325.

29. Farley, Robert M. 2014. *Grounded: The Case for Abolishing the United States Air Force.* Lexington: University Press of Kentucky.

30. The following section should not be considered a comprehensive literature review of foundational international relations texts. Rather, it is a representative sample intended to illustrate a few general points.

31. Carr, Edward Hallett. 2016. *The Twenty Years' Crisis, 1919–1939.* 2nd ed. Edited by Michael Cox. London: Springer.

32. Morgenthau, Hans J., 1985. *Politics Among Nations: The Struggle for Power and Peace.* 7th ed. Edited by Kenneth W. Thompson and W. David Clinton. New York: McGraw Hill: 47.

33. Waltz, Kenneth N. 2010. *Theory of International Politics.* Long Grove, IL: Waveland Press.

34. Keohane, Robert O. 2005. *After Hegemony: Cooperation and Discord in the World Political Economy.* Princeton: Princeton University Press; Keohane, Robert O. 1986. *Neorealism and Its Critics.* New York: Columbia University Press.

35. A foundational document being Strange, Susan. 1970. "International Economics and International Relations: A Case of Mutual Neglect." *International Affairs* 46 (2): 304–315.

36. Gilpin, Robert. 2016. *The Political Economy of International Relations.* Princeton: Princeton University Press; Gilpin, Robert. 1981. *War and Change in World Politics.* Cambridge: Cambridge University Press; Gilpin, Robert, and Jean M. Gilpin. 2001. *Global Political Economy: Understanding the International Economic Order.* Princeton: Princeton University Press.

37. Horowitz, Michael C. 2010. *The Diffusion of Military Power: Causes and Consequences for International Politics.* Princeton: Princeton University Press; Finnemore, Martha. 2013. *The Purpose of Intervention.* Ithaca: Cornell University Press.

38. Finnemore 2013: 2.

39. Von Glahn, Richard. 2016. *An Economic History of China: From Antiquity to the Nineteenth Century.* Cambridge: Cambridge University Press, 81–82. The Qin Empire lasted from 221 BCE to 206 BCE.

2

What Is the Finance Domain?

Peruse the history of Europe from its earliest period, were wars less frequent or pernicious before the system of credit was introduced than they have been since? They were more frequent and more destructive, though perhaps not of as long duration at one time.

But they did not equally produce debt. This is true, yet it remains to compare the evils of debt with those which resulted from the antecedent system of War— the devastations and extortions, the oppressions and derangements of industry in all its branches, and it remains to consider whether expedients may not be devised which may preserve to nations the advantages of Credit & avoid essentially its evils. . . .

Credit may be called a new power in the mechanism of national affairs. It is a great and a very useful one, but the art of regulating it properly, as is the case with every new and great contrivance, has been till lately imperfectly understood.

—Alexander Hamilton,
"The Defense of the Funding System," 1795

Although awareness of the role of finance in war dates to the ancient world, Joseph Schumpeter's 1918 book *The Crisis of the Tax State* marked a watershed in the scholarly analysis of the intersection between money and combat. Schumpeter defined the categories of "domain states" and "tax states," as an important step in thinking about the different ways that warmaking entities acquire, manage, and spend both liquid and illiquid resources.[1] In Schumpeter's typology, sovereign states transition from a domain state (not to be confused with a domain of strategic competition), in which a ruler has direct control over resources such as land that generates state revenues, to a tax state in which the government taxes citizens and then uses the revenue to pay for government services. Scholars such as Richard Bonney have since added to Schumpeter's typology the categories of "tribute states" that use tribute from external regions to finance themselves, "fiscal states" that have become so effective at managing taxation and expenditure that they are able to issue sovereign debt, and "fiscal-military states" that develop this fiscal infrastructure in response to military threats.[2] This typology is a product of recent literature termed *fiscal sociology* that analyzes the interaction among the development of taxes, military strength, and representative political systems.[3] Over the past few decades, these questions have become central to how the social sciences think about economic development and social order.[4] For us, these categories illuminate paths to think about how states collect, store, and use money for purposes of war.

Fiscal Regimes

Most states, even premodern ones, have attributes from several or all categories of the domain/tribute/tax/fiscal typology. Many successful premodern states depended on royal or imperial lands and tribute from conquered territories for revenue, while also having at least a rudimentary system of taxation (including in-kind revenues of staple foods, for example). Sparta and the Incan Empire are examples of premodern states with high levels of central organization that functioned with a combination of carefully managed unpaid corvée (or forced) labor by peasants and other subject peoples, state ownership of lands, and regular taxes of goods. Indeed, most provinces of the Roman Empire appear to have leaned heavily on corvée labor and taxes of foodstuffs and materials, with monetary taxes and income transfers as a supplement. The complex systems that spring up in the absence of an educated and trained group of modern bureaucrats show a mixture of personal relationships, delegated power, and careful negotiations between connected nodes on a network; in a word, they are clientelistic.[5] European feudalism showed many characteristics of the domain state, but the carefully negotiated obligations of vassals to their lords are not as centralized as we would expect in an empire or simple tax state, while more cooperative than we would expect from a tribute state.[6] Most early modern European states depended on tax farming, or the "delegation of tax collection for profit" in the words of Eugene White, where private tax collectors or "farmers" profited from their roles as intermediaries.[7]

Nevertheless, the idea of the fiscal state is helpful as a general model. In the fiscal state, there is a treasury (or fisc, from the Latin *fiscus*, originally meaning a basket or purse to hold resources) that coordinates acquisition, storage, and transmission of resources. In the fiscal state, a substantial percentage of resource flows are liquid assets—coins, bills, financial instruments—as opposed to food, material, or labor. For a fiscal state to continue to exist, it must actively manage revenue flows from these resources to its advantage. Furthermore, most of the successful historical states across different regions and periods were remarkably effective at this relatively early in their development—Chinese states before the Qin Empire, for example.

The state must develop tools for managing the three core activities—acquisition, storage, and transmission—together, as none of them is useful or feasible without the others. More complicated aspects of resource management—in particular, engaging with financial and trade flows such as minting coins, issuing or regulating currency and IOUs, and borrowing—tend to be less systematic in evolution than the other three. One of the most crucial aspects of the finance domain in the modern era—issuing long-term securitized debt—is one of the most difficult to accomplish successfully. Indeed, in the four-part typology the establishment and employment of "widespread" sovereign debt is a dividing line between developing and developed fiscal states.[8] Of these core activities, systematic revenue acquisition—usually based on taxes, fees, and tariffs—is the most crucial to the health and development of the state.[9] There is evidence that as early as 5,000 years ago governments in the Middle East were using systematic tax assessment to fund armies and navies.[10] More recently, the development of revenue sources in England over the seventeenth and eighteenth centuries has been carefully documented.[11]

Even nonstate actors attempting to create a state out of whole cloth tend to develop revenue-building mechanisms early on. For example, in November 2015 the *New York Times* reported that Iraqi terrorist group, the Islamic State in Iraq and Syria (ISIS), was raising revenues by "exacting tolls and traffic tickets; rent for government buildings; utility bills for water and electricity; taxes on income, crops, and cattle; and fines for smoking or wearing the wrong clothes."[12] These less-organized entities may be able to take advantage of high-value local economic flows in a way that governments cannot; for example, Latin American hybrid terrorist/criminal syndicates and other violent nonstate actors (VNSAs) such as the Fuerzas Armadas Revolucionarias de Colombia (FARC) have been able to raise revenue through cocaine production, refinement, and sales as well as the operation of extortion and kidnapping rackets.[13]

Storage and transmittal present their own challenges to states. With respect to storage, states needed to maintain their wealth in a form that would: facilitate transfer—that is, with a high value to weight ratio; not expire—that is, dried grain rather than bulkier foodstuffs more likely to rot or spoil; and not easily be copied, thereby preventing inflation and the consequent degradation of the value of existing financial stocks. Premodern states were in fact able to most effectively exploit precious metals for storage, although this was hardly the only currency they used. The importance of storage is evident from the accounts of Herodotus, for example, who discussed the Persian treasuries and their maintenance at some length, while Thucydides detailed the wealth storage strategies of the Athenians in the early stages of the Peloponnesian War.[14]

Regarding transmittal, while documentation of payment to Roman soldiers in the Imperial Period—roughly 27 BCE to 476 CE—is limited, payments made by the Roman Empire to its troops appear to have been made regularly and in coin.[15] Although much of this disbursement system apparently was managed at a regional or even a camp level, the Romans still managed to implement significant interregional transfers. In late Rome and Byzantium there was an extensive imperial overland transport system, including both "regular (*cursus clabularis* or *platys dromos*) and fast (*cursus velox* or *oxys dromos*)" to handle supplies and information flows, and to keep the armies well resourced.[16] Societies where money was not in common use, such as Han China under Emperor Wu, developed hybrid systems of taxation in which commodities would be used by subjects to pay taxes at the local level, at which point the commodities' value would be converted into coins or bullion to more easily transfer it from the provinces to the central state government.[17] This tax revenue could then be used in combination with the drafting of labor for local projects and military service to bolster the Han security state.

By 1500, European rulers were able to turn to bankers for help in transmitting funds from one region to another. Holy Roman Emperor Charles V used a range of bankers, frequently paying the houses of Fugger, Welser, and others exchange fees from about 20 to 25 percent.[18] To return to a previous example, more recently ISIS used the physical movement and stockpiling of cash for storage and transmission within its territories, although it also worked with a few banks whose cooperation with the group generally resulted in the banks being severed from international transactions by the international banking community.[19] In fact, VNSAs have been at the forefront of developing new methods for transmitting capital, using commodities as diverse as exotic animal species and counterfeit pharmaceuticals.[20] As we discuss below, substantial long-range trade makes the finance domain more complex and more important to determinations of national power because trade pushes the development of liquid assets and, hence, meaningful finance. As the finance domain grows in importance in international contestation, financial considerations increasingly shape the way states interact with trade and finance in their regions. As a result of the strengthening of this relationship between finance and state power, revolutions in financial affairs (RFAs) such as coins and public or central banking were in large part driven by local states' interest in tapping into trade flows to support their military interests.

There is evidence that state borrowing is simply a variant of acquisition or transmittal, at least in the early stages of development of the fiscal state.

David Stasavage notes that the Italian city-states that initiated public debt in Europe in the thirteenth century began with forced loans, even as they occasionally paid interest.[21] Charles Tilly further explains that states "have coped with the shortfall [driven by military exigency] by one form of borrowing or another: making creditors wait, selling offices, forcing loans from clients, borrowing from bankers who acquired claims on future government revenues."[22] By the end of the sixteenth century, however, Tilly points to systematic large-scale borrowing by European states from merchants and bankers. As Michael Tomz notes, this borrowing took place despite the presence of incomplete information on the part of the merchants and the states, although this activity increased in scale as state and nonstate actors developed reputations as reliable banking partners.[23] The irony here is that one of the most powerful weapons in a country's finance domain—sovereign debt—would not have developed to the extent it has without international cooperation.

These historical developments have led to a current state of affairs in which sophisticated financial systems are critical to the functioning of the modern national security state. Of all the remarkable technologies used by the armed forces of Group of 7 (G7) states, perhaps the most impressive is the backend payroll system that for decades has ensured that every employee receives salary and wage payments on schedule.[24] These systems, which depend on a combination of treasury departments that store incoming revenues in accessible form and personnel offices that take care of regular pay to employees, took centuries to develop into a regular structure. Payroll system development is also notable in its absence: the difficulty developing countries continue to have meeting their government payrolls is a reliable indicator of state fragility and an inability to compete in the finance domain. Furthermore, nonstate actors attempting to compete with states have even greater challenges, frequently having to resort to unstable—not to say illegal—methods of payment in kind like drugs or lootable natural resources to reduce the probability of a revolt or defection by their troops.

This evolution has not been without its punctuations, however. Even the United Kingdom, a previous hegemonic state and current great power in part due to its ability to fulfill this payroll requirement since the late 1800s, experienced in 1931 an unexpected reduction in government pay that triggered the Invergordon Mutiny, a two-day revolt of the crews of four Royal Navy warships docked in Invergordon, Scotland. The revolt involved about 1,000 sailors and resulted in a financial panic severe enough that it forced the United Kingdom to abandon the gold standard.[25] Arguably, the classic example of the strategic power of a fully functional fiscal state is the United Kingdom during the Napoleonic Wars of the early nineteenth century. As financial historians Michael Bordo and Eugene White have shown, the United Kingdom's combination of a well-run tax system, strong central bank, and reliable political and fiscal institutions allowed it to borrow much more easily than France, allowing the United Kingdom to increase its military might without bankrupting its public purse. Between 1770 and 1820, British debt rarely had a yield above 6 percent, while French debt was rarely below that, suggesting that prospective lenders perceived French bonds to have a higher repayment risk than English ones. From 1800 to 1820, French debt yields were at least 1 percent higher than British yields, and frequently 3 to 4 percent higher. This difference in payouts made a critical difference in their relative abilities to finance the conflict and helped lead to Britain's eventual victory in the Napoleonic Wars.[26] Understanding this victory is a task made much easier by taking the United Kingdom's maneuvers in the finance domain into account. Our hope in writing this book is to make this understanding easier for readers and, to achieve this, we must next explore the concept of the financial commons, without which the finance domain cannot exist.

Financial Commons

In 2003, Barry Posen reformulated thinking about the "commons" as a strategic concept by distilling the logic of Alfred Thayer Mahan on maritime spaces and applying that logic to other domains of state behavior. According to Posen, "the 'commons,' in the case of the sea and space, are areas that belong to no one state and that provide access to much of the globe."[27] While Mahan focused on sea spaces, Posen extended the logic to air and space. A 2010 Center for a New American Security (CNAS) report "Contested Commons: The Future of American Military Power in a Multipolar World" developed this argument and further applied it to the emerging commons of cyberspace.[28]

It is important to stipulate that this use of the term *commons* differs in important ways from how economists have normally utilized the "tragedy of the commons" concept, in that strategic theorists focus on the difficulties of exclusion and the dilemmas of shared governance rather than on problems of overuse and free riding.[29] A financial commons is a region with multiple political entities with trade significant enough to require regularized transfers of liquid assets. States embedded within such regions are then able to access resources by generating their own liquid assets—either by regularizing the flow of specie in coins and currency, or by generating tradable IOUs. The smooth functioning of the internal payments systems of the fiscal state is crucial to national security, but a fiscal state active in a shared financial commons must also handle strategic interaction with other states in that commons.

As finance and trade develop in a region, states likewise develop an interest in classes of financial assets circulating in their territory. Fluctuations in the value of coins, currency notes, and other financial instruments can help or hurt the interests of a particular state. Maintaining a particular clearly stated value—"par value," in standard financial terminology—for at least some instruments can then become of critical, potentially existential, importance to the state. From early on, we can see states intervene to change the value of a financial instrument class, or transparently improve the fiscal functions of the state to signal reliability to investors. Such operations are generally divided into two areas: operations by a treasury to support the fiscal needs of the government; and operations by a central bank to support the financial system and macroeconomy (this categorization is not at all crisp, and the exact division of labor has varied over time and between states).[30] Additionally, the flow of trade and financial assets within the commons almost invariably revolves around critical hubs, and the states that control such hubs then have the potential to restrict access to others for coercive purposes.

We argue that a number of financial commons have developed in world history. In each case, states embedded in these commons responded differently, frequently developing novel institutions and methods to take advantage of them. For basic operations, the critical issue was the development of stability in monetary or financial assets, particularly those relevant to the state. The first example is the birth of coins. While coinage allowed trade to increase and thus helped merchants, it also allowed the state to standardize revenue collection and offered more flexibility in purchasing goods. Additionally, it offered direct revenue in the form of seigniorage; that is, the amount the state gains from difference between the value of the money and the cost to produce and distribute it. This hybrid structure of a financial machinery actively used by commercial interests, with substantial maintenance done by the state for its own purposes, is a common feature of operations within the finance domain. The key service that the state offers to commerce with a well-executed coinage system, of a stable, transportable, universally accepted asset, is similarly common. In fact, one of the most powerful financial institutions in the modern world, the central bank, was for its first several hundred years of development a way for states involved in intensive ongoing military expenses to maintain par value for coins and sovereign debt.

Our strongest and most enduring example of a financial commons comes from the Mediterranean, which connected Europe, Asia, and Africa from early antiquity. The Mediterranean was the center of extensive ongoing trade for millennia and, while the historical record regarding financial instruments and institutions is incomplete, it seems likely that the flow of trade and liquid assets in the region represented a commons by the fifth century BCE if not before.

By the Middle Ages, the regions northwest of the Mediterranean also showed substantial trade and financial flows, as well as the evolution of numerous sovereign states in competition with each other, the result being that as early as the sixteenth century Northwest Europe represented a full financial commons. As we show in Chapters 4 and 5, it is here that several important finance domain technologies develop, including securitized debt and public banks. A pan-European financial commons, enabling strategic action in the finance domain, seems to have emerged by the 1600s and remains in existence today. Since economic historians have been particularly focused in looking at England, we use the 1700s English economy to establish a benchmark of the conditions necessary—what combination of money supply and international trade—to all but guarantee engagement in the finance domain. That is to say, by 1700 the English economy had evolved to the point where it is estimated to have had a money supply equal to about 15 to 25 percent of its gross domestic product (GDP) and trade representing about 7 percent of GDP.[31] These levels probably represent a point at which a financial commons is all but guaranteed, as strategic interaction between states in financial issues are visible during periods where money and trade appear to have been much less developed (there is not sufficient data to be certain). The concept generally used to discuss this interaction is "systemic interdependence," which we discuss in the next section.

After domestic financial maintenance comes the question of how one state can manipulate *systemic interdependence*—or the extent to which one member state in an international system can affect the status of another state in the system as a result of their membership in the system. Despite the topic being a popular one for Thomas Mun and other mercantilists' early work, only a few states have ever gained a significant strategic advantage via this type of large-scale financial manipulation because a system large enough to create interdependence is hard to manipulate unless the state in question either helped develop it or dominates it once it has been developed.[32]

Moreover, as Nicholas Lambert documented, a state trying to manipulate the global financial and trade system faces multiple challenges. For example, Britain in World War I was well placed to embargo imports to Germany, but due to the novelty of the method, its political unpopularity with British merchants, and pressure from neutral states such as the United States and Sweden, the British government was unable to maintain a coherent approach and quickly scaled back the strategy.[33] In contrast, during the early parts of the war the United States responded to the gold drain of the summer of 1914 by closing the New York Stock Exchange for nearly five months. This action and other operations successfully reduced the flow of gold out of the country, strategically positioning the United States as a financial power.³⁴ The United States' ability to dictate terms and help create the Bretton Woods international financial system in the wake of World War II cemented its status as a global financial power, a fiscal state able to shape a system in its own image, and one that could manipulate the finance domain to maintain its hegemonic status.

Weaponized Interdependence and Offensive Operations in the Finance Domain

Political scientist Zeev Maoz writes that interdependence can be understood conceptually as meaningful, reciprocal change among actors: "a change in *j* affects changes in *i* and a change in *i* affects changes in *j*, and both actors bear some cost for disrupting this relationship."³⁵ *Weaponized interdependence,* then, is the exploitation of this relationship by one of the actors to induce behavioral change in the other(s) to achieve a goal.³⁶ The more powerful actor in this relationship is weaponizing interdependence when it uses its power to, in Dan Drezner's words, "gain a bargaining advantage over others in a contained system."³⁷

If we conceive of the international system as a network, states that have control over central nodes in the global network can use this centrality to influence the behavior of states on the spokes to advance their foreign policy objectives. Framing the global financial system thus, the United States has control over the central nodes of this network as a result of the importance of the dollar as currency in the financial world. This importance allows the United States to "discover and exploit vulnerabilities, compel policy change, and deter unwanted actions" in other states in the system.³⁸

The weaponized interdependence literature breaks out the ability of the United States to influence the behavior of states and nonstate actors into two basic categories or "effects": panopticon and choke point. The panopticon effect references Jeremy Bentham's concept of a prison in which the guards can constantly observe the prisoners as a way of controlling them.³⁹ For example, in the case of the international financial system, the central position of the United States allows it to weaponize its "ability to glean critical knowledge from information flows" created by financial transactions and other records.⁴⁰ The United States can exploit its position to create a financial panopticon both directly, via the government's ability to influence US financial institutions to make their records available for observation, or indirectly, via its ability to influence non-US networks such as the Society for Worldwide Interbank Financial Telecommunications (SWIFT) to share information.

The choke point effect, on the other hand, needs no conceptual elaboration. States in control of a network's central nodes can "choke off" access to those nodes to other states in the system. The United States achieves this choking off through actual or threatened denial of access to the US financial system, or to networks or payment systems influenced by the United States if not directly controlled by it—again, like SWIFT—as well as more aggressive measures such as targeted financial sanctions. For example, the US government opposed the coup in Myanmar, so the US government used its access to financial networks to obtain information about the individuals involved and their finances, an example of the US government using the panopticon effect. The US government then placed these individuals on the Specially Designated Nationals List, preventing them either from accessing the funds or property they already possessed, or from using the US financial system to conduct new transactions with any persons utilizing the system.

We discuss the modern financial commons at greater length in Chapter 9. We argue, however, that the dynamics present in the modern international financial system that enable the United States to influence and coerce other countries have existed, to greater or lesser degree, at other points during world financial history. This is to say that the United States is not the first country to leverage its financial influence for coercive effect, and the late twentieth century is not the first period in which states have sought or built financial tools to shape the domain environment.

Revolutions in Financial Affairs

Treating finance as a domain of strategic competition allows us to use some of the tools analysts have developed for discussing other domains. In particular, we borrow the term *revolution in military affairs* (RMA) from the strategic literature to describe periodic transformations in the character of the financial order. We characterize these transformations as *revolutions in financial affairs* (RFAs).[41]

Tied in large part to then Soviet chief of staff Marshal Nikolai Ogarkov's concept of a "military-technical revolution," Andrew Krepinevich boils the RMA concept down to "what occurs when the application of new technologies into a significant number of military systems combines with innovative operational concepts and organizational adaptation in a way that fundamentally alters the character and conduct of conflict."[42] A classic example involves the development of the "empty battlefield" of World War I, in which overwhelming firepower prevented open maneuver and enforced entrenchment strategies, leading to what became known as "trench warfare." Any formulation of this sort inevitably introduces controversy regarding exact delineations and precise moments of transition, but the strategic community has found the concept useful. The adoption of the RMA concept by then–US secretary of defense Donald Rumsfeld in the early 2000s helped drive significant and controversial changes in technology and procurement policies.[43] Still, the idea that technological and organizational change can suddenly, materially, and irreparably alter long-standing ways of doing things, as well as having a significant impact on the balance of power in the international system, seems accurate and attractive. As such, we have adopted this conceptual framework and adapted it to the finance domain, and have analyzed this history of the finance domain as a series of RFAs over time.

Using this conceptual lens, we determined that one of the most salient RFAs is the development of the European fiscal-military state from the early 1600s to the early 1700s, which we term the *mercantilist RFA* due to its intellectual roots. At the end of the 1500s, European national leaders generally funded military operations from their own lands and property with manpower derived from feudal agreements or militia structures, supplemented by occasional taxation, seizures of property, and borrowing. By the middle of the 1700s, almost all European states had developed the state capacity to impose regular taxation of subjects, and many had central banks and were actively working to improve tax yields and financing terms. The increase in state capacity made the tools of finance central to European warmaking from that point on. This revolution coincides with the military revolution first identified by historian Michael Roberts in 1955, a revolution characterized by modernization of land power strategies and tactics, as well as an increased state capacity for war and the concomitant increased impact of war on noncombatants.[44] Although its temporal boundaries are controversial, this revolution is generally regarded as the most important transformation in the means of fighting in European history.[45] Table 2.1 shows our schema of the important RFAs, mapping each within the chapters of the book.

Relationships with Other Domains

Complex connections link finance to the other domains of strategic competition. Complex and even transformative interactions between domains are not unusual; the development of the air domain, for example, has transformed the character of both seapower and land power. Similarly, the emergence of the cyber domain wrought profound changes in the nature of warfare at sea, on land, and in the air. In this section, we discuss the relationships between the finance domain and the other strategic domains, keeping in mind that these relationships change over time as a result of social and technological factors.

Table 2.1 Revolutions in Financial Affairs (RFAs)

Chapter	Period	Symbolic End Milestone	Great Powers	RFA Drivers
3	Antiquity (to 500 CE)	Fall of Roman Empire 476	Qin Dynasty, Roman Empire	Coins, societas, bottomry loans
4	Medieval era (500–1492 CE)	Columbus arrives in Hispaniola 1492	Song Dynasty, Mongols	Bills of exchange, banking, city-state debts, city-state public banks. Within China, paper currency
5	Mercantile era (1492–1815 CE)	Congress of Vienna 1815	France	Territorial states issue tradable debts and begin public banks
6	Pax Britannica (1815–1914 CE)	Start of World War I 1914	United Kingdom	Gold standard, international private financial activity, sovereign bond issues outside home markets, central banks
7	Total War (1914–1945 CE)	End of World War II 1945	United States, Soviet Union, Germany, France, United Kingdom, Japan	Bureaucratic controls, currency blocs, exchange controls, multilateral sanctions
8	Cold War (1945–1989 CE)	Fall of the Berlin Wall 1989	United States, Soviet Union	Bretton Woods, eurocurrency market, computerized payment systems, credit cards
9	Now (1989 CE to present day)		United States, China, nonstate actors such as al-Qaeda	Networked payment systems, real-time financial messaging systems, monitoring and sanctioning technologies

Source: Authors' own.

Finance and Cyber Domains

The relationship between the finance and cyber domains is so substantial that activity in the former is often mistaken for the latter, even though the domain of finance preceded the cyber domain by several millennia. The impact of the emergence of the cyber domain on the finance domain has primarily been to increase the speed and transparency of financial transactions. The effect of these developments has been to enable state and nonstate actors—primarily the US government—to leverage their command of the financial commons to undertake or threaten coercive action against other actors within the system. We investigate the details of such action in Chapter 9, but the tools of influence include the United States employing targeted sanctions against individuals, corporations, financial institutions, and entire states to prevent the use of certain currencies to acquire illicit goods.

Finance and Maritime Domains

The relationship between the finance and maritime domains is especially complex. Evidence from ancient, medieval, and early modern sources demonstrates that the establishment of navies parallels the development of sophisticated tools within the finance domain, suggesting that RFAs and naval RMAs occur around the same time and can influence each other's development. This relationship appears to have several aspects, including the provision for capital expenditure (the construction of ships), the need for long-term maintenance (ships rot quickly when not maintained, whether constructed of wood or steel), and the need to employ professional expertise in the construction and operation of these ships. Once built and maintained, large naval vessels can advance a state's military interests as well as facilitating long-distance trade, further entwining the naval and finance domains. An RFA that influences a state to undergo a naval RMA can also independently improve the ability of actors within the system to trade internationally, thereby increasing sovereign and individual wealth, leading to increased state capacity and systemic stability.

The expansion in sophistication of the finance domain plays an important role in the development of seapower, even for nonstate actors. In a modern example, pirate vessels represent a capital investment that must show returns—a contemporary example being the "pirate stock exchange" established in the first decade of the twenty-first century in Haradheere, Somalia, in which crime syndicates accept cash from investors from all over the Horn of Africa in exchange for shares of the proceeds of multimillion-dollar kidnapping and hijacking operations—providing motivation for pirates to attack ships laden with monetary wealth, precious cargo, or well-connected passengers who can be ransomed.[46] Indeed, Somali pirates would attempt to seize the entire ship and ransom it back to its owners or their insurers. This sort of large-scale criminal enterprise triggers a response from states affected by the piracy, which can itself lead to increased government maritime expenditures that can spur technological innovations that might create another naval RMA.

The interactions between the naval and finance domains can also result in the narrowing of the gap between the government and private industry in states competitive in both domains. For example, the sheer expense involved in the design and construction of warships in the modern era led to the disappearance of wholly self-sustaining shipping companies. In fact, by the beginning of the twentieth century, private shipbuilders could not sustain the construction of warships through private lending alone and required state investment to proceed.[47] This increasingly cozy relationship between shipbuilders and governments evolved into one sector of what President Dwight Eisenhower dubbed the "military-industrial complex" in 1961 and is still a facet of the relationship between finance and military affairs.

Finance and Air Domains

The relationship between the air and finance domains shares many of the same characteristics as the relationship between the finance and maritime domains. Warplanes require significant capital expenditure to produce and to maintain, meaning that they cannot generally be acquired or sustained through systems of barter or corvée labor, especially given that the latter is now illegal in most states capable of buying and maintaining a modern air force.[48] Aircraft are particularly susceptible to technological obsolescence, meaning that actors seeking to exert power in the air domain must invest in developing the engineering, science, and technical capacity to produce, or purchase, and maintain competitive aircraft. Workers and engineers in these fields require substantial education and training, both of which require a larger system of education that itself must rest on a firm financial foundation. The development of institutions of airpower—air forces, as well as other military organizations that use aircraft—similarly requires a sustainable long-term financial commitment. These types of institutional financial outlays themselves require a state's extensive involvement in the finance domain, therefore necessitating a secure and sophisticated finance domain.

The corporations that develop technology for the use and management of aircraft benefit from high levels of liquidity in debt markets, which allows them to make long-term investments with some confidence of return. Quick and reliable movement of capital across borders enables these corporations to conduct international business with relative ease, including the acquisition of foreign technology. This ease results in increased sales of aircraft domestically and internationally, likewise increasing state capacity, which itself leads to increased participation in the finance domain.

Occasionally, actors have mitigated the financial demands of airpower in innovative ways. Many states, as well as non-state actors, have come to rely on relatively cheap unmanned aerial vehicles (UAVs)—commonly referred to as "drones"—to take advantage of the air, which tends to reduce the costs of research, development, training, and maintenance. Armenia and Azerbaijan, for example, relied heavily on UAVs, missiles, and rockets in their latest war over the Nagorno-Karabakh region in 2020.[49] However, even these efforts usually require access to producers and exporters of the relevant equipment, which in turn rewards states with access to hard currency and international liquidity markets. Thus, even sales of relatively inexpensive and obsolescing weapons and technology require activity in the finance domain, albeit with perhaps less impact than trade in modern warships and warplanes.

Finance and Land Domains

Historically, power in the land domain has had the weakest connection with power in the finance domain, as state and nonstate actors have demonstrated a capacity to develop and maintain land power in the absence of sophisticated tools for managing the finance domain. This stands to reason, as there were powerful actors in the land domain before the finance domain existed. These actors created land power through means other than finance, including conscription, tribal or ethnic solidarity, feudal obligation, revolutionary enthusiasm, and religious obligation, basically weaponizing clientelist socioeconomic community structures in the service of making or deterring war. Premodern armies of this sort could be maintained with almost minimal financial resources, as they could requisition (or loot) food and minimal equipment and enslave local populations from the territories they occupied or conquered.

A more modern example of a state acquiring and maintaining land power while attempting to limit its competition in the finance domain is the Soviet Union, which developed huge shipbuilding, aerospace, and defense industries despite having an undermonetized economy and a currency that could not be converted legally.[50] The Soviets acquired foreign technology by theft or barter instead of by purchase and earned foreign currency through the sale of military equipment, industrial goods, and raw materials rather than through the purchase or sale of sovereign debt. Domestically, Soviet currency manifested a promise from the state to workers that it would supply goods at some point in the future, rather than a representation of some reserve of precious metals. Effectively, the Soviet state played a two-level monetary game: a domestic system that enabled the relatively efficient functioning of the domestic economy, and an international system that relied on exports to generate reserves of hard currency that could be used to participate in the international economy.

That the USSR was able to make this game work for a few decades before collapsing in on itself is perhaps an indication of how difficult it is in modern times to attempt to compete across all the other domains without competing in the finance domain in any significant manner.[51]

Our assertion that a relationship between land power and the finance domain has existed throughout history should be uncontroversial, as even in premodern times wealth—however it was generated—helped enhance land power and increase state capacity. For example, Persian "archer" coins helped fund the training and equipping of real archers and helped sustain armies in garrison or on the march in distant territories across Asia Minor.[52] Centuries later in Europe and the Middle East, the Crusades required a significant financial outlay on the part of Western European monarchs and the Catholic Church. The Pope and various assorted kings financed their journeys and armed them regardless, although this may have been a financial arrangement similar to that discussed in the Somalian pirate example above.[53]

Over time, however, even land power has become more dependent on sustainable systems of finance. Conscripts demand to be paid, especially if they serve for extended periods of time. Equipment, ranging from horses to guns to artillery to advanced combat vehicles, often cannot be acquired through nonfinancial means. For example, ISIS sustained itself for a time by looting weapons depots and robbing banks in Iraq and Syria, but was unable to hold any significant amount of territory for any significant length of time.[54] More commonly, state and nonstate actors must compete significantly in the finance domain to compete in the other domains, not least the land domain. Being able to understand and compete effectively in the finance domain is necessary for modern states to exist and for nonstate actors to achieve their goals, whether they be political or monetary.

Conclusion

"Is there such a thing as the finance domain?" is not the question that we are attempting to answer in this book. Rather, we are confident that the term *finance domain* is useful for thinking about certain kinds of international competition and is productive in thinking about the relationship between resources and military power. The finance domain mediates between basic factor endowments and military capabilities. States use technologies of finance (from treasuries to coins to paper currency to central banks to digital forensics) to secure and enhance their power and influence, independently and in conjunction with tools from other domains. In the next chapters, we summarize several RFAs through history and show how using the finance domain as a lens can help increase our understanding of how states use money to pursue security.

Notes

1. Schumpeter, Joseph A. 1991. *The Economics and Sociology of Capitalism*. Princeton: Princeton University Press.
2. Monson, Andrew, and Walter Scheidel. 2015. "Studying Fiscal Regimes." In *Fiscal Regimes and the Political Economy of Premodern States*, edited by Andrew Monson and Walter Scheidel. Cambridge: Cambridge University Press, 3–27; Bonney, Richard, ed. 1999. *The Rise of the Fiscal State in Europe, c.1200–1815*. Oxford: Oxford University Press.
3. Moore, Mick. 2004. "Revenues, State Formation, and the Quality of Governance in Developing Countries." *International Political Science Review* 25 (3): 297–319.
4. North, Douglass C., John Joseph Wallis, and Barry R. Weingast. 2009. *Violence and Social Orders: A Conceptual Framework for Interpreting Recorded Human History*. Cambridge: Cambridge University Press.
5. Ezrow, Natasha M., and Frantz, Erica. 2013. *Failed States and Institutional Decay: Understanding Instability and Poverty in the Developing World*. New York: Bloomsbury.
6. Contamine, Philippe. 1986. *War in the Middle Ages*. Translated by Michael Jones. New York: Blackwell.
7. White, Eugene N. 2004. "From Privatized to Government-Administered Tax Collection: Tax Farming in Eighteenth-Century France." *Economic History Review* 57 (4): 636–663.
8. Monson and Scheidel 2015: 4.
9. A good discussion of acquisition in modern states can be found in Cappella Zielinski, Rosella. 2016. *How States Pay for Wars*. Ithaca: Cornell University Press.
10. Ellickson, Robert C., and Charles DiA. Thorland. 1995. "Ancient Land Law: Mesopotamia, Egypt, Israel." *Chicago-Kent Law Review* 71: 321–411, particularly 373–375.
11. Brewer, John. 2002. *The Sinews of Power: War, Money and the English State, 1688–1783*. Oxfordshire: Routledge; Wheeler, James Scott. 1999. *The Making of a World Power: War and the Military Revolution in Seventeenth-Century England*. Stroud: Sutton.
12. Rosenberg, Matthew, Nicholas Kulish, and Steven Lee Myers. 2015. "Predatory Islamic State Wrings Money From Those It Rules." *New York Times*. November 29. https://www.nytimes.com/2015/11/30/world/middleeast/predatory-islamic-state-wrings-money-from-those-it-rules.html. See also Clarke, Colin P., Kimberly Jackson, Patrick B. Johnston, Eric Robinson, and Howard J. Shatz. 2017. *Financial Futures of the Islamic State of Iraq and the Levant: Findings from a RAND Corporation Workshop*. Santa Monica: RAND.
13. Rollins, John, and Lianna Sun Wyler. 2013. *Terrorism and Transnational Crime: Foreign Policy Issues for Congress*. June 11. Washington, DC: Congressional Research Service; Shelley, Louise I. 2014. *Dirty Entanglements: Corruption, Crime, and Terrorism*. Cambridge: Cambridge University Press.
14. Herodotus. 2008. *The Histories*. Translated by Robin Waterfield. Oxford: Oxford University Press; Thucydides. 2009. *The History of the Peloponnesian War*. Translated by Martin Hammond. Oxford: Oxford University Press.
15. Alston, Richard. 1994. "Roman Military Pay from Caesar to Diocletian." *Journal of Roman Studies* 84: 113–123.
16. Haldon, John. "Late Rome, Byzantium, and Early Medieval Western Europe." In *Fiscal Regimes and the Political Economy of Premodern States*, edited

by Andrew Monson and Walter Scheidel. Cambridge: Cambridge University Press, 350. *Cursus clabularis* refers to a Roman wagon mail service in which the mail was delivered by oxcart, while *platys dromos* translates to "wide road," *cursus velox* refers to a Roman express mail service in which the mail was delivered by horseback, and *oxys dromos* means "fast road."

17. Von Glahn, Richard. 2016. *An Economic History of China: From Antiquity to the Nineteenth Century*. Cambridge: Cambridge University Press, 177.

18. Tracy, James D. 2002. *Emperor Charles V, Impresario of War: Campaign Strategy, International Finance, and Domestic Politics*. Cambridge: Cambridge University Press.

19. Clarke et al. 2017: 9.

20. Shelley 2014.

21. Stasavage, David. 2011. *States of Credit: Size, Power, and the Development of European Polities*. Princeton: Princeton University Press, 35–36.

22. Tilly, Charles. 1990. *Coercion, Capital, and European States, AD 990–1990*. Oxford: Basil Blackwell, 91.

23. Tomz, Michael. 2007. *Reputation and International Cooperation: Sovereign Debt Across Three Centuries*. Princeton: Princeton University Press.

24. The G7 states include Canada, France, Germany, Italy, Japan, the United Kingdom, and the United States.

25. Ereira, Alan. 2015. *The Invergordon Mutiny: A Narrative History of the Last Great Mutiny in the Royal Navy and How It Forced Britain Off the Gold Standard in 1931*. Abingdon: Routledge; Koehler, Benedikt, Mark Duckenfield, and Stefan Altorfer. 2006. *The History of Financial Disasters, 1763–1995*. Vol. 3. Oxfordshire: Taylor and Francis Group.

26. Bordo, Michael D., and Eugene N. White. 1991. "A Tale of Two Currencies: British and French Finance During the Napoleonic Wars." *Journal of Economic History* 51 (2): 303–316; Rockoff, Hugh. 2015. *War and Inflation in the United States from the Revolution to the First Iraq War*. Paper w21221. Washington, DC: National Bureau of Economic Research (NBER).

27. Posen, Barry R. 2003. "Command of the Commons: The Military Foundation of Hegemony." *International Security* 28 (1): 5–46. See also Mahan, Alfred Thayer. 1999. Vol. 4: *The Influence of Sea Power upon History, 1660–1783*, in *Roots of Strategy*, edited by David Jablonsky. Mechanicsburg: Stockpole Books, 78.

28. Denmark, Abraham, and James Mulvenon. 2010. *Contested Commons: The Future of American Military Power in a Multipolar World*. Washington, DC: Center for a New American Security (CNAS), 8.

29. See, for example, Garrett Hardin. 1998. "Extensions of 'the Tragedy of the Commons.'" *Science* 280 (5364): 682–683.

30. For a review of the technical divisions over the past few decades, see Pessoa, Mario, and Mike Williams. 2012. *Government Cash Management: Relationship Between the Treasury and the Central Bank*. Washington, DC: International Monetary Fund.

31. Palma, Nuno. 2016 *Money and Modernization: Liquidity, Specialization and Structural Change in Early Modern England*. Working Paper 2016/11. Max Weber Programme, Paris: European Union Institute, figure 7; Mitchell, Brian. R. 1988. *British Historical Statistics*. Cambridge: Cambridge University Press; Clark, Gregory. 2009. *The Macroeconomic Aggregates for England, 1209–2008*. Working Paper 09-19. Davis: Department of Economics, University of California, Davis, table 26. The earliest figures are for 1699.

32. Mun, Thomas. 1895. *England's Treasure by Forraign Trade*. London: Macmillan.

33. Lambert, Nicholas. 2012. *Planning Armageddon: British Economic Warfare and the First World War*. Cambridge: Harvard University Press.
34. Silber, William L., and Greg Kaza. 2007. *When Washington Shut Down Wall Street: The Great Financial Crisis of 1914 and the Origins of America's Monetary Supremacy*. Princeton: Princeton University Press, 333–337; Rockoff, Hugh. 2012. *America's Economic Way of War: War and the Economy from the Spanish-American War to the Persian Gulf War*. Cambridge: Cambridge University Press, 123.
35. Maoz, Zeev. 2009. "The Effects of Strategic and Economic Interdependence on International Conflict Across Levels of Analysis." *American Journal of Political Science* 53 (1), 223–240.
36. Farrell, Henry, and Abraham L. Newman. 2021. "Weaponized Interdependence: How Global Economic Networks Shape State Coercion." In *The Uses and Abuses of Weaponized Interdependence*, edited by Daniel Drezner, Henry Farrell, and Abraham L. Newman, 19–66. Washington, DC: Brookings Institution Press.
37. Drezner, Daniel. 2021. "The Uses and Abuses of Weaponized Interdependence." In *The Uses and Abuses of Weaponized Interdependence*, edited by Daniel Drezner, Henry Farrell, and Abraham Newman. Washington, DC: Brookings Institution Press, 1–18: 1.
38. Drezner 2021: 1.
39. UCL (University College London). 2021. "The Bentham Project."
40. Farrell and Newman 2021: 29.
41. Krepinevich, Andrew F. 1994. "Cavalry to Computer: The Pattern of Military Revolutions." *The National Interest* 37: 30–42; Knox, MacGregor, and Williamson Murray, eds. 2001. *The Dynamics of Military Revolution, 1300–2050*. Cambridge: Cambridge University Press.
42. Krepinevich 1994: 30; Cohen, Eliot A. 1996. "A Revolution in Warfare." *Foreign Affairs* 75 (2): 37–54.
43. See, for example, Loeb, Vernon, and Thomas Ricks. 2002. "Rumsfeld's Style, Goals Strain Ties in Pentagon; 'Transformation' Effort Spawns Issues of Control." *Washington Post*, October 16.
44. Parker, Geoffrey. 1976. "The 'Military Revolution,' 1560–1660—a Myth?" *Journal of Modern History* 48 (2): 196–214.
45. Murray, Williamson. 1997. "Thinking About Revolutions in Military Affairs." Press Release. Public Affairs, Department of Defense, Washington, DC.
46. Ahmed, Mohammed. 2009. "Somali Sea Gangs Lure Investors at Pirate Lair." Reuters, December 1.
47. Epstein, Katherine C. 2014. *Torpedo*. Cambridge: Harvard University Press.
48. The exceptions here being Saudi Arabia, Qatar, and the People's Republic of China, although they tend to use corvée labor for less-skilled jobs.
49. Shaikh, Shaan, and Wes Rumbaugh. 2020. *The Air and Missile War in Nagorno-Karabakh: Lessons for the Future of Strike and Defense*. Washington, DC: Center for Strategic and International Studies.
50. Shearer, David R. 2018. *Industry, State, and Society in Stalin's Russia, 1926–1934*. Ithaca: Cornell University Press.
51. Goldberg, Linda S., and Il'dar Karimov. 1991. *Internal Currency Markets and Production in the Soviet Union*. Working Paper w3614. Washington, DC: NBER.
52. Herodotus 2008.
53. Tyerman, Christopher. 2007. *God's War: A New History of the Crusades*. London: Penguin UK.
54. Stergiou, Dimitrios. 2016. "ISIS Political Economy: Financing a Terror State." *Journal of Money Laundering Control* 19 (2): 189–207.

3
Financial Strategies in Antiquity

For as long as they aspired to rule over their neighbours or over the Peloponnesians alone, they found the supplies and resources furnished by Laconia itself adequate, as they had all they required ready to hand, and quickly returned home whether by land or sea. But once they began to undertake naval expeditions and to make military campaigns outside the Peloponnese, it was evident that neither their iron currency nor the exchange of their crops for commodities which they lacked, as permitted by the legislation of Lycurgus, would suffice for their needs, since these enterprises demanded a currency in universal circulation and supplies drawn from abroad; and so they were compelled to be beggars from the Persians, to impose tribute on the islanders, and exact contributions from all the Greeks, as they recognized that under the legislation of Lycurgus it was impossibleå to aspire, I will not say to supremacy in Greece, but to any position of influence.
—Polybius (c. 200–118 BC), *The Histories,* Book VI

Financial competition across borders is not new. States and statelike entities have long used financial tools not only to enhance their own power, but also to shape their environments and coerce their rivals. We argue that treating finance as a domain of competition offers a useful lens for thinking about strategic competition even during antiquity. Indeed, given the extent to which analogies to the ancient world continue to inform the study of modern geopolitics, the ways in which the ancients thought about the relationship between money and war bears scrutiny. While Thucydides looms large in modern study of the ancients, the continued presence of Sun Tzu, Kautilya, Herodotus, Polybius, Cicero, and other ancients in discussions of strategic theory makes an assessment of the role of finance in the ancient world even more relevant to modern strategy, and to our understanding of international competition in general.[1]

Our effort represents a survey rather than a full recounting of the financial structures of the ancient world, a project that would run well beyond the bounds of this book. Because of the enduring relevance of the ancient Mediterranean in the contemporary strategic conversation, we concentrate first on finance in the Greco-Roman world. The city-states of the Mediterranean varied dramatically in size and sophistication and employed a correspondingly wide range of taxation and tribute schemes. While the fragmentary information available makes it hard to make definitive statements about fiscal systems and strategic manipulations of finance in this era, the dense population and the high levels of warfare, trade, and monetization suggest that the leaders of Mediterranean city-states understood the coercive potential of their tools of financial statecraft.

After a discussion of the ancient Mediterranean and its employment of financial tools in competition, we reinforce our understanding of the finance domain in the ancient world by then describing evidence of similar thought and action in premodern China. Unfortunately, as discussed earlier we are forced due to reasons of space and sources to neglect the financial statecraft of ancient India, of Africa outside the Mediterranean, and of pre-Columbian America, although there is strong evidence of similar financial statecraft in each of those areas during this period.

The Coinage Revolution in Financial Affairs in the Ancient World

Two forces determine finance's strategic significance at the international level: first, the development of structured, articulated, and powerful systems of taxation and state capacity; and, second, the development of trade and liquidity within a regional economy. Spillover effects from neighboring regions can also have an impact on the development of sophisticated financial and military structures, but this is of secondary importance. As a result of these forces, both taxation and liquidity develop considerably as a regional economy becomes more sophisticated and heterogeneous.

The primary technological development that spurred the revolutions in financial affairs (RFAs) in the ancient world was the introduction and widespread use of coins as currency. There is substantial documentation of the ways that money can spontaneously spring into existence when needed for trades, usually in the form of a generally valued good that is easy to transport. Examples of this phenomenon include: people living in frontier Appalachia used whiskey; prisoners throughout modern history have used cigarettes; and, most important for our purposes, several polities in the ancient world used metal, either precious (gold and silver, common in the Mediterranean) or base (bronze and copper, for example, common in China) to create systems of coins.

To understand why coins became the norm for currency in the ancient world, it helps to think about the nature of commerce. To complete a commercial transaction, it was necessary for merchants to check quantity and quality of the currency used for that transaction. This authentication process can be costly and difficult if the proposed currency is not widely used or if the currency is informal, such as the cigarettes or whiskey, thereby limiting trade. To remedy this problem, rulers in the ancient world began to coin official money—the kingdom of Lydia in Asia Minor (now western Turkey) being perhaps the first, although coinage seems to have emerged independently in several parts of Eurasia in the first millennium BCE.[2]

The minting of coins, to the degree that it is well done and carefully monitored, creates in money three critical functions: a unit of account, a store of value, and a medium of exchange.[3] These three functions must be performed by adjacent, but not perfectly overlapping, parts of the mint institution in most commodity money systems for a currency to be successfully circulated and adopted as a medium of exchange. The *unit of account*—that is, a measure of value, in the same way that a yardstick defines a distance—is generally a theoretical measure. In the contemporary United States, dollar bills and dollar-denominated bank accounts are valued at the going rate for dollars. This simple relationship is historically somewhat unusual and can be described as "at par value."[4] Historically, it has frequently been necessary to compute or even speculate as to the exact relationship between a physical unit of currency and its value as a unit of account. In the contemporary developed world, par value of the money supply is taken for granted, but this situation is not easily obtained. To maintain par, a unit of money must be reliably liquid; that is, convertible into other goods or services at a consistent rate.

There are roughly three ways money can maintain this liquidity: the first is for the physical value of the materials of the currency to be the same as the face value—a coin where the value of the metal that composes it is the face value of the coin; the second is for a state to set up a reliable system that allows bearers to convert the money into materials equal to the face value of the money. This was the case in the classical gold standard, where holders of paper currency or deposits could convert these into the equivalent value of gold. And third, the method in use in the United States today, is that money denominated in dollars will be accepted at par for a range of transactions. States have frequently leaned on a mixture of the first and third approaches, wherein the value of the currency's metal is below (but close to) face value; states encourage this currency's use for a number of official purposes. As money is a store of value and a medium of exchange, the value of currency as a medium of exchange is a combination of how reliable it is as a general store of value and on how rapidly it can be evaluated for this reliability. When people lose confidence in the entity issuing the currency, this value can decrease rapidly; in the case of coins of gold or silver, it can be a combination of a lack of confidence in the issuer and doubt that the value of the metal composing the coin is equal to the face value.[5]

This approach has two advantages: first, if the value of the metal fluctuates above the value of the unit of account, it creates incentives to melt down the coins for the specie; second, it allows the issuer to profit from the difference and prevents the value of the metal from going above its face value. The term *seigniorage* denotes the government's ability to capture revenue from the difference between the coin's production cost and its face value. Unless a system is operating in which the value of its money is at par, the value of seigniorage is rarely zero, and the money's issuing authorities can increase the rate of seigniorage to generate revenue or decrease it to increase the public's trust in the currency by manipulating the value of materials or the face value.[6]

Governments that practice coinage can manipulate the value of their currency via the practice of debasement, reducing the amount of precious metal in each unit of currency without lowering its face value.[7] The historical record suggests that debasement functioned for thousands of years as a crucial source of war finance for governments, despite the risks to the currency's value involved. The Roman Empire, for example, is sometimes held up as an example of the awful costs of debasement. There is no doubt that the empire reduced the fineness or percentage of silver in its coins from 1 CE to 300 CE, from close to 100 percent down to less than 50 percent by 250 CE and then further down, which is interpreted by some scholars of evidence of hyperinflation. However, the evidence from extant price data suggests much more moderate inflation; over several hundred years prices appear to have increased by an average of 3.5 percent per year (after 300 CE the rate of inflation increased to 15 percent or so a year). From the point of view of the emperors who ordered it, the debasements appear to have been generally successful.[8] Indeed, we argue that one piece of evidence of the power and success of debasement as a tool is that it faded away only as countries in Europe began to take advantage of the new financial technologies of public and central banks in the fifteenth century, a process we discuss in the next chapter.

Overall, the coinage RFA in the finance domain facilitated long-distance trade, as well as giving central rulers greater authority over territories under their control. Consistent with this increase in widespread use of coins and the concomitant political centralization, coinage took on a remarkable degree of uniformity in Eurasia from the sixth until the third century BCE.[9] In contrast to the multitude of forms that had existed a couple of centuries earlier, most coins minted or struck by states across Eurasia were round and made of a precious or base metal by the end of this period, making transmission and accounting easier for merchants and tax officials.[10] As we will show, this uniformity facilitated long-term investment structures that enabled the creation and maintenance of large fleets of warships and made possible the employment of mercenaries, thereby translating financial utility into military utility. To sum up: the coinage RFA made it easier to transform certain kinds of resource factors—precious metals, mints, mines—into ready military power. In the next sections, we detail the military implications of this RFA in the Greater Mediterranean and China.

The Impact of the Coinage RFA in the Greater Mediterranean

Although states across the Fertile Crescent did not use coinage until several centuries later, they appear to have begun using taxation to systematically fund organized military forces by about 3000 BCE.[11] In Egypt's Old Kingdom (2700–2000 BCE), censuses of specific resources of the kingdom were a critical event for the maintenance of the state, such that the regular counting of the cattle was used to track the passage of years and to determine individual tax burdens, suggesting the existence of a domain system. By the New Kingdom (sixteenth century BCE), the system had shifted toward taxation, largely in grain, making transmittal a critical issue. In Mesopotamia, by contrast, merchants frequently lent money in the form of regularized chunks of precious metal rather than government coins to individual citizens for tax payments, which contributed to substantial private debt.[12] The Neo-Assyrian Empire appears to have earned the greatest tributes of any state of the Near East or Egypt, but still required extensive internal taxes. Steady increases in trade and monetization led to greater uses of money in the tax system, but taxation in kind and through corvée labor remained important until at least 500 BCE.[13] Thus, monetary and nonmonetary systems of currency existed alongside one another, offering a useful lens for analysis of the impact of financial sophistication on state policy.

The development of a relatively sophisticated system of finance and trade in the Eastern Mediterranean is important for understanding how the great powers in the Hellenic world managed finance during war, especially considering the role of the ancient Mediterranean world as a sometimes controversial touchstone for much modern strategic literature.[14] The enduring influence of Thucydides, especially within the American strategic class, makes an exploration of the financial aspects of strategic competition in the Mediterranean particularly fruitful. Fortunately, Thucydides and several other major historians—including Herodotus and Polybius—pay considerable attention to questions of finance, and especially of the connections between finance and war.

Herodotus of Halicarnassus chronicled the Greco-Persian War of the fifth century BCE, as well as many of the social and cultural aspects of its participants. In describing the Achaemenid Empire of Persia (550–330 BCE), for example, Herodotus details the system of tribute and finance that the central government established over the various conquered territories. This description includes a list of the financial responsibilities of all the provinces, including those that have no specific tribute requirement.[15]

Herodotus thus directly associates the powers of the Achaemenid Empire with its ability to command tribute from its territories, and consequently from its ability to store great wealth.

In addition to the Achaemenid Empire's advances in tax collecting, it also made progress in coinage as a means of transforming basic resources into national power. The empire initially copied the coinage of the Lydian Kingdom that it conquered in 545 BCE, but toward the end of the sixth century BCE struck a new form of coinage, the "archer," which would remain in circulation until the Macedonian conquest of 330 BCE. Coined from gold, the Achaemenid Empire used archers for a variety of economic purposes. In the traditional historiography, the primary purpose of the coinage was understood as pay for mercenaries fighting on the western fringes of the empire, and in particular for the lethal archers of Achaemenid armies.[16] More recent scholarship has refocused on the symbolic and ideological importance of the coinage, noting that archers held greater relevance for the Persians than the mere value of the material in the coins would suggest.[17] In addition to their monetary value, archers were status symbols, demonstrating the wealth, power, and influence of the holder; consequently, control of their supply and distribution granted the ruler considerable influence over the nobility. Thus, archers may represent a halfway point between clientelist and market-based military organization; perhaps a developmental stage, or simply a hybrid example of finance and state propaganda. In any case, Persian coinage would play an important role in the Peloponnesian War, which followed the first Greco-Persian War by some forty-five years.

For their part, the city-states of Hellenic Greece varied dramatically in size and sophistication, from complex states such as Athens with a range of taxation and tribute schemes, to small units such as Melos that functioned more like domain states. The variation and the fragmentary information available make it hard to make definitive statements about fiscal systems and strategic manipulations of finance across the region.[18] However, as discussed below, the dense population and the high levels of warfare, trade, and monetization suggest that Hellenic Greece constituted a financial commons and, consequently, an area in which states could compete in the finance domain. It is ironic, then, that the two regional powers competing for hegemony—Athens and Sparta—pursued radically different financial strategies.

Athens: Hegemonic Aspirations

Athens was the largest and wealthiest of the Greek city-states during the fifth century BCE, deriving its revenue from several sources.[19] The only standard direct tax was the *metoikoin*, a tax levied on resident noncitizen free men. Although wealthy citizens were not taxed directly, there was a societal norm encouraging them to put forward money in services to the community, or liturgies. For example, the standard military form of liturgy was for citizens to directly fund the maintenance and crew of a warship. In addition to direct taxation and liturgies, Athens would also levy indirect taxes on citizens, usually in the rare case of emergencies, like the *eisphora*, a tax imposed on the wealthy in response to special military exigency. Furthermore, Athens pressured the other, weaker members of the Delian League alliance of city-states to either pay a tribute or contribute warships to bolster the Athenian military profile.[20]

By the outset of the Peloponnesian War, the Athenians had stored a large amount of wealth under the direction of Pericles, a circumstance that appears to have been unique in this period. Thucydides summarizes the finances of Athens as an annual income of 600 talents—a talent being a unit of measurement of value equal to about 6,000 drachmae, a drachma being the coin in common circulation at the time and itself worth about $US50 in 2015—from its allies, 6,000 talents in the treasury, and an additional estimated 500 talents of valuable metals in statues, reliquaries, and other *objets d'art*.[21] As a result of this storehouse of wealth, Athens could afford to pay both citizens and mercenaries relatively well; during the Peloponnesian War, each rower in a trireme crew of 200 could expect roughly a drachma a day for service, above and beyond the reward offered by completing a civic responsibility.[22] One way in which cities in the Delian League maintained this wealth was through the exploitation of its silver mines for coinage.[23] This seemingly straightforward method of revenue generation did have its pitfalls: Athens itself maintained access to silver mines for much of the duration of the Peloponnesian War, but suffered badly from curtailment of this access by the Spartans in the final years of the conflict.[24]

Another financial innovation of Hellenic Athens, as well as a link between finance and maritime trade was the sea loan, a form of debt contract that continues in some form up until the present day.[25] Also known as the maritime or bottomry loan, the advantage or "essential peculiarity" of the vehicle was that the borrower was not obliged to repay if the cargo was lost at sea.[26] Moses Finley observes of the classical era that "it seems to have been almost a fixed rule of Athenian commercial practice, attributable to the great risks of sea traffic and the inadequate accumulation of liquid capital, that merchants used borrowed funds, in whole or in part, for their maritime ventures."[27] The sea loans were short term, clearly detailed, and with interest rates that might on an annualized basis go to 100 percent, a rate that would be usurious in modern terms, but in fact reflected the level of risk involved in maritime trade at the time. Critically, the sea loan allowed the lender to demand more than the initial sum as repayment in a way that could be presented as compensation for possible losses, not interest.[28] Despite the high risk premium paid by the borrower, they appear to have been the only economically productive loans regularly made in classical Athens, in the sense that they facilitated productive commercial activity. The sea loan's effectiveness is likewise demonstrated by its widespread use: from its Athenian origins it became an important part of Roman trade, and then became part of medieval law.[29] One place in which sea loans were not in general use, however, was in Athens's main adversary: Sparta.

Sparta: Hegemonic Ambitions

Hellenic Sparta's approach to public finance appears to have been a version of the general domain state structure. There was one relatively small institutional military group, the Homoioi, governed in a generally egalitarian and democratic way by an age-class system, the *agoge*. The Homoioi were probably 5,000 strong at their most numerous and shrunk to 1,000 in late antiquity as Sparta's ambitions were likewise reduced. Kings of Sparta held domains in the communities of the free civilian Spartans, the Perioikoi, which, with the *helots* (slaves), performed the productive economic life of Sparta. The fruits of the royal domains and the drafting of the Perioikoi as soldiers supported the Homoioi as the Spartan military, seemingly without the support of a separate taxation system.[30] The comparative role of coinage in the Spartan system was likewise more limited than in Athens, as evidence suggests that Sparta did not coin its own money until after the end of the Hellenic period—possibly using iron as its metal—and that the influx of foreign wealth into Sparta after the end of the Peloponnesian War (431–404 BCE) caused some social dislocation.[31]

In contrast to Athens, the Spartans appear to have had little money on hand at the opening of the Peloponnesian War, although Michael M. Austin and Pierre Vidal-Naquet quote from a stone near Sparta that recorded what appear to be emergency loans and tributes pulled from states and individuals in the area to finance its war effort.[32] Likewise, Thucydides reports the following statements from Spartan king Archidamus as his assembly contemplated war against Athens:

> For though in respect of the Peloponnesians and our neighbour states we have equal strength and can quickly be upon them, yet against men whose territory is remote and are also expert seamen and with all other things excellently furnished, as money, both private and public, shipping, horses, arms, and number, more than any one part of Greece besides, and that have many confederates paying them tribute: against such, I say, why should we lightly undertake the war? And since we are unfurnished, whereon relying should we make such haste to it? On our navy? But therein we are too weak; and if we will provide and prepare against them, it will require time. On our money? But therein also we are more too weak; for neither hath the state any, nor will private men readily contribute. . . . What a war then will this of ours be? For unless we have the better of them in shipping or take from them their revenue whereby their navy is maintained, we shall do the most hurt to ourselves.[33]

Archidamus's concern was that Sparta would be unable to transform its basic agricultural and personnel advantages into a military system that could support distant operations, and that such operations were absolutely necessary to the defeat of Athens. In Clausewitzian terms, Archidamus identified Athens's system of finance as its "center of gravity," and expressed concern over the ability of Sparta to seriously challenge that center. This lack of a Spartan fiscal structure was not decisive in the royal decisionmaking process, however. Sovereign borrowing was reasonably well developed at the time and, after years of fighting, the Spartans were able to arrange a loan from Tissaphernes, a Persian, to buy the navy that helped them win the war.[34]

However, Polybius—a Greek historian who chronicled the rise of Roman hegemony across the Mediterranean—argues explicitly that Sparta's inability to develop sufficiently flexible financial institutions hamstrung its ability to influence events in Greece and across the Mediterranean. Polybius's judgment in this issue is hardly incontestable but, as one of the premier scholars and analysts of the rise to power of republican Rome, he was particularly attuned to the policies that enabled Rome to succeed where Greek city-states had failed. Writing in the second century BCE, Polybius offers the most important near-contemporary account of Roman victories over Carthage in the Punic Wars, and the rise of Roman influence over the Greek city-state system. As a Greek who lived much of his life in Rome, he was peculiarly qualified to make comparisons between the rise of Rome and the failure of the hegemonic aspirations of the great Greek city-states. Sparta was not poor; Polybius distinguishes between economic wherewithal and financial capacity in noting that the Spartans "found the supplies and resources furnished by Laconia itself adequate, as they had all they required ready to hand."[35] However, in his account Sparta is hamstrung by a constitutional proscription against using a universally acceptable currency, and we may infer that the inefficiencies associated with the premodern transport of bulk agricultural goods made it difficult to use barter to transform Sparta's basic factor endowment into military and diplomatic power, especially in the maritime sphere. Sparta could win the war only by engaging in a ruinous relationship with Persia and by inflicting economic pain on its allies. Persia and Athens, each of which enjoyed vastly more sophisticated systems of finance, both maintained much more extensive empires and undertook more credible efforts at achieving regional hegemony.[36] While Polybius lacked the analytical tools available to modern scholars for assessing the importance of financial, as opposed to economic, power, his analysis of the weakness of the Spartan financial system is supported by contemporary accounts.

The examples from the Peloponnesian War and its aftermath demonstrated that while mastery of the tools of finance was important to waging war, by itself it did not grant victory. Sparta defeated Athens because of the strength of its armies and the support of its allies, despite the financial sophistication of the latter. Similarly, in the immediate wake of the war, a contender for the Persian throne hired a large body of Greek mercenaries to help press his claim. Following the untimely death of Cyrus the Younger, however, the mercenaries were forced to fight their way out of the Persian Empire despite a lack of significant funds.[37] But money remained important; Aristotle describes the use of a number of stratagems by the rulers of Byzantium, including the sale of sacred lands, the sale of concessions for changing money, and the sale of "places where markets were held and traders operated, the sea fisheries, the traffic in salt, places reserved to jugglers, soothsayers, drug peddlers and other such professions."[38] While at war with the Olynthians in 364 BCE, Athenian general Timotheus engaged in a number of stratagems to raise money or keep his troops happy, including switching from silver coins to bronze coins to increase seigniorage.[39]

Sixty years after the end of the Peloponnesian War, a well-supplied Macedonian army led by Alexander the Great would conquer the entirety of the Achaemenid Empire despite the overwhelming financial resources at the command of the Persians, at least in part due to his savvy understanding of the finance domain.[40] Alexander used a variety of resources to finance his invasion, including loans from Greek city-states under Macedonian control, the minting of precious metals from silver mines, the Macedonian treasury, and taxation of occupied territories. Alexander also expected loot from Persian treasuries to provide the financial backbone for his expedition.[41] Looting represented a sort of borrowing in that soldiers fought in anticipation of receiving substantial financial gains from victory. As it happened, these expectations were rewarded, as Alexander captured major royal treasuries that significantly increased his financial wherewithal. Alexander also arranged for payments to the families of soldiers killed in action from Macedonia and elsewhere, providing incentive for his warriors to continue fighting even in dangerous situations. Following the conquest of the Persian capitol Alexander liberated the treasury, increasing the pay of soldiers substantially. On the one hand, this represented the payoff of the implicit financial debt that Alexander owed his army. On the other, it generated inflation resulting from the sudden influx of Persian bullion into the economy. The increase in the cash supply was not matched by an increase in economic productivity, consequently making precious metals relatively less valuable, thereby devaluing the currency coined from them.

The Macedonian conquest of the Persian Empire in the fourth century BCE resulted, briefly, in the existence of a single state—Seleucid—spanning from western India to the Eastern Mediterranean. However, the rapid collapse of this state precluded the development of a unified financial system.[42] The Seleucid state mainly replicated Achaemenid financial practice, using many small mints to provide coinage, mostly to the western half of the empire.[43] Overall, Alexander did not exploit the coinage RFA so much as incorporate it into an existing financial framework.

The Roman Republic and Principate

Alexander's time as hegemon ended shortly thereafter. In the third and second centuries BCE the Roman Republic would absorb much of the Greek world, defeating Macedon and the Seleucid Kingdoms in war and forcing Egypt to become a client state. This victory, added to Roman conquests in Africa and Iberia, resulted in a single financial system spanning the Mediterranean.[44] This system would last for several centuries, and its origins lay in the constitution of the Roman Republic as well as its successful exploitation of the coinage RFA. From the Roman Republic's founding in 509 BCE, it used indirect taxes to fund general administrative operations and one-time taxes (tributes, collected by *tribunii*) for military campaigns. Roman power expanded rapidly from its central Italian base, with significant effects on the financial system.[45] Roman conquests generally resulted in substantial looting and a massive increase in the availability of precious metals to the Roman state. This financial system also appears to have allowed individuals to amass enormous wealth as tax collectors or tax farmers who, standing strategically between the state and the regional taxpayers, had incentives to increase how much they collected from taxpayers and minimize how much they subsequently transmitted to the state. The tax farmers, frequently senators or other powerful men, tended not to attract the scrutiny of the state treasury so long as the receipts they transmitted were sufficient to maintain the empire's operation.[46] As with other authoritarian states to come, the Roman Empire tolerated a certain amount of corruption among its selectorate as long as they maintained their loyalty to the state.

During the early Principate (established in 27 BCE), Roman taxation included both monetary and in-kind payments. Shipments of grain from conquered provinces (primarily Egypt, but also other parts of the Mediterranean) were collected and distributed to urban populations.[47] Monetary contributions were also collected from the provinces and from Italy directly. As would be expected for a state without a permanent financial bureaucracy or a body of strong fiscal theory, state policy varied over time. Augustus, for example, favored easy credit and substantial state investment, while his successor Tiberius tightened the money supply and hoarded the resulting surplus.[48] While there is debate over the extent and sophistication of Roman monetary policy, there is little doubt that the establishment of the Principate led to significant changes in the nature of monetary flows in the empire.[49] In particular, Romans were aware of the relationship between the prices, the availability of precious metals, and interest rates, and the ability of the household of the emperor to manage and account for financial flows gave the state the capacity to monitor and stabilize prices across the empire.[50]

Regarding the internal component of financial competition, fiscal management, the Principate appears to have been too strongly oriented toward tribute from its early years of conquest and had trouble consistently raising internal revenues. In later years the state would grant remissions and tax relief to entire regions, focusing its taxation efforts on productive regions such as Egypt or state domains like mines.[51] By the late third century CE, tensions along the northern and eastern borders of the empire made fiscal and financial demands more stringent. Reigning in the east from 284 until 305 CE as part of a tetrarchy, Emperor Diocletian undertook a raft of reforms to the administrative and economic systems of the empire, including a wholesale transformation of the system of taxation. Diocletian's attempt to reform coinage and prices included devaluing the coinage and undertaking an effort at price controls, actions that avoided hyperinflation but not destabilization.[52] Authority fragmented across the empire, leading to increasing differences in fiscal policy in the east and the west. Western emperors began to offer low taxes to particular regions as they bid for support and power, progressively reducing the tax base. There were multiple debasements (reductions in the amount of metal in a coin), partially due to limits on access to specie but also likely to have been attempts to use seigniorage as an emergency financing measure. In contrast, and despite the policy failures mentioned above, Diocletian stabilized and bureaucratized the government financial system in the east, implementing "the most comprehensive and rational fiscal regime in the Mediterranean world until modern times," saving the Eastern Roman Empire for "another millennium."[53]

At its peak, the ability of the Roman Empire to provide a stable and predictable financial environment facilitated the expansion of trade across the Mediterranean and, consequently, the ability of Rome to effect its political and strategic preferences.[54] The development of banks with transregional reach and of social organizations that spread risk across multiple individuals and families significantly lowered household financial risks relative to what had existed prior to the establishment of Roman hegemony.[55] These financial networks likely increased the general prosperity of the Mediterranean, while simultaneously allowing the Roman state to capture a greater portion of the gains from trade and thus to transform economic productivity into military power. Furthermore, the association of the prosperity of families and trade groups with the health of the empire helped soften the harsher aspects of Roman imperial rule, reducing incentives for rebellion and, consequently, the costs of imperial maintenance. In short, the development of sophisticated tools within the finance domain enabled Rome to expand its military, economic, and political power across the Mediterranean.[56]

The fiscal impact of the Roman Empire was felt across Eurasia.[57] Han China and the Roman Empire conducted a vigorous trade, albeit usually through Parthian (Iranian) and Indian intermediaries.[58] Peter Frankopan's work details the extensive commercial, social, and cultural connections between Asia and Europe during the ancient period.[59] Archaeological and primary source analysis also supports the idea that both Han and Roman authorities regarded the maintenance of commercial connections as a high policy priority.[60] The consolidation of Roman control over the Mediterranean and the transition between the republic and the empire led to a massive increase in trade contacts between China and Rome. While Han China was more densely bureaucratized than the Roman Empire, the Roman economy appears to have been more monetized than its Chinese counterpart.[61] Indeed, the military expansion of the Roman Empire provided for the existence of a financial commons that enabled the development of sophisticated systems of credit and finance across the empire and beyond.[62]

China in Antiquity

Over the past several thousand years, China has tended to dominate the politics of East Asia in a way that is dramatically different than any power in Europe. An imperfect European analogy for China's multiple periods of unification after the ascension of the Qin Dynasty in 221 BCE might be the Roman Empire from Augustus to the fall of the Western Roman Empire, although the latter did not reconstitute itself in the same way as later Chinese dynasties. Although in a number of cases China is the first—or among the first—to use a particular financial technology, most famously in the development of paper money, fiscal and financial methods often failed to survive the collapse of particular dynasties. Thus, the methods used by Chinese governments to fund their military shifted from something like feudalism, to something like the late Roman garrisons, to sophisticated fiscal-military states, and then back again. At the same time, the most sophisticated interactions in the finance domain rival anything seen elsewhere to at least the nineteenth and possibly the twentieth century.

As states across the Mediterranean and the Levant began to develop systems of taxation and some storage and transmission capability, Chinese states were forging similar tools. By the fourth century BCE—the middle of the Warring States Period—most states in China had adopted fairly complex systems of centralized taxation, labor impressment, and expenditure that attempted greater control of the economy than that attempted by the empires of the west at the time.[63] And this centralization only grew more comprehensive; by the second century BCE, the Han Dynasty had advanced beyond this capacity to a taxation system that covered much of the geographical equivalent of modern-day China in a single state.[64] Effectively, this centralization brought most of the regional trade system under the authority of a single government, making strategic use of finance less important in external relations. Despite this level of bureaucratic operation, however, organized taxation and public finance remained critical challenges throughout the period; for example, at several points in the early Imperial Period, maintaining sufficient coinage was a challenge, limiting how well resources could flow across provinces.[65] Nevertheless, these attempts at control provide evidence that early Chinese policymakers were aware of the relationship between money supply and prices, as well as the relationship between fiscal policy and state power, and acted accordingly.[66]

The origins of China's monetary economy are complex and contested, but some scholars at least have argued that the shape—if not the production process—of early coinage across Eurasia is not accidental. While early Chinese coins came in a multiplicity of shapes, by the third century BCE coins were usually round, like their counterparts in the Mediterranean.[67] As we further discuss, this similarity suggests a complex set of financial relationships that enabled cultural and economic exchange across Eurasia during premodern times. The primary differences between Chinese and Mediterranean coinage involved the metal used—bronze as opposed to gold and silver—and the presence of a hole in the middle of the Chinese coins, as well as its purpose: while bullion existed as a store of value in China, it was not widely used as currency.

While both the Han and Roman Empires understood the importance of managing their financial affairs, and made efforts to control the amount of coined currency circulated through (and out of) their economies, Roman coins were not as useful to the Chinese as bullion or the other goods that Parthian and other intermediaries could provide.[68] Indeed, Chinese states from the Qin Dynasty on exclusively employed bronze coinage over precious metals, using the latter only as bullion.[69] Nevertheless, the fact that the Romans had established a robust system of coinage was deeply important to Chinese traders, and to the Han state. The system that developed during the late republic and early Imperial Period differed substantially from the Hellenistic period, during which the successors of Alexander established competitive, mutually antagonistic kingdoms on the ruins of the Persian Empire. These kingdoms lacked a unified coinage, preventing the establishment of systems of finance that enabled borrowing across distance and time and, thus, facilitated long-distance trade.

Conclusion

One of this chapter's purposes is to illustrate the extent to which strategic competition in antiquity demanded the development of financial institutions of sufficient sophistication to enable states to productively exploit their resource and human endowments. Additionally, we hope to demonstrate here that early states used tools of finance to buy or borrow military power from others, as well as to deter or terminate conflict. Money, in short, was critical to how the ancients thought about war.

The ability of states to use finance to mobilize resources, shape competition, and coerce their enemies is nearly as old as the international system itself. Generations of students at all manner of educational institutions have cut their strategic teeth on Thucydides, reading in detail about Athenian and Spartan finances. Despite its significance and ubiquity, rarely do financial issues become the core of the story when discussing these conflicts. Even less often do we consider the core insight of Polybius, perhaps the premier analyst of empire in the ancient literature. While financial competition does not explain the entirety of the course of the Peloponnesian War, it does help explain, for example, the nature and limits of Spartan hegemony at the end of the conflict.

This chapter's primary purpose, however, is to illustrate the ways in which the coinage RFA enabled several related military developments in antiquity. The RFA enabled states to raise and maintain military forces for extended periods of time at long distances from their imperial centers. Specifically, the Achaemenid, Qin, and Roman Empires used coined currency to pay soldiers in short- and long-term deployments on distant borders, and the Roman Empire maintained such forces on a permanent bases, using currency to transform the gains associated with long-distance trade into military power.

The coinage RFA also likely enabled the maintenance and construction of large-scale naval forces, which required significant capital investment in yards for maintenance and construction, harbors for basing, and professional crews for sailing. Coinage likewise facilitated long-distance maritime trade, which helped to build a cadre of expertise and professionalism in the maritime domain and create the basis for substantial navies. As a result, Persia, Athens, Carthage, and Rome were all able to use naval forces to extend their power and ensure control over territory.

However, while dominance in the finance domain gave tremendous advantages to its possessor, it could not always prove decisive. Despite Athens's financial wherewithal and sophistication, for example, it failed to defeat Sparta in the Peloponnesian War, losing its empire in the process. Likewise, the vast sums of money at the command of the Achaemenid Empire could not produce sufficient military power to overcome Greek resistance in the fifth century BCE and failed to mobilize enough power in the fourth century to defeat Alexander's invasion. Finally, while the Roman Empire collapsed for complicated reasons, the lack of a sophisticated institutional understanding of the relationship between financial and economic policy led to repeated political crises over the course of the Imperium, crises that money was only occasionally able to solve and that could not stave off Rome's eventual fall.

Notes

1. See, for example, US Army War College. 2017. "Theory of War and Strategy Course Directive," and Palmer, James. 2020. "Oh God, Not the Peloponnesian War Again." *Foreign Policy,* July 28.

2. Scheidel, Walter. 2008. *The Monetary Systems of the Greeks and Romans: The Divergent Evolution of Coinage in Eastern and Western Eurasia*. Palo Alto: Stanford University Press, 267–286.

3. Mishkin, Frederic. 2014. *The Economics of Money, Banking and Financial Markets* 11th ed. London: Pearson, chap. 3.

4. See Chapter 1 for a fuller discussion of this concept.

5. For a discussion of the links between par value and the actual value of a coin, see Rolnick, Arthur J., François R. Velde, and Warren E. Weber. 1996. "The Debasement Puzzle: An Essay on Medieval Monetary History." *Journal of Economic History* 56 (4): 789–808. For a discussion of how banknotes can deviate from par, see Gorton, Gary. 2012. *Misunderstanding Financial Crises: Why We Don't See Them Coming*. Oxford: Oxford University Press, chap. 2.

6. Goff, Brian L., and Mark Toma. 1993. "Optimal Seigniorage, the Gold Standard, and Central Bank Financing." *Journal of Money, Credit and Banking* 25 (1): 79–95; Sussman, Nathan. 1993. "Debasements, Royal Revenues, and Inflation in France During the Hundred Years' War, 1415–1422." *Journal of Economic History* 53 (1): 44–70; Sussman, Nathan, and Joseph Zeira. 2003. "Commodity Money Inflation: Theory and Evidence from France in 1350–1436." *Journal of Monetary Economics* 50 (8): 1769–1793; Li, Yiting. 1995. "Commodity Money Under Private Information." *Journal of Monetary Economics* 36 (3): 573–592; Sargent, Thomas J., and Bruce D. Smith. 1997. "Coinage, Debasements, and Gresham's Laws." *Economic Theory* 10 (2): 197–226.

7. Alternatively, states could increase the face value of the coin while maintaining the same quantity of metal.

8. Temin, Peter. 2012. *The Roman Market Economy*. Princeton: Princeton University Press, chap. 4; Butcher, Kevin, 2015. "Debasement and the Decline of Rome." *Studies in Ancient Coinage in Honor of Andrew Burnett*, edited by Richard Ashton, Silvia Hurter, and Caroline Petit, 181–205. London: Spink and Son.

9. Horesh, Niv, and Hyun Jin Kim. 2011. "Why Coins Turned Round the World over? A Critical Analysis of the Origins and Transmission of Ancient Metallic Money." *China Report* 47 (4): 279–302.

10. Scheidel, Walter. 2010. "Coin Quality, Coin Quantity, and Coin Value in Early China and the Roman Empire." *American Journal of Numismatics* 22: 93–118.

11. Ellickson, Robert C., and Charles DiA Thorland. 1995. "Ancient Land Law: Mesopotamia, Egypt, Israel." *Chicago-Kent Law Review* 71: 373–375.

12. Warburton, David A. 1997. *State and Economy in Ancient Egypt: Fiscal Vocabulary of the New Kingdom*. Vol. 151. Freibourg: University Press; Gottingen: Vandenhoeck and Ruprecht.

13. Jursa, Michael, and Juan Carlos Moreno Garcia. 2015. "The Ancient Near East and Egypt." In *Fiscal Regimes and the Political Economy of Premodern States,* edited by Andrew Monson and Walter Scheidel. Cambridge: Cambridge University Press, 142.

14. Palmer, Michael A. 1988. *Origins of the Maritime Strategy: American Naval Strategy in the First Postwar Decade*. No. 1. Washington DC: US Navy, Naval Historical Center.

15. Herodotus. 2008. *The Histories*. Translated by Robin Waterfield. Oxford: Oxford University Press, 250–251.

16. Hamilton, Charles D. 2016. *Plutarch's "Life of Agesilaus."* Berlin: De Gruyter.

17. Nimchuk, Cindy L. 2002. "The 'Archers' of Darius: Coinage or Tokens of Royal Esteem?" *Ars Orientalis,* 55–79.

18. Emily Mackil writes "We do know a little about a lot of states." Mackil, Emily. 2015. "The Greek *polis* and *koinon*." In *Fiscal Regimes and the Political Economy of Premodern States,* edited by Andrew Monson and Walter Scheidel. Cambridge: Cambridge University Press, 473.

19. Ober, Josiah. 2015. "Classical Athens." In *Fiscal Regimes and the Political Economy of Premodern States,* edited by Andrew Monson and Walter Scheidel. Cambridge: Cambridge University Press, 492–522.

20. Finley, Moses I. 1982. *Economy and Society in Ancient Greece.* New York: Viking Press, 90, 46–47; Daley, Jason. 2016. "Archaeologists Uncover Massive Naval Bases of the Ancient Athenians." *Smithsonian Magazine,* June 17.

21. Thucydides. 2009. *The History of the Pelopennesian War.* Translated by Martin Hammond. Oxford: Oxford University Press, 98.

22. Torr, Cecil. 1906. "Triremes." *Classical Review* 20 (2): 137.

23. Austin, Michael M., and Pierre Vidal-Naquet. 1977. *Economic and Social History of Ancient Greece: An Introduction.* Berkeley: University of California Press, 118–123.

24. Rankin, David I. 1988. "The Mining Lobby at Athens." *Ancient Society* 19: 189–205.

25. Ziskind, Jonathan R. 1974. "Sea Loans at Ugarit." *Journal of the American Oriental Society* 94 (1): 134–137. Hoover, Calvin B. 1926. "The Sea Loan in Genoa in the Twelfth Century." *Quarterly Journal of Economics* 40 (3): 495.

26. Rathbone, Dominic W. 2019. "Maritime Loans." In *Oxford Classical Dictionary,* edited by Simon Hornblower and Antony Spawforth. Oxford: Oxford University Press.

27. Finley, Moses I. 1982. *Economy and Society in Ancient Greece.* New York: Viking Press.

28. Hoover 1926: 498–501.

29. Usher, Abbott Payson. 1943. *The Early History of Deposit Banking in Mediterranean Europe.* Vol. 1. Cambridge: Harvard University Press: 64–69; Rathbone, Dominic. 2007. "Merchant Networks in the Greek World: The Impact of Rome." *Mediterranean Historical Review* 22 (2): 309–320.

30. Austin and Vidal-Naquet 1977: 24–40; Finley 1982: 78–93.

31. Michell, H. 1947. "The Iron Money of Sparta." *Phoenix* 1: 42–44.

32. Austin and Vidal-Naquet 1977: 297–300.

33. Thucydides. 2009: 80–81.

34. Mickelson, Karen. 2015. "Greek *polis.*" In *Fiscal Regimes and the Political Economy of Premodern States,* edited by Andrew Monson and Walter Scheidel, 53–77. Cambridge: Cambridge University Press.

35. Polybius. n.d. "The Histories." University of Chicago.

36. Thucydides 2009; Herodotus 2008.

37. Xenophon. *Anabasis.* 1998. Cambridge: Harvard University Press.

38. Austin and Vidal-Naquet 1977: 304.

39. Austin and Vidal-Naquet 1977: 303–307.

40. Kallianiotis, Ioannis N. 2016. "The Economic History of Alexander the Great Expedition." *International Journal of Economics and Financial Research* 2 (2): 16–32.

41. Holt, Frank Lee. 2016. *The Treasures of Alexander the Great: How One Man's Wealth Shaped the World.* Oxford: Oxford University Press.

42. Mørkholm, Otto. 1991. *Early Hellenistic Coinage from The Accession of Alexander to the Peace of Apamaea (336–188 BC).* Cambridge: Cambridge University Press; Kroll, John H. 2012. "The Monetary Background of Early Coinage." In *The Oxford Handbook of Greek and Roman Coinage,* edited by William E. Metcalf, 39-52. Oxford: Oxford University Press.

43. Aperghis, Gerassimos George. 2004. *The Seleukid Royal Economy: The Finances and Financial Administration of the Seleukid Empire.* Cambridge: Cambridge University Press: 208.

44. Howgego, Christopher. 1992. "The Supply and Use of Money in the Roman World 200 BC to AD 300." *The Journal of Roman Studies* 82: 1–31.

45. Howgego 1992: 3.
46. Tan, James. 2015. "The Roman Republic." In *Fiscal Regimes and the Political Economy of Premodern States*, edited by Andrew Monson and Walter Scheidel, 208–228. Cambridge: Cambridge University Press.
47. Thornton, Mary K., and Robert L. Thornton. 1990. "The Financial Crisis of AD 33: A Keynesian Depression?" *The Journal of Economic History* 50 (3): 655–662.
48. Thornton and Thornton 1990: 657.
49. Oldroyd, David. 1995. "The Role of Accounting in Public Expenditure and Monetary Policy in the First Century AD Roman Empire." *Accounting Historians Journal* 22 (2): 117–129.
50. Nicolet, Claude. 1971. "Les variations des prix et la 'théorie quantitative de la monnaie' à Rome, de Cicéron à Pline l'Ancien." In *Annales: Histoire, Sciences Sociales*. 26 (6): 1203–1227.
51. Scheidel, Walter. 2015. "The Early Roman Monarchy." In *Fiscal Regimes and the Political Economy of Premodern States*, edited by Andrew Monson and Walter Scheidel. Cambridge: Cambridge University Press, 229–257.
52. Wassink, Alfred. 1991. "Inflation and Financial Policy Under the Roman Empire to the Price Edict of 301 AD." *Historia: Zeitschrift fur Alte Geschichte* 40 (4): 465–493; Temin 2012: chap. 4.
53. Bransbourg, Gilles. 2015. "The Later Roman Empire." In *Fiscal Regimes and the Political Economy of Premodern States*, edited by Andrew Monson and Walter Scheidel. Cambridge: Cambridge University Press, 258–281, at 270.
54. Scheidel, Walter. 2009a. *A Comparative Perspective on the Determinants of the Scale and Productivity of Maritime Trade in the Roman Mediterranean*. Paper 040902. Princeton: Princeton/Stanford Working Papers in Classics.
55. Rankin, David. 2003. "The Financing of Maritime Commerce in the Roman Empire, I–II AD." In *Credito e Moneta nel Mondo Romano*, edited by Elio Lo Cascio, 197–229. Bari: Edipuglia; Temin, Peter. 2004. "Financial Intermediation in the Early Roman Empire." *Journal of Economic History* 64: 705–733.
56. Lacey, James. 2015. *Gold, Blood, and Power: Finance and War Through the Ages*. Carlisle: US Army War College | Strategic Studies Institute: 5.
57. Farley, Robert. 2021b. "What Han China's Financial Relations with Rome Can Teach Us Today." *The Diplomat*, May 28.
58. Howgego 1992: 6.
59. Frankopan, Peter. 2019. *The New Silk Roads: The Present and Future of the World*. New York: Knopf.
60. Galli, Marco. 2017. "Beyond Frontiers: Ancient Rome and the Eurasian Trade Networks." *Journal of Eurasian Studies* 8 (1): 3–9.
61. Scheidel, Walter. 2009b. *Rome and China: Comparative Perspectives on Ancient World Empires*. Oxford: Oxford University Press; Horesh and Kim 2011.
62. Scheidel 2009a.
63. Von Glahn, Richard. 2016. *An Economic History of China: From Antiquity to the Nineteenth Century*. Cambridge: Cambridge University Press, 81–82.
64. Von Glahn 2016: 84–128.
65. Lewis, Mark E. 2015. "Early Imperial China, from the Qin and Han through Tang." In *Fiscal Regimes and the Political Economy of Premodern States*, edited by Andrew Monson and Walter Scheidel. Cambridge: Cambridge University Press, 282–307.
66. Scheidel 2010: 93–118.
67. Horesh and Kim 2011: 279–302.
68. Scheidel 2010.
69. Scheidel 2010: 93–118.

4
Medieval Money, Markets, and Mayhem

> *The consuls had instructed their warriors that when they heard the signal from the trumpets they should enter the city ready to fight, but in silence and without shouting. And so it was done. The knights followed after them, and within three hours, with the help and favor of God, and with much Saracen blood shed by the swords of the Genoese, the whole city was captured apart from the citadel. Twenty thousand Saracens were killed that day; and from one part of the city ten thousand were captured, and in the citadel twenty thousand, and then ten thousand women and children were brought to Genoa. Within four days the Saracens surrendered the citadel and themselves, and gave thirty thousand marobotini to ransom themselves. The consuls retained some of the captured money, namely sixty thousand marobotini, for the benefit of the commune, and they paid the debt that the commune owed, namely seventeen thousand pounds. They had the rest of the money divided up among the galleys and other ships. They left Ottone de Bonovillano with a thousand men to guard the city, and after holding a council they instructed everyone [else] to leave the city with their galleys and other ships, and this was done. They arrived unharmed, gloriously and triumphantly, at Barcelona; there they beached the galleys and ships and appointed a new consulate. With the agreement and permission of their fellows, two of the consuls, Oberto Torre and Ansaldo Doria, went with two galleys to Genoa, and with the money that they had brought they paid the commune's debt, and they made a new consulate at Genoa.*
> —Caffaro di Rustico (1080–ca. 1164),
> "The Genoese Capture of Almería"[1]

The collapse of the Western Roman Empire in late antiquity transformed the relationship between money and war. Major factors shaping the relationship included the regional dominance of the Roman Catholic Church, the fragmentation of secular power and authority in Western Europe, the early Islamic conquests in the Mediterranean, and the enduring strength of the Byzantine Empire in the Eastern Mediterranean. Despite the collapse of

Rome in the West, sophisticated systems of trade and finance persisted across the Mediterranean and Eurasia, setting the terms on which princes could contemplate and make war. At the same time, proto-states in the Americas began to flex their financial muscles.

Post-Roman Western Europe

The collapse of the Western Roman Empire led to two critical changes in the finance domain. First, the organized fiscal system that maintained the Roman legions in the west collapsed, and with it any regular standing army. Second, the resultant collapse of civil order caused cascading financial disruptions that rippled across Eurasia for centuries. Western Europe after the sixth century saw not so much a revolution in financial affairs (RFA) as a devolution, resulting in the abandonment of advanced financial techniques and technologies.

In the centuries leading up to the collapse, Rome was defended by a mobile field army (*comitatenses*), fixed frontier troops, and allied forces of non-Romans (*foederati*). In all, the Roman troops numbered perhaps half a million at their peak. With the fall of the empire, Germanic kingdoms displaced Roman rule across the west, absorbing language, technology, and even the names for critical feudal roles such as duke and count. Our understanding of the technologies and tactics of the medieval era is constantly in flux, but in general heavy cavalry tended to displace the disciplined infantry of antiquity—an example of an RMA—as states lacked the capacity to raise and train the kind of large, permanent infantry formations of the empire.[2] Over time, sophistication in the arts of fortification and weaponry advanced, even as fiscal and financial technologies remained limited.

A brief discussion of British history illustrates the development in post-Roman taxation methods. As discussed in Chapter 3, the Roman taxation system was generally ad hoc before the fall of Western Roman Empire, but still more expansive than those that survived in its wake. The Victorian historian of British taxation Stephen Dowell notes that the tax systems that were in place in England under Roman rule departed with the triremes when the legions were withdrawn. Over time a system developed in Britain that depended on local officials, in particular the *scirgerefa* (or sheriff) assigned to each shire who administered the feudal demesne (or properties) and collected fines and occasional taxes from its serfs.[3]

After their conquest of Britain in 1066, the Normans further developed the system of royal administration with such innovations as the Doomsday Book—the first recorded survey of English land and other holdings—and the Court of the Exchequer. For the first century of Norman rule, such money as was collected was linked to feudal obligations such as the fee that was accepted instead of a knight's service (scutage), or the fee paid by tenants of the demesne to support military expeditions (tallage). In the roughly 250 years between the time of the Norman conquest and the fourteenth century, payments linked to feudal obligations and taxes to fund wars began to blend together even as they became increasingly common, although without as much state coercion as perhaps is portrayed in popular culture; for example, in 1243 the king's officers "went from citizen to citizen saying, 'You must accommodate the king, who is carrying on war in foreign parts for the good of the kingdom, and is greatly in want, with such and such monies.'" By the mid–fourteenth century, this relatively ad hoc system was more routinized, with king and citizen reaching the compromise of an irregular assessment of a fifteenth of wealth of rural residents and a tenth of that of town residents set as a standard source of revenue.[4] It is estimated that around 1200 CE taxation provided at most one-quarter of the crown revenue in England and France, the rest being revenue from the demesne and from feudal prerogatives; overall this period was one in which European governments were transitioning from domain states to tax states.[5]

Given the limitations of funding from demesne resources and the still nascent methods of taxation, feudalism became the primary method for funding military operations across northwestern Europe in the medieval period. The system developed over several centuries and was characterized by a lord assigning land to military specialists who, in turn, owed the lord military duties (the exact terms of which were carefully negotiated and varied considerably). As discussed above, this system functioned as a workaround to deal with the lack of regular tax income. The costs of war—horses, fortifications, arms, training—were pushed onto local communities. For any operations requiring mobility, the medieval sovereigns frequently had to exert their utmost simply to put several thousand soldiers in the field for a month or two. As the historian Philippe Contamine writes, war "was the *guerre guerroyante*, made up of losses and recaptures, surprises, incursions, ambushes and sallies" where "'a campaign brought to a conclusion constitute[d] an exception . . . which defie[d] the rule.'"[6] All the carefully negotiated contracts of loyalty that allowed the lord to push the cost of training and armament outward usually had serious written limits and were difficult to fully enforce. These systemic weaknesses and inefficiencies led to levels of violence and instability exceeding those of late antiquity.

This disorder in the west interrupted the extended networks of trade for much of the second half of the first millennium CE and broke up the financial commons that had facilitated long-distance exchange. However, ongoing trade in the Eastern Mediterranean, East Asia, and the areas in between offered opportunities for continued advances in financial techniques. As discussed in the previous chapter, while Hellenic Athens had depended on the maritime loan to facilitate trade, Rome added the *societas* as a standard contract of long-term partnership. By 1000 CE, there were multiple contract types across the Eastern Mediterranean to facilitate complex trading and financial enterprises—in addition to the maritime loan, there was the *qirād* or (*quirad*) in the Islamic world, the '*isqa* (or *isqua*) used by Jewish traders, the Byzantine *chreokoinōnia* (or *chreokoinonia*), and the *commenda* centered around the Italian city-states. These instruments are similar enough to suggest the continued presence of a financial commons—however attenuated—although the fracturing of this commons is likewise suggested by the different cultures' use of diverse instruments. Of these various instruments, however, the *commenda* played the most important role in Europe; scholars believe it followed the design of other contract types, but there is an unresolved debate as to exactly which ones were the key inspiration. For our purposes, the critical issue is that the *commenda*'s existence and structure allowed labor and capital in Italian city-states to partner in extended and complicated projects (usually voyages). The contract linked an investor, called a *commendator*, and a traveling or carrying partner (the *tractator* or *socius portat*) who was responsible for the work of the enterprise. Overall, the developing selection of legal contracts in the Mediterranean show the recovery of financial and trade systems, which then led to the RFA among city-states by the fourteenth century.[7]

The Crusades, Church Power, and the Levant

While much of our story involves the increasing efficacy of state financial institutions, nonstate and semistate actors can also play a significant role in the finance domain. The Catholic Church, for example, successfully used the finance domain to build and rebuild a coalition of forces that pursued the conquest of the Holy Land. While the church's financial strategies did not evolve into financial institutions of long-term importance and were arguably dead ends, they are a useful example of nonstate use of the finance domain. From the late eleventh century until the fourteenth century, knights and mercenaries from all across Western and Central Europe—including heretics and pagans, as the more worldly concerns of military campaigns overtook the more spiritual ones—undertook a series of economically and religiously motivated wars against Islamic proto-states from the Middle East to the Western Mediterranean. Authorities of the Catholic Church sanctioned and partially organized these wars, in conjunction with local secular clientelist leaders, who organized the armies and often personally commanded them in the field. The Crusaders sometimes collaborated with local Christians in the Eastern Mediterranean, but not always; Crusaders sometimes (as in the Fourth Crusade) targeted their fellow Christians. In addition to the vast wealth looted from the supposed infidels, the Crusaders managed to capture and hold parts of the Middle East for some two centuries, as well as enjoying more enduring successes on the Iberian Peninsula and in Eastern Europe.

In part due to the lucrative haul of the Crusades, the Catholic Church wielded significant financial power, both in terms of its direct control over economic resources (including rich agricultural areas) but also because of its capacity to alter the structure of trade and finance.[8] For example, in support of the Second Crusade Pope Eugene III detailed several earthly privileges that Crusaders could be expected to enjoy should they join the holy conflict such as: restrictions on the ability of moneylenders to collect interest on their debts even if they had sworn to pay such interest; an absolute right to hold property—including that of their families—until the death of the Crusader could be conclusively demonstrated to the satisfaction of the church; and the ability to mortgage their land and other property for financial support, either to other local nobles or to the church itself.[9]

Later Popes extended these privileges, for example, when Pope Innocent III extended the moratorium on interest collection on debts, meaning that interest already incurred and paid could be reclaimed by the Crusader or his family. Although these restrictions were sometimes honored in the breach and had unpredictable side effects (crusading soldiers immediately losing practical access to credit, for one example, and financially weakening European Jews such that they could not escape the Inquisition for another), they nevertheless represented a significant incursion by the church into the finance domain. While the church's sale of indulgences was not central to the fund-raising for the Crusades overall, there are a number of cases of their being used to finance specific groups and some of the Crusades within Europe. The Crusades thereby expanded the moral, legal, and political influence of the church and enhanced its ability to accomplish its goals through military force, in no small part because of the dexterity that church authorities exhibited in navigating the finance domain.

Financial gain was one of several motivations for a Crusader, but most of them required a significant economic investment to generate any hope of a return, either financially or geographically. For example, a Crusader required money for travel, equipment, and often retainers, meaning that a personal crusade often began with the Crusader selling assets, expropriating property from the more vulnerable members of his community, calling in debts, and sometimes taking on loans.[10] Local church properties such as monasteries frequently acted as lending agents for these loans and usually required the Crusader's property be used as collateral.

Other funding methods put the financial burden more directly on ordinary citizens: in preparation for the first Crusade in 1096, for example, a number of kingdoms implemented an early tax on movable properties like currency or jewelry, in which the king ruled that his subjects must pay a certain percentage—it varied by region—of their movable property at their church and swear that their payment was correct. In England, this arrangement was the precursor to the Saladin Tax of 1188, which the king claimed was used to fund the campaign to expel Saladin from Jerusalem. In the intervening century, however, English state capacity had grown to the point where the king and assembled nobles and clergy were able to monitor and enforce full payment by subjects, with the final assessment decided by a jury.[11]

The impact of the Crusades was felt not just in the Middle East or in the coffers of the church; they appear to have started or accelerated a number of political and financial changes in areas across Europe, even as some of the methods that the church used to generate military power turned into evolutionary dead ends. One unintended consequence of the Crusades was the removal of the more bellicose European nobles from domestic politics, reducing political infighting among elites. Another set of consequences was that the Crusades also allowed rulers to develop new financing methods and increase the liquidity of land markets, helping in turn to increase government revenues. As a result, the areas of Europe that sent large numbers of Crusaders to the Middle East showed greater political and financial stability in the following centuries.[12]

Early Islamic Nations and the Eastern Roman Empire

In Mecca in the sixth century, local merchants began to use the *ilaf*, a commercial agreement that allowed several individuals to pool their resources in caravans. Like the *commenda* and similar maritime agreements, the *ilaf* was a dramatic example of the power of a financial contract to combine resources in new and extraordinary ways. Within a few decades, this new contract allowed the merchants of Mecca to attain an entirely new level of power and wealth relative to other communities across the Arabian Peninsula.[13]

Beginning in 622, Arab armies began to expand the territories they controlled at the expense of the Byzantine and Sassanid Empires, the former headquartered in Constantinople and representing the eastern half of the Roman Empire, and the latter a successor to the Parthian Empire that had dominated Persia for much of late antiquity. The Roman Empire endured in the east well after the collapse of the western provinces, remaining the dominant power in the Mediterranean until the seventh century. The collapse of the Western Roman Empire did not lead to an immediate transformation of conditions in the east, and the Byzantine Empire continued to enjoy a sophisticated monetary economy with substantial long-distance trade across Eurasia and the Mediterranean. Both the Sassanids and the Byzantines had been weakened by extensive wars with one another and, in the case of the Romans, a financially ruinous effort to reconquer Italy. Both empires were also weakened by an outbreak of bubonic plague, which followed trade networks and caused significant death and disruption.

At the same time, the Arabian polity incorporated merchants who could fund and supply armies, facilitating their advance.[14] In short order, Arab forces seized the Levant (including Jerusalem), Egypt, Mesopotamia, Persia, and parts of Anatolia. As a result, the Sassanid Empire ceased to exist, and the Byzantine Empire lost control of large portions of its territory. Over the next century, what became an Islamic caliphate expanded into Central Asia and the Caucasus, as well as across North Africa and Iberia. Unlike the Sassanid Persians, the Byzantine Empire survived these invasions, but the Islamic conquests had the three-pronged effect of sharply reducing the size of the empire (and thus the prospects for long-distance trade), reducing imperial access to the mines and mints necessary for coin production, and providing competing markets for exports from East Asia.[15]

In addition to establishing an empire of their own, the Islamic conquest of much of the Mediterranean world resulted in the widespread distribution and use by the caliphate of Byzantine coinage, a practice which continued for roughly a century.[16] In addition to this advancement in financial sophistication, the leaders of the Islamic empire had established institutions of credit and banking by no later than the eighth century CE.[17] This latter development facilitated long-distance trade across the Islamic world, as well as between Islamic and non-Islamic merchants.[18]

The innovations in the Muslim empire of the seventh and eighth centuries did not end with using merchant capital to bankroll military actions, the adoption of widespread coinage, and the increase in credit availability. Immediately after its conquest by Islamic forces in the 700s, the leadership of Iraq created a bureaucratic system of taxation used to pay the Islamic veterans in the towns of Basra and Kufa. The caliphs of the Islamic empire then adapted this system and utilized it in other regions of the caliphate for the next several hundred years. Using a mixture of local bureaucrats from the preexisting Sasanian state and veterans of the conquests, the system appears to have done a better job of maintaining a central bureaucracy than the Merovingian and Carolingian descendants of the Western Roman Empire.[19] While it is not clear that this early capability in fiscal state management continued to develop as the Arab empire fragmented into multiple states, the rapidity of the early Islamic conquests shows the importance of financial flows and management in military administration.

The Public Debt and Public Banking RFA

There are two major developments in the finance domain in medieval Europe that constitute the RFA that helped pull the world out of the post-Roman Dark Ages: the development of long-term public debt; and the public bank, a precursor to a central bank. Both began in a few city-states in the medieval era and then migrated in the early modern period to territorial states (this latter development is covered in Chapter 5).

While there is general agreement that the European economy was in decline from 1300 to 1450 and that, by the middle of the sixteenth century, Europe was experiencing substantial inflation, the reasons for this turbulence are in dispute.[20] The price revolution was originally pinned to the conquest of the Americas and the resulting increase in gold and silver in royal coffers, but prices began to increase in the 1400s. Other explanations put forward range from improved mining techniques in Central Europe, increases in population and the attendant increase in monetary velocity, and the expanded use of credit instruments.[21]

Even as the medieval European economy fluctuated in strength, it grew in sophistication as legal and financial forms were developed and put into wide use—such as the *commenda* discussed above—forms often derived from Roman legal foundations. One factor in this development was the rise in popularity in Western Europe of the fair—a version of the *souk* that had been a feature of life in the Arab Middle East for several thousand years and that made its way to Europe in the seventh century—an institution that facilitated the growth of complex interregional trade. Crucially, even as individual fairs waxed and waned in importance, fairs in general were a locus of development for a variety of legal, contractual, and financial arrangements that began to diffuse. So while the fair is not an RFA in itself, it created an environment for the instruments and institutions that became the public banking RFA.[22]

Another factor that led to the public banking RFA, albeit through its failure, was the intentional debasement of metal coins by European princes as a method of defense spending during the medieval and early modern periods.[23] John Munro notes the important role of debasement—which he defines as "the reduction of the amount of pure gold or silver represented in each unit of the country's money-of-account pricing system"—as a financing technique for Europe's war machines:

> Monarchs from Marcus Aurelius in the second century A.D. to Henry VIII in the sixteenth waged their wars by this fiscal aid. In the later Middle Ages, Philip IV of France reportedly received 50 per cent of his total revenues in seignorage in 1299; his grandson Philip VI, 70 per cent in 1349. In the 1350s, Count Louis de Male's debasements of the Flemish coinage earned him revenues amounting to perhaps one-fifth of his total income.[24]

Munro explains the process with an example from Burgundy in 1387. The coin being debased is the double gros, which had a unit of account value (traite) defined within the classic pound/livre system of England, the Low Countries, and France: 1 pound/livre = 20 s (shillings/sous) = 240 d (pence/deniers). Table 4.1 is a slightly edited version of Munro's example.[25]

Traite is the buying power of the coin that the sovereign or mint master declares for it, and would like it to have. Brassage is the production cost, and the seigniorage is what remains for the king at the end—assuming that households accept the price, and bring their bullion or old coins to be minted into new double gros. Thus, by the spring of 1387 the seigniorage had gone up by 6 deniers for each coin, an increase in seigniorage of 240 percent per coin. If the debasement worked, households made money as well—note the increase in the mint price paid to those bringing bullion (2s. 11d.) was 17 percent. But if the coins were viewed as suspect, the king, the mint, and householders might have trouble getting them accepted by others, hence the risk.

Another approach to raising funds quickly was borrowing. To maximize the yield of this approach, it was helpful to borrow from many people, for an extended period of time, and be able to borrow again in the future. Pulling this off was complicated, and the first successful examples were the relatively smaller city-states (after several centuries, the larger territorial states began to do it as well). Munro writes, "The first evidence for organized public debts is to be found in towns of twelfth-century

Table 4.1 Example of Coin Debased in Burgundy

	Double Gros of October 1386	% of the traite	Debased Double Gros of April 1387	% of the traite
Traite (unit of account)	19s. 0d.	100.0	23s. 1/2d.	100.0
Brassage (production cost)	1s. 1 1/2d.	5.2	1s. 7d.	6.9
Seigniorage (king's share)	2 1/2d.	1.1	8 1/2d.	3.0
Total Charges (Brassage and Seigniorage)	1s. 4d.	6.3	2s. 3 1/2d.	9.9
Mint price for bullion	17s. 8d.	93.7	20s. 9d.	90.1

Source: Munro, John H. 2020. *Wool, Cloth, and Gold.* Toronto, Ontario, Canada: University of Toronto Press.

Italy."[26] David Stasavage is quite clear about the purpose of this debt: "The ability to borrow was critical in medieval and early modern Europe because it allowed states to participate in wars, either defensive or offensive." Stasavage demonstrates that long-term debt was first in wide use in city-states in the Mediterranean region in the thirteenth century, much earlier than the territorial states that started to use it only in the very late fifteenth century as it spread across Europe.[27] For those states that were able to organize it, long-term debt became popular as it was easier for city-states to raise funds rapidly by borrowing than it was to collect the equivalent large amounts via tax revenue, a tactic Stasavage views as critical to their survival.[28] Steven Epstein provides an example in his discussion of an urgent financial retrenchment in the city-state of Genoa in 1214, as tax revenues are hypothecated to pay off debts more than a century before it began true long-term debt:

> Local financial expertise, usually applied to building individual fortunes, was marshaled to address what by then must have amounted to massive fiscal problems. . . . The men directing the affairs of the commune knew that debt tied their hands, and they used a respite from war to clear the debts that would cripple any effort to raise money quickly in a crisis. . . . Futures revenues were the closest thing to actual savings, so the commune sold them at a discount during war and redeemed them during war.[29]

The Genoan fiscal system, like many of the city-states, developed centralized records of debt ownership, which in turn allowed for trade in debt securities. This system's successful operation was only temporarily disrupted by a fire set during a popular revolt in 1339 to burn the central records listing debt holders.[30]

The development of the public bank—the second innovation fueling the RFA as well as the evolution of state building in Europe in the Middle Ages—was directly connected to the first, public debt, and was also very much a product of war finance. The early public banks were founded in part to deal with problems created by city-states using currency debasement as a strategy for raising war funds.[31] Consider, for example, the first public bank, the Table of Change (Taula de Canvi) founded in Barcelona in 1401.[32] Medieval Barcelona was a thriving port city and as such was the major source of liquidity for the Aragón-Catalonian kings, who were matched only by the Italian princes in the scope of their ambitions.[33] The descendants of Guifre the Hairy, who was made Count of Barcelona in 878 by Louis the Stammerer, married into the Crown of Aragon in 1150. The combined titles of King of Aragon and Count of Barcelona allowed the Aragonese rulers to use Barcelona as a major source of funding, making it possible for them to build a large navy during the thirteenth and fourteenth centuries,[34] with "expeditionary fleets of up to around 80 galleys."[35] These expenditures led the Crown of Aragon to take drastic measures in the 1350s that resulted in what has been described as "Europe's first 'financial revolution.'"[36] This sort of creativity in the face of financial catastrophe is, as we will show, a common pattern: the founding of the public bank in the wake of a period of intense warmaking, during a period of temporary peace, but with the state under intense financial pressure.[37]

The next public bank to be founded was the Bank of St. George (Casa di San Giorgio) in the Republic of Genoa in 1407. The bank was founded after the War of Chioggia—the latest in a series against the Republic of Venice—whose impact on the Genoese was so ruinous that the Doge of Genoa handed the defense of the realm over to France, and whose impact also necessitated the substantial restructuring of public debts.[38] Within the century the Casa had acquired enormous power and directly governed a number of Genoese colonies. A then naïve Niccolo Machiavelli was struck by the power of the Casa, and suggested, perhaps in jest, that the bank might take control of the city-state itself, thereby creating a truly unique republic.[39]

Genoa's rival, Venice, did not launch its public bank, the Banco della Piazza, until 1587, more than a hundred years before the Bank of England but over a century later than its rival city-states in the Mediterranean region.[40] Local worthies had floated proposals for a public bank as early as the 1300s as a way to mitigate banking crises and the constant stream of financial flows to fund their many military operations.[41] But even though the need for a bank was appreciated, the pressures to create one were less than in Genoa. Venice had access to funding from its conquests on the Italian mainland, and Alvise Pisani's banking house was able to lend to the Venetian government. Together, this meant that Venetian finances were stable enough without a true public bank during the critical period of the early 1500s, after the crushing defeat at the Battle of Agnadello and the issuance by the Venetians of a number of new bonds.[42] As we see from Table 4.1, all of this put Venice after Basel, Genoa, and Barcelona, but contemporaneous with Hamburg, Nuremburg, and Holland as well as Mediterranean rivals Naples, Milan, and the Papal States. Building on Stasavage's point that city-states were first to adopt public debt with territorial states following,[43] we can see in Figure 4.1 that public or central banks were slower to arrive, and their foundations more focused around the seventeenth century. At the same time, the importance of overall financial sophistication comes through as well. The correlation between date of first public debt and date of the founding of a public bank is 0.73. The transition of public banks from city-states to territorial states is discussed further in the next chapter, when we review the mercantilist RFA of the seventeenth and eighteenth centuries in Europe.

Figure 4.1 The Relationship Between Public Debts Before 1800 and Public Banks

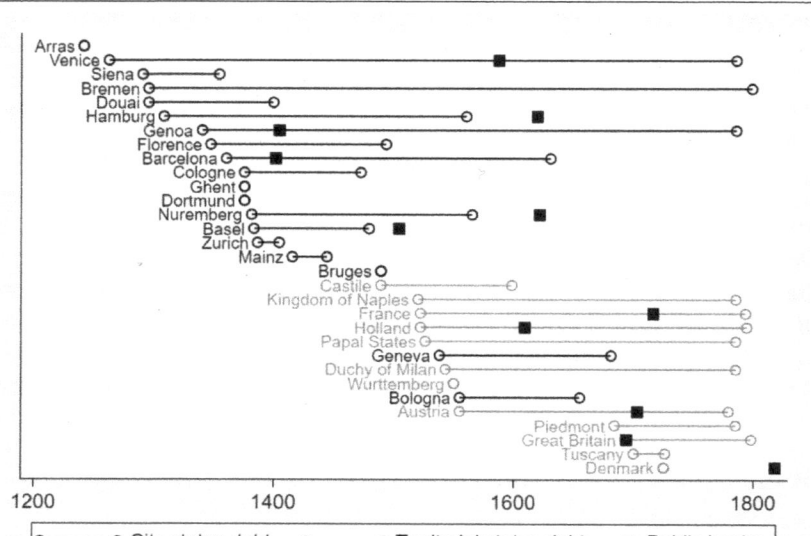

Sources: Stasavage, David. 2011. *States of Credit: Size, Power, and the Development of European Polities.* Princeton: Princeton University Press; Roberds, William, and Francois R. Velde. 2016. "The Descent of Central Banks (1400–1815)." In *Central Banks at a Crossroads: What Can We Learn from History,* edited by Michael D. Bordo, Øyvind Eitrheim, Marc Flandreau, and Jan F. Qvigstad, 34–35. Cambridge: Cambridge University Press; Capie, Forrest, Charles Goodhart, and Norbert Schnadt. 1994. "The Development of Central Banking. Appendix B" In *The Future of Central Banking: The Tercentenary Symposium of the Bank of England,* edited by Forrest Capie, Stanley Fischer, Charles Goodhart, and Norbert Schnadt, 123–232. Cambridge: Cambridge University Press; and Kindleberger, Charles. 1999. "Currency Debasement in the Early Seventeenth Century and the Establishment of Deposit Banks in Central Europe." In *Essays in History: Financial, Economic, Personal,* by Charles Kindleberger, 49–58. Ann Arbor: University of Michigan Press.

State Consolidation in the Pre-Columbian Americas

While Europeans were coping with the slow-motion collapse of the Roman order, proto-states in the New World were developing the financial tools necessary to the command of empire. In fact, pre-Columbian American empires were tax states of increasing sophistication and organization in the centuries leading up to 1492. Although categories such as "domain state," "tax state," and "fiscal-military state" are sometimes hard to apply across periods and with imperfect data, it seems that the Incas had a high level of tax organization and achieved the regular payments of labor and goods to the state. Part of this high level of development was the result of the Incas' trading with other groups nearby, but it was also due to their unusually high level of imperial restraint: military expenditure "became increasingly less significant as the Incas reached the frontiers of the world that they deemed worth civilizing or that could threaten their hegemony" and this strategic restraint preserved the stability of their empire over most of western South America until their conquest by the Spanish in the late sixteenth century.[44]

By contrast, the Aztec Empire did not show as much restraint in its ambitions. The Aztecs could fulfill these ambitions because of their financial sophistication; indeed, while at its peak the Aztec Empire most resembled a domain state it had a well-developed systems of taxation. Structurally, the Aztec Empire of the sixteenth century CE in many ways resembled the Athenian Empire, with a number of city-states required to pay taxes to the Aztecs, albeit with goods and labor (textiles were a primary form of payment and represented a commodity money of the period) rather than metallic coinage. In addition, the state conscripted young men for specific military campaigns as needed rather than maintaining standing armies, thereby allowing the Aztecs to achieve military power without spending as much.[45]

This sophistication and flexibility were no remedy against the European conquerors of the Americas in the fifteenth and sixteenth centuries, who possessed the ability to consistently raise funding and transform that funding into maritime power. Moreover, it was this ability that transformed the political structure of the Americas and financial institutions in Europe. We continue our discussion of these transformations in the next chapter.

China from the Period of Disunion to the Ming Dynasty

Much like the West, the story of financial technology in China starts with a retrogression: the collapse of the Han Dynasty in the third century CE was followed by the Period of Disunion in China from 220 to 589 and the devolution of fiscal and financial methods of government. Over the next several centuries, both rulers and commoners repeatedly attempted to use the physical and methodological artifacts from the Han Dynasty in financial transactions, but with limited success. For example, when the Jin Dynasty attempted to follow the Han precedent and conduct a census of the population in 280 CE as a precursor to developing a fiscal system, they were able to tally up only one-quarter the population of the last Han census a century earlier. While this failure to conduct an accurate census illustrates the reduced state capacity of the Jin Dynasty, it also demonstrates how most of the population had become dependent on local aristocrats who stepped into the power vacuum, and who "sheltered themselves behind [a] barricade of privilege and vanished from the tax registers."[46] Similarly, while coins were minted sporadically throughout this period, it was frequently done by private parties and never in sufficient quantity, forcing continued use of the heavy bronze wuzhu coins minted in the early centuries CE as well as use of commodity currencies such as bolts of cloth for long-distance trading and the settling of debts.[47] In addition, although the Northern Wei made major steps toward political reunification of China, including a substantial push toward an effective fiscal bureaucracy in the fifth century, it is notable that they made little use of coins and collected all revenues in commodities.[48]

In the eighth century the Tang Dynasty reestablished patterns of financial innovation, paving the way for some of the most impressive monetary and financial advances in world history, including, over the next several hundred years, some of the most sophisticated and aggressive uses of defensive financial operations in conflict. A number of the improvements in trade, finance, productivity, and fiscal management in the early stages of the Tang-Song transition were the result of disruption caused by the An Lushan Rebellion of 755 to 763 CE. The conflict led to internal displacement of civilians, causing a substantial migration from the north to the south, with the concomitant shift from dry land agriculture of wheat and other crops to a focus on rice production. Likewise, political deadlock before the rebellion gave way to substantial shifts in land tenure, tax collection, and fiscal policy; in particular, previous efforts to maintain equitable landholdings led to a compromise wherein unequal private holdings were mitigated by progressive taxation. In addition, the conflict resulted in a loss of central government revenues and power, but regional governors stepped into the breach and were able to maintain order while encouraging economic growth and commerce. Aggressive use of a government monopoly on salt production and sales, begun at the onset of the rebellion, facilitated a transition to taxing in coin rather than in kind. Finally, this period also saw an expansion of the availability of credit, with an efflorescence of "counting houses" (*guifang*) and perhaps the first paper money in the world, "flying cash" (*feiqian*), a system for intercity payments.[49]

Many of the patterns of this period and the later Tang Dynasty continued during the Song Dynasty from 960 to 1279 CE, including economic and commercial advancement as well as substantial political centrifugal forces. As steppe peoples such as the Tangut, Khitan, Lao, Jurchen Jin, and Mongols began to attack, Chinese policymakers turned to financial statecraft to shore up their defenses. One of the first challenges the Song faced on taking power was expanding the money supply, a move urgently needed for three reasons: first, to support the continued expansion of the economy; second, to coordinate payments for the standing armies needed to defend their borders; and finally, to make up for almost eight centuries of little or no coinage. The Song relentlessly increased coin production for over 100 years until by 1080 they were producing the largest amount of coins in Chinese Imperial history, mitigating their security and commercial problems.

The Song state's vulnerability in the finance domain combined with the increasing commercial and financial sophistication of their economy forced the Song to develop the first verifiable paper currency, a key component of the instantiation of an RFA. This currency innovation—the *jiaozi* credit bill—was achieved by the government regulating the use of existing private notes in 1024. Military pressure on the state led to further innovation in fiscal and financial administration to increase the military budget, culminating with the New Policies under royal councilor Wang Anshi from 1060 to 1076. Wang focused on "regulating wealth" (*licai*) as "the defining feature of the art of government," bureaucratizing taxation on landowners, mining concerns, and trading companies among others while cutting government spending and introducing price controls. While the New Policies had mixed results, they greatly increased revenues during Wang's tenure.

With Wang's retirement, the fiscal administration of the Northern Song rapidly collapsed, and the capital, Kaifeng, fell to the Jurchen Jin people of Manchuria only a few decades later in 1127. As the Jurchen Jin were in the process of sacking Kaifeng, however, they came across a huge stock of coins, raising the question of why these coins had not been deployed by the Northern Song to stabilize government finances and prevent the collapse of the state. Defeated but not conquered, the Song leadership fled south of the Huai River and began the Southern Song dynasty. Thus rebranded, the Southern Song continued their sophisticated and largely successful use of paper money, keeping hundreds of millions of notes in circulation—while maintaining the currency's face value—throughout the mid-thirteenth century.[50]

The Southern Song's success with currency circulation was rooted in an understanding by policymakers of monetary policy, including the dangers of inflation, as Yuan Xie, a Southern Song (1127–1279) minister, demonstrates: "Paper notes are a matter that will be of lowly esteem when aplenty, and become prized when scarce; thus redeeming some of them out of circulation, will make them appreciate in value; for when it is lowly its circulation languishes; when it is prized, it will be widely used; thus redeeming some of it will boost its circulation."[51] In the end, however, the Southern Song's financial sophistication did not protect them from defeat by the Mongols in 1279. As is the case across history, high performance in one domain such as finance, even for an extended period, does not guarantee overall victory.

The steppe successors to the Song, the Jurchen Jin and the Mongols—the latter of whom formed the Yuan Dynasty in China in the thirteenth and fourteenth centuries—had varying degrees of success with these financial tools. The Jin attempted to continue use of paper currency, their variant called jiaochao, but were hampered by the combination of external military pressure and lack of copper mines, both of which caused the currency to devalue. Military defeats led to the Jin losing bronze and other metal mining territory to neighboring enemies, which in turn may have triggered hyperinflation, with one batch of Jin notes losing 1/200th of their value between 1217 and 1221. By the time the Jin were conquered by the Mongols in 1234, they had abandoned the use of their paper currency.

By contrast, the Mongols were better masters of paper currency than the Jurchen Jin, but much less capable than the Song. The Mongols made use of paper currency even before taking full control of Jin and Southern Song territories, with local usage as early as the 1220s. In 1260, Yuan emperor Kublai Khan launched the paper currency, the Zhong-tong chao, across his khanate. Instability led the Yuan to issue replacement currencies over the next eighty years and at times reduced the notes to 10 percent or less of their face value. Since the Song faced military and material crises at least as extreme as the Yuan, the differences in performance seem to come down to know-how.[52]

This lack of expertise on the Mongols' part could help explain the way in which fiscal discipline disintegrated under the Mongol Yuan Dynasty (1279–1368), even as the "Pax Mongolica"—a period of relative stability brought by the predations of Genghis Khan and the rule of his successor Kublai Khan that united the Asian continent under the Chinggisid Empire—produced a significant increase in trade across the Eurasian landmass. Indeed, according to Ayse Zarakol, the Khans were not so much defeated by the Ming Dynasty in 1369 as that the first Ming Dynasty was Chingissid in character.[53]

In any event, the first Ming emperor, Hongwu, set a reactionary course: "to restore the autarkic village economy of the idealized past as envisioned by Mencius and other Confucian philosophers and to minimize (if not eliminate) the market economy and the inequalities it fostered." As part of this program, Hongwu attempted to use paper currency in a purely fiat manner, decoupled from commercial drivers, as a force of state control. The Mings' fiscal and economic policies are generally regarded by historians as unsuccessful, with the paper currency losing value and eventually abandoned. The Ming Dynasty did, however, succeed in largely restoring domestic order in the short term, thereby enabling an eventual economic recovery.[54]

The role of paper currency within the larger dynamics of political and military struggle in eleventh- to fifteenth-century China is one of the more dramatic episodes in the history of the finance domain. The evidence suggests that the monetary and financial knowledge of the Southern Song was extremely strong and that they successfully maintained an advanced form of currency as a tool of internal fiscal control and transfer, as well as external trade in the face of relentless attack. As this success also involves some of the most sophisticated monetary management methods seen before the 1800s, it is worth a brief discussion comparing and contrasting it with contemporaneous developments in Europe. In particular, paper currency in China appears to have played a role roughly similar to debasement in Europe: a way to wring additional finance out of existing currency.[55] While one of the reasons medieval European states did not implement paper currency likely came down to low operational capacity, it is also true that they were able to achieve their fiscal goals fairly well with debasement.

The reasons Chinese states only rarely turned to debasement (a major exception being the late Ming period)[56] are more opaque to modern observers. They sometimes credit conservative Confucian principles as an explanation, but it is hard to see how the Northern Song (to 1127), the Jurchen Jin (to 1234), and the Southern Song (to 1279)—all of whom turned to paper money as a way to handle problems with coinage—would have let an adherence to Confucianism block a possible avenue of dynastic survival. A more plausible, if quotidian, explanation is that Chinese states overwhelmingly favored base coinage, particularly bronze, and used it substantially even past the end of the Yuan Dynasty, and it is probable that it is simply harder to debase a base metal coin than a precious metal coin.[57] A final contributing factor was two pieces of simple bad luck that Chinese states suffered: first, neighboring states seem to have placed a high value on the Chinese coins, leading to their continual export and resultant coin shortages;[58] second, China may have had less access to precious metals than European states, forcing the Chinese dynasties to rely on the more volatile base metal coins and paper money for currency.[59] The Chinese dynasties of the period did undergo a currency and banking RFA similar to states in Europe and the Levant but, as this chapter illustrates, developments in the finance domain must be considered in a larger context with other issues such as the level of overall state conflict and regional patterns in political and economic development.

Conclusion

The collapse of the western half of the Roman Empire led to revolutionary military and financial transformations in the Mediterranean world, transformations that had ripple effects as far as China. Long-distance trade in Western Europe collapsed during this period, and this collapse reduced the commercial prospects of merchants across the rest of Eurasia. At the same time, the advent of coinage from the Roman and Byzantine Empires, as well as new polities in Western Europe and in the Levant helped generate a financial commons in Eurasia, even if trade and financial flows had dropped dramatically.

In military terms, the standing, infantry-based armies of the Roman Principate gave way to generally smaller, more temporary armies that favored light infantry and cavalry. Especially in Western Europe, these forces were bound by bonds of personal and religious obligation rather than either money or civic duty, although the state use of mercenaries remained common, especially on the outer edges of their territories. In Northwest Europe, the lack of currency made it difficult to maintain standing navies of the size and sophistication seen in antiquity and in Italian city-states.

Still, the major political units of the period also used financial tools to pursue their military and security objectives. In Europe, the Catholic Church took advantage of its economic assets in the form of the extensive holdings of monasteries—to control finance and credit. The ability of the church to manipulate the terms of credit gave it the capacity to engineer a succession of military campaigns in the Levant. Genoa and Venice, with their advanced fiscal institutions, supplied seapower to the Crusades. And by 1500, many of the territorial states of Northwest Europe had sufficient state capacity and tax systems to build the first permanent armies the region had seen since the seventh century.[60] For its part, the Song Dynasty in China made the first extensive use of paper money to generate military power to fight off invaders on its northern border. The Songs encountered problems of inflation that later policymakers would have found quite familiar.

The most significant event of the era for the development of a finance domain, in addition to being one of the turning points of world history, was Christopher Columbus's expedition to find a shortened route to the Indies, which led to the invasion and occupation of the Americas at the end of fifteenth century. The expedition is important for the way it demonstrates the accumulating tools of European finance, and for the way it transformed the finance domain going forward. While it did not involve a sea loan (Columbus was not sailing west to sell merchandise), the financial structure shows millennia of accumulated experience in sharing risk in a maritime environment. The expedition cost 2 million Iberian maravedis to launch—substantial but an order of magnitude less than standard loans and costs for military expeditions at the time. King Ferdinand and Queen Isabella of Spain put forward half of the money, borrowing in turn from a network of Genoese merchants in Seville, which was then repaid with sales of indulgences in the western province of Extremadura. Columbus was responsible for 500,000 maravedis, borrowed from some of the same investors as Ferdinand and Isabella. Two court officials, Alonso de Quintanilla and Luis de Santangel, helped to build the links between government, church, and merchants enabling these loans.[61] The transformations that enabled the Columbian expeditions also set the stage for the mercantilist revolution of the seventeenth and eighteenth centuries, which we discuss in the next chapter.

Notes

1. Jansen, Katherine L., Joanna H. Drell and Frances Andrews, eds. 2010. *Medieval Italy: Texts in Translation*. Philadelphia: University of Pennsylvania Press, 120–121.
2. Contamine, Philippe. 1986. *War in the Middle Ages*. Translated by Michael Jones. New York: Blackwell, 3–29.
3. Dowell, Stephen. 1884. *History of Taxation and Taxes in England from the Earliest Times to the Present Day*. London: Longmans, Green, 5–7.
4. Dowell, Stephen. 1884. *History of Taxation and Taxes in England from the Earliest Times to the Present Day*. London: Longmans, Green, 13–88, at 52.
5. Barzel, Yoram, and Edgar Kiser. 2002. "Taxation and Voting Rights in Medieval England and France." *Rationality and Society* 14 (4): 473–507, at 481.
6. Contamine 1986: chap. 7, at 219.
7. Van Doosselaere, Quentin. 2009. *Commercial Agreements and Social Dynamics in Medieval Genoa*. Cambridge: Cambridge University Press, subsection 3.1, 63–78; Pryor, John H. 1977. "The Origins of the Commenda Contract." *Speculum* 52 (1): 5–37; Udovitch, Abraham L. 1962. "At the Origins of the Western Commenda: Islam, Israel, Byzantium?" *Speculum* 37 (2): 198–207.
8. Tyerman, Christopher. 2007. *God's War: A New History of the Crusades*. London: Penguin UK.
9. Bramhall, Edith Clementine. 1901. "The Origin of the Temporal Privileges of Crusaders." *American Journal of Theology* 5 (2): 279–292; Brundage, James A. 1997. "Crusaders and Jurists: The Legal Consequences of Crusader Status." *Publications de l'École Française de Rome* 236 (1): 141–154.
10. Cazel, Fred. 1989. "Financing the Crusades." In *A History of the Crusades, Volume VI: The Impact of the Crusades on Europe*, edited by Harry Hazard and Norman Zacour. Madison: University of Wisconsin Press, 116–149.
11. Dowell 1884: 44–48.
12. Blaydes, Lisa, and Christopher Paik. 2016. "The Impact of Holy Land Crusades on State Formation: War Mobilization, Trade Integration, and Political Development in Medieval Europe." *International Organization* 70 (3): 551–586.
13. Ibrahim, Mahmood. 1990. *Merchant Capital and Islam*. Austin: University of Texas Press, 41–42.
14. Morony, Michael G. 2017. "Trade and Exchange: The Sasanian World to Islam." *Late Antiquity and Early Islam, Fifth Workshop: Trade and Exchange in the Late Antique and Early Islamic Near East*, 17–18.
15. Metcalf, David Michael. 2001. "Monetary Recession in the Middle Byzantine Period: The Numismatic Evidence." *Numismatic Chronicle (1966–)* 161: 111–155.
16. Siegfried, Nikolaus A. 2001. "Concepts of Paper Money in Islamic Legal Thought." *Arab Law Quarterly* 16: 319.
17. Udovitch, Abraham L. 1975. "Reflections on the Institutions of Credits and Banking in the Medieval Islamic Near East." *Studia Islamica* 41: 5–21.
18. Udovitch, Abraham L. 1967. "Credit as a Means of Investment in Medieval Islamic Trade." *Journal of the American Oriental Society* 87 (3): 260–264.
19. Kennedy, Hugh. 2015. "The Middle East in Islamic Late Antiquity." In *Fiscal Regimes and the Political Economy of Premodern States*, edited by Andrew Monson and Walter Scheidel. Cambridge: Cambridge University Press, 290–403.
20. Aerts, Erik. 2006. "The European Monetary Famine of the Late Middle Ages and the Bank of San Giorgio in Genoa." *Ligurian Society of Homeland History Conference Proceedings*, 27–62.

21. Hamilton, Earl J. 2013. *American Treasure and the Price Revolution in Spain, 1501–1650*. Cambridge: Harvard University Press; Munro, John H. 2003b. *The Monetary Origins of the "Price Revolution": South German Silver Mining, Merchant Banking, and Venetian Commerce, 1470–1540.* Working Paper. Toronto, Ontario, Canada: Department of Economics, University of Toronto; Fisher, Douglas. 1989. "The Price Revolution: A Monetary Interpretation." *Journal of Economic History* 49 (December): 884–902; Goldstone, Jack A. 1991. "Monetary Versus Velocity Interpretations of the 'Price Revolution': A Comment." *Journal of Economic History* 51 (1): 176–181.

22. The fairs are essential to medieval economic history, but appear to be somewhat peripheral to military finance. A schematic source is Johnston, Ruth A. 2011.Vol. 1: Fairs. In *All Things Medieval: An Encyclopedia of the Medieval World.* Santa Barbara: Greenwood, 227–231. More detailed discussions include Usher, Abbott Payson. 1943. *The Early History of Deposit Banking in Mediterranean Europe.* Vol. 1. Cambridge: Harvard University Press; Munro, John H. 2001. "The 'New Institutional Economics' and the Changing Fortunes of Fairs in Medieval and Early Modern Europe: The Textile Trades, Warfare, and Transaction Costs." *VSWG: Vierteljahrschrift für Sozial-und Wirtschaftsgeschichte* 88 (1): 147.

23. Munro 2020: chap. 1; Spufford, Peter. 1988. *Money and Its Use in Medieval Europe.* E-book. Cambridge: Cambridge University Press, chap. 13.

24. Munro 2020: 22.

25. Munro 2020: table 1 at 27, chap. 1.

26. Munro, John H. 2003a. "The Medieval Origins of the Financial Revolution: Usury, Rentes, And Negotiability." *International History Review* 25 (3): 505–562 at 505.

27. Stasavage 2011: Chapter 2 at 30; Epstein, Stephan, 2000. *Freedom and Growth: The Rise of States and Markets in Europe, 1300–1750.* London: Routledge.

28. Stasavage 2011.

29. Epstein, Steven. 1996. *Genoa and the Genoese, 958–1528.* Chapel Hill: University of North Carolina Press, 106–107.

30. Steven Epstein 1996: 204.

31. Kindleberger, Charles. 1999. "Currency Debasement in the Early Seventeenth Century and the Establishment of Deposit Banks in Central Europe." In *Essays in History: Financial, Economic, Personal,* by Charles Kindleberger, 49–58. Ann Arbor: University of Michigan Press;Munro 2020: chap. 1; Spufford 1988: 289–318.

32. Usher 1943: 129.

33. Payne, Stanley G. 1973. *A History of Spain and Portugal.* Vol. 1. Madison: University of Wisconsin Press, 112.

34. Bensch, Stephen P. 2002. *Barcelona and Its Rulers, 1096–1291*. No. 26. Cambridge: Cambridge University Press, 50, 313–325.

35. Thompson, I. A. A. 2020. *The Military Revolution and the Trajectory of Spain: War, State, and Society, 1500–1700.* Trowbridge: Paragon, 114.

36. Fynn-Paul, Jeff. 2014. "Military Entrepreneurs in the Crown of Aragon During the Castilian–Aragonese War, 1356–1375." In *War, Entrepreneurs, and the State in Europe and the Mediterranean, 1300–1800,* edited by Jeff Fynn-Paul. Leiden: Brill, 32–62 at 35.

37. Payne 1973: 160–161.

38. Aerts 2006: 27–62.

39. Steven Epstein 1996: 280.

40. Lane, Frederic C. 1973a. *Venice, a Maritime Republic.* Baltimore: Johns Hopkins University Press, 329; Lane, Frederic C. 1973b. "Venetian Bankers, 1496–

1533: A Study in the Early Stages of Deposit Banking." *Journal of Political Economy* 45 (2): 187–206.

41. Mueller, Reinhold C. 1997. *The Venetian Money Market: Banks, Panics, and the Public Debt, 1200–1500*. Baltimore: Johns Hopkins University Press, 110118.

42. Lane 1973a: 324–329.

43. Stasavage 2011: 33–34.

44. D'Altroy, Terence N. 2015. "The Inka Empire." In *Fiscal Regimes and the Political Economy of Premodern States,* edited by Andrew Monson and Walter Scheidel. Cambridge: Cambridge University Press, 31–70, at 65.

45. Smith, Michael E. 2015. "The Aztec Empire." In *Fiscal Regimes and the Political Economy of Premodern States,* edited by Andrew Monson and Walter Scheidel. Cambridge: Cambridge University Press, 71–114.

46. Von Glahn, Richard. 2016. *An Economic History of China: From Antiquity to the Nineteenth Century.* Cambridge: Cambridge University Press, 156–166.

47. Von Glahn 2016: 156–166.

48. Von Glahn 2016: 170–181.

49. Von Glahn 2016: 208–217.

50. Von Glahn 2016: 236–242, 255–265; Von Glahn, Richard. 2010. "Monies of Account and Monetary Transition in China, Twelfth to Fourteenth Centuries." *Journal of the Economic and Social History of the Orient* 53 (3): 463–505. In both of these writings, Von Glahn describes huizi notes depreciating to 25 percent of nominal value, which for several decades of intense warfare is not an unusual inflation level and might even be considered exemplary. In an earlier review essay, Von Glahn references a 95 percent fall in market value for the huizi notes, which would count as a more serious problem. Von Glahn, Richard. 2004. "Revisiting the Song Monetary Revolution: A Review Essay." *International Journal of Asian Studies*. 1 (1): 159–178, in particular 175.

51. Xiao, Qing. 1984. *Zhong-guo gu-dai huo-bi shi*. Ren-min chu-ban-she, 248–257, via Horesh, Niv. 2014. *Chinese Money in Global Context: Historic Junctures Between 600 BCE and 2012.* Palo Alto: Stanford University Press, 55.

52. Von Glahn.2016: 236–242, 255–265; Von Glahn 2010.

53. Zarakol, Ayse. 2022. *Before the West: The Rise and Fall of the Eastern World Orders*. Cambridge: Cambridge University Press.

54. Von Glahn 2016: 284–312 at 285.

55. Horesh 2014: 53.

56. Von Glahn, Richard. 1996. *Fountain of Fortune: Money and Monetary Policy in China, 1000–1700.* Berkeley: University of California Press, 173–206.

57. See, for example, Scheidel, Walter. 2010. "Coin Quality, Coin Quantity, and Coin Value in Early China and the Roman Empire." *American Journal of Numismatics* 22: 93–118, in particular 103: "In the words of Kevin Butcher and Matthew Ponting, the Roman minting authorities were experts at disguising the declining silver contents of their coin ages: 'they endowed silver coins with an artificially produced surface layer that was heavily enriched with silver, thereby creating an impression of elevated fineness where it was visible to coin users.'"

58. Von Glahn 2010: 465, 470.

59. See Cribb, Joe. 1979. "An Historical Survey of the Precious Metal Currencies of China." *Numismatic Chronicle*. 19: 185–209, in particular 189. The dramatic levels of silver imports also support this assumption; see Von Glahn, Richard. 1996b. "Myth and Reality of China's Seventeenth-Century Monetary Crisis." *Journal of Economic History* 56 (2): 429–454. As discussed, base metals

prices fluctuated substantially, leading to periods when the metal of the coin was worth more than its unit of account value, hence encouraging people to melt down the coins in large quantities.

60. Contamine 1986: 165–172.

61. Wyman, Patrick. 2021. *The Verge: Reformation, Renaissance and Forty Years that Shook the World*. New York: Hachette Book Group, 45–47.

5
The Mercantilist Revolution

And so it came about that each one of those lords to whom he sent gave very freely when he was asked, whether jewels, small bars and plates of gold and silver, or other valuables which he possessed; of all this treasure gathered together the fifth due to your Majesty amounted to over two thousand four hundred pesos of gold, exclusive of all the ornaments in gold, silver and featherwork, the precious stones and other costly articles which I set aside for your Majesty, which would be worth some hundred thousand ducats and more; and which apart from their value were so marvellous on account of their novelty and strangeness as to be almost without price, for it is doubtful whether any of all the known princes of the world possesses such treasures and in such quantity. And let this not appear fabulous to your Majesty, for in truth there was not a living thing on land or sea of which Muteczuma could have knowledge which was not so cunningly represented in gold, silver, precious stones or featherwork as almost to seem the thing itself; of all of which Muteczuma gave me great store for your Majesty, not to mention others of which I gave him examples to copy, and he had them reproduced in gold, such as images, crucifixes, medallions, carved jewels and necklaces, and many other ornaments belonging to us which I persuaded him to have copied.

—Hernando Cortés, ca. 1520

Developments in the finance domain in the period 1500–1815 CE were almost exclusively focused in Europe; even the United States is only of interest here in that it echoes European developments of the time. The combination of increased maritime trade, improvements in agricultural productivity, an influx of specie from the Americas, and competitive pressure in warfare triggered a significant increase in state revenues between the early 1600s and the early 1700s. The linkage between trade, taxation, finance, and national security set the stage for the next revolution in financial affairs (RFA): mercantilism. This revolution was due in part to a general increase in business sophistication, a flowering of economic thought, the launch of central banking, and the success of a number of public-private financial partnership schemes. Although the transformation of the finance domain during this period was extraordinary, it had clear antecedents in the recent past.

Europe on the Brink of the Mercantilist RFA

As discussed in the previous chapter, city-states were already issuing debt by the 1200s, setting the stage for the evolution of more complicated financial instruments. Larger and more complicated states now competed in the finance domain by working to maintain their ability to create liquid assets that maintained their value. Following the example of the public deposit banks of the city-states such as the Banco della Piazza in Venice and the Taula de Canvi in Barcelona, these proto-states also began launching central banks—first in Sweden in 1668 and then the Bank of England in 1694, allowing for the creation and trading of public debt. As Margolein C. Hart writes, "Before the sixteenth century few European [territorial] states contracted substantial long-term debts at all. By the eighteenth century almost all were permanently indebted."[1] By the end of the seventeenth century, relatively primitive versions of the instruments with which states today use to compete in the finance domain were in place.

These attempts by states to utilize the new financial tools at their disposal were not, however, wholly successful; in fact, state military financing triggered severe financial crises such as the South Sea Bubble, in which the English government created a public-private partnership to swap government debt for equity in a company previously dedicated to generating revenue through the slave trade with Africa and South America. The South Sea Company stock septupled in value between February and June 1720 but then crashed, leading to a dramatic economic and political crisis. Despite these setbacks, this period saw the growth of national financial competition into a continental arena. In previous periods, limitations on trade flows and financial links had kept the financial commons limited to fairly small regions such as classical Greece and adjacent areas, or the early Chinese states on the Yellow and Yangtze Rivers. By the end of the 1600s, however, all of Europe was linked by a financial commons, and management of the finance domain as an ingredient of national defense became critical for states across the entire world.

This evolution of the European finance domain was in part fueled by the increased ability of states to buy and sell public debt. By the sixteenth century, territorial states in Europe had a range of means by which to borrow money; financing by sale of institutional debt instruments became common to fund state security, supplemented by a mixture of voluntary and forced loans from the nobility and from merchants and bankers. Spain, France, German principalities, and city-states in Catalonia and Italy, made use of various instruments in addition to revenues derived from tax streams or income from royal lands.[2]

As a result of this growing financial sophistication in state behavior, states across Europe became increasingly focused on acquiring and maintaining liquidity, although not necessarily in the interest of cultivating financial interdependence; in a word, states were moving on to a form of protectionism called "mercantilism." This evolution was driven by a combination of intellectual ferment, monetary gamesmanship, and policy integration on the state level, and resulted in a more sophisticated international financial system and a broader financial commons.

Taxation Comes of Age

European proto-states in the early modern period were forced by circumstance to make myriad trade-offs between direct taxes (on income and wealth) and indirect taxes (on excise and customs). For example, French king Phillip VI first imposed the *gabelle* (duty) tax on salt in France in 1331, which had the dual consequence of creating a government monopoly on salt as well as raising revenue for the crown. In fact, by 1641 this salt tax alone brought in twice as much in tax revenues as all the taxes levied by their competitor, the English Crown. So much more powerful was the French state, however, that the salt tax did not even represent the bulk of its revenue at the time, 60 percent of which came from the *taille*, a direct tax on land. The taxes succeeded despite the prevailing view among the French nobles that *contribuer est consideré comme ignoble*—"to contribute is despicable."[3]

Aristocratic carping aside, the fuse had been lit on the mercantilist RFA, as we can see from the spectacular growth in tax revenues across European states from 1500 to 1789 in Table 5.1. Spain's advantage from its conquests in the Americas in the 1500s begins to show in the early 1600s, as revenues double from to fifty-one tons of silver from 1500–1509 to 107 tons from 1550–1559, and then more than quadruple to 430 tons from 1600 to 1609. France also shows a strong revenue performance, largely due to size, raising 1,053 tons of silver from 1600 to 1609 alone. The Dutch Republic holds a high position in the 1600s, a remarkable feat considering that, despite British concerns in the seventeenth century that, in the words of Samuel Pepys, "the Devil shits Dutchmen," the Dutch Republic in fact had at most one-quarter of the population of England at the time.[4] The Dutch Republic was able to leverage its ability to rapidly tax, borrow, and deploy a robust economy whose gross domestic product (GDP) per capita

Table 5.1 Revenues of European States and Related Series, 1500–1789

Annual Average Total Revenue (tons of silver)

	United Kingdom	Dutch Republic	France	Spain	Venice	Austria	Russia	Prussia	Ottoman Empire	Poland Lithuania
1500–1509	20.7		86.9	51.0	44.1					11.3
1550–1559	35.9		151.6	107.1	48.9				106.1	6.5
1600–1609	65.7	116.8	294.2	430.8	67.6			3.5	122.6	15.2
1650–1659	196.1	213.9	1053.7	412.7	68.0	74.6		6.3	150.1	39.9
1700–1709	559.4	400.6	878.2	219.2	95.0	206.3	89.8	44.5	163.0	10.8
1750–1759	821.1	367.6	1081.2	439.3	83.3	349.3	275.2	202.3	179.4	9.5
1780–1789	1627.3	466.8	1962.0	642.5	98.5	858.7	661.7	294.9	147.2	86.3

Sources: From the online appendix https://ata.boun.edu.tr/sites/ata.boun.edu.tr/files/faculty/sevket.pamuk/database/a-_web_sitesi.xls for Karaman, K. Kivanç, and Şevket Pamuk. 2010. "Ottoman State Finances in European Perspective, 1500–1914." *Journal of Economic History* 70 (3): 593–629. Because data is assembled from multiple sources, authors focus on years where all states have data; hence, the gaps in time periods.

was more than double England's into a brief period of European military supremacy before the lack of clear political unity, disputes between different provinces, and the aforementioned relatively small population eventually pulled it down by 1700.[5] The ability of a state to quickly raise revenue is not by itself necessarily predictive of longer-term political power, however; several of the European powers who would come to dominate by the late 1800s—Prussia, Russia, and Austria—could in the 1600s barely compete with Venice and the Dutch. The rapid development of the revenue systems in England and France over the course of the 1600s puts them solidly at the top of the European table through the 1700s, evidence of which we can also see in Table 5.2.

As Table 5.2 also shows, by 1700 England had become a financial competitor to France, Germany, and Italy. The struggle of these states to rise to—or stay in—a position of prominence is closely correlated to the efflorescence of mercantilist thought, a development we discuss in the next section.

The Emergence of Mercantilist Thought

The seventeenth century was a time of significant change in the development of the links between trade, taxation, finance, and national security. Many aspects of this period—as well as the significance of this development for strategic competition—become clearer when viewed through the lens of the finance domain. In particular, developments in economic thought and the launch of central banking—as well as a number of public-private financial schemes—show the strategic importance of finance in this period.

The rise of the British economic school of mercantilism and two closely related Continental schools—Colbertism and cameralism, about which there is more below—is evidence of this significant change in strategy and philosophy. Despite the substantial disagreement about the school of mercantilism's exact intellectual parameters, a number of themes have been noted by

Table 5.2 Annual Gross Domestic Product (GDP) Estimates, Historic Territories of Modern States (in billions of 2011 US dollars)

	France	Germany	Italy	Netherlands	Portugal	Spain	Sweden	United Kingdom
1500	25.4	21.9	28.4	2.2	1.3	8.6	1.0	6.7
1600	29.8	20.6	31.5	6.4	1.4	10.4	1.0	10.4
1700	36.4	22.5	34.6	6.4	3.1	11.0	2.5	20.7

Source: Bolt, Jutta, and Jan Luiten van Zanden. 2020. *Maddison Style Estimates of the Evolution of the World Economy: A New 2020 Update*. Working Paper WP-15. Maddison-Project. Gronigen, University of Gronigen.

scholars such that its theoretical boundaries can be broadly defined. In particular, there is a clear link between mercantilist ideas and the effect of competitive pressures of nationalism on trade and commerce. For example, German economist Gustav Von Schmoller, writing in 1884, notes of mercantilism: "The essence of the system lies not in some doctrine of money, or the balance of trade[,] not in tariff barriers, protected duties, or navigation laws, but in something far greater: namely in the total transformation of society and its organisation, as well as of the state and its institutions, in the replacing of a local and territorial policy by that of the national state."[6] Some fifty years later, Swedish political economist Eli Heckscher, in his summary of mercantilist ideas refers to mercantilism as "the body of thought focused on nation-building."[7] Finally, Lars Magnusson summarizes the political nature of mercantilism, writing that "the ultimate *ends* of mercantilist policies were to strengthen the external power of the state."[8]

Consistent with the idea that state economic policy should serve state power first and promote prosperity second, many mercantilist works of this period focus on states and kings maintaining an essential supply of liquid assets, particularly in the years before the fiscal revolutions of the late 1600s. In one of the first and most important works of English mercantilist thought, *England's Treasure By Forraign Trade or The Ballance of Our Forraign Trade Is the Rule of Our Treasure*, Thomas Mun, director of the East India Company and member of the Crown's Privy Council to King James I, writes "a Prince that will not oppress his people, and yet be able to maintain his Estate, and defend his Right, that will not run himself into Poverty, Contempt, Hate, and Danger, must lay up treasure, and be thrifty."[9] The enlightened prince, Mun writes, should not be entirely focused on thrift, however: "For if he should mass up more money than is gained by the over-ballance of his forraign trade, he shall not Fleece, but Flea his Subjects, and so with their ruin overthrow himself for want of future sheerings."[10] These ideas did not appear from nowhere: in medieval Europe, there was already substantial focus among rulers on gaining access to bullion for state purposes in a vague doctrine of "bullionism" that is a clear precursor of mercantilism.[11] Authors like Mun debated and formalized these ideas, arguing for an enlightened form of authoritarianism during this period, echoing the work of philosopher contemporaries like Thomas Hobbes.

While much discussion of mercantilism focuses on English texts (in part because Adam Smith was one of the first to discuss it as a school of thought), similar ideas took hold across the continent. As early as the 1580s, Lus Ortiz, controller of Spanish public finance, argued that specie should not leave the country.[12] Among the states of Germany in the 1600s, "monetary manipulations by enhancing, debasing and clipping . . . coins" were so common "this period has been named the *Kipper- und Wipper-*

zeit."¹³ As part of this movement, in 1625 German author Jacob Borniss emphasized the importance of bullion and, in a reference to Cicero and Machiavelli's "sinews of power," termed liquid assets the *Nerv der Dinge* (nerve of things).¹⁴ The study of fiscal management, dubbed cameralism, became a major academic discipline in universities across the Holy Roman Empire. In France, Jean Baptiste Colbert greatly increased tax yields as minister of finances (1661–1683), while likewise increasing military expenditure as minister of the navy (1669-1683)—a prime example of the close links between fiscal policy and military policy.¹⁵

From City-State to Territorial State: The Dutch Republic

While still under Habsburg control, the Netherlands was affected by the pressure of the military and financial revolutions. Describing the system of the Habsburg Netherlands from 1506 to 1567, James Tracy notes that the fiscal system "was eclectic and in many ways creative, even if it never achieved the blessed state of solvency."¹⁶ Indeed, the Habsburgs initiated a number of ways for the Netherlands government to raise money on credit, including to sell shares on the relatively new Antwerp stock exchange, where financiers might raise 60,000 pounds for the crown within twenty-four hours.

As the costs of fighting the Eighty Years' War increased pressure on the Habsburgs in the 1500s, however, they leaned more and more on the sale of *rentes*—annuities funded by local government taxes.¹⁷ Ironically, the *rentes* system turned out to be the most important financial development for the Habsburgs, as well as one that would ensure the end of their rule in the Netherlands. Tracy describes this as a financial revolution and points to three specific stages of the system's development. First, in the early 1500s, the Dutch states began to take collective responsibility for *renten*, bureaucratizing the system and devolving power away from the Habsburgs. Second, the states undertook a series of regular taxes called the "novel expedients" to support the *rentes,* further cementing local control of the tax collection process. Finally, the states stopped requiring purchase of the *rentes,* allowing the yield of the *rentes* to create voluntary demand.¹⁸ The result was an instrument that enabled the construction of a modern state. As Tracy notes,

> In sum, the combination of initially high rates, freedom from constraint, and some assurance of repayment led to an explosion of interest in provincial *renten* among urban wealth-holders in Holland. Together with the opening of new markets, particularly in Zeeland, it was this extraordinary expansion of 'domestic' urban markets which enabled the States of Holland to raise unprecedented sums through the sale of *renten* during the 1550s.¹⁹

Although the Dutch Republic would acquire enormous power over the seventeenth century based in part on the financial innovations pushed by the Habsburgs, its political success was far from preordained. The republic's entire existence was a rejection of centralization—"the [Dutch] revolt . . . was very much a war against the Spanish centralization policy."[20] As with most successful revolutions, this switch to the new methods of organizing and financing was not smooth. Even as sophisticated bureaucracies grew in the provinces, the role of private individuals and their readiness to pay on behalf of the state was still crucial. For example, a colonel would be commissioned by the paymasters and use his own funds to begin recruitment of his army; soldiers would be responsible for purchasing their uniforms, but could borrow from the colonel or his captains against their future pay; and if captains lacked sufficient private capital to cover these and other expenses, they could borrow from a dedicated category of officers called *solliciteurs-militair,* who by providing funding to units "virtually prevented mutinies in the army."[21] Although these practices are key to understanding the public-private nature of the Dutch military at the time, they are by no means unique, and other countries furnish similar examples.

The Rise of the Central Banks

Another key piece of the mercantilist RFA was the development in Europe of the first central banks, the Riksbank in Sweden and the Bank of England. While it took centuries for the tools of central banking to be developed, we can see these banks developing the tool kit for maintaining currency at par (Riksbank) and creating a stable demand for government debt (Bank of England). The finance domain was becoming increasingly complex, requiring increasingly complex tools to negotiate it.

The development of the central bank was not entirely novel, however, but instead part of the long-term evolution of financial institutions. As discussed in the previous chapter, the public deposit banks of the European city-states in the late medieval era acted in a number of ways to protect the government-issued coinage or debt instruments.[22] Additionally, private consortia or individuals also played critical roles in some of the city-states, again maintaining the value of coins, notes or debt instruments.[23] The Dutch Republic experienced similar innovations, creating multiple social institutions that might be described as "proto-central banks" or precursor components.

One of these institutions, similar to the first approaches in Venice, was a small pool of wealthy noblemen enlisted as proxy agents of the state to help fund long-term debt. In particular, the Doubleth family; Philips Doubleth became the first family member to serve as receiver-general for the republic, an ill-defined position serving a nascent state government. In addition to acting as the Council of State's accountant, Doubleth also acted in part as the state's central banker, importuning his other wealthy friends and acquaintances to loan the state money to fight for Dutch independence from Spain.[24] When Philips died in 1612 after having served since 1586, three other Doubleths served in the position, two of whom were also named Philips. In all, a Doubleth served as receiver-general for the Dutch until 1666, or eighty years.

Again following the example of a later stage of public banking in Venice, the Dutch created the Bank of Amsterdam in 1609, to stabilize the value of their currency.[25] The establishment of an institution devoted just to monetary policy was necessitated by the federated structure of the Dutch Republic, which led to a proliferation of nearly 1,000 different types of coins. Combined with the exigencies of war, this diversity led to a series of debasements by provinces trying to finance military operations.[26] The half-century leading up to the bank's founding was the most intense period of debasement in the 1500-1800 period, with the 1570s being particularly extreme.[27] The Bank of Amsterdam helped to lessen the chaos in the Dutch marketplace by generating bank money as a stable unit of account, allowing provincial coins to maintain value and commerce to continue.[28]

By the late 1600s, the first actual central banks were created—first the Swedish central bank the Riksbank in 1668 and then the Bank of England in 1694, both charged by their respective crown with helping to fund public debt.[29] The Riksbank had replaced a putatively private bank, Stockholms Banco, which had been founded by serial entrepreneur Johan Palmstruch in 1657 to prevent devaluation and the loss of copper coin during the Thirty Years War.[30] While the French government would not create a stable central bank until Napoleon's reign, it made use of comparable institutions before then, including the ill-fated and short-lived Banque Royale discussed below. For a period, the city of Paris took control of royal tax revenues, in 1522 issuing *rentes sur l'hotel de ville* for the benefit of the crown. Analogous to Paris's role, the Vienna City Bank was created in 1706 to assist the Austrian monarchy under the reign of the Habsburgs in financing public debt.[31] Indeed, the entire period of the 1600s and early 1700s saw several dramatic experiments by territorial states in raising debt for public finance and military funding, most of which resulted in growing institutionalization and routinization in the financing process. This evolution in public banking reflects the learned discussions of finance of the late 1600s and early 1700s discussed earlier in this chapter, showing that states had a clear understanding of the new state of affairs in international competition.[32]

The War of Spanish Succession and Its Legacies

The War of Spanish Succession, fought between an alliance of France and Spain on the one side and the Grand Alliance of the Kingdom of Great Britain, the Dutch Republic, and the Holy Roman Empire (itself an amalgamation of Central European territories under the control of the Habsburgs) on the other, marked another transition point in the evolution of national debt instruments. Great Britain gained a substantial strategic advantage by allowing public debtholders to trade directly with each other, increasing the liquidity and attractiveness of state IOUs, allowing for increased state military spending.[33]

Great Britain and the South Sea Company

The case of the South Sea Company is worth reviewing briefly to give a sense of how competition in the finance domain drove some of the more aggressive funding decisions warring states made. As a result of fighting the War of Spanish Succession and the Great Northern War more or less simultaneously, the British government was more than 4 million pounds in debt to the Board of Ordnance—government supplier of weapons, ammunition, and fortification —and the Navy Board—government supplier of ships and manager of the Royal Navy—by 1711. Additional obligations were due to a broad range of individuals in a broad range of contracts. A solution of sorts was proposed by, among other people, John Blunt of the Hollow Sword Blades Company, a bank that had originally been established as a joint stock company to make rapiers.

 The solution Blunt and then chancellor of the exchequer Robert Harley proposed was that the creditors could be repaid in the stock of a new company, to be called "the Governor and Company of Merchants of Great Britain Trading to the South Seas and other parts of America and for encouraging the Fishery"—the South Sea Company, dedicated to trade with South America. After the company's incorporation in 1711, it gained concessions to trade in the Americas, the one with the greatest economic promise being the right to sell slaves there. While the name and general business of the company echoed storied joint stock companies of the past, such as the East India and Royal Africa Companies, the company was only modestly successful at making money between company managers relatively inexperienced in the risks of trade, aggressive competition from other companies, and uncooperative Spanish officials in the Americas.

 In the hands of the experienced Exchange Alley operators managing the company, the hybrid revenue streams of the company—South American trade and British government interest payments—became not a problem but a virtue, exciting investors. The South Sea Company stock's price rose steadily and quickly, buoyed by the trading of government debt for shares of stock. By 1719, with the stock price still rising and the UK government facing increasing pressure from creditors on other debt, the government went back to the well. In early 1720, the government passed an act allowing creditors to trade British government debt for the appreciating South Sea Company stock. Critically, in this period the stock was purchased (either by cash or British government debt) at a premium over the 100 pound par value, and the act allowed that premium to be reserved for previous stockholders, not shared equally across all. This seemingly minor tweak created a Ponzi scheme dynamic, with earlier investors gaining substantial amounts of equity from the purchases of later investors. As a result of the passage of the act, as well as the circulation of rumors about the stock's future value, in January 1720 the stock's price jumped from 128 pounds to over 300 as the scheme was enacted. By July, the price had jumped to a high of 950 pounds before collapsing to below 200 by October. The crash was so spectacular that a new term was invented by the British public to describe it: the *bubble*. The collapse led to an investigation, numerous suicides, and political scandal. However, a series of compromises allowed the basic structure to continue and develop, paving the way for British triumphs in the eighteenth and nineteenth centuries.[34]

France and John Law

Across the channel, the Scotsman John Law was orchestrating a parallel finance domain operation that offered the French crown comparable relief from its military debts. Law's methods were much more complex and extravagant than the South Sea Company, and much less documentation survives, so it is hard to make definite claims about how it worked and what contributed to its failure. As with the South Sea Company, a complex mix of revenue sources—in this case trade with North America and payments from French debt, but also West African and East Asian trade along with mints and tax farms—appear to have enticed and confused subscribers. For a brief moment Law gave France its first central bank, the Banque Royale, and Europe's first paper currency. It all collapsed at roughly the same time as the South Sea Company stock, but arguably more catastrophically. Most importantly, unlike the British government, the French government turned completely away from the cutting-edge finance domain practices for nearly a century.[35]

As chaotic and destructive as these episodes were, they are nevertheless illustrative of the pressures of the mercantilist RFA. In each of these cases, a mixture of a hybrid public-private structure, novel financial contracts, and large-scale purchases of state IOU's (as tallies, shares, bills, and other instruments) by the general public were used to raise large sums for military purposes by both Britain and France. One way to think about these efforts is as akin to the atomic bomb testing at Bikini Atoll; they represented tests of powerful new technologies of national security, and the collateral damage for individuals swept up in the experiments should not blind us to the real long-term strategic advantages gained in the process.

The Exception of French State Finance

Looking across the intensely competitive landscape of Europe in the 1600s and 1700s, the case of France is striking. Many have noted the remarkable contrast between the general grandeur of Ancien Régime France and the Achilles' heel that was its fiscal system, the vulnerability that eventually took down the monarchy in the French Revolution.[36] It was a system that was remarkably complicated and inefficient, difficult to adjust, and only barely up to the task. At its worst, the system was extremely dysfunctional, a morass of fraud and self-dealing. There is, however, no way to be sure as to the extent of the damage: the records are so fractured, with separate accounts and large gaps, that there is no hope of recovering a full picture, even at the overall level.[37] Despite these shortcomings, the system functioned for centuries and, as Eugene N. White demonstrates, if the government had made only slightly better decisions in the 1780s, there was nothing to keep it from rolling forward indefinitely, at least in terms of economics.[38]

Additional factors put France at a competitive financial disadvantage: though large, it started the early modern period more oriented toward agriculture than trade; it was less monetized; and it had weaker internal transportation links. These shortcomings combined to make it more challenging for France's rulers to pull liquid assets out of their kingdom. In addition, as with other large states, France had been assembled from many smaller polities; during this process of consolidation, the king granted many exceptions and liberties favoring the rich and powerful, thereby leading to a regressive tax system.[39] So regressive, in fact, that Philip Hoffman argues that the term "liberty" in Ancien Régime France became synonymous with "privilege."[40]

These factors set France on a dysfunctional path of fiscal development, but additional national security demands forced the crown to adopt increasingly risky and complicated financing methods over the course of the early modern period. Whereas in the early 1500s, French king Louis XII could put money into a literal war chest to maintain a liquid reserve, as the financing demands of war increased, and as a number of civil wars cut into the functions of the tax system, the king turned in part to a mixture of forced loans on loyal towns and asking tax officials to advance money. Martin Wolfe refers to these options as "inside credit" (i.e., inside crown control) and the king's ability to lean on tax officials as "squeezing the fiscal sponge." Wolfe argues that in the 1400s and 1500s, tax officials were selected on the basis of their existing wealth and there was little need to turn to bankers for loans. As we will show, this practice seems to have changed with the Thirty Years' War.[41]

In addition, the French crown took increasingly drastic measures, making special deals at pegged interest rates. As Hoffman writes:

> The needs of the moment . . . undoubtedly justified defaulting on the *rentes* in 1602-4, seizing the *droits alienes* in 1634, and cutting payments due rentiers and office holders in 1648. But the political consequences were considerable and not always predictable: the *paulette* [making venal offices inheritable for a payment], the intendants [special agents of the crown with extraordinary powers to collect taxes], the Fronde [a series of major civil wars], and an enduring concern with the sensitive politics of government debt.[42]

The frantic royal responses to exigent circumstances seem to come from the disjointed nature of the negotiation: on the one hand, the bulk of the revenues were brought in via piecemeal negotiations with different parties; on the other, the king was an autocrat with few if any legal limits on his actions.

The extent of the complex financial, political, and legal tactics that the French crown needed to deploy to succeed are apparent in the increase in revenues occurring during the Thirty Years' War, 1618–1648, and how well the financiers involved in taxing and lending to the crown fared.[43] As French tax revenues quadrupled in the early seventeenth century, the king's financiers indulged in a one-off burst of luxury home building, suggesting that the actual net lending by financiers in this period was probably limited—as much as they were providing liquidity to the crown, they were able to use some combination of tax farming and high interest payments to vault into higher income categories, at least in the 1630–1660 period.[44] This is a striking contrast to the earlier patterns of the 1500s, when, according to Wolfe, tax officials really did transfer substantial amounts of liquidity to the crown during stringent periods, sometimes losing money or going long periods with reduced income. The financiers' burst in mansion building is made even more interesting by Julius Dent's finding in his study of the careers of the financiers that only some of the seventeenth century financiers came to the work with substantial amounts of money—a number of them started out as servants, for example.[45]

The French crown thus faced three challenges. First, it needed to keep enough of the financiers happy enough to be able to maintain access to funds. Second, it needed to reduce actual payments to save money. Finally, it needed to regain control of the flow of money in the long term—the grand houses that were springing up are just one bit of evidence that the crown was giving away the store. Two tools, a carrot and a stick, helped the crown meet these challenges. The carrot was the *Ordonnances de Comptant*, a specialized means of making secret payments from the crown to financiers quickly, that was in theory designed for the most urgent interests of state, but by 1660 was largely a way to pay financiers interest that seemed for legal or political reasons "too high." Annual use of the *Ordonannces de Comptant* rose nearly two orders of magnitude in the eighty years from 1582 (752,538 livres) to 1659–1660 (70 million livres or more).[46] The stick was the *chambre de justice*, a special court that investigated "maladministration which had harmed the interests of the king or those of his subjects."[47] E. N. White notes that *chambre* used strategic applications of criminal indictments and substantial fines[48] to create some equity between short-term lenders who achieved high returns early on and long-term lenders who had been ready to wait, as well as by reducing payouts to the short-term lenders.[49] These two instruments allowed the crown to expand revenues even as financiers reduced their real estate spending in the best cases, and went bankrupt or died in prison in the worst.

These adjustments preserved the French system almost into the nineteenth century. As E. N. White notes, it is possible that the system could have survived the French Revolution of 1789 with slightly better decisions by government officials but, once the revolution started, the situation continued to destabilize, helping to drive the political upheaval until Napoleon instituted major reforms on taking power.[50]

The United States: Hercules in the Cradle

The founding of the United States in the late eighteenth century offers a unique opportunity for studying how policymakers accommodated themselves to the new fiscal realities of the mercantilist RFA. The War of Independence pushed the small country to extremes and left it with inflation and debt. For the first forty years of its existence, the United States fought a series of wars against the giants of Europe, including the War of 1812 but also an undeclared naval war with France from 1798 to 1800, as well as continual skirmishes with Spain and other countries.[51] After the United States successfully concluded the War of 1812, however, it was secure from attack until it began to initiate international combat in the late 1800s. We can see that US finance domain operations, particularly central banking, become fitfully more sophisticated from the founding to the issuance of War of 1812 debt, but then stall.

Even before the founding, the founders were deeply aware of the importance of the finance domain. Alexander Hamilton in particular argued for the importance of the finance domain in the Federalist Papers, advocating for the role of a solid institutionalized revenue system and the ability to borrow. Hamilton's work in *Federalist No. 31* shows a remarkable sensitivity to the role of credit in government, particularly in war:

> As revenue is the essential engine by which the means of answering the national exigencies must be procured, the power of procuring that article in its full extent, must necessarily be comprehended in that of providing for those exigencies.
>
> As theory and practice conspire to prove that the power of procuring revenue is unavailing, when exercised over the States in their collective capacities, the Federal government must of necessity be invested with an unqualified power of taxation in the ordinary modes.[52]

Starting from the general idea that a government should be able to do its job, part of which is defense, A. Hamilton notes the intense pressures that states encounter in war, requiring access to taxes and credit. In fact, competing in the finance domain required as much vigilance and preparation from the state as in the terrestrial or maritime domains. In A. Hamilton's unpublished "Defense of the Funding System," he wrote "[credit] is so immense a power in the affairs of war that a nation without credit would be in great danger of falling a victim in the first war with a power possessing a vigorous and flourishing credit."[53]

The US Constitution, ratified in 1788, manifests the tensions between ideals of limited government and the demands of national security, in particular the differential financial requirements of armies and navies. While the Constitution provides Congress with the authority to raise funds for an army, it does so on only a limited basis, with the term of funding lasting just two years. Despite this funding provision being an improvement over the Articles of Confederation, which decentralized military spending to the individual colonies, this limitation reflects the founders' concern over the antidemocratic effects of a standing army and the belief that armies did not require a permanent institutional foundation—and, consequently, a permanent financial allocation—to be effective. The Constitution imposes no such limitation on the financing of navies, in part because navies had historically not threatened the existence of democratic government, but also because navies represented a capital expenditure in construction, maintenance, and training that could not be realized in a short time frame. The early frigates of the US Navy, for example, each required more than three years for construction, in addition to ongoing maintenance and employment.[54]

As A. Hamilton successfully argued, increased revenue was necessary to build a state strong enough to avoid being drowned by the British.

Richard Sylla notes that the US government was "effectively bankrupt" before 1790, collecting "a grand total of $162,200 in custom duties" in 1789. This situation changed completely between 1790 and 1792, with a "Federalist financial revolution," and in 1793 the "government collected almost $4.7 million tax revenue."[55] Sylla further tracks the US financial revolution to a series of letters A. Hamilton wrote during the War of Independence that show a deep grasp of the finances of the Dutch Republic and Great Britain and gave a schematic version of the system he would put in place a decade later.[56]

The development of the modern central bank is closely related to the pressure to protect the nation from attacks via the finance domain. The United States, however, seemed impervious to this pressure, at least for the bulk of the eighteenth and nineteenth centuries. The United States was a wealthy, generally developed economy with a relatively sophisticated financial system, so why then did it not have a central bank between 1836 and 1913? We argue, in brief, that the lack of a central bank resulted from the lack of a serious external military threat. During this period, the wars fought by the United States were generally against much weaker opponents—Mexico, the Confederacy, Paraguay, pre-Meiji Japan, and the Indian nations—and, with the exception of the Civil War, were cheap to fight.[57] By the early 1900s, however, the United States was starting to compete with established great powers on the international stage and required a more sophisticated national financial system. Until then, the United States had no real need to compete in the finance domain.

There is a remarkable overlap between periods where American national security policy was concerned with major wars against foreign adversaries and the existence of a US central bank. Figure 5.1 plots federal interest expenditure as a percentage of GDP, federal interest expenditure if the most recent major US war was foreign but zero if the most recent conflict was the Civil War or other rebellion, and the existence or absence of a central bank. The interaction variable, "interest greater than 0.5 percent of GDP and most recent war against a foreign adversary" has a correlation of 82 percent with the existence of a central bank, a number that falls to 72 percent if we limit it to the period before 1900.[58]

The First Bank of the United States was chartered over substantial opposition as a means to fund the War of Independence. Robert Morris led the development, which A. Hamilton viewed as vital and perhaps essential to the war effort.[59] With the election of Thomas Jefferson in 1800, Albert Gallatin became secretary of the treasury. Despite being an outspoken critic of A. Hamilton, Gallatin ended up accepting much of his system, at least in practice. The War of 1812 reversed any success in reducing military expenditures, and he made no clear progress in reducing the national debt beyond the process A. Hamilton put in place. Gallatin in fact supported the

Figure 5.1 The Interaction of Foreign War and Government Debts in US Central Bank History

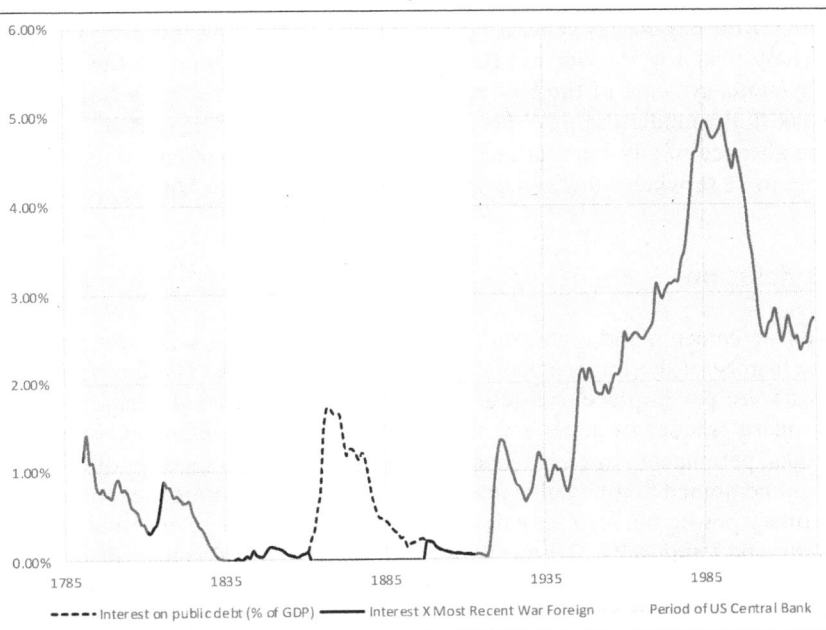

Sources: US gross domestic product (GDP) data are from measuringworth.com. Data on interest payments before 1947 are from Series Y457-465. US Bureau of the Census. 1975. *Historical Statistics of the United States, Colonial Times to 1970, Bicentennial Edition, Part 2.* Washington, DC: US Government Printing Office. Data from 1947 onward are from FRED2. 2021. "Federal Government Current Expenditures: Interest Payments (A091RC1Q027SBEA)," Data on dates of American wars are from Congressional Research Service. 2020. *Instances of Use of United States Armed Forces Abroad, 1798–2020.* Report R42738. Washington, DC: Congressional Research Service.

Bank of the United States for its ability to secure public money, remit funds rapidly, and generally monetize the US economy. The one area Gallatin was able to alter A. Hamilton's system was to eliminate large sections of the tariff and taxation system he had built up.[60]

As the Revolutionary War debts were paid down, the US Senate let the bank's charter expire in 1811, and Jefferson was dead set against the creation of another one. However, the financial demands of the War of 1812 forced the issue. Even under extreme financial pressure, it took Congress "seven attempts, after more than two years of almost constant endeavor" before the bank was in place.[61] The difficulty in raising money turned a political nonstarter into the crucial issue of national defense, and the Second Bank of the United States was born in 1816. By the time the bank was enacted, the War of 1812 was over, but the debt from it remained, and maintaining a stable and national currency for the federal government was crucial for day-to-day federal operations and amortizing the debt. Over its twenty-year life the Second Bank helped to greatly improve the internal payments systems of the United States, but did not become a full central bank in the modern sense.[62] For various reasons, including—as we argue—the absence of any international threat, the Second Bank ended its official role in 1836 when Congress again allowed its charter to lapse.

Conclusion

The seventeenth and eighteenth centuries saw a critical inflection point in the history of the finance domain: the mercantilist RFA. The developments that were put in place in a few city-states in the medieval period became standard practice by states across the continent. The development of central banks, permanent armed bureaucracies, and mercantilist theories of employment combined to give policymakers tools not just for turning resources into military power, but also for gaining access to a wider range of resources spatially and temporally. Central banks and the ancillary financial institutions that accompanied them gave states the ability to rent military power from abroad and from the future to an unprecedented extent. This capacity in turn helped spur innovation in other military domains, with armies and navies seeing radical doctrinal and technological improvement. The interaction between these financial and military advancements led to the Pax Britannica and the gold standard RFA, which we discuss in the next chapter.

Notes

1. 't Hart, Marjolein C. 1993. *The Making of a Bourgeois State: War, Politics and Finance During the Dutch Revolt*. Manchester: Manchester University Press, 158.

2. Tilly, Charles. 1990. *Coercion, Capital, and European States, AD 990–1990*. Oxford: Basil Blackwell; Drelichman, Mauricio, and Hans-Joachim Voth. 2016. *Lending to the Borrower from Hell: Debt, Taxes, and Default in the Age of Philip II*. Princeton: Princeton University Press; Tracy, James D. 1985. *A Financial Revolution in the Habsburg Netherlands: Renten and Rentiniers in the Country of Holland, 1515–1565*. Berkeley: University of California Press, 7–27.

3. 't Hart 1993: 119–120

4. Samuel Pepys quoting Sir William Batten in his diary, Friday, July 19, 1667, at *The Diary of Samuel Pepys Daily entries from the 17th century London diary*. https://www.pepysdiary.com/diary/1667/07/19/. Thanks to Brad Delong for the note. See, for example, Tables 5.1 and 5.2.

5. 't Hart 1993: in particular chaps. 4 and 5.

6. Robbins, Lionel. 1998. *A History of Economic Thought: The LSE Lectures*. Princeton: Princeton University Press, 47.

7. Robbins 1998: 48.
8. Magnusson, Lars. 1994. *Mercantilism*. Abingdon: Taylor and Francis, 34. Emphasis in original.
9. Mun, Thomas. 1664. *England's Treasure by Forraign Trade*: 91.
10. Mun, Thomas. 1664. *England's Treasure by Forraign Trade*: 92–93.
11. Munro, John H. 2020. *Wool, Cloth, and Gold*. Toronto, Ontario, Canada: University of Toronto Press, chap. 1.
12. Magnusson 1994: 202.
13. Magnusson 1994: 64. The literal meaning of "kipper and wipper-zeit" is disputed, but references a frantic clipping of coins and handing them to a sucker. According to political scientist Florian Justwan, its opacity is due to it being a slang term unique to northern Germany; Dash, Mark. 2012. "'Kipper und Wipper': Rogue Traders, Rogue Princes, Rogue Bishops and the German Financial Meltdown of 1621–23." *Smithsonian Magazine Blogs*, March 29.
14. Magnusson 1994: 190.
15. Wakefield, Andre. 2014. "Cameralism: A German Alternative to Mercantilism." *Mercantilism Reimagined: Political Economy in Early-Modern Britain and Its Empire*, edited by Andre Wakefield. Oxford: Oxford University Press, 134–150.
16. Tracy 1985: 29–30.
17. Tracy 1985: 38–46.
18. Tracy 1985: in particular "Conclusion."
19. Tracy 1985: 138.
20. A process aided by the marvelously named Pragmatic Sanction of 1549 that effectively created the Netherlands as an administrative body and that led ultimately to the Habsburgs' removal from power over the states. 't Hart, Marjolein C. 1989. "Cities and Statemaking in the Dutch Republic, 1580–1680." *Theory and Society* 18 (5): 667.
21. 't Hart 1993: 32–39. Quotation regarding *solliciteurs-militair* is on 38.
22. Kindleberger, Charles P. 1999. "Currency Debasement in the Early Seventeenth Century and the Establishment of Deposit Banks in Central Europe." In *Essays in History: Financial, Economic, Personal*, by Charles P. Kindleberger. Ann Arbor: University of Michigan Press, 49–58; Neal, Larry. 2018. "The Variety of Financial Innovations in European War Finance During the Thirty Years' War (1618–1648)." In *Financial Innovation and Resilience: A Comparative Perspective on the Public Banks of Naples (1462–1808)*, edited by Lilia Costabile and Larry Neal. London: Palgrave Macmillan, 127–145.
23. Lane, Frederic Chapin. 1973a. *Venice, a Maritime Republic*. Baltimore: Johns Hopkins University Press, 324–329.
24. 't Hart 1993: 166.
25. Quinn, Stephen, and William Roberds. 2007. "The Bank of Amsterdam and the Leap to Central Bank Money." *American Economic Review* 97 (2): 263.
26. Dehing, Pit, and Marjolein t' Hart. 1997. "Linking the Fortunes: Currency and Banking, 1550–1800." In *A Financial History of the Netherlands*, edited by Marjolein 't Hart, Joost Jonker, and Jan Luiten van Zanden. Cambridge: Cambridge University Press, 3840.
27. Quinn and Roberds 2007: 7, table 1.
28. Quinn, Stephen, and William Roberds. 2014. "How Amsterdam Got Fiat Money." *Journal of Monetary Economics* 66: 1–12; Quinn, Stephen, and William Roberds. 2019. "A Policy Framework for the Bank of Amsterdam, 1736–1791." *Journal of Economic History* 79 (3): 736–772.
29. Bordo, Michael. 2007b. "A Brief History of Central Banks." *Economic Commentary*, December. Cleveland: Federal Reserve Bank of Cleveland.

30. Wetterberg, Gunnar, and Patrick Hort. 2009. *Money and Power: From Stockholms Banco 1656 to Sveriges Riksbank Today.* Stockholm: Sveriges Riksbank, 24–45.

31. Velde, François R., and David R. Weir. 1992. "The Financial Market and Government Debt Policy in France, 1746–1793." *Journal of Economic History.* 52 (1): 12; Hoffman, Philip T. 1994. "Early Modern France, 1450–1700." In *Fiscal Crises, Liberty, and Representative Government, 1450–1789,* edited by Philip T. Hoffman and Kathryn Norberg. Palo Alto: Stanford University Press, 233, 172; Pieper, Renate. 2012. "Financing an Empire: The Austrian Composite Monarchy, 1650–1848." In *The Rise of Fiscal States: A Global History,* edited by Bartolome Yun-Casallila, Patrick O'Brien, and Francisco Comin Comin. Cambridge: Cambridge University Press, 164–190.

32. Anonymous. 1695. *Some Observations upon the Bank of England.* London: John Whitlock. Cited by Roseveare, Henry G. 1992. *The Financial Revolution 1660–1750.* London: Routledge; Murphy, Anne L. 2013. "Financial Markets: The Limits of Economic Regulation in Early Modern England." In *Mercantilism Reimagined: Political Economy in Early Modern Britain and Its Empire,* edited by Philip J. Stern and Carl Wennerlind. Oxford: Oxford University Press, 263–281.

33. Carlos, Ann M., Erin K. Fletcher, Larry Neal, and Kirsten Wandschneider. 2013. "Financing and Refinancing the War of the Spanish Succession, and then Refinancing the South Sea Company." In *Questioning Credible Commitment: Perspectives on the Rise of Financial Capitalism,* edited by D'Maris Coffman, Adrian Leonard, and Larry Neal. Cambridge: Cambridge University Press, 147–168.

34. Dickson, Peter George Muir. 2017. *The Financial Revolution in England: A Study in the Development of Public Credit, 1688–1756.* Abingdon: Routledge, in particular 67–71, table 17 on 139, and chaps. 5 and 6; Levenson, Thomas. 2020. *Money for Nothing: The Scientists, Fraudsters, and Corrupt Politicians Who Reinvented Money, Panicked a Nation, and Made the World Rich.* New York: Random House, in particular chap. 11.

35. Levenson 2020.

36. Bonney, Richard. 1981. *The King's Debts: Finance and Politics in France, 1589–1661.* New York: Clarendon Press; Oxford: Oxford University Press; White, Eugene. 2001a. "France and the Failure to Modernize Macroeconomic Institutions." In *Transferring Wealth and Power from the Old to the New World: Monetary and Fiscal Institutions in the Seventeenth Through the Nineteenth Centuries,* edited by Michael D. Bordo and Roberto Cortes-Conde. Cambridge: Cambridge University Press, 59–99.

37. E. N. White 2001: 59–99. Eugene White summarizes the figures that are available, but puts forward as well a list of wars, which he believes are at least as reliable a guide to the overall picture.

38. White, Eugene N. 1989. "Was There a Solution to the Ancien Régime's Financial Dilemma?" *Journal of Economic History* 49 (3): 545–568.

39. At the same time, it was sometimes necessary to pay the rich lenders their full interest rates in secret for political reasons. Bonney, Richard. 1976. "The Secret Expenses of Richelieu and Mazarin, 1624–1661." *English Historical Review* 91 (361): 825–836.

40. Hoffman 1994: 226–252.

41. Wolfe, Martin. 1972. *The Fiscal System of Renaissance France.* New Haven: Yale University Press, 63–66, 86–91.

42. Hoffman 1994: 226–252.

43. Hoffman 1994: 238–239, tables 1 and 2 for tax receipts; Dent, Julian. 1973. *Crisis in Finance: Crown, Financiers, and Society in Seventeenth-Century France.*

New York: St. Martin's Press, tables 4 and 5, 183, 187, for information on grand home building.

44. Julian Dent notes that the tresoriers de l'Epargne (savings treasurers) literally burned their tax receipts during the early 1600s, which supports his general discussion of opportunities for profit and fraud by the financiers.

45. Wolfe 1972: 63–66; Dent 1973: chap. 5.

46. Bonney 1976: 825836; Dent 1973: 84–85. While Richard Bonney and Julian Dent's work differs in many respects, and Bonney is critical of Dent's work (footnotes on 825, for example), the picture they offer on quantities is similar.

47. Dent 1973: 103–108.

48. Dent 1973: 103–108, 158–162.

49. E. N. White 2001: 24.

50. E. N. White 1989: 545–568; White, Eugene N. 1995. "The French Revolution and the Politics of Government Finance, 1770–1815." *Journal of Economic History* 55 (2): 227–255.

51. Congressional Research Service. 2020. *Instances of Use of United States Armed Forces Abroad, 1798–2020.* Report R42738. Washington, DC: Congressional Research Service; See also Edling, Max M. 2014. *A Hercules in the Cradle: War, Money, and the American State, 1783–1867.* Chicago: University of Chicago Pres, in particular 88 but also chap. 3.

52. Hamilton, Alexander. 1788. *Federalist No. 31.* January 1.

53. Hamilton, Alexander. 2019. "The Defense of the Funding System." In *Alexander Hamilton on Finance, Credit, Debt,* edited by Richard Sylla and David J. Cowen. New York: Columbia University Press, 297–298.

54. Toll, Ian W. 2008. *Six Frigates: The Epic History of the Founding of the US Navy.* New York: Norton.

55. Sylla, Richard. 2011. "Financial Foundations: Public Credit, the National Bank, and Securities Markets." In *Founding Choices*, edited by Douglas A. Irwin and Richard Sylla. Chicago: University of Chicago Press, 59-88, at 59. See also Cowen, David, and Richard Sylla. 2018. *Alexander Hamilton on Finance, Credit, and Debt.* New York: Columbia University Press, "Introduction."

56. Sylla 2011: 63–66.

57. Congressional Research Service 2020.

58. Testing the hypothesis that the true correlation is in fact zero gives a t-statistic of 21.7 (d.f. of 227) in the first case and 10.7 (d.f. of 108) in the second, both of which are statistically significant.

59. Morgan, H. Wayne. 1956. "The Origins and Establishment of the First Bank of the United States." *Business History Review* 30 (4). 472–492, at 476–477.

60. Edling 2014: 102–120.

61. Catterall, Ralph Charles Henry. 1902. *The Second Bank of the United States.* Chicago: University of Chicago Press, 21. Chapter 1 details the political battles; Walters, Raymond, Jr. 1945. "The Origins of the Second Bank of the United States." *Journal of Political Economy* 53 (2): 115–131, details the critical role of concerns about war in the push by John Calhoun and others.

62. The functions of the bank and how they helped commerce and federal payments is detailed in Knodell, Jane Ellen. 2016. *The Second Bank of the United States:"Central" Banker in an Era of Nation-Building, 1816–1836.* London: Routledge.

6
Pax Britannica and the Gold Standard

American Credit and the Folly of Repudiation!
This new and vain people can never forgive us for having preceded them 300 years in civilisation. They are prepared to enter into the most bloody wars in England, not on account of Oregon, or boundaries, or right of search, but because our clothes and carriages are better made, and because Bond Street beats Broadway. Wise Webster does all he can to convince the people that these are not lawful causes of war; but wars and long wars, they will one day or another produce; and this, perhaps, is the only advantage of repudiation. The Americans cannot gratify their avarice and ambition at once; they cannot cheat and conquer at the same time. The warlike power of every country depends on their Three per Cents. If Caesar were to return to earth, Wettenhall's list would be more important than his Commentaries; Rothschild would open and shut the temple of Janus; Thomas Baring or Bates, would probably command the Tenth Legion, and the soldiers would march to battle with loud cries of Scrip and Omnium reduced, Consols, and Caesar! Now, the Americans have cut themselves off from all resources of credit. Having been as dishonest as they can be, they are prevented from being as foolish as they wish to be. In the whole habitable globe they cannot borrow a guinea, and they cannot draw the sword because they have not money to buy it.
We all know that the American can fight. Nobody doubts their courage. I see now in my mind's eye a whole army on the plains of Pennsylvania in battle array, immense corps of insolvent light infantry, regiments of heavy horse debtors, battalions of repudiators, brigades of bankrupts, with Vivre sans payer, ou mourir, on their banners and oere alieno on their trumpets: all these desperate debtors would fight to the death for their country, and probably drive into the sea their invading creditors.
—*The Wit and Wisdom of the Rev. Sydney Smith*, 1860

The end of the Napoleonic Wars and the Congress of Vienna of 1814–1815 can be thought of as a rough milestone for the beginning of the next revolution in financial affairs (RFA): the success and spread of a gold standard.

The sophistication of world trade and finance, relative peace on the European continent, and British hegemony in the maritime and finance domains led to a new era. British dominance resulted in active conflict in the domain moving to more peripheral areas such as financing of conflicts outside of Europe, or use of finance by France and Germany for an edge in contestation around the world.

The development of the gold standard increased liquidity for great powers and created greater dependencies between them. The United Kingdom, for example, enacted liberal policies, such as openness to trade and limited public budgets, while its citizens invested substantially in business enterprises in the Crown colonies. Although the United Kingdom was the largest actor in world trade and finance in this period, it tended to use its power to maintain stability and trade flows. While there was the potential for the British financial system to profoundly affect other regions and the world overall, it does not seem to have been deliberately used for this purpose by the Crown.[1] In fact, given that the gold standard required similar behavior from all participant countries, there is considerable doubt among economic historians as to whether the Bank of England played a commanding role during normal operation of the standard.[2] Even though this approach was slower to catch on with Britain's rivals—particularly France and Germany, whose investors were more tightly constrained by their governments' more nationalistic policies—the overall philosophy of outward-facing growth and trade interdependence had taken hold in the finance domain.

The Continental System and The Gold Standard RFA

France's failed attempt at domination through the imposition of the Continental System during the latter stages of the Napoleonic Wars was another key indicator of changes in the finance domain. By the resumption of hostilities signaled by the expiration of the Treaty of Amiens in 1803, France struggled to maintain parity with the United Kingdom, with the establishment of Napoleon's Continental System representing its most serious effort to challenge British influence in Europe.[3] The Continental System was Napoleon's attempt at financial warfare (albeit one based on a strategic miscalculation) in which France launched a general embargo and naval blockade against the United Kingdom in 1806. Napoleon, recently crowned emperor of France, hoped that the British would need to send increasing amounts of money overseas to pay for imports, leading to their financial and economic collapse and forcing them to end the war. Napoleon substantially underestimated actual British wealth, however, and the scheme failed as the French learned an early lesson in the difficulty of unilaterally imposing financial sanctions, especially against a target as wealthy and influential as the United Kingdom.[4] This mistake did not single-handedly lose Napoleon the war, but it did influence his decisions to invade Spain and Russia, two even more costly miscalculations.

The allies of the victorious Sixth Coalition—Austria, Great Britain, Prussia, and Russia—decided that France should pay war reparations of 700 million francs in the Second Treaty of Paris in November 1815, one of the earliest cases in Europe of the imposition of large-scale postwar reparations payments.[5] The restored French monarchy of Louis XVIII made the first payment of 140 million francs out of taxes already collected, almost completely draining the public treasury. When it became clear to the French crown that it would be necessary to obtain outside financing to make the payments, the French took out a loan underwritten by the Dutch bank of Hope and Co. and the Barings Bank in the City of London, an innovative arrangement that provides a key example of the change to the finance domain in the early nineteenth century.[6]

Ironically, France's ability to pay the debts imposed—and, thereby, push the progress of the finance domain—was enabled by the very states that imposed the debts in the first place. The French were able to finance their debt in this manner through tools developed by the United Kingdom and other European states for trade and public finance. Over time, these public financing tools became more effective, and this effectiveness, combined with an increase in trade with gold-backed currency and the emergence of multiple large financial centers, resulted in the creation of a more orderly global financial commons. This creation offered ample benefits to the great powers, but also afforded new opportunities to peripheral players: several small states and substate regions began to float large bond issues to finance themselves, thereby allowing them to field armies and navies for domestic and foreign use. These innovations required the creation of a gold standard to truly transform the international financial system into a financial commons.

As with other RFAs, maintenance and development of the gold standard—defining the unit of account as a fixed quantity of gold—was driven in substantial part by national conflicts. For example, Great Britain, at the behest of Master of the Royal Mint Sir Isaac Newton, went on the gold standard in the wake of the War of Spanish Succession in 1717. The major interruptions were the Napoleonic Wars and World War I, with high costs that forced Britain off the formal gold standard for extended periods. Returning to the standard was a high priority for policymakers, with full convertibility of notes achieved within a decade after each conflict. Britain was finally forced off the standard in 1931, when for the first time in centuries the currency was devalued in peacetime as a consequence of the Great Depression and the Invergordon Mutiny.[7]

Similarly, a unified Germany went on the gold standard in 1871 at the end of the Franco-German War using the stores of gold it won as a way to take economic advantage of its new status as a great power in Europe. The Franco-German War also had an impact on France's financial policy: France had been using a bimetallic standard—meaning the government defined the unit of account in fixed quantities of both silver and gold—until 1878, when it stopped coining silver in an attempt to prevent Germany from buying gold by selling silver. The result was, instead, the collapse of the price of silver and its effective end as a currency as pervasive as gold.[8]

The Gold Standard and International Borrowing

Given the expansion of the gold standard to include larger and larger sections of the world in this period, it is worth taking a moment to understand the general links between economic growth and increases in gold stocks from 1700 to the collapse of the Bretton Woods system in 1972. Figure 6.1 shows the growth of world gold stocks and the growth of the world economy.

Figure 6.1   Annual Growth in World Gross Domestic Product (GDP) and Gold Stocks, 1700–1980

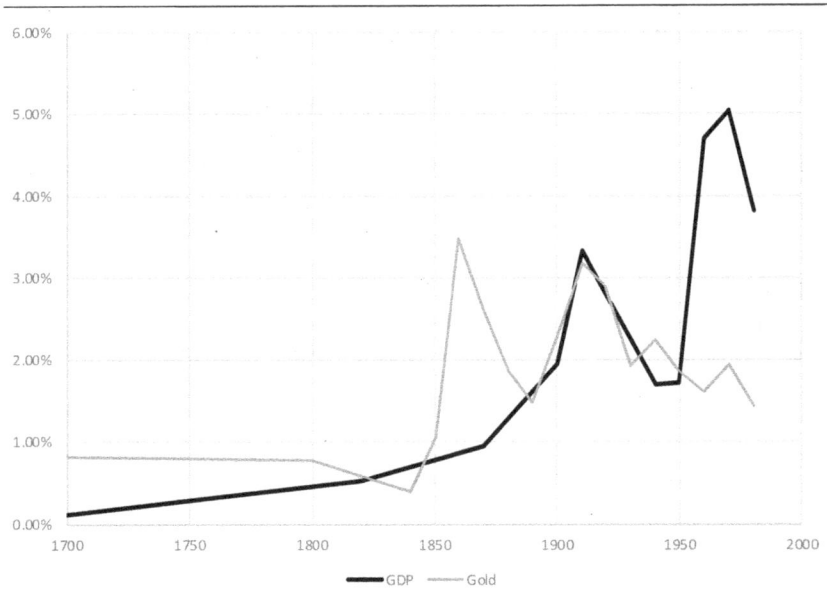

Sources: Cooper, Richard N., Rudiger Dornbusch, and Robert E. Hall. 1982. "The Gold Standard: Historical Facts and Future Prospects." *Brookings Papers on Economic Activity* 1: 1–56; Our World in Data. 2017. "World GDP over the Last Two Millennia."

Up to roughly 1890, gold stocks tended to grow faster than world gross domestic product (GDP).[9] From about 1890 to 1950, gold stocks and world GDP grew at roughly the same speed. After 1950, however, world GDP grew much faster. This broad pattern helps to explain much of the rise and fall of the gold standard and gives perspective on the instability of the world financial system for much of the twentieth century. As a brief reminder, the closely related ideas of the velocity of money and monetary demand suggest a relationship between money supply and economic activity given by the equation of exchange:[10]

$$MV = PY$$

Where M is monetary stock, V is velocity of money, P is price level, and Y is GDP.[11] With some algebra, we can convert this into the formula for monetary demand,

$$M = \frac{P}{V}Y$$

$$M = F(P, Y)$$

As the above equations demonstrate, there is a close link between the money supply and GDP, mediated by shifts in the price level and velocity/money demand. When states impose a practice of maintaining consistent gold reserves—how much gold banks keep for each dollar in deposit accounts or other short-term liabilities—then this should result in a close relationship between growth in gold and growth in money supply.[12] If, in addition, velocity and the price level show long-term stability, there should also be a close relationship between gold and growth in GDP.

Using this model, the overall performance of the gold standard from 1700 onward demonstrates the existence of three discrete epochs: (1) 1700 to 1890, where the growth in gold outstrips the growth in GDP and encourages trade, decreases monetary velocity, and fulfills increased demand for gold-based money; (2) 1890 to 1950, where the growth in GDP and gold is roughly equal, halting the previous fall in monetary velocity with possible effects on trade; and (3) 1950 to 1980, where the growth of the world economy so far outstrips gold stock growth that the gold standard forces states to either increase velocity or decrease reserves to maintain the previous smooth flow of payments.

Granted, this analysis ignores endogeneity, in particular the ways that changes in technology and financial methods will increase velocity, thereby facilitating more transactions and, hence, GDP for any specific quantity of gold; that GDP will directly affect gold stocks by encouraging further gold exploration; and that various national currency policies affect and are affected by gold and GDP stocks. With that said, it seems likely that there are exogenous factors such as the total amount of accessible gold deposits and population growth rates that limit the range of possible increases of gold stocks and GDP.

International Lending in the Nineteenth and Early Twentieth Centuries

The international sovereign debt market became so vigorous that, by the end of the 1820s, the list of states issuing bonds in London included Prussia, Russia, Colombia, Chile, Brazil, and Greece, as well as nonstate entities such as the city of Buenos Aires, the Order of St. John of Jerusalem—a chivalric order dating back to the Crusades that was headquartered at the time in Russia—and the fictitious country of Poyais, in whose name General Gregor McGregor raised funds to create a new British colony in Central America that he would rule.[13] In the somewhat less fictitious new American republic, a spending impasse that existed at the time between the nascent federal government and the states over the question of public spending on internal improvements was broken in part by foreign banks lending to individual American states.[14] Likewise, foreign lending to the Russian throne in the late nineteenth century and again in the wake of the Russo-Japanese War of 1905 may have helped the czar hold his empire together as revolutionary groups like the Narodnaya Volya (The Peoples' Will) agitated for its destruction.[15]

The establishment of a gold standard did not simply increase the availability of funding for state actors, however; it also created a system of rules that incentivized states. The need to keep what Michael Bordo and Hugh Rockoff refer to as a "Good Housekeeping Seal of Approval" to maintain access to the international financial system forced states to limit the range of government expenditures.[16] This access became increasingly important as military competition drove increased state expenditure, and for many states this meant borrowing on a large scale. The more a state could persuade lenders that its economy was strong and growing, its rulers would avoid profligacy, and its finance ministry was capable, the more it could borrow, thereby further guaranteeing its survival. In this way, the link between military strategy and all other domestic political and economic issues was tightened at the state level in Europe in the nineteenth century.

Finance in the American Civil War

The American Civil War offers a case study in competition in the finance domain between two governments with only limited experience of military conflict. The onset of hostilities in the American Civil War created enormous and complex financial problems in Washington and the confederate capital of Richmond, Virginia.[17] In the same way that war in the American maritime and land domains trailed state-of-the-art European practice, policymakers in Washington and Richmond struggled in the finance domain to assemble the financial tools that European governments had developed decades before.

Prior to the Civil War, the US government collected revenue primarily from customs and tariffs, which it continued to do throughout the war. The United States was hardly flush with cash at the beginning of the war, in part because of the sectional tensions that preceded the conflict.[18] To make up for this shortfall, Congress authorized over the course of the war several major bond sales, a small income tax, and—with the National Bank Acts of 1863–1864—the creation of national banks that issued their own federally regulated paper currency and used federal bonds as "safe assets."[19] The funds raised from these methods contributed to the new federal government's ability to put down the rebellion and reunite the country.

US state capacity also benefited from some extraordinary individual fund-raising efforts, most notably those of serial entrepreneur and banker Jay Cooke. Cooke had previously sold bonds for the state of Pennsylvania and others in his role as the president of his own private banking house in Philadelphia, before playing a crucial role in supporting the Union during the Civil War. In Cooke's first effort, he spent twenty times more on advertising than was suggested in selling the "seven-thirty" Treasury bonds[20] in 1861 and, as a result, was responsible for selling a full 20 percent of that series. In October 1862, Treasury Secretary Salmon Chase asked Cooke to lead the sales of the "five-twenty" bond series.[21] Cooke responded by launching an aggressive, but precise, public relations campaign targeting newspapers across the North, which enabled Cooke and his agents to sell $362 million out of an oversubscribed loan that brought in $511 million to the Union.[22]

Cooke's efforts and the critical role of finance to the Northern war effort in general did not go unnoticed in the press. The *Philadelphia Inquirer* wrote in 1861 of a group of 800 subscribers: "Their charge of money bags is quite as efficient as a charge of bayonets."[23] Cooke, never shy, had a banner set up in his Washington, DC, office with the words:

> The Bravery of Our Army
> The Valor of Our Navy
> Sustained by Our Treasury
> Upon the Faith and
> Substance of
> A Patriotic People.[24]

The Confederate States of America faced a considerably more complicated set of problems in financing their rebellion. Prior to the war, most of the major banks and the bulk of the nation's bullion were located in the North. The Confederacy funded itself primarily through the creation of non-interest-bearing notes, supplementing this with private bank loans, taxation, customs receipts, and bond sales. The Confederacy's most immediate financial problem was identifying sources of revenue: not surprisingly for the proponents of anti-federalism, the Confederacy struggled to bring in direct taxes and these furnished only 10.5 percent of tax revenues over the war.[25] In addition to this structural problem, there were those caused by the war, a prime example being that the US Navy blockade of Confederate ports dramatically reduced customs revenue, meaning that there was little indirect tax revenue to make up for low direct tax revenue.[26] As a result, its debt was generally not backed by existing streams of revenues, but by the prospect of the possible future revenues conditional on Confederate victory; Confederate debts and notes were in large part bets on the course of the war.[27] By 1863, the Confederacy resorted to a tax-in-kind policy on agricultural products, which saw some success, as did the effort to raise foreign funding with bonds guaranteed by cotton.[28]

Seeking foreign credit overseas was problematic for several different reasons; in addition to the practical difficulty of transporting cotton to Europe in the face of federal blockades, there was the general problem of the Confederacy's reputation as a bad credit risk.[29] This stigma was due in part to the role President Jefferson Davis and other Confederate leaders had played earlier in their careers, urging the repudiation of state debts in the 1840s referenced in this chapter's epigraph. As a result, European countries were hesitant about throwing in their lot with a breakaway republic with leaders who had a reputation for not paying their bills. Overall, the Confederacy raised enough to fund only 2 percent of its warfighting expenditures with European bonds.[30]

The Confederacy attempted to shore up its solvency through the creation of a paper currency.[31] These treasury notes were not backed by gold, cotton, or any other commodity, meaning that their value—like that of many Confederate bond issues—depended on the future trade of a victorious Confederate States of America. Consequently, the currency's value fluctuated based on Confederate military fortunes. At the same time, the Confederacy suffered from substantial inflation, averaging 10 percent per month during its existence.[32] Although it does not appear that the US government engaged in an intentional program to inflate the Confederate currency, it certainly took no steps to prevent speculators from taking action that increased the supply of paper currency in the South.[33] Confederate policymakers undertook several efforts to remedy this problem by reducing the supply of money, including putting deadlines on the convertibility of currency into bonds.[34]

Altogether, the state of Confederate finance and the state of the Confederate war effort were inextricably linked. The US government was able to therefore weaken the Confederates militarily by inflicting financial pain on the Confederacy in several ways, including reducing customs revenue through naval blockades and facilitating the counterfeiting of Confederate currency.[35] US battlefield victories also acted to inflict financial pain by removing territory from Confederate control and destroying transportation networks, making it difficult to collect taxes in kind, as well as undermining confidence on the part of the Southern populace in the government and the currency.

Eventually, the deteriorating financial situation in the Confederacy resulted in citizens of the South rejecting the nearly worthless Confederate currency, instead preferring to use US "greenbacks," further undercutting the Confederacy's state capacity and ability to govern. The federal government had key structural advantages, including access to most of the country's banking and financial know-how, control of most of the nation's gold, and no serious difficulties in maintaining a robust export profile. The continued existence of the country was not in question, giving borrowers more confidence in the currency. In addition to these inherent advantages, the war was fought primarily on the territory of the Confederacy, meaning that the Northern economic and taxation systems suffered only a few disruptions.

One legacy of the American Civil War was financial, altering the US systems of currency, banking, and taxation. Gary Gorton credits the National Bank Acts with creating the first stable money in the United States, bank notes backed by federal bonds that reliably traded at face value (or par value) instead of fluctuating with the commercial reputation of the issuing bank.[36] In addition, the financial realities of the US system were altered for the next centuries by the impoverishment of the South, in part by the systemic inequality that already existed, in part by the devastation brought to the territory by the rebellion, and in part by the personal bankrupting of its most prominent citizens in keeping the war effort going.[37] Problems that existed before the war were exacerbated, and the hamstringing of postwar attempts to pacify and reconstruct the South ensured that the tensions that led to the war would continue to exist.

The Pax Britannica: A Brief History

The term *Pax Britannica* references the relatively pacific 1815–1914 period. Economic theorists posit that this peace is the result not of a universal embrace of Kantian principles of democracy and cooperation, but instead out of a reluctance by financiers of the period to fund war, an explanation reinforced by Sardinian prime minister Camillo de Cavour, who complained in 1859 that "bankers of all countries have organized a kind of conspiracy in favor of peace." Economic historians Marc Flandreau and Juan Flores demonstrate that in this period the high risks of war made the most prestigious financiers, in particular the House of Rothschild, demur much more often than not when presented with the opportunity to finance yet another revolutionary nationalist movement or desperate royal in their efforts to grab or hold power.[38]

Unable to borrow from Rothschilds or other elite houses, these states were forced to seek out less prestigious underwriters for bonds with much higher interest payments—not quite the junk bonds of their day, but definitely riskier. As a result, war became more expensive to prosecute, and thus a less desirable foreign policy option. For example, a war between Belgium and Holland was avoided in the 1830s despite the former's secession from the latter, and the Rothschilds' explicit refusal to finance Belgium's side was critical to new Belgian king Leopold I's demurral. At the same time, however, Flandreau and Flores note the Rothschilds did finance a small number of wars in the New World, including Brazil and Argentina's participation in the Triple Alliance war from 1864 to 1870. In this case, because victory by these two countries seemed certain, the Rothschilds were happy to lend: "Haute Finance was not the Red Cross . . . prestigious banks [did not] dislike wars—they disliked only losers, or more precisely the risk of being found in losers' company." The peace of Pax Britannica was not the complete absence of interstate conflict, but its relative absence.[39]

As referenced by its name, the Pax Britannica also froze the power structure in the finance domain where it was in 1815—with Britain as hegemon. By the turn of the twentieth century, however, the Pax Britannica's rule of the finance domain had started to collapse. The British government's policy approach as hegemon—pushing for a liberalized system and generally trying to avoid intervening in financial matters—was under pressure, in particular from France and Germany.[40] The governments of these two countries systematically guided their bankers to invest in specific projects around the world to gain a strategic advantage—in the Balkans, Persia, Italy, Turkey, and China, among others, and the United Kingdom began to follow their lead. As Jacob Viner would write of this pre–World War I competition at the turn of the twentieth century: "For the claim . . . that the bankers exercised a controlling influence over pre-war diplomacy . . . [there is] not the slightest degree of support . . . [instead] diplomacy exercised a controlling influence over pre-war international finance."[41] Or as Herbert Feis was to write on the eve of US involvement in World War II, quoting Adam Smith, "Defense is more important than opulence"—national security concerns overrode economic goals.[42]

In Table 6.1, we present a rough summary of the stocks of overseas investment in select regions from Britain, France, and Germany in 1914. All amounts are in billions of 2011 dollars.[43] Also computed are: (1) the ratio of the stock of the investment by country X in region Y to estimated GDP of the region at that time; and (2) percentage of the investment stock in region Y of all overseas investments by country X in 1914.

As Table 6.1 demonstrates, Britain's overseas investments were much greater than France's or Germany's, at twice that of France and almost three times that of Germany. It is not clear that this hierarchy was preordained: Maurice Levy-Leboyer found that in the early 1800s France kept neck and neck with Great Britain and it was only after French defeat in the Franco-Prussian War in 1871 that the two countries diverged in their overseas investment habits.[44] In addition, Table 6.1 shows that Britain's investments are focused away from Europe, with more than half going to colonies or the former colonies (the United States). In contrast, France and Germany are much more focused on Europe, with the majority of their international investments staying on the continent.

The data in Figure 6.1 also reinforce the pattern described by Herbert Feis and D.C.M. Platt, among others, that the United Kingdom's overseas investments are focused largely on profit, while France and Germany have a split focus of profit and political alliances. The fact that one-quarter of French investment is in Russia and one-eighth of German investment is in Austria Hungary speaks volumes. Pushing this point further, there is evidence of the effort to gain influence in the former Ottoman Empire in the fact that all three countries, but particularly France and Germany, are focused on Turkey and the Balkan States. As the Turkish "Sick Man of Europe" was on his deathbed, the continental powers did not want to let the opportunity pass.

Finally, the data in Table 6.1 show that the further the investments get from Europe, the more all three countries seem to use some mix of colonial preference and profit focus to make decisions. Latin America, with no substantial true colonies, appears to be relatively neutral for all of them. Africa and Asia are more complicated, but here France and Germany appear to be following the British semimercantile lead, investing in colonies but also likely business environments. It is not possible to come up with reliable comparison data for China, but it seems to have been a backwater in many ways, with no more than 1.5 percent of UK investment flows and only a slightly higher percentage for France and Germany.

There is a range of reasons the British government generally took a hands-off approach to financial matters; the combination of strong trade, healthy trade financing, and the most powerful navy in the world at the time led the country to favor the expansion of trade and liberal financial policies globally. In addition, as the United Kingdom was literally and

Table 6.1 Summary of Overseas Investments for Britain, France, and Germany, 1914

	GDP	Britain			France			Germany		
	2011$	2011$	%R GDP	% Outflow	2011$	%R GDP	% Outflow	2011$	%R GDP	% Outflow
Europe	1,561.5	23.4	1.5	5.8	123.2	7.9	61.1	69.0	4.4	53.2
Russia	336.1	11.8	3.5	2.9	50.6	15.1	25.1	9.9	3.0	7.7
Spain and Portugal	72.4	2.9	4.0	0.7	17.5	24.1	8.7	9.4	13.0	7.
Italy	143.9	1.3	0.9	0.3	5.8	4.0	2.9			
France and Germany	536.2	1.5	0.3	0.4						
France and Great Britain	588.4							7.18	1.2	5.5
Austria	31.2	0.9	2.7	0.2						
Austria-Hungary	57.4				9.9	17.2	4.9	16.6	28.9	12.8
Balkan States	51.9	1.8	3.5	0.5	11.2	21.6	5.6	9.4	18.1	7.2
Turkey	22.1	2.6	11.6	0.6	14.8	66.9	7.3	9.9	45.0	7.7
Latin America	197.0	81.0	41.1	20.1	26.9	13.6	13.3	21.0	10.7	16.2
Argentina	41.5	34.2	82.4	8.5						
Brazil	24.3	15.8	65.3	3.9						
Mexico	30.0	10.6	35.3	2.6						
Chile	14.1	6.5	46.2	1.6						
Uruguay	4.6	3.9	83.7	1.0						
Peru	7.0	3.7	52.1	0.9						
Cuba	5.4	3.6	65.2	0.9						
Other Latin America	58.4	2.7	4.7	0.7						

continues

Table 6.1 Continued

	GDP	Britain			France			Germany		
	2011$	2011$	%R GDP	% Outflow	2011$	%R GDP	% Outflow	2011$	%R GDP	% Outflow
Africa	99.8									
Egypt	20.3	4.8	23.6	1.2						
South Africa	11.3	39.6	350.8	9.8						
Egypt, Suez, and South Africa	64.2				14.8	23.0	7.3			
Colonies		190.5		47.3	17.9		8.9	11.05	11.1	8.5
World	4,318.4	402.7	9.3	100.0	201.5	4.7	100.0	129.8	3.0	100.0

Sources: Investment stock data for each country from Feis, Herbert. 1930. *Europe, the World's Banker 1870–1914: An Account of European Foreign Investment and the Connection of World Finance with Diplomacy Before the War*. New Haven: Yale University Press. Britain 23, France 51, Germany 74. Conversion from pounds to 2011$ using measuringworth.com, conversation for francs and marks using 1910–1914 exchange rates from National Bureau of Economic Research, Macrohistory Database. n.d. "NBER Macrohistory: XIV. Money and Banking." Cambridge: NBER. https://www.nber.org/research/data/nber-macrohistory-xiv-money-and-banking Macrohistory data series m14004a and m14002 respectively, converted to 2011$ using Measuring Worth Foundation. n.d. "Measuring Worth," measuringworth.com. Country and regional GDP values from Maddison Project Database, version 2020. Bolt, Jutta, and Jan Luiten van Zanden. 2020. *Maddison Style Estimates of the Evolution of the World Economy: A New 2020 Update*. Working Paper. Maddison-Project. Groningen: University of Groningen. For GDP 1914 estimates used when available at country level, when 1914 estimates not available 1910–1913 estimates were used, when 1910–1914 were not available 1920 estimates (particularly for non-European regions) were used. In the table "R" = "recipient" GDP.

Note: GDP = gross domestic product.

figuratively a modest distance from continental politics, it had less incentive to find leverage against adversaries in Europe. Finally, the prejudice of the aristocrats against trade and finance was uniform across Europe, but appears to have played a particularly important role in putting distance between aristocratic Whitehall and the financial strivers of the City of London.[45]

At the same time, Britain leaned heavily on its empire, which in 1914 represented half of all investment overseas with Canada, Australia, New Zealand, South Africa, and India representing more than 90 percent of investment in the empire and roughly 45 percent of all overseas investment. The Colonial Stocks Act of 1900 further encouraged these tendencies, making the securities of colonies that followed Crown Treasury orders "Trustee Securities" and, thus, highly secure assets suitable for investment by the more established institutions, not just speculators.[46] Additional evidence of this strategy is the United Kingdom's behavior in what was called "the Orient" at the time; Feis argues that the UK government intervened aggressively in finance in China, Turkey, Persia, Egypt, and its possessions in Africa. In these cases, where the British government believed governments were not strong enough to keep out rival powers or to maintain basic market institutions, it became more actively engaged.[47]

By contrast, as the second-largest overseas investor in this period France pursued a much more hands-on financial policy, allowing government control of foreign listings on French exchanges and, thus, creating a tool for linking financial power to national interest and enabling the French state to be more aggressive in the finance domain. In 1912, French prime minister Raymond Poincare told the Chamber of Deputies he would "combine with French military and naval power, as converging and connecting forces, the financial power which is so great an aid to France."[48] After the Franco-Prussian War in 1871, for example, the French government placed an "official but tacit ban" on the purchase of German securities by French citizens and firms. There were efforts before World War I to overturn the ban, but this was derided by bellicose French politicians as "financial pacifism" and came to nothing.[49] Similarly, the French government continued to invest in Austria-Hungary for decades after this ban on German loans, but as the political tensions that would lead to World War I increased, the French began to perceive the Austro-Hungarian Empire as an enemy and banned the purchase of first Austrian and then Hungarian securities. Financiers on both sides made one final attempt in 1911 to arrange loans from France to the dual monarchy, but it came to nothing.

Wilhelmine Germany employed a financial policy strategy more similar to France's than the United Kingdom's, in which the government used a range of levers to control securities listings and investment by German banks. While the intervention by Chancellor Otto von Bismarck to stop

German lending to Russia is the most dramatic example of this strategy, many other interventions occurred to support and build alliances, in particular efforts to woo Italy in 1882, Turkey and Hungary in 1910, and more generally in China and states in South America.[50]

In the face of the political jockeying by these three large players, other states, including great powers, could find their access to financial resources suddenly constrict. Russia, for example, with a combination of a large population and geographic size, a weak economy, and chaotic politics including the frequent pogroms, triggered a range of strong negative responses from other European governments, banking houses, and bondholders. This negative impulse was not universal, however; in the middle of the 1800s, when the Congress of Vienna held more power and Britain was able to keep as purely as possible to its liberal financial ideals, British investors were subscribing to a loan that funded Russian armies actively deployed against British forces in Crimea.[51]

One of the more dramatic moments of the use of finance in the service of European power politics occurred in November 1887. Up to that point, German financiers—with the encouragement of the German government—had invested considerable amounts in Russia, due to a combination of geographic proximity, political amity, and the economic complementarity relating the two countries. By 1886, however, there were doubts in Germany about Russia's economic and financial strength, and loan negotiations between the Russian state and German bankers over debts accrued by the former began to fall apart. At the same time, several controversies over Russo-German relations emerged, including tariff disputes, a failure to renew their alliance, and a Russian *ukase*—a czarist edict—that seemed designed to push German landowners out of Russian western territories (modern-day Poland). Finally, on November 10, 1886, German chancellor von Bismarck ordered the Reichsbank to stop lending against Russian securities, likely to show German influence over the Russian economy. In the event, the decision backfired—although German investment in Russia reduced by an estimated 3 billion marks, French investors quickly took Germany's place in the Russian market.[52] From then on, French investment would dominate foreign lending to Russia, and Russia's stock of franc reserves would represent one-quarter of all its foreign reserves by 1913.[53]

The French bailout did not solve all of Russia's financial problems, however. Czarist Russia's pogroms aimed at displacing and exterminating their Jewish population resulted in a reduction of its access to finance and, hence, hurt it militarily. For example, Jewish American banker Jacob Schiff of the American banking house Kuhn Loeb worked to punish Russia by going out of his way to help Japan raise money on Wall Street for the Russo-Japanese War, putting Japan in a much better financial position than it otherwise would have been in 1905. Between the war and increasing domestic protest and instability, a desperate Czar Nicholas II finally granted a few liberalizing concessions, which he then reversed the next year. Russia tried to improve its finances by floating a bond issue in France, which became the target of a large political protest campaign by a newly tolerant France in the process of reversing the injustice of the Dreyfus affair. While the protests did not block the bond issue, they temporarily increased yield spreads, forcing Russia to pay a modest financial penalty for its oppressive policies.[54]

Conclusion

If a giant like Russia could be caught short when European diplomats ordered their bankers around, then there was no way smaller countries such as the Balkan states could avoid even more extreme bullying. Adam Tooze and Martin Ivanov detail the way Bulgaria's allegiances and national politics were continually under pressure, if not actually crushed and molded, before World War I. Trying to raise money in 1902, Bulgaria chose to ally itself with France and Russia, thus enabling it to raise money via the French bank Paribas in exchange for giving over control of its tobacco tax and accepting a bondholder's representative in Sofia. Additional loans in the next few years required giving bondholders increasing control over tax revenue, further ceding Bulgarian sovereignty to build up its financial health. This strategy was politically unpopular with the Bulgarian people, and after several changes in political leadership Bulgaria tried in 1908 to gain a new loan without the controls. France refused and Bulgaria then raised money from Germany and Austria, effectively switching allegiances. The First and Second Balkan Wars of 1912 and 1913 muddied things further as Bulgaria fought the Austro-Hungarian-allied Ottoman Empire even as it needed greater lending to stay solvent. This sort of scrambling and changing partners became the Bulgarian template for the next few years and up to the start of World War I, as Bulgarian diplomacy was a welter of efforts to gain funds from one or another external alliance by promising loyalty and giving up control.[55] This chaos was emblematic of the state of the finance domain at the beginning of the twentieth century, as putative hegemons scrabbled for purchase in a world of uncertain alliances and violence.

World War I marked the end of Pax Britannica and the overall calming influence of the gold standard RFA. If the finance domain was to stabilize, the impetus for that stabilization was going to have to come from the New World. We discuss the impact of the war and the rise of this new influence in the next chapter.

Notes

1. The potential use of British financial centrality to shut down German trade is discussed further in Chapter 7. Lambert, Nicholas. 2012. *Planning Armageddon: British Economic Warfare and the First World War.* Cambridge: Harvard University Press, 169–172. There is evidence that fluctuations in British country banking had an outsized influence on the American financial system. Williams, Geoffrey. 2020. *Lending Money to People Across the Water": The British Joint Stock Banking Acts of 1826 and 1833, and the Panic of 1837.* Working Paper. Lexington: Transylvania University.

2. See, for example, Eichengreen, Barry. 1987. "Conducting the International Orchestra: Bank of England Leadership Under the Classical Gold Standard." *Journal of International Money and Finance* 6 (1): 5–29. An illustrative contradiction of the idea of Bank of England leadership can be found in McCloskey, D. N., and J. R. Zecher. 2005. "How the Gold Standard Worked, 1880–1913." In *Gold Standard in Theory & History,* edited by Donald N. McCloskey and J. Richard Zecher. Abingdon: Routledge, 47–60. McCloskey and Zecher argue that far from being the conductor, the Bank of England may have simply been the triangle player.

3. Bordo, Michael, and Eugene N. White. "A Tale of Two Currencies: British and French Finance During the Napoleonic Wars." *Journal of Economic History* 51 (2): 303–316; White, Eugene N. 1995. "The French Revolution and the Politics of Government Finance, 1770–1815." *Journal of Economic History* 55 (2): 227–255.

4. Davis, Lance E., and Stanley L. Engerman. 2006. *Naval Blockades in Peace and War: An Economic History Since 1750.* Cambridge: Cambridge University Press, 29–33; Aaslestad, Katherine. 2014. "Revisiting Napoleon's Continental System: Consequences of Economic Warfare." In *Revisiting Napoleon's Continental System: Local, Regional, and European Experiences,* edited by Katherine Aaslestad and Johan Joor. New York: Springer, 1–22; O'Brien, Patrick. 2006. "The Hanoverian State and the Defeat of the Continental System: A Conversation with Eli Heckscher." In *Eli Heckscher, International Trade, and Economic History,* edited by Ronald Findlay, Rolf G. H. Henriksson, Håkan Lindgren, and Mats Lundahl. Cambridge: MIT Press, 373–406; Daly, Gavin. 2007. "Napoleon and the 'City of Smugglers,' 1810–1814." *The Historical Journal* 50 (2): 333–352.

5. White, Eugene N. 2001. "Making the French Pay: The Costs and Consequences of the Napoleonic Reparations." *European Review of Economic History* 5 (3): 337–365.

6. Dawson, Frank Griffith. 1990. *The First Latin American Debt Crisis: The City of London and the 1822–25 Loan Bubble.* New Haven: Yale University Press, 17–18.

7. The Invergordon Mutiny was a strike by British sailors at the Royal Navy base in Invergordon, Scotland, to protest a 25 percent cut in salary. The strike lasted from September 15 to September 16, 1931, and caused a bank run in Britain that forced the United Kingdom off the gold standard for fear of bankrupting the government.

8. Bordo, Michael D., and Anna J. Schwartz, eds. 2009. *A Retrospective on the Classical Gold Standard, 1821–1931.* Chicago: University of Chicago Press; Bordo, Michael D., and Finn E. Kydland. 1990. *Gold Standard as a Rule.* Series w3367. Cambridge, MA: National Bureau of Economic Research (NBER),

9. GDP is the market value of all final goods and services produced and sold in a prescribed time period.

10. For a more extensive discussion, see Mishkin, Frederic. 2014. *The Economics of Money, Banking and Financial Markets.* 11th ed. London: Pearson, chap. 19.

11. The velocity of money is the average number of financial transactions within a specific time period.

12. Note that velocity is inversely related to monetary demand—the more money people hold on to (greater demand) the lower the frequency at which that money is changing hands (lower velocity).

13. Short-run inflation and deflation were extremely common under the gold standard, see Bordo, Michael D. 1981. "The Classical Gold Standard—Some Lessons for Today." *Federal Reserve Bank of St. Louis Review* 63 (5): 2–17.

14. Dawson 1990.

15. Wallis, John Joseph, and Barry R. Weingast. 2005. *Equilibrium Impotence: Why the States and Not the American National Government Financed Economic Development in the Antebellum Era.* Series w11397. Cambridge, MA: NBER.

16. Garvy, George. 1972. "Banking Under the Tsars and the Soviets." *Journal of Economic History* 32 (4): 869–893; Malik, Hassan. 2018. *Bankers and Bolsheviks: International Finance and the Russian Revolution.* Princeton: Princeton University Press.

17. Bordo, Michael D., and Hugh Rockoff. 1996. "The Gold Standard as a 'Good Housekeeping Seal of Approval.'" *Journal of Economic History* 56 (2): 389–428.

18. Burdekin, Richard C. K., and Farrokh K. Langdana. 1993. "War Finance in the Southern Confederacy, 1861–1865." *Explorations in Economic History* 30 (3): 352–376.

19. Martorelli, Michael A. n.d. "Financing the Civil War." Essential Civil War Curriculum; Flaherty, Jane. 2009. "The Exhausted Condition of the Treasury on the Eve of the Civil War." *Civil War History* 55 (2): 253.

20. Giroux, Gary. 2012. "Financing the American Civil War: Developing New Tax Sources." *Accounting History* 17 (1): 92; Blue, Frederick J. 1987. *Salmon P. Chase, A Life in Politics.* Kent: Kent State University Press, 157; Mishkin 2014: 236.

21. So named for their interest rate of 7.30 percent.

22. So named for being a bond callable in five years, but which fully matured in twenty years.

23. Edling, Max M. 2014. *A Hercules in the Cradle: War, Money, and the American State, 1783–1867.* Chicago: University of Chicago Press, 197–204, in particular 197–198.

24. Edling 2014: 203.

25. Edling 2014: 204.

26. Davis, George K., and Gary M. Pecquet. 1990. "Interest Rates in the Civil War South." *Journal of Economic History* 50 (1): 135.

27. Burdekin and Langdana 1993: 356.

28. G. K. Davis and Pecquet 1990: 135.

29. Burdekin and Langdana 1993: 359; Weidenmier, Marc D. 2000. "The Market for Confederate Cotton Bonds." *Explorations in Economic History* 37 (1): 76–97.

30. "To exchange the bonds for cotton, the bondholder first had to obtain warrants from the Confederate European representative in Paris. The investor then ran the Union blockade, took possession of the cotton in the South, and returned to Europe, running the blockade a second time. To facilitate the exchange, the Confederate government agreed to transport the cotton within 10 miles of a navigable river or port." Weidenmier 2000: 79.

31. Weidenmier, Marc D. 2005. "Gunboats, Reputation, and Sovereign Repayment: Lessons from the Southern Confederacy." *Journal of International Economics* 66 (2): 407–422.

32. Rothman, Jordan. 2009. "'A Pledge of a Nation': Charting the Economic Aspirations, Political Motivations, and Consequences of Confederate Currency Creation." PhD dissertation, Brandeis University.

33. Burdekin and Langdana 1993: 354.

34. Rector, Raymond. 2018. "Northern Entrepreneur's Counterfeiting of Confederate Currency and the Impact It Had on Inflation." Undergraduate Honors Thesis, Butler University; and Weidenmier, Marc D. 1999. "Bogus Money Matters: Sam Upham and His Confederate Counterfeiting Business." *Business and Economic History* 28 (2): 313–324.

35. Burdekin, Richard C. K., and Marc D. Weidenmier. 2000. "The Option Value of Confederate Currency and Inflation Control, 1861–1865." Unpublished manuscript, Claremont Colleges Working Paper in Economics, July.

36. Burdekin and Langdana 1993: 362.

37. Gorton, Gary. 2012. *Misunderstanding Financial Crises: Why We Don't See Them Coming*. Oxford: Oxford University Press, 17–19.

38. Rosenblum, Joshua, and Brandon Dupont. 2016. *Impact of the US Civil War on Southern Wealth Holders*. Brussels: Center for Economic and Policy Research, June 19.

39. Flandreau, Marc, and Juan H. Flores. 2012. "The Peaceful Conspiracy: Bond Markets and International Relations During the Pax Britannica." *International Organization* 66 (2): 211–241 at 217.

40. Flandreau and Flores 2012, at 235.

41. Platt, Desmond Christopher Martin. 1968. *Finance, Trade, and Politics in British Foreign Policy, 1815–1914*. Oxford: Clarendon Press. Feis, Herbert. 1930. *Europe, the World's Banker 1870–1914: An Account of European Foreign Investment and the Connection of World Finance with Diplomacy Before the War*. New Haven: Yale University Press, 83–117.

42. Viner, Jacob. 1929. "International Finance and Balance of Power Diplomacy, 1880–1914." *Southwestern Political and Social Science Quarterly* 9 (4): 407–451, at 451.

43. Feis, Herbert. 1940. *Changing Pattern of International Economic Affairs*. New York: Harper and Bros, epigraph on iii and at 14.

44. For context, British, French, and German GDP in 1914 in adjusted 2011 US dollars were $374.4 billion, $213.9 billion, and $322.2 billion, respectively.

45. Levy-Leboyer, Maurice. 1977. "La Balance des Paiements et L'Exportation des Capitaux Francais." In *La Position Internationale de la France: Aspects Economique et Financiers XIX–XX siecles*, edited by Maurice Levy-Leboyer, Ecole des Haute Etude en Sciences Sociales, Paris: Librairie Jean Touzot. 75–142, in particular figure 1 on 80.

46. Feis 1930; Platt 1968.

47. Feis 1930: 83–117.

48. Mitchener, Kris James, and Marc D. Weidenmier. 2010. "Supersanctions and Sovereign Debt Repayment." *Journal of International Money and Finance* 29 (1): 19–36; Mitchener, Kris James, and Marc Weidenmier. 2005. "Empire, Public Goods, and the Roosevelt Corollary." *Journal of Economic History* 65 (3): 658–692; Feis 1930: 98.

49. Feis 1930: 123.

50. Feis 1930: 199–200.

51. Feis 1930: 175.

52. Viner, Jacob. 1928. "Political Aspects of International Finance." *Journal of Business of the University of Chicago* 1 (2): 141–173, in particular 156–157.

53. Laves, Walter H. C. 1928. "German Governmental Influence on Foreign Investments, 1871–1915." *Political Science Quarterly* 43 (4): 498–519, 500–502; Feis 1930: 212–215.

54. Eichengreen, Barry, Arnaud Mehl, and Livia Chiţu. 2019. "Mars or Mercury? The Geopolitics of International Currency Choice." *Economic Policy* 34 (98): 315–363. The one-quarter estimate is based on figure 3 on 325.

55. Collet, Stephanie, and Kim Oosterlinck. 2019. "Denouncing Odious Debts." *Journal of Business Ethics* 160 (1): 205–223.

56. Tooze, Adam, and Martin Ivanov. 2011. "Disciplining the 'Black Sheep of the Balkans': Financial Supervision and Sovereignty in Bulgaria, 1902–38." *Economic History Review* 64 (1): 30–51, in particular 33–37.

7

From the Great War to World War II

In view of the decline in international commercial relations, the more important countries have fallen into the habit of exploiting more intensively the economic territories at their disposal. Much is said nowadays to the effect that Germany is striving for autarchy. People entirely forget that this autarchy has long since been achieved by such countries as France and Great Britain, not to mention Russia and the United States. Autarchy can be easily achieved - in fact it naturally exists - in an economic region which is supplied with almost all raw materials, provided it enjoys the same monetary system throughout. The British devaluation would never have had the success which it achieved if Great Britain had not been able to bring the monetary system of the Dominions onto the same basis as her own. France could never have used her colonial empire so successfully if it had not been administered under the same monetary system as the mother country.

—Hjalmar Schacht,
"Germany's Colonial Demands," 1937[1]

World War I inspired revolutions in every domain of strategic competition, including finance. At the outset of the war, the British government contemplated both economic and financial means to completely choke the German economy, although due to condemnation both at home and abroad it was forced to relax this considerably.[2] Ostensibly neutral parties also reacted to the incipient crisis caused by the war; in July 1914, US treasury secretary Williams Gibb McAdoo responded quickly to the gold drain created by the belligerents of the new war selling their holdings in US companies and converting the resultant cash into gold by closing the New York Stock Exchange for four months.[3] Financial considerations likewise motivated the entry of the United States into the war, an action that cemented an allied victory and was at least somewhat affected by the sympathies and loans provided by J. P. Morgan and other elite WASP financiers for the British.[4]

The conclusion of hostilities in November 1918 was not the conclusion of these dramatic changes and world crisis, however. While many regions enjoyed growth and prosperity in the 1920s, international conflict was endemic and by 1930 the world economy was in a slump that lasted for years, caused enormous misery directly, and indirectly led to the rise of Adolf Hitler. While there is ongoing discussion among scholars as to the causes of the Great Depression, some general themes are clear: the United Kingdom was too weak to keep its central role in world trade and finance; the United States was not yet interested in a hegemonic role; international efforts to move back to the gold standard set currency values too high; Germany bucked at an objectively steep reparations bill imposed by the allies; and recovery after a financial crisis can be difficult.[5] While a full discussion of the proposed cures to the Great Depression is beyond the scope of this book, a brief list includes: a negotiated revaluation of major currencies at lower gold prices; earlier and more general devaluations of major currencies; and a more aggressive role by the United States generally in the international economy, including more aggressive interventions by the Federal Reserve in American bank failures.[6]

Our focus in this book, however, is on the finance domain and developments in practice, not optimal macroeconomic policy. The period of total war (1918–1945) demonstrates the continued close linkage between national security and finance; for example, the impact that reparations and German borrowing to repay them had on European politics; and the British difficulties in paying naval personnel that triggered the UK devaluation and the dissolution of the gold standard, both of which we discuss in greater detail below.

The scrambling that states did to overcome these two problems and others during the period of total war resulted in the development of a constellation of tools, tactics, and strategies that constituted a new revolution in financial affairs (RFA), one that used increasing state capacity and monetary sophistication to project power via the finance domain in concert with controls on trade on goods. In a sense, the basic principles of these tools were very old: "all the fusty relics of medieval trade regulation," as Lionel Robbins termed them.[7] At the same time, improvements in state capacity and a clearer sense of monetary issues gave these tools a new lease on life. Some of these tools were exploited and developed in colonial administration, where the relatively porous monetary systems of the nineteenth century gave way to more carefully managed colonial currencies and currency exchange systems from the 1890s onward.[8] Other parts were developed in the wartime blockade by the allies, as the conflict led them to build an unprecedented administrative system tracking trade and financial flows.[9] There was no common suite of methods deployed, but the themes of colonialism (or super-colonialism[10]), autarchy, and sanction are pervasive. To be clear, we do not quote Hjalmar Schacht in the epigraph that begins this chapter because his views were right, but because his views were representative.

The unifying feature that made the RFA possible was large-scale professional bureaucracy—the bureaucratic RFA. Max Weber provides the key theoretical lens for understanding this, arguing that the professionalization of bureaucracies is an extension of the Enlightenment principle of rationalism. Weber further argues that by rationalizing government bureaucracies— organizing them according to principles of hierarchy, specialization, explicit rules, and merit—they become more competent and more stable, thereby creating an environment in which economies can flourish.[11] Despite other researchers' skepticism of the limits of bureaucracy, there is no doubt that bureaucratic capacity in major powers grew considerably in the centuries up to 1918.[12] While statistical measures are hard to come by, there is a clear pattern of reform and professionalization across the major Western powers. The earliest steps in the process seem to have been the development of the Prussian civil service in the 1600s and 1700s, followed by Napoleon's reforms after 1800, and then Anglo-American turning points such as the Northcote-Treveleyan reforms (1853) and the Pendleton Act (1883).[13] While developments in bureaucratic evolution over any particular decade might have been slow and haphazard, the long-term trajectory toward increased size, professionalization, and sophistication is clear. It is striking to compare, for example, the enforcement of the laws on the Maximum in revolutionary France with Schacht's administration of the New Plan in Nazi Germany in the 1930s: the former was directed at the top by two committees of fewer than a dozen men and depended on already busy local officials and ad hoc revolutionary militias for enforcement; the latter had a dedicated staff of 18,000.[14]

The development of colonial currency regimes in the two decades leading up to 1914 give some impression of what this evolution meant for the use of the finance domain. The British colonial administrators in India never achieved a control of the rupee that satisfied them, but from the 1890s onward they worked harder on ordering the Indian monetary system, shifting it slowly toward the gold standard.[15] The currencies of other British colonies were brought into order with greater ease, such as those in West Africa with the implementation of a currency board just before the war.

The British were not alone in using colonial conquest for financial gain and stability: one of the first things the Japanese did on taking over Taiwan in 1895 and Korea in 1905, to name two examples, was to reform the local monetary system.[16] In the Philippines, budding American money doctor Edwin Kemmerer was able to design an approach that brought the colony onto a gold exchange standard in the early 1900s.[17] Most such reforms depended on shifting to token currencies that were not tradable outside the region. In each of these cases, the motivations of the colonial administrators were complex—a worldwide move away from bimetallic and silver standards to gold played a significant role—and no doubt in many cases there was a real expectation that the reform would benefit all the colonial subjects. By putting in place a more legible and centralized financial system, and shutting down existing flows, however, the colonial administrators also were able to build up their own power. The colonial currency reforms suggest an important variant of weaponized interdependence, where political authority is used to redesign a trade network in a way that further empowers that authority; where weaponization does not follow interdependence but arrives hand in hand. The potential for abuse of these reforms becomes particularly clear in the occupations by Germany and Japan during World War II, discussed later in this chapter.

The War Is Now Ended

There were extensive diplomatic, economic, and social changes in Europe in the aftermath of World War I. In the first instance, it took more than six months to move from the end of hostilities to a negotiated treaty, agreed to in Paris and signed at Versailles, during which the allies continued to impose a blockade on the Central Powers in an attempt to force them to accede. The treaty itself appears to have been problematic in numerous respects. It has been criticized from the start as excessively harsh to Germany, asserting German guilt for the war and requiring reparation payments for a total of approximately US$33 billion (current dollars) that would be set in 1921. John Maynard Keynes famously prophesied long-term problems from this arrangement and popular sentiment has tended to view the horrors of the next twenty-seven years as proof he was correct.[18] Reviewing major historical episodes of enforced reparations, Eugene White shows that the post–World War I reparations imposed on Germany were larger by almost any measure than all other comparable cases before or since; the payments imposed, however, were within a comparable range of other reparation demands and, hence, could have been covered by the German state had it chosen to.[19]

The Versailles Treaty also was the contractual basis for the more clearly forward-looking proposal: the founding of the League of Nations. This proposal has its own ambiguous legacy, however, as its creation marked a step toward greater international cooperation and a vision of nonviolent dispute resolution, as well as being a significant development of the finance domain, as it indicated a general desire among states to establish a strategically and financially stable international system that might prevent future conflagrations by using a prosocial system of rules.[20] Unfortunately for its architects, including US president Woodrow Wilson, this dream suffered a severe blow when the US Senate voted against American membership.[21] The League continued operating until the start of World War II, albeit without the world's hegemon-in-training, thereby limiting the extent of the League's impact on international relations. On the positive side, the League developed and helped fund structural adjustment programs for Southern and Eastern European countries trying to stabilize their currency during this period.[22] On the negative side, as Nicholas Mulder explains, the League developed the modern version of sanctions and, at least within Europe, may have helped exacerbate the economic and political splits between the United Kingdom, France, Germany, and Italy.[23]

As Europe moved into the 1920s, the restrictions of the Versailles Treaty and the limited power and influence of the League were invitations to chaos. In Germany, for example, wealth is estimated to have fallen from 648 percent of national income in 1910 to 354 percent after World War I. Britain, despite sustaining no loss of territory, saw capital fall even more precipitously from 679 percent to 288 percent over the same period.[24] In addition, the mobilization and subsequent destruction of an entire generation of young men in the war resulted in an anger at the governments responsible that led to a radical remaking of European politics, overturning autocratic governments in Germany and Austria, and an expansion of the voting franchise to women in Austria, Germany, Hungary, Poland, the USSR, and the United Kingdom, among other European states. This democratization led in turn to an expansion of social insurance programs and a change in the priorities of public economics, but also contributed to an increase in economic, political, and social turmoil as well as restraining some of the standard methods for handling trade imbalances.[25]

While it is beyond the scope of this book to resolve the role of German reparations in the issues of the interwar period, it should be said that in the 1920s and early 1930s there is no clear example of another international issue—economic, political, or social—that remained so contentious throughout. Though it is true that German politicians used the issue to build grievances among their voters, it is also true that the allies failed to take advantage of several opportunities to clarify the issue.[26] With France's occupation of the Ruhr region of Germany in 1923, the issue came to a head; Germany's angry response exacerbated the revanchist instincts of its polity and may have played a role in exacerbating the hyperinflation. These hostilities led to the Dawes Plan of 1924 and a modus vivendi that dominated the rest of the 1920s: US loans to Germany being used to pay reparations to Britain and France, which would then use this money to pay war debts to Americans. This cycle of payments illustrates the growing importance of the United States in the finance domain despite its reluctance to assume the mantle of hegemony.[27]

The United States: Ready for Power, but Not Hegemony

The many long-standing debates over how to handle different aspects of the US financial system —central banking or not, gold standard versus silver versus bimetallic—appeared to be temporarily resolved by the passage of laws codifying the establishment of a central bank and adherence to a gold standard in the years immediately before World War I.[28] Indeed, the passage of the Gold Standard Act of 1900 and the Federal Reserve Act of 1913 were part of a loose consensus in Washington and New York City that tried to move the United States closer to the structures of European economies, in particular those of the United Kingdom.

A Permanent Central Bank

Analysis of central banking in general and of the need for an American central bank in particular usually focus on domestic concerns. In the US case specifically, there is no evidence that the purpose of the Federal Reserve was primarily related to war or national security. Instead, the US effort to create a central bank was aimed at addressing critical state capacity issues like financial stability and resolving domestic political struggles over hard money versus soft money. As the United States had at least one financial crisis every decade of the nineteenth century, political and financial elites were anxious to improve financial stability. Similarly, these elites saw it as increasingly vital to maintain a balance between capital holders—who desired a gold standard to stabilize future payment values—and borrowers, in particular farmers, who wanted to spur inflation to devalue the dollar and reduce the financial burden of the loans they had taken out. At the time, the creation of a US central bank seemed like a solution to these problems.[29]

Just because problems are not acknowledged, however, does not mean they do not exist. As Lawrence J. Broz argues, central banks entail two public goods: the first is the bank itself; and the second is the work of negotiating and designing the blueprint of the bank—the compromises required before it can be brought into being.[30] A central bank can have a significant effect on the distribution of wealth within a polity, so creating a central bank's organizational structure must be undertaken with great caution and with as much consensus by its creators as possible. Previous US efforts at creating a central bank—the First and Second Banks of the United States—succeeded at creating the first public good but failed at the second, mainly by failing to secure the agreement among elites as to how the banks should operate. As a result, the banks quickly wore out their welcome and Congress allowed their charters to lapse.

By the late nineteenth century, American international trade was ripe for a more active role by American banks; for the previous century, financing of US companies' participation in international trade had largely been handled by British or Anglo-American merchant banks. Large "money center"[31] banks, such as National City Bank in New York, knew they could make money supporting American businesses overseas, but that this would require a number of legal and institutional changes to happen. In particular, US banks required the legalization of overseas branches by the US government and allowing trade paper to be discounted by banks. The large money center banks and their leadership put substantial resources into the long, sometimes fraught negotiations over the architecture of the Federal Reserve because it was a key step toward these goals. In the main, the US banks and the merchants who borrowed from them got what they wanted. As one of the early Federal Reserve governors observed to the press, the Federal Reserve System "was designed in large part to expand our trade with foreign countries."[32]

International issues played an important role in another sense. It was not simply the opportunities that a successful central bank could offer the money center banks and their wealthiest clients that drove the Federal Reserve's creation. Another key influence was US international strategic ambitions: in 1916, three years after the Federal Reserve Act's passage into law, US president Wilson wrote, "We have got to finance the world in some important degree, and those who finance the world must understand it and rule it."[33] From the beginning, the Federal Reserve was intended to be a key element to this strategy.

The Federal Reserve's role in national security is evident from the 1898 report of the Indianapolis Monetary Commission's Convention. The report was the first major effort at creating a blueprint for the future Federal Reserve:

> Modern Warfare is so expensive that it is almost as much a matter of money as of men. A nation suddenly confronted by the alternative of war or dishonor would be greatly handicapped by a large demand debt which it must provide for at once. Great additional force is given to this consideration by the fact that it would be scarcely possible for this nation to engage in war in its present situation. . . . In countries where the government has no demand debt outstanding, and the gold reserve is held by banks, the nation's stock of gold is capable of some degree of protection through the rate of interest charged for loans. But our government has no such resource. Its great gold reserve is an open mine free to all who bring its notes. The exigencies of war or commerce are liable to create sudden and great demands for gold. And as the entire monetary system of the country hangs upon that one reserve, the situation is one of uncertainty and hazard against which no insurance is possible, and which is bound to continue while the government demand obligations are extant in large volume.[34]

While war finance was not the focus, it was on the agenda.

As discussed in Chapter 6, the United States is the exception that proves the rule that central banking was driven by war finance issues until recently. While wealthy, very involved in trade, with a developed finance sector, the United States established central banks only for those periods when it was concerned with international competition. Internal divisions such as the American Civil War, and relatively low-cost wars such as the Mexican-American War, did not rouse the United States to act. Only when the United States was struggling against the major European powers, and once it had set its course for empire and engaging in European conflicts, did the United States work to establish the Federal Reserve.[35]

A Source of Global Capital

While the United States was not yet at its position of hegemony after World War I, it was more active in international finance than it had been before. As a result, the US governmental approach in this period was similar to that of the United Kingdom's prior to the war—a belief that government policy should focus on basics such as balancing the budget, maintaining the gold standard, and allowing private parties to take charge of lending and investment decisions.[36]

Whatever the strengths and weaknesses of the British prewar approach, the United States over the 1920s and 1930s seems to have had worse results. Presumably, part of this failure was due to the complex global economic environment, although part of the problem was the naïvete and parochialism of American officials, bankers, and businessmen, at least compared with their nineteenth-century British counterparts. This relative lack of expertise revealed itself through the US government's considerable shifts over time and in its approach to different regions—sometimes avoiding even the image of engagement, at other times jumping in as a missionary or a rescuer.[37]

Within the US government, the State Department took the lead on formulating and implementing international financial policy, with a focus on encouraging private investment overseas to stabilize the postwar international system, as the department associated international financial stability with the national interest. The US Departments of Treasury and Commerce deferred to the State Department on this issue, effectively making private foreign loans a question of national strategy. Latin America became the primary target of these strategic loans, issued from private banks, in part because of US disenchantment with Europe after the Treaty of Versailles, and in part to reinforce the Roosevelt Corollary to the Monroe Doctrine. The purpose of this version of dollar diplomacy was to give the US government a measure of control over its "good neighbors" to the south without creating the appearance—or assuming the responsibility—of imperial expansion. The policy was successful, inasmuch as it gave the US government and the private banks significant influence on the political and financial systems of the borrowers, thereby increasing US influence in the Western Hemisphere.[38]

A combination of four domestic developments since the turn of the century enabled this foreign policy, according to historian Emily Rosenberg: "A government that saw stabilization of the international economic environment as central to the national interest; a zealous cadre of experts eager to become financial advisers abroad; cooperative investment bankers; and a public that had been schooled to buy bonds by the war-bond campaigns of 1917–18."[39] The drawback to effectively privatizing foreign policy in the finance domain was that State Department priorities such as increasing US investment, improving governments' fiscal policies, and bringing as many countries as possible on to the gold standard conflicted with those of American bankers and businessmen, who were more focused on profit. For example, a loan to El Salvador negotiated between 1921 and 1923 was backed by the State Department as a way to encourage Americans to invest overseas. However, after the department had helped to arrange a legally dubious "exchange of notes" between governments as a sign of official approval for the loan, the American bankers then radically tightened their terms on San Salvador. Similar maneuvers on a Bolivian loan and negotiations for a loan to Guatemala left the State Department increasingly wary about this approach as well as leaving an increasingly sour taste in Latin American mouths.[40]

Despite problems and some heavy-handedness in the US government role, the overall pattern in cross-border lending is clear: after World War I, flows from private US investors represented the largest source in the 1920s and 1930s, whereas before 1914 flows from British citizens had been the largest source.[41] Wall Street banks may have seen this business as a way to sell assets to retail investors; sovereign lending from Wall Street took off in the 1920s, and ratings agencies, which in some cases had been around since the 1860s, began to rate sovereign bond issues between 1918–1924.[42] The United Kingdom's cross-border lending was still high; indeed, the United States and the United Kingdom were still at the top of the lending table, representing nearly two-thirds of overseas lending during this period.[43] By contrast, France and Germany, the two countries that had engaged in large-scale politically oriented lending in the prewar period largely sat on the sidelines during this Anglo-American banking spree. As a result, the international cross-border loan business was for the most part centered in New York and London during this time. The United Kingdom, as ever, focused on lending to its imperial client territories, while the United States focused on its neighbors in the Americas. The impact of these foci was to raise the debt levels of their trading partners; Canada became one of the world's most heavily indebted nations during the interwar period, followed closely by Australia, India, Argentina, and Brazil. Other heavily indebted countries during this time included China, the Netherlands East Indies, Germany, and the successor states to the Austro-Hungarian Empire. While the United States and the United Kingdom were surely suffering during the Great Depression, their lending policies may have led to even greater suffering in their loan partners.[44]

Latin America and the United States

The pattern of US behavior during the interwar period did not represent a change in policy for the United States, but rather a change in form. While an aggressive mixture of military and financial controls continued in some countries—such as Haiti, which was occupied by US troops until 1934—the mixture of bankers, diplomats, and other experts that had driven aggressive approaches of US financial diplomacy from 1900 to 1918 reconfigured significantly in the 1920s. The State Department continued to be involved in US overseas investments in Latin America, but focused less on controlled loans and more on encouraging US lending activity in the region as a way of putting underutilized American investment capital to work. These overtures found a willing audience, as a number of Latin American countries looked to use these US funds for infrastructure, public funds, and private investment. As the networks necessary to link Wall Street with the public and private financial needs of Latin America did not previously exist and had to be created out of whole cloth on the ground in real time, private citizen money doctors such as Kemmerer were necessary to play a critical bridging role.[45]

Kemmerer was one of a small clique of Americans and European economic advisors who linked the imperial background of American dollar diplomacy with the 1920s more bureaucratic approach to financial policy. Having helped manage the Philippine money supply, then coming to Princeton as a professor of economics, Kemmerer was well placed to bring an American economics elite cachet to the advice he gave in every country he visited. This advice, however, tended to be the same regardless of the government he was advising: a strong believer in the gold standard and vehemently opposed to inflation, Kemmerer recommended the formation of central banks, spending cuts, and strict currency controls during his many trips in Latin America and Central Europe, policies that the World Bank would recommend as "austerity measures" seven decades later to these same clients.

Kemmerer's confidence in his own genius meant he could be harsh and dismissive of local institutions in his conferences with State Department officials and given to favoring authority at the expense of the promotion of democracy. For example, in his work in Ecuador, Kemmerer favored the dictatorial junta of the July Revolution that overthrew President Gonzalo Cordova in 1925, telling the State Department that the Ecuadorian legislature—which Kemmerer dismissively characterized as "a Latin American Congressional debating society"—would never settle with US bondholders.[46] By helping to provide a narrative of reform and improvement, Kemmerer played a critical role in the investment of millions of US dollars in Latin America in the 1920s. Despite Kemmerer's narrative—one echoed by his fellow "doctors"—this flow of capital had the opposite effect to the one he guaranteed; these incoming dollars in that decade represented a "capital flow bonanza," leading to inflation and exploding debt and helped to destabilize and unsettle these economies and contributed to—or at least exacerbated—the depression that hit the region in the 1930s.[47]

In all this activity, only a few Latin American countries issued sovereign debt on international markets in a way that would facilitate military expenditure. This hesitance is in part the result of the State Department's warning off of any Wall Street lending to Latin American countries explicitly for the purchase of weapons. While this warning curtailed military funding in Latin America, it did not eliminate it:[48] for example, the Chaco War between Bolivia and Paraguay, lasting from 1932 to 1935, was the bloodiest interstate conflict in South America of the twentieth century, with combined battle deaths of over 92,000 representing 2 percent of Bolivia's overall population and 3.5 percent of Paraguay's.[49] This war was no surprise to either state or to its backers (Czechoslovakia and Argentina/Italy, respectively), as both states had been active on the foreign markets for the better part of a decade. They did, however, have different approaches; Paraguay carefully made use of the expansive bond markets of the 1920s to buy equipment from around Europe, while Bolivia focused on a single large contract with the British engineering firm Vickers.

Despite the carnage caused by this particular arms race, it barely registers in comparison with the major players at the time; Paraguay's expenses on equipment imports are estimated at roughly 5 million British pounds, Bolivia's at roughly 3 million pounds.[50] While these sums represented substantial sacrifices by the two countries, it is barely a blip in international borrowing of the time, when Argentina, Brazil, and Mexico were borrowing hundreds of millions of British pounds.[51] This rush to borrow was in part due to the substantial ease of borrowing in the 1920s, and this funding fueled public sector expansion and state building across Latin America. Once the Great Depression hit, however, these states may have attempted to use war as a way to divert public attention away from their suffering brought on in part by this borrowing spree—a number of militarized interstate disputes flared up on the continent in the 1930s, primarily between Colombia and Peru, Peru and Ecuador, Brazil and Paraguay, and Paraguay and Bolivia.[52] But the political instability in the Americas in the 1930s was not nearly as globally significant as the instability in Europe, as we discuss in the next section.

The Depression and Europe

The Invergordon Mutiny and the Shift to Devaluation

On September 15, 1931, the crews of four British Royal Navy battleships mutinied at their base in Invergordon, Scotland.[53] The week before, the British government had cut the pay of naval officers and sailors by up to 25 percent, depending on grade and seniority, in an effort to manage the dire economic consequences of the Great Depression. The pay cuts, implemented by the Tory government of Prime Minister Ramsay MacDonald, were part of an across-the-board spending reduction to all public sector employees, civilian as well as military, a fact relayed to the sailors by their superior officers in an attempt to quell the mutiny. It failed, and by September 16 all of His Majesty's Ships then docked at Invergordon were involved in the mutiny to at least some degree, with crews on the *Hood, Nelson, Valiant,* and *Rodney* performing only essential duties while sailors on the other ships provided moral support.

Quick, nonviolent action on the part of the Admiralty ended the mutiny on September 16 with pay partially restored and the ships dispersed, although 200 sailors were discharged from the navy as a result. However, the damage to the public faith in the British financial system was done; the mutiny caused a panic on the London Stock Exchange and a run on the pound. Only five days later, the United Kingdom left the gold standard, the first instance of a major European power doing so.[54]

Germany Bureaucratizes Its Fetters

While the United States and the United Kingdom resolved their problems with the gold standard in the early 1930s by going off it, other great powers such as France and Germany stayed on it but were pressed to more extreme financial measures to do so.[55] As world trade and financial flows decreased and became more regionally focused in the early 1930s, competitors in the finance domain evolved into a group of blocs—the British sterling bloc, the French gold standard bloc, and a Central European bloc, among others. In each case, high historic trade flows were important in defining the trade bloc. The sterling bloc seems to have been a response to country devaluations and membership did not, in itself, lead to reduced trade flows with other regions.[56]

In contrast, the German trade bloc was a response to the dramatic pressures Germany was under in trying to stay on the gold standard. Of all the toxic consequences of reparations, perhaps the most serious one was its role in the large stock of foreign-denominated debt that Germany owed in the early 1930s, making devaluation intolerable to the Weimar government, which instead chose to stay on the gold standard and implement exchange controls in 1931.[57] The rise of Hitler, Germany's default on its debts, and international outrage at Nazi brutality exacerbated the situation, reducing reserves to a historically low level.[58] In August 1934, German reichminister of economics Hjalmar Schacht launched his New Plan as a solution, eventually employing 18,000 people to control currency exchange and trade flows with other countries and minimize reserve loss.[59] The plan is sometimes presented as a scheme to squeeze surplus value out of Germany's southeastern neighbors but seems instead, in the 1930s, to be a defensive response to a critical lack of reserves; Germany's terms of trade steadily deteriorated as it tried to maintain the mark's value.[60] Alan Milward argues that not only did the small members of the mark bloc do much better than any other primary goods producers in that period, but Germany frequently failed to hit its most critical international trade goals.[61] Michael Kitson likewise argues that Nazi financial and economic policies do reasonably well when judged based on their political goals of maintaining the mark's value (critical after the hyperinflation of the 1920s) and building sources of supply that would be stable during a major war.[62]

In general, the consensus of economic historians appears to be that Germany played the hand it was dealt fairly well, managing to maintain the value of the mark, achieve substantial economic recovery with expanded spending, and secure sources of raw materials that were necessary for rearmament and future conflict, all in the face of a worldwide collapse in trade. If anything, the parties most exploited by Schacht's Reichsbank were the creditors whose German IOUs he systematically bought out at low prices.[63] This condition changes in World War II, when Germany began to occupy neighboring countries, and the combined leverage of military occupation and the financial control allowed it to extract surplus. By early 1941, for example, the Germans were deploying the exchange control system of the New Plan as part of their occupation of France, using it for control and resource extraction.[64]

The worldwide frustration with currency blocs and devaluations managed to survive World War II, leading to the Bretton Woods system and the European Common Market as potential solutions among other institutions discussed below. More recent research suggests that while exchange controls, currency blocs, and other bureaucratic controls may have caused substantial harm, devaluation was in fact a reasonable second-best solution; devaluing countries generally were able to adjust more smoothly without imposing substantial problems on neighbors.[65]

Japanese Colonization and the Bureaucratic RFA

Between Japan's relatively limited role in World War I and an unexpected economic boom due to the collapse in European exports, it was able to fund its participation in World War I through austerity programs and taxation rather than relying on borrowing, and in fact the expansion of exports allowed it to reduce its debt levels.[66] This self-reliance was a piece of good fortune for a country that had started formal relations with the West only less than a century before, especially given the tight credit situation created by heavy borrowing on the part of Italy, France, the United Kingdom, and former rival Russia.

By World War II the Japanese model had changed again, as its leaders worked to build a semiautarkic empire.[67] Japan was still not depending on international sources of finance, in part due to efforts at self-reliance and in part because it had gone to war against the countries that dominated the financial markets. As before, the Japanese government funded itself internally, borrowing from its citizens. Japanese industry had advanced to the degree that it could provide the basic necessities for waging war, at least for a time. The Japanese Empire was much larger than in World War I and so it made much greater and more extensive use of colonial currencies and military scrip to finance its war effort. The Japanese government had experience managing currency within a colony since taking over Taiwan and Korea at the turn of the century, and was readily able to implement similar systems in its new territories, taking advantage of seigniorage. Freely printed, unbacked currency allowed Japan to acquire resources through market means, with enforcement of monetary monopoly holding inflation in check.[68] These currencies were not backed by metal or any other reserve, were not convertible into any foreign currency, and could be used only for trade with Japan. This effort was of a piece of Japan's overall strategy within what it called the "Greater East Asia Co-Prosperity Sphere" and worked well enough temporarily, although the entire system was rendered moot by the destruction of the Japanese merchant marine during the war. In any case, at the end of the World War II the Japanese government defaulted on all public debt, leaving the country in a state of immiseration, a condition made worse by the complete destruction of two of its key industrial centers by the US atomic bombs in 1945.[69]

China in Japan's Shadow

Unlike Japan, China had only a fledgling defense industry in the first few decades of the twentieth century, and required hard currency to purchase weapons, not only for the continuing civil war against the Chinese Communist Party (CCP), but also for funding an anticipated future conflict against Japan. Most importantly, China required a stable, convertible currency to help knit the disparate provinces together and offer legitimacy in the face of challenges from both the CCP and the Imperial Japanese invaders. Reserves of metal and US dollars enabled the Nationalist government to stabilize prices and maintain its own currency, but its inability to prevent the different provinces from mining their own precious metals and printing their own currency led to China suffering from increasing inflation during the interwar period.[70]

Price instability was not Nationalist China's only problem during this time. By 1937, the physical security of China's remaining silver reserves had come under threat from the Imperial Japanese Army, further motivating the Nationalist government to export silver to the United States. As the war proceeded and Japan occupied a greater portion of Chinese territory, Japan began to offer its own regional fiat currencies, intending to replace the yuan, limit the extent of international and interregional trade, and redirect Chinese resources into the Japanese Empire while at the same time undercutting the legitimacy of Chiang Kai-shek's regime in Chongqing. The US and UK governments appreciated the threat that Japanese efforts represented to the stability of the Nationalist government, and even acted in a token manner to stem these efforts. In March 1939, the United States and the United Kingdom agreed to create a stabilization fund that would back the yuan against further attack by the Japanese, although this was quickly dissipated. In addition, the United Kingdom also helped the Nationalist regime smuggle currency into Japanese-occupied Chinese territories, offering at least some competition with the Japanese fiat currencies. This particular effort was not sufficient to repel the Japanese occupation, which continued until Japan's imperial bellicosity and overreach led to its collapse in the 1940s and Japan's formal surrender on September 9, 1945.[71]

Soviet Finance: Bureaucratic Hypertrophy

The Soviet financial system was unique even for this unusual period in global financial history.[72] The Communist Party of the Soviet Union sought a wholesale reconstruction of the Soviet economy along ideological lines. In the immediate wake of the Bolshevik Revolution in the early 1920s, the USSR sought recognition, trade, and loans from the West, especially the United States.[73] The destruction inflicted by World War I, the revolution, and civil war had left the USSR with little in the way of the modern technology, infrastructure, or machine equipment it would need to rebuild and realize its collectivist vision. Much of this technology and equipment had to be imported from abroad, meaning that the USSR would have to create a stable currency with which to purchase these goods. The USSR could not entirely isolate itself from the corrupting influence of the industrialized nations of the West, even as the entente demanded that the Soviets accept the burden of the aforementioned loans taken by the czar's government.[74] That the Western powers regarded the Soviet Union as fundamentally illegitimate did not help matters: for example, the United States initially refused to accept Soviet gold as payment, regarding it as stolen.[75] Foreign owners of property confiscated during the Russian Revolution made it difficult for the USSR to conduct normal business abroad, as lawsuits and threats of property forfeiture made the maintaining of accounts difficult.[76] By the mid-1920s, however, international financial relations began to normalize, and US firms regularly began to extend credit to Soviet firms under terms progressively more favorable to the Soviets.[77] Pragmatism briefly won out over ideology in the Soviet leadership, and encouraging foreign capital investment was one of the core aspects of the New Economic Policy (NEP), although it did not meet with easy success.[78]

By 1930, Joseph Stalin had won the factional wars in the Communist Party and took control of the USSR. Stalin was able to recover a degree of stability in the Soviet economy, making the importation of capital and technology from the West less critical, although Stalin's willingness to ignore the needs of Soviet citizens also played a role in this recovery. The Soviets abandoned the NEP and, instead, pursued a policy of centralization and autarky intended to limit the influence of foreign countries and especially of foreign financiers, while also enabling central planners to appear to achieve their goals. In addition, the state operated Torgsin stores in the USSR between 1931 and 1935, in which customers could pay for consumer goods with hard currency, gold, or jewelry, which the state then used to help purchase industrial resources from other countries.[79]

Part of this new centralization was the increase in power and influence of Gosbank—a central bank established under the NEP in 1922. As Gosbank's bureaucratic structure shifted over time, it gained administrative control over the advance of credit to internal and external clients. This centralization was designed to limit inflation, which had become a serious problem in the relatively disorganized period of the NEP, as multiple actors within the USSR had the effective authority to extend credit and increase the supply of currency.[80] To attempt to solve this problem, Soviet planners built the new system around two principles: (1) preventing inflation; and (2) ensuring that resources and planning drove finance rather than the other way around.[81] The planners' intention was to generate self-discipline on the part of enterprise executives while also maintaining a tight money policy and avoiding enterprise bankruptcy, an impossible task even in stable economies. While its autarkic aspects kept the USSR relatively insulated from the financial catastrophes of the Great Depression, it did not prevent and likely exacerbated inflation and regional famines.

Conclusion

World War I placed enormous strain on the ability of European states to successfully convert basic factor endowments into practical military power. The global system of finance that had been established under the classical gold standard continued to function even as the combatants engaged in total war with one another. But while the war saw unprecedented mobilization of resources on the part of the combatants, it also destroyed immense wealth across Europe because of the physical destruction of combat and because of the distortions required to channel vast resources to military action.

States responded to the destruction of wealth by attempting to reorganize their trade and finance along more systematic lines, along the way taking advantage of improvements in state capacity to exert greater control in the finance domain, the result of which we term the *bureaucratic RFA*. The methods of this RFA such as exchange controls and sanctions seem to have contributed to the Great Depression, putting even former hegemon the United Kingdom in dire economic and military straits. States frequently responded to this pressure by pursuing even more competitive policies that worsened things. The one "beggar-thy-neighbor" policy practiced in this period that economic historians view as constructive was devaluation, a policy that meant effectively leaving the gold standard. The devastation of World War II cleared the international system of these unilateral actors, creating an opportunity for a new hegemon to take center stage and remake the finance domain in its own image.

Notes

1. Schacht, Hjalmar. 1937. "Germany's Colonial Demands." *Foreign Affairs* 15 (2): 223–234.

2. Lambert, Nicholas. 2012. *Planning Armageddon: British Economic Warfare and the First World War.* Cambridge: Harvard University Press; Mulder, Nicholas. 2022. *The Economic Weapon.* New Haven: Yale University Press, chap. 1.

3. Silber, William L., and Greg Kaza. 2007. *When Washington Shut Down Wall Street: The Great Financial Crisis of 1914 and the Origins of America's Monetary Supremacy.* Princeton: Princeton University Press, 333–337;

4. Thompson, John A. 2002. *Woodrow Wilson.* London: Taylor and Francis Group, 100.

5. Kindleberger, Charles. 1986. *The World in Depression, 1929–1939.* Berkeley: University of California Press; Eichengreen, Barry J. 1996. *Golden Fetters: The Gold Standard and the Great Depression, 1919–1939.* Oxford: Oxford University

Press; Eichengreen, Barry J. 2019. "Versailles: The Economic Legacy." *International Affairs* 95 (1): 7–24; Reinhart, Carmen M., and Kenneth S. Rogoff. 2009. *This Time Is Different: Eight Centuries of Financial Folly.* Princeton: Princeton University Press; Friedman, Milton, and Anna Jacobson Schwartz. 2008. *A Monetary History of the United States, 1867–1960.* Princeton: Princeton University Press, chap. 7.

6. Friedman and Schwartz 2008; Kindleberger 1986; Eichengreen 1996; Bernanke, Ben S., 1983. *Non-monetary Effects of the Financial Crisis in the Propagation of the Great Depression.* Series w1054. Cambridge: National Bureau of Economic Research (NBER); Eichengreen, Barry, and Douglas A. Irwin. 2009. *The Slide to Protectionism: Who Succumbed and Why.* Series w15142. Cambridge: NBER. The argument that more aggressive devaluation was the actual path to recovery for most countries, including the United States and the United Kingdom, seems the most persuasive.

7. Nenovsky, Nikolay, and Kalina Dimitrova. 2007. *Exchange Rate Control in Bulgaria in the Interwar Period: History and Theoretical Reflections.* Discussion Paper. Sofia: Bulgarian National Bank. (61).

8. Helleiner, Eric. 2002. "The Monetary Dimensions of Colonialism: Why Did Imperial Powers Create Currency Blocks?" *Geopolitics* 7 (1): 5–30; North, Douglas. 1991. "Institutions." *Journal of Economic Perspectives* 5 (1): 97–112.

9. Mulder 2022.

10. Milward, Alan S., 1985. "The Reichsmark Bloc and the International Economy." In *Aspects of the Third Reich,* edited by Hannsjoachim W. Koch. London: Palgrave, 331–359.

11. Gerth, Hans H., and C. Wright Mills, eds. 1946. *Max Weber.* Oxford: Oxford University Press.

12. This criticism involves both the construction and the impact of bureaucracy, and the economic problems of the interwar period certainly show as much of the costs of bureaucracy as they do of the virtues. Among the many critiques in public choice economics, one of the most canonical would be Niskanen, William A. 1971. *Bureaucracy and Representative Government.* Chicago: Aldine-Atherton.

13. Lynn, Laurence E., Jr. 2006. *Public Management: Old and New.* New York: Routledge.

14. White, Eugene. 1995. "The French Revolution and the Politics of Government Finance, 1770–1815." *Journal of Economic History* 55 (2): 244. Sargent, Thomas J., and François R. Velde. 1995. "Macroeconomic Features of the French Revolution." *Journal of Political Economy* 101 (3): 505–506; Tooze, Adam. 2007: *The Wages of Destruction: The Making and Breaking of the Nazi Economy.* New York: Viking Penguin, 94.

15. Piatt, Andrew A. 1901. "Indian Currency Problems of the Last Decade." *Quarterly Journal of Economics* 15 (4): 483–516; Keynes, John Maynard. 1913. *Indian Currency and Finance.* London: Macmillan.

16. Helleiner 2002; Schiltz, Michael. 2012. *The Money Doctors from Japan: Finance, Imperialism, and the Building of the Yen Bloc, 1895–1937.* Cambridge: Harvard University Press; Mitchener, Kris James, and Marc Weidenmier. 2008. *Trade and Empire.* Series w13765. Cambridge: NBER.

17. Mulder 2022.

18. Scholarly views have been somewhat more conflicted, with Etienne Mantoux countering that the issue was not the economic consequences of the peace, but "the economic consequences of Mr. Keynes." White, Eugene. 1999. *Making the French Pay: The Costs and Consequences of the Napoleonic Reparations.* Series w7438. Cambridge: NBER, 1 and 42.

19. White, Eugene. 1999. *Making the French Pay: The Costs and Consequences of the Napoleonic Reparations*. Series w7438. Cambridge: NBER, 19–28 and table 5 at 23. The one measure by which the 1921 reparations are not the largest is debt service as percentage of exports, where the 1815 reparations for France were bigger; on most other measures, the 1921 reparations dwarf all others.

20. Tooze, Adam. 2015. *The Deluge: The Great War, America and the Remaking of the Global Order, 1916–1931*. New York: Penguin Group. There are other problems as well, including unevenness in the ability of financial centers to evaluate sovereign debt risks. Flandreau, Marc, Juan H. Flores, Norbert Gaillard, and Sebastián Nieto-Parra. 2009. *The End of Gatekeeping: Underwriters and the Quality of Sovereign Bond Markets, 1815–2007*. Series w15128. Cambridge: NBER; Flandreau, Marc, Norbert Gaillard, and Frank Packer. 2011. "To Err Is Human: Rating Agencies and the Interwar Foreign Government Debt Crisis." *European Review of Economic History* 15 (3): 495–538.

21. Woodrow Wilson's speech on "The Fourteen Points" laid out the vision of the League and the way forward toward peace and stability. Office of the Historian, Foreign Service Institute, US Department of State. 2022. "Wilson's Fourteen Points."

22. Eichengreen 2019.

23. Mulder 2022.

24. Piketty, Thomas. 2017. *Capital in the Twenty-First Century*. Translated by Arthur Goldhammer. Cambridge, MA: Belknap Press, technical appendix, tables S4.1 and S3.1. Years of comparison after World War I are 1920 for Britain, 1930 for Germany.

25. Eichengreen 1996.

26. Lamont, Thomas. 1930. "The Final Reparations Settlement." *Foreign Affairs* 8 (3): 336–363; Kindleberger 1986.

27. Tooze 2007: 2, 5–6; Eichengreen 2019: 14.

28. Roberts, Priscilla. 1998. "Quis Custodiet Ipsos Custodes?' The Federal Reserve System's Founding Fathers and Allied Finances in the First World War." *Business History Review* 72 (4): 585–620.

29. Forder, James. 2003. "'Independence' and the Founding of the Federal Reserve." *Scottish Journal of Political Economy* 50 (3): 297–310.

30. Broz, Lawrence J. 1997. *The International Origins of the Federal Reserve System*. Ithaca: Cornell University Press.

31. A "money center" bank focuses the vast majority of its activity on institutional or other large clients like governments, major corporations, or other similar banks.

32. Abrahams, Paul Philip. 1968. *The Foreign Expansion of American Finance and Its Relationship to the Foreign Economic Policies of the United States, 1907–1921*. Dissertation. Madison: University of Wisconsin:18.

33. Sebok, Miklos. 2011. "President Wilson and the International Origins of the Federal Reserve System—A Reappraisal." *White House Studies* 10 (4): 441.

34. Laughlin, James Laurence. 1898. *Report of the Monetary Commission of the Indianapolis Convention of Boards of Trade, Chambers of Commerce, Commercial Clubs, and Other Similar Bodies of the United States*. Chicago: University of Chicago Press, 41–42.

35. Kang, Sung Won, and Hugh Rockoff. 2015. "Capitalizing Patriotism: The Liberty Loans of World War I." *Financial History Review* 22 (1): 45–78.

36. Rosenberg, Emily S. 2004. *Financial Missionaries to the World*. Durham: Duke University Press, 100–101.

37. Rosenberg 2004.

38. Rosenberg 2004: 98–105.

39. Rosenberg 2004: 98.

40. Rosenberg 2004: 98–105.
41. Eichengreen, Barry J., and Richard Portes. 1985. *Debt and Default in the 1930s: Causes and Consequences*. Series w1772. Cambridge: NBER.
42. Eichengreen, Barry, and Richard Portes. 1990. "The Interwar Debt Crisis and Its Aftermath." *World Bank Research Observer* 5 (1): 69–94, at 72; Flandreau, Gaillard, and Packer 2011: 495–538, at 508.
43. Eichengreen and Portes 1985: 4.
44. Eichengreen and Portes 1985: 8–9.
45. Rosenberg 2004; Drake, Paul W. 1989. *The Money Doctor in the Andes*. Durham: Duke University Press; Flandreau, Marc, ed. 2005. *Money Doctors: The Experience of International Financial Advising, 1850–2000*. Vol. 26. London: Routledge.
46. Drake 1989: 163.
47. Drake 1989; For amounts of investment in select countries, see Fernandez, Andres. 2008. "Capital Flows and Business Cycles in Latin America During 1920s and 30s: A Second Look from a Neoclassical Perspective." Working Paper. New Brunswick: Rutgers University; For the definition of *capital flow bonanza*, see Reinhart, Carmen M., and Vincent R. Reinhart. 2009. "Capital Flow Bonanzas: An Encompassing View of the Past and Present." *NBER International Seminar on Macroeconomics* 5 (1): 9–62.
48. Hilton, Stanley E. 1973. "Military Influence on Brazilian Economic Policy, 1930–1945: A Different View." *Hispanic American Historical Review* 53 (1): 71–94; Rosenberg 2004: 106–107.
49. Sarkees, Meredith Reid, and Frank Wayman. 2010. *Resort to War: 1816–2007*. Washington, DC: CQ Press.
50. Hughes, Matthew. 2005. "Logistics and the Chaco War: Bolivia Versus Paraguay, 1932–1935." *Journal of Military History* 69 (2): 411–437.
51. Kaminsky, Graciela L. 2010. *Two Hundred Years of Financial Integration: A New Database with an Example from Latin America*. Working Paper. Washington: George Washington University: 1–33, in particular figure 7. Kaminsky, Graciela L. 2016. *International Borrowing Cycles: A New Historical Database*. Series w22819. Cambridge: NBER.
52. Drake 1989; Hensel, Paul R. 1994. "One Thing Leads to Another: Recurrent Militarized Disputes in Latin America, 1816–1986." *Journal of Peace Research* 31 (3): 281–297.
53. Ereira, Alan. 2015. *The Invergordon Mutiny: A Narrative History of the Last Great Mutiny in the Royal Navy and How It Forced Britain Off the Gold Standard in 1931*. London: Routledge.
54. Whalley, Philip. 2009. "The Invergordon Mutiny and the National Economic Crisis of 1931: A Media and Parliamentary Perspective." *Journal for Maritime Research* 11 (1): 1–23.
55. Eichengreen, Barry J., and Jeffrey Sachs. 1985. "Exchange Rates and Economic Recovery in the 1930s." *Journal of Economic History* 45 (4): 925–946; Eichengreen and Irwin 2009.
56. Eichengreen, Barry J., and Douglas A. Irwin. 1995. "Trade Blocs, Currency Blocs, and the Reorientation of World Trade in the 1930s." *Journal of International Economics* 38 (1–2): 1–24, at 4.
57. Tooze 2007: 21–22; Eichengreen and Irwin 2009..
58. Tooze 2007: 71–75; Eichengreen and Sachs 1985: table 4 at 944.
59. Tooze 2007: 76–79.
60. Kirshner, Jonathan.1997. *Currency and Coercion: The Political Economy of International Monetary Power*. Princeton: Princeton University Press, 121–140;

Neal, Larry. 1979. "The Economics and Finance of Bilateral Clearing Agreements: Germany, 1934–8." *Economic History Review* 32 (3): 391–404.

61. Milward 1985.

62. Kitson, Michael. 1992. "The Move to Autarky: The Political Economy of Nazi Trade Policy." Department of Applied Economics Working Paper 9201 Cambridge: Cambridge University, January.

63. Tooze 2007: 90–94.

64. Occhino, Filippo, Kim Oosterlinck, and Eugene N. White. 2008. "How Much Can a Victor Force the Vanquished to Pay? France Under the Nazi Boot." *Journal of Economic History.* 68 (1): 1–45.

65. Eichengreen and Sachs 1985; Eichengreen and Irwin 2009.

66. Much of this material appeared in different format in Farley, Robert. 2021c. "What Does Finance Have to Do with War?" *The Diplomat,* March 31. Regarding Japan's wartime boom, see Schiltz 2012: chap. 3.

67. Huff, Gregg. 2007. "Financial Transition in Pre–World War II Japan and Southeast Asia." *Financial History Review* 14 (2): 149.

68. Huff, Gregg, and Shinobu Majima. 2013. "Financing Japan's World War II Occupation of Southeast Asia." *Journal of Economic History* 73 (4): 937–977; Schiltz 2012.

69. Shizume, Masato. 2011. "Sustainability of Public Debt: Evidence from Japan Before the Second World War." *Economic History Review* 64 (4): 1113–1143.

70. Kirshner 1997.

71. Kirshner 1997.

72. Gregory, Paul R., and Aleksei Tikhonov. 2000. "Central Planning and Unintended Consequences: Creating the Soviet Financial System, 1930–1939." *Journal of Economic History* 60 (4): 1017–1040.

73. Siegel, Katherine Amelia Siobhan. 1996. *Loans and Legitimacy: The Evolution of Soviet-American Relations, 1919–1933.* Lexington: University Press of Kentucky.

74. Malik, Hassan. 2018. *Bankers and Bolsheviks: International Finance and the Russian Revolution.* Princeton: Princeton University Press; Lenin, Vladimir I. 2010. *Imperialism, the Highest Stage of Capitalism.* London: Penguin.

75. Siegel 1996: 18.

76. Siegel 1996: 89.

77. Siegel 1996: 100.

78. Arnold, Arthur Z. 1937. *Banks, Credit, and Money in Soviet Russia.* New York: Columbia University Press; Siegel 1996: 111.

79. Osokina, Elena. 2021. *Stalin's Quest for Gold: The Torgsin Hard-Currency Shops and Soviet Industrialization.* Ithaca: Cornell University Press.

80. Gregory and Tikhonov 2000: 1020.

81. Gregory and Tikhonov 2000: 1018.

8

Bretton Woods and the American Century

> *These proposals for an International [Monetary] Fund and International Bank [for Reconstruction and Development] are concrete evidence that the economic objectives of the United States agree with those of the United Nations. They illustrate our unity of purpose and interest in the economic field. What we need and what they need correspond—expanded production, employment, exchange, and consumption—in other words, more goods produced, more jobs, more trade, and a higher standard of living for us all. To the people of the United States this means real peacetime employment for those who will be returning from the war and for those at home whose wartime work has ended. It also means orders and profits to our industries and fair prices to our farmers. We shall need prosperous markets in the world to ensure our own prosperity, and we shall need the goods the world can sell us. For all those purposes, as well as for a peace that will endure, we need the partnership of the United Nations.*
> —Franklin D. Roosevelt, "The President's Message to Congress on Bretton Woods," 1945

This chapter explains how the finance domain dropped into the background of international affairs after World War II, why it is underdiscussed in the strategic literature, and how the temporarily reduced visibility of strategic finance was a mixture of design and chance. In this chapter, we also discuss the creation of the Bretton Woods revolution in financial affairs (RFA), the factors that led to the finance domain's resurgence in the wake of the end of the formal Bretton Woods currency system in 1971, and the implications for the endurance of US hegemony.

As we show, the global financial system was redesigned in part to eliminate the destructive aspects of finance domain competition. The primary adversary of the United States was the USSR, a country with an idiosyncratic economic and financial system resembling a simple tax state, which insulated it from global financial pressure. The development of nuclear deterrence as the primary strategic doctrine of both the United States and the USSR meant that large-scale wars were largely limited, and local wars, wars of independence, and civil wars were more prevalent. Finally, most strategic preparation by major powers assumed that any major war would quickly become nuclear, and the focus became deployment of defensive forces sufficient to justify the escalation of war, hence deterring global war and the economic devastation such a war would bring. Together, these factors pushed finance to the sidelines of great-power competition.

The Bretton Woods monetary system of fixed exchange rates formally ended in the 1970s, but we argue that this only partially reduced the impact of the RFA. The collapse of the USSR was more important in that it obviated the primary focus on nuclear deterrence as the specter of global nuclear annihilation receded into the background, resulting in the return of increased national security competition in the finance domain by the end of the twentieth century. The institutional pieces in the epigraph excerpted from US president Franklin D. Roosevelt's speech remain in place, as does the international cooperative network of which they are important components, ensuring that many of the strengths of the Bretton Woods RFA endure into the present day. It is therefore important that we discuss the origin of this RFA and its consequences.

In the Wake of Total War: The Bretton Woods RFA

Determined to learn from the chaos of the first forty-five years of the twentieth century, the Allied victors of World War II attempted to create a benevolent financial hegemony undergirded by American economic power—what John Ikenberry calls a "liberal international order" as a way of distinguishing it from previous hegemonies that existed primarily for conquest—known as the Bretton Woods system.[1] The delegates from the Allied powers attempted to preserve the best parts of the previous financial system, specifically the British-centered classical gold standard, and mitigate the effects of the worst parts. The Bretton Woods system performed well in many ways, and pieces of it remain in effect well into the twenty-first century. This system represents the RFA for the post–World War II period, an RFA created by the United States, a state powerful enough at the time to exert enough influence on other states to cooperate in its construction and implementation. As such, it is possible that Bretton Woods represents the first truly intentional, collaborative RFA in history, which may help explain the durability of its institutions.

Resilient as the institutional features of the Bretton Woods system have proven, even in its heyday it was hardly flawless; indeed, the rapid changes in the global economy and power structure in the postwar period forced its stewards in the United States, United Nations, and global banking bureaucracy to make continual adjustments. Shocks to the system both external—the rise of Organization of Petroleum Exporting Countries (OPEC)—and internal—the pressure of maintaining the United States' military commitments and weakness in containing inflation—were more than the system could easily bear. By the 1970s, the United States itself had dismantled one of the key components of the system by going off the gold standard, and by the 1980s the world had turned away from the dream of a carefully managed global trade system with stable exchange rates. Instead, even as the United States maintained its role as the linchpin of the system, other governments became increasingly ready to let market forces—rather than careful central management—adjust exchange rates and, hence, influence trade flows.

A New Institutional Environment

By the late 1940s, the world had transitioned from a multipolar to a bipolar international system as former great powers decimated by World War II were incapable of reclaiming their leadership roles. This system was characterized by the two poles—the United States and the USSR—engaging in an ideological Cold War. While the United States moved into leadership of the Western bloc, it worked to create a collective security organization of European allies, and the establishment of an organization—the North Atlantic Treaty Organization (NATO)—as a bulwark against Soviet aggression. This creation required a complex negotiating process among members to maintain logistical and financial support for European forces.[2] At the same time, the United States worked in partnership in a "first among equals" role with the former great powers to create multilateral diplomatic and financial institutions such as the United Nations and the Bretton Woods system designed to maintain stability through nonviolent dispute resolution, international cooperation, and economic growth via managed capitalism.

Interest in establishing a new liberal international order marked by the rule of law and cooperation dated to the end of the World War I and US president Woodrow Wilson's ill-fated attempt to create a League of Nations. As the Allies began to look toward eventual victory in World War II, discussions began in earnest—especially within the Roosevelt administration—on the nature of the postwar order and the position of the United States at its center. Putting a plan into action met with relatively little resistance; the failures of institutions in the interwar period and the hope that something good might come from the horrors of the war played a critical role in herding decisionmakers in Washington and London toward substantive compromise. The primary intellectual architect of this new system was John Maynard

Keynes; as a popular author, academic, and political advisor, his diagnosis of the flaws in the Treaty of Versailles, and of the cyclical issues behind the Great Depression were, if not completely accepted, well known and taken seriously in the United States and the United Kingdom.[3] Keynes's experiences at Versailles, in the City of London, at Cambridge, and within the British civil service made him a natural fit for his central role in the design of the Bretton Woods system and its institutions such as the World Bank and the International Monetary Fund (IMF) mentioned above.[4]

As Michael Bordo writes, Bretton Woods was designed in the hopes of combining "the advantage of the classical gold standard (i.e., exchange rate stability) with the advantage of floating rates (i.e., independence to pursue national full employment policies)."[5] In fact, this conceptual flexibility caused friction between the system's founders; for example, Ikenberry notes that in the negotiations from 1943 to 1944, the critical split was between a pro-free-trade US State Department and a British cabinet oriented toward full employment policies, even at the expense of a certain amount of prosperity.[6] However, there was greater consensus between the negotiators than there was disagreement, primarily because of the severity of the problems the world faced.

Specifically, three issues of the interwar period were of particular concern to the committee: the collapse of the gold exchange standard; a race to the bottom by states in currency devaluation; and the prevalence of unilateral thinking and action by decisionmakers at the state level.[7] The collapse of the gold exchange standard was itself driven by three developments: competition between states with a gold surplus (e.g., the United States and France) and states with a gold deficit (e.g., the United Kingdom) combined with a general unwillingness within the interwar finance domain to cooperate; economic and trade expansion outpacing the world's gold supply, the result of which was a contraction of the global money supply; and a crisis of confidence in the ability of certain state financial centers to pay their debts in gold, leading to "bank runs" such as the United Kingdom's suspension of convertibility in 1931 in the wake of the Invergordon Mutiny.[8]

Many prominent economists of the time, including Ragnar Nurkse, argued that currency devaluations—the second issue listed above—were primarily the result of floating currency exchange rates. Rampant arbitrage led to currency speculation, the argument ran, which would lead to short selling–induced currency devaluation first in one state and then in others in the system, leading to general currency crisis. The most problematic of the three issues listed, however, was the state tendency to think and act unilaterally; that is, instead of cooperating on a systemic level to create institutions that would promote economic growth and financial stability, individual states imposed their own domestic currency controls or, at the most, entered into bilateral agreements with one other state. As we argued in

Chapter 7, the development of bureaucracy gave states capacity to pursue a range of such aggressive goals. This reaction naturally led to isolationism and a decrease in trade and economic growth in general. The goal at the Bretton Woods conference was to create a global financial system that would mitigate these problems, as well as adhering to the general principles of promoting free trade and economic prosperity.[9]

Although Keynes was prominent and respected by the Bretton Woods conference participants and was central to these discussions, his ideal approach—a world bank with true central banking capabilities—was not adopted. In Keynes's 1943 plan, he called that bank the "International Clearing Union" and wanted to give it the ability to issue a currency called "bancor." Keynes suggested the bank have $25-$30 billion in liquidity facilities, or a stock roughly equal to about 5 percent of world gross domestic product (GDP) flow in 1943.[10] This money could be lent out by the bank to states with currency deficits to give them the time and ability to get their fiscal-monetary house in order. Contrary to the monetarist criticism that Chicago School economists like Frank Knight directed at Keynes and his adherents, this was not just a scheme whereby the rich states of the world would play Santa Claus and, thereby, risk runaway inflation. Instead, the Keynes plans included strict controls to limit capital flows from shifting exchange rate parities.[11]

The Keynes plan struck its opponents as too ambitious. For example, Harry Dexter White, senior Treasury official and leader of the US delegation to Bretton Woods, proposed a more limited stabilization fund about 20 percent the size of Keynes's and careful oversight of exchange rate valuations.[12] The final compromise had slightly more generous funding than the White plan, but no international currency. Instead, the United States managed the gold value of the dollar, and all other countries managed the dollar value of their currency. In addition, the final compromise included near-term capital controls and, in harmony with both plans, the new Bretton Woods system focused on fixed parities; that is, a state's currency valuation is fixed to that of another state's.[13]

Bretton Woods: Peacemaker in the Financial Commons

In Chapter 6 we looked at the increasing use of the tools of the finance domain as France, Germany, and other powers slowly whittled away the Pax Britannica in the years before 1914. We reviewed discussions by the economists Herbert Feis and Jacob Viner and others who documented politicization of finance and trade flows in the late nineteenth and early twentieth centuries. Both Feis and Viner were prominent enough to play a direct role in the construction of Bretton Woods, as well as to inform other architects of the institutional design. Feis pursued a multifaceted career in academia, including stints at the University of Cincinnati, Harvard, and the Institute of Advanced Studies at Princeton, and Viner was a leading economist of trade, president of the American Economic Association in 1939, and also held substantial government positions.[14] Both were involved with the Council on Foreign Relations and a number of projects, including *Europe, the World's Banker 1870–1914* by Feis, were published by the council. They apparently were close friends and the fact that both published their work on this issue in a fairly tight window of time—1929–1930—suggests they were actively discussing it with each other.[15] Regardless, it is striking that two of the more high-profile Americans writing about international trade during the interwar period spent considerable time looking back at the prewar period, and then worked hard within the Roosevelt administration to help plan the postwar architecture.

Among the economists who worked on Bretton Woods, Viner was one of the least Keynesian, most Chicago School in philosophical orientation. Viner also had significant impact on the design, as his intense correspondence with Keynes in 1943 discussing the system persuaded Keynes to adjust his proposal.[16] Viner also appears to have helped the revised plan succeed by ginning up critical support among American economists for Keynes's vision of Bretton Woods, in substantial part because Viner hoped it would avoid the destructive power struggles of the prewar period.[17] Viner continued to defend Bretton Woods assiduously after the war, writing in 1947 of the IMF and World Bank, "These agencies will enable economically and politically weak countries to receive financial aid without thereby becoming entangled in the political net of a great power."[18] Viner's defense of the system was useful politically in creating a coalition in the economics community, and combined a Chicago School enthusiasm for markets and suspicion of politics with a desire to resolve the worst parts of political conflict with multilateral organizations.[19]

The Impact of the Bretton Woods System

The launch of the Bretton Woods system, the Bretton Woods Institutions, and their sister institution the United Nations resulted in the establishment of a new international system aimed at fostering peace and prosperity through the advancement of international cooperation and the promotion of democracy and capitalism. Michael Bordo points out that the Bretton Woods era, in its pure form, showed remarkable macroeconomic stability; the downside is that this period, with fixed exchange rates linked to gold, lasted at most twenty-five years and arguably only nine. Here, we review some of the issues of the fixed exchange rate system and the transition to floating exchange rates; following a number of researchers, we are more impressed by the post-1971 continuity than the change.[20]

From the point of view of the US executive branch in the 1950s and 1960s, the critical issue of financial statecraft was to limit the loss of US gold reserves. Indeed, President John F. Kennedy said, on multiple occasions, "The two things which scared [me] the most were nuclear weapons and the payments deficit."[21] Although the latter problem was not as significant a threat as the former during his presidency, Kennedy was right to be concerned: by the late 1950s, the United States had become to some extent the world's banker, holding substantial gold reserves and lending out in dollars to other states. Managing this role meant the United States had to strike a delicate balance: the more dollar reserves that were in the hands of other countries, the greater the world money supply and the less limited the world economy was by the relatively slow growth of gold stocks. However, if dollar reserves in the hands of other countries grew at a significantly greater rate than the United States' monetary gold stock, the result could be a bank run where dollars were sold for gold, the value of the dollar collapsed, the system fell apart, and the end product would be another global depression.[22]

An additional impact of the United States assuming the role of world's banker was that a US official settlements balance of payments deficit became the rule rather than the exception after 1958, with only a brief surplus in fiscal year 1968–1969.[23] This deficit was not driven by international trade—the current account remained in surplus for the bulk of this period—but by foreign aid programs like the Marshall Plan in the early 1950s and then by private investment by US companies as they raced to take advantage of the postwar chaos. Nevertheless, the US government perceived this deficit as a threat to its financial stability. The Dwight D. Eisenhower, John F. Kennedy, and Lyndon B. Johnson administrations focused on several solutions, among others limiting expenditure on troops in Europe and persuading Germany to "offset" spending by the United States with purchases of American weapons or other dollar-denominated items.[24] Despite these and many other interventions, the US monetary gold stock declined at a fairly steady pace from the mid-1950s onward.[25]

In the end, what seems to have been the primary cause of the system's downfall was the weakness of US monetary policy. Exactly the source of this weakness is debatable, but the escalation of the Great Inflation around 1965 in the United States and the lack of a proper Federal Reserve response pushed the capital account of the United States further into deficit.[26] As gold stocks depleted for over a decade, the US government took increasingly drastic measures tried to staunch the flow but, because the fundamental issue was with the dollar valuation, none of the strategies focused on capital flows made a dent. Seeing no other viable alternative, on August 15, 1971, President Richard M. Nixon took the United States off the gold standard and the fixed parities of Bretton Woods shifted to floating rates. However, in the following fifty years the dollar has generally held or increased its role in the world economy, and recent work suggests that while strict currency pegs are much rarer, the number of currencies worldwide that anchor themselves to the dollar has actually gone up since the end of the formal Bretton Woods system.[27]

Overall, the fixed exchange system always had a core tension in its desire to balance capitalism with stability and control, and financial repression was common in the early period.[28] It is reasonable to ask how much the financial repression helped to stabilize the financial commons; for example, the focus on fixed exchange rates, combined with a release of capital controls, created a lopsided setup that incentivized speculators to bet against overvalued currencies and led to violent devaluations. However, in the decades after the war regulations loosened up and workarounds were found, greater pressures built up. Starting in the mid-1950s Britain became the epicenter of so-called eurodollar and then eurocurrency accounts, regulatory arbitrage that allowed banks more freedom with accounts denominated in foreign currencies. Eurocurrency transactions became a substantial part of international lending in the 1960s. With the end of fixed exchange rates and fueled by petrodollars in the wake of the 1973 oil embargo, eurocurrrency trading acted to substantially privatize sovereign lending. An early part of what is sometimes called the "shadow banking system," eurocurrency accounts have been important in international finance ever since, including a central role in the financial crisis of 2008. As discussed below, eurocurrency finance played a critical role in a number of less-developed regions in the 1970s and 1980s, particularly in Africa and Latin America.[29]

In the background lay US involvement in the Vietnam War, with mounting costs leading to inflation and putting pressure on the system.[30] As Hugh Rockoff notes, "It turns out, then, that the current international financial system is a byproduct of war. . . . The inflations of the Vietnam era led to the discontinuance of the Bretton Woods system and the establishment of a new international financial system based on flexible exchange rates."[31] The irony here is that US hegemony in the finance domain was threatened not by external forces, but by the US government's attempt to assert its hegemony in the terrestrial domain. The Bretton Woods agreement, however, placed the United States at the center of the finance domain, and the RFAs of the late twentieth and early twenty-first centuries solidified this position.

Bretton Woods, the Cold War, and the USSR

In addition to the hegemonic role of the United States in the finance domain and the structure and institutions of Bretton Woods, the nature of great-power competition in the Cold War limited the role of financial competition. The United States and the USSR prepared for a short, high-intensity conflict, one that could start with almost no warning at all. Therefore, every resource either power hoped to use had to be in place the moment the war began, so stockpiling weapons and other supplies became the top priority. The ability to maintain liquid reserves to purchase supplies in an ongoing conflict was unimportant for the two major powers, pushing finance domain issues to the back burner. Allies and dependent states, such as NATO or Warsaw Pact countries, also sought to lay everything in store, although their struggle for liquidity was usually focused on terms of trade or economic support from the two superpowers.

An American textbook looking at the Soviet economy notes that "the volume of Soviet foreign trade was significantly less than one would find in market economies at similar levels of economic development." This lag by the USSR was the result of a combination of the implementation of a command economy and a distrust of capitalism, which in turn led to a bent toward autarkic or quasi-autarkic trade patterns. The fact that the Soviet currency, the ruble, was not convertible meant the USSR was required to balance trade with each of its Council for Mutual Economic Assistance (COMECON) partners such as Albania and Cuba, most of whom were financially dependent to some degree on the USSR.[32] The USSR was a remarkable throwback in its imperial approach to trade and finance, in some ways looking more like the Inca or Aztec Empires than any major European power since the 1600s. However, the USSR did avail itself of some tools of the finance domain, using markets and trade to protect its interests, borrow and trade on world markets, and gather intelligence.

As with the United States, the USSR used economic power to build alliances and partnerships. Since the USSR had outlawed private investment, any flow of resources to another country was government controlled and tended to be in the form of loans rather than grants. As of the mid-1960s, the standard conditions for one of these loans was a twelve-year term paying 2.5 percent interest. When the USSR did provide aid to its client states, it was frequently in the form of a barter arrangement, with the USSR trading military technology or a major civil engineering project for specific local commodities.[33] Also similar to the United States, this aid was a form of soft power to win cooperation from countries with particular strategic value such as Indonesia. The greatest successes were dramatic and remain famous—the Aswan Dam being the prime example—but the number of planned projects that actually came to fruition was low; for example, only 11 percent in the case of Indonesia in the 1950s and early 1960s. And because almost all Soviet aid was in kind, any equipment that survived the transit intact was likely to be climatically inappropriate, such as the aid package of tractors with sealed, heated cabs sent to sub-Saharan Guinea and Mali, an act that prompted a commentator to remark that at least they did not send snowplows. All foreign aid has limitations, and the history of US aid has numerous stories of such mishaps, but overall it appears that Soviet financial and trade limitations translated into a less successful imposition of soft power, compared to its US adversaries.[34]

Although the USSR had relatively low levels of trade with the US-led financial commons, it was not zero. Dating back to the revolution, the USSR owned banks in Europe and used them to handle trade and financial flows. Indeed, one of them, Banque Commerciale pour l'Europe du Nord (BCEN or Eurobank), is believed to have been an early core of the eurodollar market, keeping Soviet dollar assets in Paris-based accounts to protect them from US seizure.[35] Economic engagement with the West was high at the end of World War II, fell (but still accounted for about one-seventh of all trade for the 1950s and 1960s), and rebounded with détente in the 1970s. By the 1980s, Soviet hard currency trade was about $30 billion a year—about 5 percent—in an economy producing probably less than $600 billion per year. The trade gave the Soviets access to grain to supplement poor harvests and to maintain access to high technology coming out of the West. In addition, as a gold-producing nation, the USSR could remedy short-term liquidity problems by selling gold. Finally, one-third to one-half of hard currency imports in any particular year were paid for with oil and gas exports, and the Soviets rode the high 1973–1986 energy price wave to a certain level of financial stability.

This USSR dependence on exports to prop up its economy created a profound degree of vulnerability, however, and the fall in oil prices in 1986 seems to have forced Moscow to drastically tighten its belt, which contributed to the fall of the USSR.[36] While the Soviet collapse had other sources, including the war in Afghanistan, a sclerotic domestic industrial economy that could not innovate at the same rate as its Western competitors, and a regime survival strategy out of place with global trends on human rights, the financial austerity undoubtedly played a significant role in the economic and political pressure that preceded the dissolution of the USSR.[37] In short, the lack of sophisticated tools for managing and manipulating the finance domain is one of the reasons for the USSR's inability to compete with the United States in the late Cold War, and led to its eventual downfall.

Europe and the Adaptation of the Bretton Woods RFA

At the end of World War II, Europe was in a state of collapse. Competition in the finance domain—in any domain—was a practical impossibility for the former great powers of the previous four centuries. Indeed, it was those centuries of competition that had brought European states to this pass. The two superpowers had, however, brought with them new paradigms for state behavior focused more on cooperation than competition. One of these superpowers, the United States, was able to reify such a paradigm through the Bretton Woods RFA, and the overwhelmed states of Europe were in no position to challenge it. So European states capitalized on the Bretton Woods RFA and associated institutions like the United Nations that were explicitly designed to encourage financial recovery through cooperation and adapted the ideas to create institutions of their own to further promote peace and prosperity on their continent. A key piece of this project was the development of a common economic market and currency to facilitate trade and other financial transactions across borders.

A benchmark in the formation of the European Union (EU) was the Schuman Declaration of 1950, a compact binding together France, West Germany, Italy, the Netherlands, Belgium, and Luxembourg with an agreement to create a common market for coal and steel production, two materials critical for rebuilding economies and waging war.[38] This effort was relatively successful, playing a role in Europe's economic recovery and the maintenance of political stability throughout the remainder of the twentieth century. Once the Bretton Woods fixed exchange system ended, a natural evolution for the EU was to develop its own currency: transfer costs associated with currency exchange across the community produced a deadweight loss in trade productivity. By replacing existing currencies and thus eliminating transfer costs, the euro would increase trade productivity, economic integration, and consequently political integration. The euro would also provide policymakers at the center of the EU with additional tools to discipline and manage the economic policies of member states (although not sufficient for effective macroeconomic stabilization). Finally, the euro offered Europe the chance to create an alternative to financial hegemony of the dollar, as the reduction in political tensions with the USSR in the late 1980s gave Europe greater flexibility to find its own geostrategic path.[39]

The euro was established in 1992 and officially adopted on December 31, 1998, when it replaced the currency of eleven European countries, creating a currency zone that could rival the United States in size and prosperity.[40] An additional part of this effort was the June 1998 establishment of the European Central Bank (ECB), which managed the currency with a writ that focused on inflation and on the monitoring of national economic policy. Unlike most other central banks, the ECB had no explicit security or defense role, in large part because the armed forces remained the responsibility of the individual member national governments.[41] Since 1999, eight other countries have been added to the eurozone, although (as we show in the next chapter) maintaining the euro has become socially and politically fraught, and the euro has yet to rival the political power of the dollar.[42]

The Developing World and the Cold War Financial System

Many states were not comfortably in either the US or Soviet camp, however, or shifted their position over the Cold War. For some states, the new system meant a return to more traditional modes of financing military operations, in particular support from stronger states and sales of raw materials. Leaders or governments-in-exile would woo the leadership of a superpower for financial support. Jonas Savimbi's National Union for the Total Independence of Angola (UNITA) rebels in Angola, for example, leveraged the combination of Cold War politics and the relatively recently created art of public relations to use the infamous Washington firm of Black, Manafort, Stone, and Kelly to lobby the US Congress for foreign aid to attempt to unseat the Soviet- and Cuban-backed regime.[43] But for a range of countries, the Cold War meant an idiosyncratic path to sufficient financial resources. Here, we offer a representative selection of accounts from the group of states Brazil, Russia, India, China, and South Africa (now referred to as BRICS) intended to illustrate the range of strategies that developing countries pursued to manage their position in the finance domain.[44]

China

One of the most important stories of this period involves the development of the Chinese financial system since the late 1940s, when the People's Bank of China (PBOC) was founded in 1948 and the Chinese Communist Party (CCP) seized power in 1949. Under a Maoist system and before the reforms of Deng Xiaoping of the late 1970s, "the PBOC was a mere subordinate to the Ministry of Finance (MOF) and a cashier of the government under the central planning regime."[45] As a closed, centrally planned economy, China insulated itself for the most part from international financial influence. This insulation was no guarantee of smooth financial operations, however: in the 1950s, the CCP attempted in vain to use the PBOC to direct local enterprises in support of planning goals. This attempt failed because of a lack of well-trained personnel and a lack of an organizational structure that could allow top PBOC leadership to manage local efforts. The failure of the mid-1950s reforms seems to have led to the use of the PBOC as effectively a political actor; instead of using banking and finance knowledge to guide local economic growth, the technical knowledge became a backstop to support initiatives already under way. This arrangement did not change between 1956 and the beginning of additional reforms in 1978.[46]

As a result of these failures, among other factors, the first decades of CCP rule were financially disastrous. Carl Walter and Frazier Howie relate a story that, after the opening of China, Deng Xiaoping and other senior officials needed hard currency for travel to New York to speak at the United

Nations, but the nation's coffers were so depleted that after withdrawing everything to be found in the banks, state-owned financial enterprises, and government ministries "they could scrape together only US$38,000."[47] Despite its poverty and other competitive disadvantages, China attempted to strengthen its position as a rising power by lending strategically throughout the second half of the twentieth century.[48] The reforms Deng spearheaded led to enormous economic growth and expansion in a relatively short time—its hard currency reserves alone went from a mere $38,000 in hard currency in the 1970s to $3 trillion forty years later, a real increase of over seven orders of magnitude.[49] As we will see in the next two chapters, it is in the twenty-first century that Chinese activity in the finance domain really took off.

India

After India formally declared its independence from the United Kingdom in 1947, its external debt increased rapidly and its debt service ratio went from effectively zero in the early 1950s to 30 percent by the late 1960s. As a founding member of the nonaligned "third way" bloc, India maintained a certain rhetorical independence from the two superpowers that allowed it to borrow from the United States, from its former colonial master the United Kingdom, from the USSR, and from the Bretton Woods Institutions established specifically to help stabilize financially vulnerable states. This independence had its drawbacks as well, as despite India's careful work fostering multiple sources of loans there was a continuous tension between its effort to foster internal development and its competition with neighboring powers. Specifically, India's aggressive use of external debt for internal development made it vulnerable to US and World Bank pressure with regard to its foreign policy. Not only did the Sino-Indian War and Indo-Pakistani War of the 1960s create substantial expenses, but the United States cut off aid in response to the war with Pakistan, likely the precipitant for the Indira Gandhi administration's devaluation of the rupee in 1966.[50] India had changed its borrowing strategy by the early 1980s to lessen foreign influence on its finances, borrowing more from private sources than government ones, thereby reducing its dependence on the United States, United Kingdom, and the rapidly collapsing USSR. Apparently, Feis and Viner's plan for using Bretton Woods Institutions succeeded in this instance, giving India space to build state capacity: by the early 1990s, roughly India's peak period of borrowing, it had switched to borrowing more from private sources than state-backed ones.[51]

South Africa

Since the formation of the Union of South Africa in 1910, the nation's armed forces alternated their attention between internal and external threats. Between World War II and the early 1960s, the military more than tripled its manpower and focused on violently suppressing internal dissent. After the Sharpeville uprising and subsequent massacre in 1960, international protests over the South African government's apartheid policies began to threaten the country's access to arms with the first UN arms embargo in 1963. South Africa compensated for the subsequent weapons shortage by beginning to substantially invest in domestic arms manufacturing. As South Africa continued to use force to solve its internal security problems, and as a result became a pariah state in the eyes of the international community, the South African government increasingly used military responses to crises in neighboring Angola and Namibia in the 1970s, which in turn required an increase in financing. As the real price of gold increased over the 1970s, South Africa was able to finance its defense budget though a complicated mixture of policies and so did not have to accumulate excessive debt. The combination of the fall in the price of gold at the opening of the 1980s and aggressive economic and financial pressure from the United States during the 1980s, including a July 1985 Chase Manhattan Bank demand for the immediate repayment of all its loans to South African entities, however, knocked the legs out from under the apartheid regime. Unable to finance its armed forces and increasingly isolated from the global economy, the apartheid regime yielded power in 1994.[52] Ultimately, South Africa's subsequent regime overhaul created the opportunity for it to be welcomed back into the community of nations and given renewed access to the financial commons.

Pan-Africa and International Lending

A striking pattern over the 1970s and 1980s is the overall growth in international sovereign lending, fueled in large part by eurocurrency accounts. In Africa especially, this trend contributed to increasing government deficits across the continent, with total external debt rising from about $8 billion in 1970 to about seven-and-a-half times that by 1987.[53] Expert opinion in African states and international organizations since 1979 held that debt was building up in problematic ways, an opinion expressed with increasing force as time wore on and the debts mounted.[54] The mix of debt sources changed considerably between 1970 and the late 1980s, as the market that had been dominated by private lenders in the 1970s shifted to bilateral government loans and financing by Bretton Woods RFA organizations like the World Bank and the International Monetary Fund, loans that continued to grow in the 1980s even as private sources dried up.

The result of this shift was in part to further destabilize African debtor states by these institutions' insistence on making austerity measures a condition of loan repayment or debt forgiveness, making a region in the process of decolonizing that much more chaotic.[55] That both the United States and the USSR used this decolonization process as an opportunity to fight proxy wars in Eritrea, Zimbabwe, Angola, Chad, Ethiopia, and Mozambique, among others, led to knock-on effects like an increase in arms purchases across the continent in the late 1970s and a general increase in intrastate armed conflict in Africa that continued from the mid-1970s to 2021.[56] Add to that instability the exacerbating effect of African dictators such as Mobutu Sese Seko of the Congo and their cronies siphoning off billions of dollars in loans from the public coffers to personally enrich themselves, and Léonce Ndikumana and James Boyce's 2010 estimate that capital flight from sub-Saharan Africa between 1970 and 2004 totaled at least $443 billion, and we can appreciate the extent to which the Bretton Woods RFA in Africa has been a mixed blessing at best.[57]

The Latin American Debt Crisis: A New Dollar Diplomacy?

A seismic shift occurred in the relationship between the United States and its Latin American "good neighbors" with the creation of nationalized oil companies in states like Venezuela and Argentina in the mid–twentieth century. These nationalized companies, as well as other smaller independent private firms, broke the chokehold the "seven sisters"—Chevron, Exxon, Gulf, Mobil, Texaco, British Petroleum, and Royal Dutch Shell—held on the market during the first half of the twentieth century; by 1972, a market that had effectively been an oligopoly was transformed by the entry of 300 independent firms and 50 nationalized ones.[58]

Part of this change is due to the shift in thinking that brought about the Bretton Woods RFA, and the US-led international community's emphasis on promotion of democracy and capitalism. This movement would not have had much impact, however, if it were not accompanied by a significant increase in oil prices: a barrel of crude oil jumped from an average of $16.64 in 2021 US dollars between 1946 and 1973 to an average of $65.71 between 1974 and 1990.[59] As a result of the price jump and the resultant boom in oil production, banks in New York and London came under pressure to expand lending to international partners because of the need to profitably attract and maintain deposits from now wealthy oil-producing countries, and, as with Africa, much of this was coming via eurocurrency accounts. Money flowed into Latin American government accounts, leading to a spree in infrastructure spending. As most Latin American countries were commodity producers at the time, they attempted to service these loans by increasing commodity production. Combined with the 1982 recession (which drove down demand), this had the predictable effect of glutting the commodity markets, resulting in depressed prices and the threat of loan defaults across Latin America.

In contrast with the relatively laissez faire attitude adopted by the United States in the 1920s, Washington regarded the potential for default in Latin

America as an economic and a political crisis, with the twin threats of global recession and losing Latin America to Soviet influence uppermost in the US government's mind in the early 1980s.[60] As a result, the US government pressured domestic and foreign banks to accept restructuring of loans and debt forgiveness plans for Latin American governments to ease the immediate burden and buy time.[61] The International Monetary Fund then stepped in to provide relief and restructuring to several Latin American countries during the 1990s under the condition that the countries accept austerity and reform their economies in more market-friendly directions. As in Africa, however, these austerity programs combined with corrupt leadership of several Latin American countries to worsen conditions economically and politically as governments were forced to cut domestic spending to service loans for infrastructure projects that never occurred. In the end, Latin America was not "lost" to the USSR because the USSR had ceased to exist, but the impact of decades of poor decisions and squandered wealth was severe nevertheless.

Conclusion

The Bretton Woods RFA had two major components: the financial system based on a new gold standard; and the creation of a network of organizations dedicated to promoting the expansion of prosperity, political stability, and international cooperation. While the financial system did not survive the United States' entry into the Vietnam War, the innovations of the era extended past 1973 and into the twenty-first century as the institutions of financial stabilization and coordination remained largely the same. While the Bretton Woods gold standard may not have survived, the management institutions that did ensured that radical changes and innovations that occurred in finance across the globe - including eurocurrency markets, securitization, a shift to more open capital accounts and flexible exchange rates - would not destabilize the finance domain. In the 1980s the United States, Japan, and Western Europe weathered a series of financial crises in ways that suggested the development of new tools of financial management, even as governments moved ideologically away from state intervention.

After 1992, the collapse of the Soviet Union made clear the dominance of the United States as a military and financial hegemon. After 2001, the US government became increasingly aware of the lethality of the financial tools that it possessed, turning these tools toward the monitoring of terrorist finances and smart sanctions to undermine the capability of rogue states to use money. In 2008, the United States used its financial might in ways both delicate and overwhelming to prevent the wholesale collapse of the global financial system, while at the same time employing the same tools to neutralize violent nonstate actors. We discuss these changes and their impact in the next chapter on the digital RFA.

Notes

1. Named after the Mount Washington Hotel in Bretton Woods, New Hampshire, where the conference establishing the system took place during July 1–22, 1944; Ikenberry, G. John. 2020. *A World Safe for Democracy: Liberal Internationalism and the Crises of Global Order*. New Haven: Yale University Press.
2. Gavin, Francis J., 2002. "The Gold Battles Within the Cold War: American Monetary Policy and the Defense of Europe, 1960–1963." *Diplomatic History* 26 (1): 61–94; Zimmermann, Hubert. 2002. *Money and Security: Troops, Monetary Policy, and West Germany's Relations with the United States and Britain, 1950–1971*. Cambridge: Cambridge University Press.
3. Keynes, John Maynard. 2018. *The Economic Consequences of the Peace*. London: Routledge. See also Feis, Herbert. 1951. "Keynes in Retrospect." *Foreign Affairs* 29 (4): 564–577: 564–568.
4. Skidelsky, Robert. 2000. *John Maynard Keynes: Fighting for Britain, 1937–46*. London: Macmillan; Ikenberry, G. John. 2007. "The Political Origins of Bretton Woods." In *A Retrospective on the Bretton Woods System*, edited by Michael D. Bordo and Barry Eichengreen, 155–198. Chicago: University of Chicago Press.
5. Bordo, Michael D. 2007a. "The Bretton Woods International Monetary System: A Historical Overview." In *A Retrospective on the Bretton Woods System: Lessons for International Monetary Reform* edited by Michael D. Bordo and Barry Eichengreen, 5. Chicago: University of Chicago Press. Another issue driving the design of the system was concern for economic development, see Helleiner, Eric. 2014. *Forgotten Foundations of Bretton Woods: International Development and the Making of the Postwar Order*. Ithaca: Cornell University Press.
6. Ikenberry 2007: 157.
7. As discussed in Chapter 7, recent work has suggested that devaluations, while disruptive in some ways, on net improved the international situation.
8. Chapter 7 has a more full discussion of the mutiny and other related issues.
9. This analysis of the problems of the interwar period was not universally accepted, however. Monetarists like Milton Friedman argue that it was actually government intervention in the currency markets that destabilized the money supply rather than the floating rates. Less dogmatic economists like Barry Eichengreen and Michael D. Bardo argue that the problems were caused more by adherence to the gold standard rather than the weaknesses of the system created by that standard. For more, see Bordo 2007a: 28–31.
10. An equivalent figure in 2022 would be over $5 trillion.
11. Bordo 2007a: 32–37.
12. Harry Dexter White was also a Soviet spy, although this probably had no impact on his actions at Bretton Woods.
13. Bordo 2007a: 32–37.
14. *New York Times*. 1972. "Herbert Feis, Historian, Dies; Awarded Pulitzer Prize in '61." March 3, 43. Nerozzi, Sebastiano. 2011. "From the Great Depression to Bretton Woods: Jacob Viner and International Monetary Stabilization (1930–1945)." *European Journal of the History of Economic Thought* 18 (1): 55–84, 56; Nerozzi, Sebastiano. 2009. "Building Up a Multilateral Strategy for the United States: Alvin Hansen, Jacob Viner, and the Council on Foreign Relations (1939–45)." In *American Power and Policy* edited by Martin S. Alexander and William J. Philpott, 24–68, at 27. London: Palgrave Macmillan.
15. On their friendship, see Nerozzi 2009: 70n.
16. Nerozzi 2009: 42–45.
17. Nerozzi 2011: 78–79.

18. Viner, Jacob. 1947. "International Finance in the Postwar World." *Journal of Political Economy* 55 (2): 97–107, at 102.
19. See, for example, Viner, Jacob. 1944. "The Economic Problem." In *New Perspectives on Peace,* edited by George B. De Huszar, 13-45. Chicago: University of Chicago Press.
20. Bordo 2007a: 3–4.
21. Gavin, Francis J. 2004. *Dollars and Power: The Politics of International Monetary Relations, 1958–1971.* Chapel Hill: University of North Carolina Press, 59.
22. As is generally true with leverage issues, there was no clear ratio of external dollar liabilities to US gold stock at which point a crisis would develop; in fact, external dollar liabilities were greater than US monetary gold stock by 1959, and external liabilities held by monetary authorities were greater than gold stock by 1964. Bordo 2007a: figure 1.10 at 39, and discussion at 55–56.
23. Bordo 2007a: 55–58.
24. Gavin 2004.
25. Bordo 2007a: figure 1.10 on page 39.
26. For a discussion of various theories, see Bordo, Michael D., and Barry Eichengreen. 2013. "Bretton Woods and the Great Inflation." In *The Great Inflation: The Rebirth of Modern Central Banking,* edited by Michael D. Bordo and Athanasios Orphanides, 449-498. Chicago: University of Chicago Press; Meltzer, Allan H. 2013. *Comment on Bretton Woods and the Great Inflation.* Comment c9175. Cambridge MA: NBER.
27. For a discussion of the transition, Eichengreen, Barry. 2011. *Exorbitant Privilege: The Rise and Fall of the Dollar and the Future of the International Monetary System.* Cary: Oxford University Press. Regarding the increased role of the dollar, Izetzki, Ethan, Carmen M. Reinhart, and Kenneth S. Rogoff. 2017. *Exchange Arrangements Entering The 21st Century: Which Anchor Will Hold?* Cambridge MA: NBER.
28. Reinhart, Carmen, and Jacob Kirkegaard. 2012. "Financial Repression: Then and Now." VoxEU, 16; Diaz-Alejandro, Carlos, 1985. "Good-Bye Financial Repression, Hello Financial Crash." *Journal of Development Economics* 19 (1–2): 1–24.
29. Midlands Bank seems to have started eurocurrency trading with a series of foreign exchange operations that allowed it to borrow dollar deposits at 50 basis points less than the UK bank rate. See Schenk, Catherine R., 1998. "The Origins of the Eurodollar Market in London: 1955–1963." *Explorations in Economic History.* 35 (2): 221–238; de Grauwe, Paul. 1975. "The Development of the Euro-Currency Market." *Finance and Development* 12 (3): 12–17. Altamura, Carlo Edoardo. 2017. "The Paradox of the 1970s: The Renaissance of International Banking and the Rise of Public Debt." *Journal of Modern European History* 15 (4): 529–553; Griffith-Jones, S. 1980. "The Growth of Multinational Banking, the Euro-Currency Market and Their Effects on Developing Countries." *The Journal of Development Studies* 16 (2): 204–223. For a discussion of the role of European dollar accounts and transactions in the 2008 crisis, see Tooze, Adam. 2018. *Crashed: How a Decade of Financial Crises Changed the World.* London: Penguin. There may have been Soviet banks using eurodollars before Midlands, see Author Redacted. 1975. *The Changing Role of Soviet-Owned Banks in the West.* Central Intelligence Agency.
30. A recent discussion of the process is Bordo, Michael D., Eric Monnet, and Alain Naef. 2019. "The Gold Pool (1961–1968) and the Fall of the Bretton Woods System: Lessons for Central Bank Cooperation." *Journal of Economic History* 79 (4): 1027–1059.
31. Rockoff, Hugh. 2012. *America's Economic Way of War: War and the Economy from the Spanish-American War to the Persian Gulf War.* Cambridge: Cambridge University Press.

32. Gregory, Paul, and Robert Stuart. 1994. *Soviet and Post-Soviet Economic Structure and Performance.* New York: HarperCollins, 210–216.
33. Gulhati, Ravi I. 1972. "India's External Debt." *India Quarterly* 28 (1): 3–11, at 5–6.
34. Holbik, Karel. 1968. "A Comparison of US and Soviet Foreign Aid, 1961–1965." *Weltwirtschaftliches Archiv* 100 (2): 320–340; Boden, Ragna. 2008. "Cold War Economics: Soviet Aid to Indonesia." *Journal of Cold War Studies* 10 (3): 110–128; Goldman, Marshall I. 1965. "A Balance Sheet of Soviet Foreign Aid." *Foreign Affairs* 43 (2): 349–360.
35. Author Redacted CIA (Central Intelligence Ageency). 1975. "The Changing Role of Soviet-Owned Banks in the West."
36. McIntyre, Joan. 1987. "The USSR's Hard Currency Trade and Payments Position." *Gorbachev's Economic Plans* 2: 474–488; Gregory and Stuart 1994: 210–216. Size of 1980s Soviet economy extrapolated from FRED2 data series "Gross Domestic Product for Russian Federation (MKTGDPRUA646NWDB)."
37. Easterly, William, and Stanley Fischer. 1994. "What We Can Learn from the Soviet Collapse." *Finance and Development* 31 (4): 2–7.
38. European Union Home Page. 2023. "Principles, Countries, History."
39. Dinan, Desmond. 1994. *Ever Closer Union.* Boulder: Lynne Rienner, 454.
40. Belgium, Denmark, France, Germany, Greece, Ireland, Italy, Luxembourg, Portugal, Spain, the Netherlands, and the United Kingdom.
41. Dinan 1994: 469.
42. Austria, Finland, Slovenia, Cyprus, Malta, Slovak Republic, Estonia, Latvia, and Lithuania.
43. Brogan, Pamela. 1992. *The Torturers' Lobby.* Washington DC: Center for Public Integrity.
44. BRICS states include Brazil, Russia, India, China, and South Africa.
45. Bell, Stephen. 2013. *The Rise of the People's Bank of China.* Cambridge: Harvard University Press, 7.
46. Walter, Carl E. 1985. "Dual Leadership and the 1956 Credit Reforms of the People's Bank of China." *China Quarterly* 101: 277–290. Carl Walter notes (at 283 and 283n) that that the PBOC had 300,000 employees in the 1950s, of which only 3,000 had been trained at a college level, and another 5,000–6,000 had been trained at the high school level, for any type of banking work. There were 20,000 employees deployed in the mid-1950s to work with local enterprises.
47. Walter, Carl, and Fraser Howie. 2012. *Red Capitalism: The Fragile Financial Foundation of China's Extraordinary Rise,* Hoboken: Wiley, 3. Carl Walter more pungently describes the situation in 1978 in an interview for the Asia Society: "When I say that China was bankrupt in 1978–9, it was bankrupt. If you look at all the statistics books and so on, they go back to then and they don't go before. There was nothing before then." Carl E. Walter interviewed by Ben Stone for the Asia Society's China Boom Project, August 10, 2010.
48. Horn, Sebastian, Carmen M. Reinhart, and Christoph Trebesch. 2021. "China's Overseas Lending." *Journal of International Economics* 133: 1–32.
49. For Chinese currency reserves, see International Monetary Fund, Total Reserves excluding Gold for China [TRESEGCNM052N], retrieved from FRED, Federal Reserve Bank of St. Louis; https://fred.stlouisfed.org/series/TRESEGCNM052N, April 12, 2023. For a discussion of Deng Xiaoping's reforms, see Hofman, Bert. 2018. *Reflections on Forty Years of China's Reforms.* Washington, DC: World Bank.
50. Gulhati 1972: 3–11; Brecher, Michael. 1977. "India's Devaluation of 1966: Linkage Politics and Crisis Decision-Making." *Review of International Studies* 3 (1): 1–25.

51. Bajpai, Nirupam. 1994. "India's External Debt: Retrospect and Prospects." *Economic and Political Weekly,* 2232–2245. See table 2 and compare to table II in Gulhati 1972. For borrowing as a percent of gross national income (GNI), see *World Bank Data.* 2023. "External debt stocks (% of GNI), India".

52. Goedhuys, Diederik. 1994. "South African Monetary Policy in the 1980s: Years of Reform and Foreign Financial Aggression." *South African Journal of Economic History* 9 (2): 145–164; Aron, Janine, Ibrahim Elbadawi, and Brian Kahn. 1997. *Determinants of the Real Exchange Rate in South Africa.* Oxford: Centre for the Study of African Economies, Institute of Economics and Statistics, University of Oxford; Batchelor, Peter, Paul Dunne, and Guy Lamb. 2002. "The Demand for Military Spending in South Africa." *Journal of Peace Research* 39 (3): 339–354.

53. Simson, Rebecca. 2019. "Africa's Clientelist Budget Policies Revisited: Public Expenditure and Employment in Kenya, Tanzania and Uganda, 1960–2010." *Economic History Review* 72 (4): 1409–1438; Ndikumana, Léonce, and James Boyce. 1998. "Congo's Odious Debt: External Borrowing and Capital Flight in Zaire." *Development and Change* 29 (2): 195–217.

54. Curry, Robert L. 1979. "Africa's External Debt Situation." *Journal of Modern African Studies* 17 (1): 15–28; Greene, Joshua. 1989. "The External Debt Problem of Sub-Saharan Africa." *IMF Staff Papers* 36 (4): 836–874; Greene, Joshua E., and Mohsin S. Khan. 1990. *African Debt Crisis.* Nairobi: Initiatives.

55. Curry 1979: 1528, table 3; Greene 1989.

56. Batchelor, Dunne, and Lamb 2002: 339–354, figure 2. More detailed numbers available on request, based on Stockholm International Peace Research Institute (SIPRI) arms import data from *World Bank Data* 2023 at "Arms imports (SIPRI trend indicator values)—Sub-Saharan Africa (excluding high income)"; and debt levels from Greene 1989.

57. McGowan, Patrick J. 2003. "African Military Coups D'état, 1956–2001: Frequency, Trends, and Distribution." *The Journal of Modern African Studies* 41 (3): 339–370, table 2 and figure 1; Collier, Paul, and Anke Hoeffler. 2002. "On the Incidence of Civil War in Africa." *Journal of Conflict Resolution* 46 (1): 13–28, figure 1; Palik, Julia, Anne Marie Obermeier, and Siri Aas Rustad. 2022. *Conflict Trends in Africa, 1989–2021.* Working Paper. Oslo: Peace Research Institute Oslo (PRIO); Dessy, Sylvain E., and Desire Vencatachellum. 2007. "Debt Relief and Social Services Expenditure: The African Experience, 1989–2003." *African Development Review* 19 (1): 200–216; Dainoff, Charles. 2021. *Outlaw Paradise: Why Countries Become Tax Havens.* Lanham, MD: Lexington Books; Cobham, Alex, and Petr Jansky. 2020. *Estimating Illicit Financial Flows: A Critical Guide to the Data, Methodologies, and Findings.* Oxford: Oxford University Press.

58. Kobrin, Stephen J. 1985. "Diffusion as an Explanation of Oil Nationalization: Or the Domino Effect Rides Again." *Journal of Conflict Resolution* 29 (3): 3–32.

59. British Petroleum. 2022. "Statistical Review of World Energy–Commodity Prices."

60. Sheinin, David. 1999. "The New Dollar Diplomacy in Latin America." *American Studies International* 37 (3): 81–99.

61. Sims, Jocelyn, and Jessie Romero. 2013. "Latin American Debt Crisis of the 1980s." *Federal Reserve History,* November 22.

9

The Digital Revolution in Financial Affairs

We've said all along, and I've told Putin to his face more than a month ago, that we would act together and the moment Russia moved against Ukraine. Russia has now undeniably moved against Ukraine by declaring these independent states.

So today, I'm announcing the first tranche of sanctions to impose costs on Russia in response to their actions yesterday. These have been closely coordinated with our allies and partners. We will continue to escalate sanctions if Russia escalates. We're implementing full blocking sanctions on two large Russian financial institutions, VEB and their military bank.

We're implementing sanctions on Russia's sovereign debt. That means we've cut off Russia's government from western financing. It can no longer raise money from the West and cannot trade in its new debt on our markets or European markets either.

Starting tomorrow, and continuing in the days ahead, we'll also impose sanctions on Russia's elites and their family members. They share in the corrupt gains of the Kremlin policies and should share in the pain as well.

—Joe Biden, as quoted by Azi Paybarah, *New York Times*, 2022[1]

On July 2, 2021, the US Department of the Treasury's Office of Foreign Assets Control (OFAC) launched an attack on individuals in the junta government of Myanmar.[2] This attack was a follow-up on the issuing of Executive Order (EO) 14014 earlier that year on February 12, in which US president Joe Biden ordered—among other actions—that the US-held bank accounts or other possessions of anyone involved in the coup of February 2 in overturning a democratic election from the previous November were to be frozen. This EO included everyone involved in the coup, anyone working for the junta after February 2, anyone involved in human rights abuses connected with the coup, and anyone related to any of these individuals such that they would attempt to circumvent this order.[3]

The July attack was part of a multipronged coordinated assault on the Myanmar junta, including the Department of Commerce's Bureau of Industry and Security (BIS) adding four Myanmarese companies to its Entity List.[4] The BIS uses the list to restrict export and in-country transfer activity of persons (both individual and corporate) "reasonably believed to be involved, or to pose a significant risk of becoming involved, in activities contrary to the national security or foreign policy interests of the United States."[5] Adding the companies was a follow-up to BIS actions in the wake of the coup, which included export restrictions placed on what the BIS classifies as "sensitive items"; that is, weapons and military technology. BIS took these actions to ensure that the junta—which has killed nearly 900 Myanmarese civilians and displaced 200,000 more, according to UN High Commissioner for Human Rights Michelle Bachelet—did not get stronger militarily, or that Myanmarese companies—or their investors or customers—were not profiting from the coup.[6]

OFAC's attack on July 2 added to this campaign. They placed twenty-two people on the Specially Designated Nationals (SDN) List, all of whom were connected to the junta.[7] Being placed on the SDN List means that these individuals lose control of any property they own, either directly or indirectly, in the United States, as well as any property they own that is controlled by US citizens, and any property in which they own a majority share. In addition, individuals on the SDN List are prohibited from making any financial or commercial transactions within the United States, transiting the United States, or with "US persons" (meaning, in this case, both individual and corporate). This last section is the most important, as it prohibits people on the SDN List from using branches of US-based banks and, in effect, using the US financial system at all.[8] The purpose of the combined attacks by the US government on the Burmese junta was not just to express anger at the subversion of democracy in Myanmar and the ensuing human rights abuses, but also to weaken the regime and make it possible for opposition to retake control of the government. In effect, the United States is using its financial power to effect political change in other countries. That is to say, the United States employed the tools of financial statecraft to achieve foreign policy goals. The United States would not be able to achieve these goals without weaponizing the financial interdependence Myanmar has with it. In this chapter, we survey the current array of financial tools the United States can use to further its foreign policy interests. These tools comprise the digital revolution in financial affairs (RFA) and represent the ways in which advances in computing and telecommunications have enabled the sort of instant transmission of information—as well as the instant monitoring of those transmissions—that have fundamentally changed the global financial system in the twenty-first century. This chapter also focuses in depth on the use of the digital RFA in combatting the Russian invasion of Ukraine in February 2022.

Twenty-First Century Financial Statecraft

The US Joint Doctrine Note 1-18 discusses strategy as a blueprint for a state to employ the instruments of power at its disposal to achieve its policy objectives. The note defines these instruments as traditionally defined as diplomatic, informational, military, and economic (DIME). A newer, broader understanding of these instruments has led the national security community to include finance, intelligence, law, and development, leading to the more accurate if less catchy acronym for military, informational, diplomatic, financial, intelligence, economic, law, and development (MIDFIELD) (vii–viii).[9] This broader understanding of the instruments of state power creates a powerful incentive to understand how finance is used by states to advance their interests.

At this point, some review would be worthwhile. Statecraft involves the use of these instruments by a state to "pursue foreign policy," according to Benn Steil and Robert E. Litan. *Financial statecraft,* then, is the use of the flow of money into and out of the state to achieve that state's foreign policy goals. To properly understand exactly what this type of statecraft entails, it is useful to distinguish the tools of financial statecraft from those of economic statecraft.[10]

As Table 9.1 demonstrates, it is possible to conceive of financial statecraft as a subset of economic statecraft, but as we have argued the subject of financial statecraft itself a rich enough subject on its own to make it worthy of study. We believe the previous chapters establish as well that it is important and beneficial to think about issues using the finance domain lens, almost completely separate from the general ideas of economic statecraft for three reasons: (1) the speed with which financial issues affect state access to resources; (2) the strategic interdependence the financial commons creates; and (3) the focused institutional capacity required for success in finance. Given the ever increasing amount of money in circulation globally, as well as the diversity of opinion about the United States' current place in the global hierarchy of states and the role finance plays in securing the United States'

Table 9.1 Financial and Economic Statecraft Tools

Economic Statecraft	Financial Statecraft
Trade privileges, tariffs, and quotas	Capital flow guarantees and restrictions
Trade sanctions on states	Financial sanctions on nonstate actors
Foreign aid in drought and disaster	Underwriting debt in a foreign currency crisis
Regional trade agreements	Currency unions or dollarization

Source: Steil, Benn, and Robert E. Litan. 2006. *Financial Statecraft: The Role of Financial Markets in American Foreign Policy.* New Haven: Yale University Press, 4.

place, we likewise believe an understanding of financial statecraft is critical to appreciating the nature of US hegemony in the international system.

As the international financial system becomes larger, more complex, and more interdependent, more crucial is the centrality of the United States' position in this system and its role in helping to create it. In particular, the United States' ability to influence other states through the use of financial statecraft is driven by two conditions: (1) the importance of banks to the international financial system; and (2) the centrality of the dollar in the global financial system. Echoing Cicero on money and war, Juan C. Zarate observes that "banks are the ligaments of the international system."[11] According to the *Financial Times*'s research arm *The Banker*, the top 1,000 of the world's banks held $128 trillion in assets at the end of 2020, $20 trillion of which resides in US banks.[12] The 2017 World Bank Global Findex reports that roughly seven out of every ten adults—over 5.5 billion people—in the world have a bank account. That proportion rises to 94 percent in countries the World Bank classifies as "high-income economies,"[13] meaning that nearly every person over the age of fifteen has a bank account in the United States and its Group of 7 (G7) partners.[14] In addition, if this money moves across borders, there is a high probability it will be denominated in dollars and interact with the US financial system at some point.[15] According to the Bank for International Settlements, foreign exchange trading volume reached $6.6 trillion per day in April of 2019, with dollars being involved in at least one side of those trades 88 percent of the time, and nearly two-thirds of all foreign exchange reserves held in dollars.[16] In 2017, 80 percent of international trade involved the dollar.[17] While the majority of these dollars are held by banks outside of the United States, they are still highly dependent on US institutions. As Perry Mehrling notes, a network of central bank currency swap lines anchored by the Federal Reserve has expanded since the 2008 financial crisis, providing a critical dollar backstop to global finance.[18] While there have been shifts in the dollar's position since 1945, they have been, if anything, surprisingly minor.

If, like Henry Farrell and Abraham Newman, we apply network theory to our understanding of the centrality of US finance and the dollar in the way in which the international system operates, we see that the United States controls the central nodes of the global financial network, making it "uniquely positioned to impose costs"[19] on the other states in the network, and therefore project its power. Rather than use the blunter and more defensive instruments of mercantilism employed at the dawn of the modern finance domain, the United States uses a more complex and aggressive strategy embodied in the concept of "weaponized interdependence," which the next section of this chapter explores.[20] The remainder of the chapter discusses specific tools at the US government's disposal in weaponizing interdependence to achieve foreign policy goals; specifically, the accessing of financial messaging and payment systems, and the use of financial sanctions, with special attention given to the Society for Worldwide Interbank Financial Telecommunication (SWIFT) system and Section 311 of the USA PATRIOT Act, as well as a case study on sanctioning Russia in the wake of its 2022 invasion of Ukraine.

Payment Systems

As we have discussed in previous chapters, historically the use by states of financial destabilization as a foreign policy tool is common, although it generally involved counterfeiting the target state's currency, a tool which "unsettles its political and legal structures and undermines the state's ability to maintain internal order and security against external threats."[21] A recent example of this tactic was uncovered in the first decade of the twenty-first century, as the United States discovered that North Korea was counterfeiting approximately $45 million worth of $100 "supernotes" and circulating them.[22] However, new tools in the finance domain have given the United States far more sophisticated ways of destabilizing and otherwise interfering with the use of currency in the global financial commons.

Since the end of the twentieth century, the US government has harnessed the impact of globalization to use electronic payments systems for panopticon (mapping the system) and choke point (controlling the flow of assets) purposes. That the United States was at the center of the global interbank payment system network was no accident: payment system technology underwent a "harmonization" in the late 1990s as European Union (EU) states adopted the real-time gross settlement (RTGS) system modeled in part on the US-developed Fedwire system implemented in the 1970s.[23] By 2007, 93 of the world's 174 central banks were using the RTGS system, despite the utility emerging market states might have gained from adopting the cheaper and less onerous deferred net settlement (DNS) system. This harmonization is either an example of efficient technology diffusion and economies of scale, or of the United States and Europe exerting its financial hegemony, or both.[24]

A by-product of this harmonization is that it makes it easier for the US government to obtain information and enforce any choke point edicts. The use of the RTGS is so widespread that it has become, in Jennifer Jeffs's words, an "institutionalized underpinning for the global financial framework."[25] The real-time settlement of transactions means that there is less noise for analysts to sort through in the system in search of useful information; in addition, there is less information lost than there might be as transactions cross from one type to system to another. Between these network efficiencies and the central position the United States occupies in this network, the ease with which information can be harvested enables the United

States to operate from a position of strength with respect to other states in the system.

Messaging Systems

In addition to weaponizing the financial world's dependence on foreign exchange transaction systems, the United States has also used financial messaging systems to create panopticon and choke point effects that allow it to achieve foreign policy goals. Specifically, the most important system is SWIFT. From the beginning in 1973, SWIFT has been a cooperative effort by the world's major central banks, a level of cooperation that extends to its headquarters in Brussels, whose location was chosen "to sidestep the emerging rivalry between London and New York as the hub of global banking."[26]

SWIFT's messaging system is a primary component of the network that connects banks to each other around the world. It is an example of members of the international banking community coming together to create a public good that would allow them all to be more successful without privileging the leading banking centers of the day when it was created. SWIFT's structure reflects this ethos: not only is it headquartered in Brussels, but the lead overseer of the system is the National Bank of Belgium (NBB). Group of 10 (G-10) central banks provide additional oversight, including the Bank of Canada, Deutsche Bundesbank (Germany), European Central Bank (ECB),[27] Banque de France, Banca d'Italia, Bank of Japan, De Nederlandsche Bank (Netherlands), Sveriges Riksbank (Sweden), Swiss National Bank, Bank of England, and the Federal Reserve System (United States).[28]

SWIFT's success as an interbank messaging system has made it almost ubiquitous in the banking world. From its first message sent in 1977, SWIFT has grown exponentially to become, in Henry Farrell and Abraham Newman's words, "the dominant provider,"[29] increasing from 10 million messages sent in 1979, to 296 million in 1989, to over 1 billion in 1999, to nearly 6 billion by 2016 among over 11,000 banks in over 200 countries.[30] Although it is, as Joanna Diane Caytas notes, "just a secure messaging system that does not provide settlement," SWIFT is nevertheless a system without which banks around the world could not function.[31]

As the "the switchboard of the international financial system," it was perhaps only a matter of time before the United States chose to use its influence to weaponize SWIFT.[32] The United States had been sticking its nose under the tent in the 1990s, responding to the growing use of the international financial system by violent nonstate actors such as organized crime syndicates and terrorist groups to, in Thomas Oatley's words, "extra-territorialize US anti-money laundering law to safeguard the integrity of the American financial system."[33] This effort included the focused action of the

US Department of the Treasury's Office of Foreign Assets Control, explicitly designed to operationalize panopticon and choke point strategies through the observation of foreign persons both individual and corporate and, assuming OFAC found them a threat, either put them on the Specially Designated Nationals blacklist or froze any assets these persons had in US banks.[34] US government action grew in intensity after the September 11 terror attacks, as the United States moved to disrupt terrorist financing networks that utilized the international financial system, leveraging global sympathy in the wake of the attacks to gain increased access to networks, including SWIFT, to improve efforts to observe these financial flows and choke them off.

Section 311 and Other Sanctions Applied by the United States in the Twenty-First Century

Nearly universal outrage in the United States at the attacks al-Qaeda carried out on 9/11 coalesced into nearly universal support for government retaliatory measures. The George W. Bush administration took advantage of this support to create an entire new executive branch department, one of the largest and most ambitious expansions of government size and power in decades. In addition to creating the Department of Homeland Security, the USA PATRIOT Act—passed just six weeks after 9/11—included Section 311, which "allows for identifying customers using correspondent accounts, including obtaining information comparable to information obtained on domestic customers [panopticon] and prohibiting or imposing conditions on the opening or maintaining in the US of correspondent or payable-through accounts for a foreign banking institution [choke point]."[35]

Section 311 allowed the US government to further widen the scope of its search and ability to punish persons who were not US citizens and who resided outside the United States. This power was not wielded immediately or promiscuously; indeed, the US government did not use it until Boxing Day 2002, when it designated Ukraine and Nauru as "primary money laundering concerns" and even then revoked the designation by 2003 and 2008, respectively.[36] In November 2003, however, FinCEN designated Myanmar a primary money laundering concern and, as of this writing, has yet to rescind the designation, instead intensifying its attacks as discussed above. With the exceptions of North Korea and Iran, the 311 designation has been applied mainly to banks as opposed to countries.[37]

Exceptions they may be, but the campaigns against North Korea and Iran that included the 311 designation were successful in that they influenced both countries to briefly abandon the behaviors that led the international community to label them as pariah states, bringing them both back to the bargaining table to resume negotiations on limiting their nuclear programs and allowing for outside inspections.[38] These designations were part of a concentrated strategy on the part of the US Treasury Department to attack two-thirds of what President George W. Bush called the "axis of evil" in his 2002 State of the Union address by denying them access to the international financial system.[39] Indeed, the US government used the 311 designation and its leverage over the international banking system in its attack on Iran, creating a sanctions regime with the EU to prevent Iranian financial institutions from gaining access to SWIFT or any Iranian assets frozen in US institutions in 2012. Thus effectively frozen out of the international financial system, Iran returned to the bargaining table with the UN Security Council member countries and Germany to offer compliance in exchange for the lifting of the sanctions.[40]

Tax Havens: Dark Territories

Not every state was vulnerable to this system; there was one group that was able to more or less successfully resist US and Group of 20 (G-20) attempts to leverage financial interdependence against their interests: tax havens such as the Cayman Islands, Liechtenstein, and Samoa. According to a study conducted by Charles Dainoff, states that become tax havens do so in response to domestic economic pressures and external marketplace demand. Moreover, they do so even in the face of international disapproval and organized campaigns designed specifically to punish tax haven behavior, primarily because the cost borne from such campaigns by tax havens is significantly lower than the financial gains they reap from attracting foreign direct investment.

While the international community considers the tax avoidance and evasion that tax havens enable by persons both individual and corporate significant, the most serious problem tax havens create for the United States and the G-20 vis-à-vis financial interdependence is that they allow these persons to avail themselves of banking and corporate secrecy. This secrecy blunts the panopticon effect, allowing tax haven customers to obscure their actions from the sight of regulatory, taxation, and law enforcement organizations, as well as choking off capital flows into US and G-20 government coffers. These flows are significant: according to Annette Alstadsaeter, Niels Johannsen, and Gabriel Zucman, 10 percent of the world's wealth—around $40 trillion—is held in tax havens; in addition, according to International Monetary Fund (IMF) data, approximately 22 percent of annual foreign direct investment—around $480 billion dollars—flows through tax havens. With this much money appearing and disappearing at will, whatever panopticon and choke point effects the United States and the G-20 have through their manipulation of the international financial system are significantly blunted.[41]

The Financial War on Russia

The previous sections detail the components of the digital RFA and their use as tools of US finance domain operations and successful deployment against relatively isolated state actors like North Korea and Iran and nonstate actors like al-Qaeda. The Russian invasion of Ukraine in 2022 gives an example of these weapons used against a larger actor with a larger economy in a conflict centered around conventional kinetic operations and provides important new evidence regarding their strengths and weaknesses. The United States and its allies used tools of the finance domain in a coercive effort to change Russian policy toward Ukraine for nearly a decade of the twenty-first century. The effort began even before the Russia's 2014 invasion of Ukraine, but escalated in intensity after the seizure of Crimea and again following Russia's full invasion of Ukraine in February 2022. This campaign offers a unique lens into how modern states compete in the finance domain and how that competition relates to actions in other strategic domains.

Prelude

The United States began using tools of financial statecraft against Russia well before 2014. Generally suspected to be a tax haven for Russian government officials, oligarchs, and organized crime figures going back to the days of the USSR, Latvia was designated a "jurisdiction of primary concern" in a 2005 US Department of State International Narcotics Strategy Control Report (INSCR). The United States had not previously designated Russia as a whole under Section 311, although it had done so against banks that did business with Russia, including ABLV Bank, Multibanka, and VEF Banka, all headquartered in Riga, Latvia. Despite this finding, the United States eventually rescinded the 311 designations of Multibanka and VEF Banka.[42]

Mounting and maintaining a sustained financial sanctions campaign against stronger states like Russia is much more difficult than one against weaker states like North Korea. Unlike Iran and North Korea—effectively pariah states in the system of G-20 countries—Russia, in the words of Noah Cross in *Chinatown*, still has "a few teeth in my head . . . and a few friends in town."[43] Even though several of Russia's "friends" were relatively small financial players, Russia was still able to wield enough influence for a coordinated sanctions program to founder.

Moscow's 2014 invasion of Ukraine jumpstarted the US attempt to sanction Russia. Russia invaded Crimea in March 2014 to, in President Vladimir Putin's words, "restore unity."[44] Despite Putin's rhetoric, the Ukrainians did not see the situation in the same light and went to war against Crimean separatist forces, resulting in over 10,000 battle deaths and almost

24,000 injuries. The G-20 nations were not forced into action, however, until Malaysia Airlines flight 17 was blown out of the sky over Ukrainian airspace with what turned out to be a Russian-made surface-to-air missile whose firing rig vanished across the border into Russia immediately thereafter. Two hundred ninety-eight civilian deaths were more than the international community could bear, apparently, and the United States and European Union agreed to launch a sanctions campaign to "force Russia to 'abide by its international obligations and return its military forces to their original bases and respect Ukraine's sovereignty and territorial integrity.'"[45]

Forcing a relatively weak power like Iran back to the bargaining table is one thing; forcing a relatively strong power like Russia to reverse a foreign policy decision involving troops and territorial sovereignty is quite another and required a much more ambitious effort. The sanctions package put in place by the United States started narrowly, banning travel and freezing assets for any "'individuals and entities' responsible for the Russian military intervention" in Crimea.[46] It later broadened to include travel bans; arms embargoes; export controls; and restrictions on Russian banks Sberbank, VTB, Vnesheconombank, Gazprombank, and Rosselkhoz, and energy companies Gazprom, Gazprom Neft, Lukoil, Surgutneftegas, and Rosneft. The European Union, Australia, and Japan joined the campaign at this early stage.[47] These sanctions had a significant economic effect, combining with falling oil prices (caused in large part by US pursuit of fracking technology) to throw Russia into a recession, weaken the ruble, and cost Russia "tens of billions of dollars" according to Prime Minister Dmitry Medvedev.[48] The combination of the impact of the sanctions and the sheer number of states participating in the sanctions regime led the United States and the United Kingdom to take the next step and approach SWIFT about denying Russian banks access to the service. The threat was serious enough that Medvedev deemed it "equivalent to a declaration of war," and pushed Russia to develop its own payment system.[49]

SWIFT's board took Russia's threat seriously too, especially given that Russia was a larger, more powerful target than Iran or North Korea and had a more powerful cadre of allies as well. The board declined to exclude Russia from the system both the first time the United States and the European Union asked in 2014, and again in 2018, but radically limited Russia's access after the 2022 invasion. Medvedev's response to this step was more aggressive, asserting that that "our economic reaction and generally any other reaction will be without limits."[50] The United States had met an adversary in the finance domain capable of offering a strong resistance to its attacks, an adversary with enough leverage of its own to create opposition in the EU and skepticism within SWIFT.

The United States kept up the sanctions campaign, despite the 2016 presidential election, which put an administration more amenable to Russian demands in the White House. By 2021, the United States had broadened the sanctions regime to include those related to "malicious cyber activities and influence operations (including election interference), human rights abuses, use of a chemical weapon, weapons proliferation, illicit trade with North Korea, support to the governments of Syria and Venezuela, use of energy exports as a coercive or political tool, and other harmful foreign activities."[51]

This situation held in 2021 as Russia began visible preparations for a military campaign against Ukraine. Washington warned Moscow against aggressive military action and established the framework for an even more aggressive set of economic and financial sanctions against Russia's interests. The extent of the invasion on February 26, 2022, surprised nearly everyone and triggered this financial campaign.

Russian Preparations

In the years prior to the war, Russia accumulated some $600 billion in central bank reserves, with some half of the total held in the United States, the European Union, the United Kingdom, and Japan. Moscow could use these reserves to intervene in currency markets and maintain the value of the ruble, or to buy weapons from foreign producers.[52] Russia also maintained a conservative sovereign debt load, making these debts easier to service and making it possible to take on new debt as the circumstances of war required.[53] Finally, Russia established the SFPS alternative international payment system that would enable its banks to continue to process payments with certain customers in the event of a cut-off from the SWIFT system.[54]

While Moscow expected a sharp, short war, these measures imply that Moscow also understood that its invasion would provoke sanctions from the West. Moscow hoped that a quick victory and the prospect of high energy prices would result in the relaxation of the impending sanctions regime before the sanctions could do serious, long-term financial damage. In the immediate wake of the invasion, Russia imposed capital controls to prevent further capital flight, and substantially raised interest rates.[55] These actions gave holders of the ruble an incentive to hold on to it, and made it difficult to dump ruble assets even if they wished. Russia took further steps to protect the ruble by requiring Russian exporters to convert 80 percent of their foreign exchange earnings into rubles, propping up the demand for rubles and ensuring state access to foreign currency.[56] Moscow judged that Russian energy was too important to Europe to sanction completely, which would leave open a door for the acquisition of more Western currency. In addition, Russia began to insist that energy customers pay for gas and oil with rubles rather than with dollars to force foreign customers to buy rubles, shoring up the value of the currency.[57] Finally, Russia made it illegal for Russian brokers to sell foreign-owned Russian securities, ensuring that foreign investment capital remained in the country.[58]

Western Tools of Financial War

The Western campaign resulted in sanctions of a number and magnitude previously unseen in world financial history.[59] For example, in the immediate wake of the invasion, US, EU, British, and Japanese sanctions effectively froze the $300 billion in currency reserves that Russia held abroad.[60] However, the sanctions allowed Russia to use its frozen foreign reserves to pay interest on its sovereign debt, avoiding a default.[61] Thousands of individuals, businesses, and nongovernmental organizations were sanctioned by Western countries, including individuals associated with the Russian government as well as individuals and groups associated with President Putin's inner circle.[62] Western countries also seized the assets of individual Russians associated with the regime, resulting in the appropriation of yachts and other luxury items owned by Russian oligarchs.[63] A wide range of countries joined these sanctions, including states such as Japan and South Korea that have historically shied away from such action.[64]

The SWIFT lockout discussed above was intended to make it difficult for Russian banks to continue processing payments on an international scale, but without crippling the European economy. Sberbank, the largest bank, was initially excluded from the cutoff, but was placed on the list following revelations of atrocities at Bucha.[65] Gazprombank, on the other hand, was not sanctioned due to its importance to international energy markets.[66] The impact of the SWIFT lockout was to reduce the flow of international financial transactions from inside Russia by increasing the amount of time processing the transactions take in absence of real-time messaging, as well as sending a signal to SWIFT member banks that Russian banks were no longer members of the SWIFT community.

An additional sanction the United States put in place was the imposition of an oil price cap. On December 4, 2022, the United States and the European Union agreed to a $60 price cap on a barrel of oil, well below international trading prices and making it difficult for Russian to sell above this price.[67] The rationale for the cap was to limit the damage inflicted on the global economy by an oil shortage while, at the same time, limiting the extent to which Russia can profit from its bad behavior.[68] We discuss the impact that these sanctions had on Russia in the next subsection.

The Impact

The impact of the Western financial campaign against Russia is difficult to determine at the time of writing. In the short term, the campaign of financial coercion has neither made it impossible for Russia to continue its war nor dissuaded the Kremlin from continuing to pursue its invasion. The financial campaign has not destroyed the Russian economy, and it is difficult to isolate the economic, financial, and military components of the damage that the economy has suffered thus far. The financial campaign has not prevented Russia from accessing foreign military technology, although it may have limited the extent to which Russia could do so and the partners with whom Russia could work.

In addition, the ruble has not collapsed. Indeed, the ruble remains strong relative to most foreign currencies, although this is, in large part, because of the difficulty of conversion as a result of Russian policies propping up its value. Inflation in Russia has dropped substantially since the first days of the war when it reached 17.8 percent. Interest rates are also down considerably, not far off from the prewar norm.[69] Especially given that most Western countries are also suffering high inflation, the Russian experience does not seem completely outside the norm.

These sanctions have, however, made it difficult for Russian companies to raise funds from international sources, and largely impossible for the Russian government to do so, although the Kremlin did not borrow much in Western capital markets before the invasion.[70] Russia still has access to domestic bond markets, which have continued to attract some foreign investment.[71] The Russian stock market has taken a beating, but not one out of line with other recent Russian market crashes.[72] Russia's use of the Service for Transfer of Financial Messages (SPFS) and several other tools to evade the SWIFT cutoff have limited the extent of damage to Russia's financial system, and to the domestic holdings of Russian citizens.[73]

Russia's economy is dependent on its export of energy, and the beginning of the war created international instability that drove energy prices up. Although Russia's energy export options became more limited under the impact of sanctions, it continued to deliver to some customers (even in Europe) and has found new customers to take on at least part of the slack in demand.[74] The price increases more than made up for the decline in exports, at least in the early months of the conflict.[75]

The sanctions package also did not prevent Russia from gaining access to weapons it needed to continue the war. Russia has developed alternative means, including a deal with Iran for drones and ballistic missiles that involved the transfer of some hard currency—probably delivered on pallets as a way to get around the SWIFT sanctions—along with captured examples of a variety of Western military technology.[76] Russia also acquired ammunition from Belarus and North Korea, although the details of those deals remain unclear. In any case, energy sales have ensured that Russia has the financial capacity to buy weapons from abroad, even if other elements of the sanctions regime (primarily export controls) hinder Russian ambitions.[77]

Russia has absorbed the blows that the sanctions campaign dealt by stabilizing the financial system and the government revenue system at the expense of living standards of ordinary citizens.[78] In September 2022, Russia announced deep cuts to government spending in all areas other than defense, much as it did during the Cold War in its guise as the USSR.[79] While interest rates are well down from their peak, they remain high and in the long run risk strangling economic activity. The energy exports the Russian economy depends on might be damaged by changes in the terms of contracts with Western energy consumers.[80] While the sanctions campaign may not have forced Russia out of Ukraine, it has had an impact: in September 2022, a retired Russian central bank official estimated that the sanctions turned what was expected to be 5–6 percent growth that year into a 4 percent contraction, and that the sanctions were 30–40 percent effective.[81]

How Has Ukraine Survived?

An equally important question concerning the digital RFA and the intervention in the finance domain by the coalition led by the United States is: how will this intervention benefit Ukraine? This question is important because the war with Russia inflicted immense economic damage on Ukraine in terms of infrastructure damage, the costs of mobilization and lost labor, the transfer of refugees internally and externally, and the general costs of fielding the military forces needed to defend against and defeat Russia. Therefore, in addition to using the tools of the digital RFA to punish Russia, the United States and its allies must also use them to help Ukraine.

Ukraine is financing the war by printing money, and through international financial support.[82] Even before the war, the Ukrainian state suffered from a weak tax base, with relatively low, nonprogressive tax rates.[83] In the first days of the war, Ukraine fixed its exchange rate and imposed capital controls, limiting the immediate impact of a financial panic. However, the Ukrainian government was careful to carve out exceptions and limitations to those controls to avoid frightening away foreign investment.[84] Ukraine has financed the war in part by running down its foreign currency reserves, but the inflationary policy of printing more money was probably inevitable. Ukraine froze debt service payments in July, with the general agreement of its creditors.[85] Taking advantage of this respite, the National Bank of Ukraine (NBU) adjusted the currency peg to the dollar, devaluing it by 25 percent (the official rate had largely held until then).[86] Ukraine has struggled to pay its soldiers, although the immediate military impact of this is not obvious given conscription and the generally high morale of Ukrainian military forces.[87]

While Ukraine has received military assistance from the coalition, they are undoubtedly counting on international financial support as well.[88] However, disbursement of financial aid has lagged, probably because Ukraine's Western partners have themselves faced economic difficulties caused by the war.[89] Uncertainty about the course of the war has also made it difficult for Ukraine to access international financial institutions such as the International Monetary Fund.[90] There has also been some discussion of using Russian assets seized or frozen abroad as a form of reparations for Ukraine.[91] The move would be largely unprecedented and may be illegal in some countries, in particular the United States.[92]

In addition to these factors limiting the ability of the coalition to aid Ukraine, Ukraine's management of its finances also has its problems. For example, October 2022 saw the messy resignation of the chair of the NBU, who fled abroad in advance of an apparent corruption investigation. Although the corruption allegations may be legitimate, some figures in the government had been critical of the management of the bank for pursuing macroeconomic stability at the expense of the war effort.[93] The chair was replaced by an individual closely associated with President Volodymyr Zelensky's inner circle, suggesting a tighter connection between the government and the finance sector.[94]

Next Steps

The US-led coalition has not yet exhausted the potential tools for financial conflict. As discussed above, the recently imposed oil price cap may decrease Russian state revenues. The United States could also designate Russia a "State Sponsor of Terror," which would open up other avenues for squeezing the Russian financial system, including giving US plaintiffs access to frozen Russian assets.[95]

For its part, in November 2022 Russia began to lay the legal foundation for the establishment of a national cryptocurrency exchange, which would make it easier for individuals and firms to evade financial scrutiny.[96] Russia could also opt to carve out an even deeper path of financial austerity, further reducing domestic spending. Finally, Russia could undertake additional steps to build out a new financial commons that would not feature the US dollar as its centerpiece. Moscow is hardly the only country in the world to chafe at the financial power of the United States, although it remains unclear that China, India, and others are willing to take risks to support Russia.

Evaluation

To what extent can the United States and its allies use financial tools to undercut Russia's capacity to wage war?[97] Let us begin with what financial tools have not done. Financial sanctions have not frozen the Russia economy and have not prevented Russia from exporting energy. Financial sanctions have not brought the Russian defense industry to a standstill, although they have had a part in making it difficult for Russia to source some components internationally. Financial sanctions have not forced Russia to abandon the war, or seriously undercut Russia's ability to pay for the conflict. Moreover, the finance campaign has (along with the war itself and the trade and economic sanctions) disrupted global flows of goods and capital and helped drive up inflation around the world.[98]

However, financial sanctions have cut a huge slice out of Russia's international assets. Russia may never have access to those assets again, and the ability of Russia to hold money abroad has been sharply curtailed. Russian imports and exports have dropped substantially, if not all the way to zero. Wealthy Russian citizens, including members of President Putin's inner circle, have lost control of the assets that they held abroad. Long term, projections of the growth of the Russian economy have grown grim.

On the other hand, financial tools have enabled the United States and its allies to keep Ukraine's economy and war effort afloat. In some ways Ukraine is in a fundamentally better position than Russia, if only because Ukraine's creditors are friendly with Kyiv in a way that Moscow's creditors are not. If Ukraine survives the war as a sovereign territorial unit it will have access to Western credit markets, and will also likely continue to receive substantial financial grants from many of the most wealthy nations in the world. Depending on the nature of the war's settlement, Ukraine may also have access to the markets and regulatory expertise of the European Union.

A very schematic comparison of the states discussed in this chapter and their ability to weather a sanctions regime, outlined in Table 9.2, may be useful. North Korea represented around 0.01 percent of world trade in 2019, and Iran 0.1–0.2 percent—before the latest round of sanctions. Both

Table 9.2 Comparison of 2019 State Trade Shares of World Market (in billions of US dollars and percentage)

	North Korea	Iran	Russia	China
Country Exports + Imports	3	56	662	4,340
Country Exports + Imports as % of Total World Trade	0.01%	0.15%	1.75%	11.49%

Source: IMF (International Monetary Fund). IMF Direction of Trade Statistics (DOTS) dataset, 2023.
Note: Total world trade = 37,756.

were effectively cut off from the financial commons with little collateral damage. The Russian economy, between 1.0 and 2.0 percent of global trade, is suffering badly from financial sanctions but with considerable secondary effects on inflation and global trade flows. The People's Republic of China represents 11.5 percent of world trade, making the type of sanctions package used on North Korea, Iran, and Russia an exceedingly touchy prospect to contemplate.[99]

The United States and its allies have not (yet) won their financial proxy war against Russia, but they have exploited the innovations of the digital RFA to create set of tools for inflicting damage on Russia and for keeping the Ukrainian war effort viable. As Richard Oscar notes, the fact that so many countries have joined the sanctions regime has required those countries to develop the administrative capacity to execute the sanctions, meaning that future efforts may become even more effective in punishing rogue states.[100] It is also possible in the long term that the combination of differing interests and increasing sanctions could split the world economy into two or more blocs, with only limited trade between them but complex trade and financial links within them. The ability to impose—and resist—international sanctions regimes represents one of the critical manifestations of financial power in the 21st century. We continue to explore this question in the final chapter.

Conclusion

The United States—and, to a lesser extent, the G-20 countries—was instrumental in creating the current digital RFA, and this instrumentality gives the United States unique access to the international financial system, allowing it to weaponize the financial interdependence the system creates to advance its foreign policy goals. The United States has used this access to create this weaponization in the following effects: the choke point effect, allowing it to limit other states' access to the system as a way of influencing those states' behavior; and the panopticon effect, which allows it to observe other countries' behavior to prepare the appropriate weapon to influence that behavior. This weaponization can have a significant impact on target state behavior but, according to Oatley, only under the following three conditions: 1) the target states must be relatively weak (like North Korea) rather than relatively strong (like Russia); 2) the target state itself must not have access to choke points of its own that it can weaponize, as is the case with tax havens or Russia; and 3) weaponizing financial interdependence is successful only if there is agreement among the states doing the targeting and their allies about what the weaponization is meant to achieve and how it is meant to achieve it.[101] In the next chapter, we discuss what developments should occur in the next fifty years in the finance domain, what role future RFAs will play, and how the international system will change as a result.

Notes

1. Paybarah, Azi. 2022. "None of Us Should Be Fooled: President Biden's Speech on Russia." *New York Times,* February 22.
2. Official US government documents refer to Myanmar by its former name of Burma. For clarity's sake, we continue to use Myanmar.
3. EOP (Executive Office of the President). 2021. Executive Order 14014. *Federal Register,* February 12; DOT (US Department of the Treasury). 2021. Press Releases. July 2. https://home.treasury.gov/news/press-releases/jy0260.
4. King Royal Technologies Ltd., Wanbao Mining, and Wanbao subsidiaries Myanmar Mining Copper Ltd. and Myanmar Yang Tse Copper Ltd., all of which have revenue-sharing agreements with previously sanctioned Myanmar Economic Holdings Limited. BIS sanctioned these companies because of their role in financing the coup. DOC (US Department of Commerce). 2021. Press Releases. July 2. https://www.commerce.gov/news/press-releases/2021/07/commerce-increases-restrictions-burmese-military-adding-four-entities.
5. DOC 2021.
6. DOC 2021.; UN. 2021. "Myanmar: From Political Crisis, to 'Multi-Dimensional Catastrophe.'—Bachelet." *UN News,* July 6.
7. DOC 2021. The twenty-two include seven members of the illegitimate government and fifteen spouses or children of the junta who were already on the Specially Designated Nationals List. The seven are: Saw Daniel, Banyar Aung Moe, Aye Nu Sein, Chit Naing, Aung Naing Oo, Myint Kyaing, and Thet Thet Khine. The fifteen are: Kyu Kyu Hla (spouse of Min Aung Hlang), Than Than Nwe (spouse of Soe Win), Thet Thet Aung (spouse of Mya Tun Oo), Than Than Aye (spouse of Tin Aung San), Aung Mar Mint (spouse of Maung Maung Kya), Khaing Pa Pa Chit (spouse of Mo Mint Tyun), Moe Htet Htet Tun (adult child of Moe Myint Tun), Khang Moe Myint (adult child of Moe Myint Tun), Yadanar Moe Myint (adult child of Moe Myint Tun), Daw Nilar (spouse of Ye Win Oo), Theit Thinzar Ye (adult child of Ye Win Oo), Ohn Mar Myint (spouse of Aung Lin Dwe), Shwe Ye Phu Aung (adult child of Aung Lin Dwe), Hlaing Bwar Aung (adult child of Aung Lin Dwe), and Phyo Arkar Aung (adult child of Aung Lin Dwe).
8. DOC 2021.
9. USJFD (US Joint Force Development). 2018. "Strategy." Joint Doctrine Note.
10. Economic statecraft being the state's use of various economic instruments to achieve foreign policy goals. Steil, Benn, and Robert E. Litan. 2006. *Financial Statecraft: The Role of Financial Markets in American Foreign Policy.* New Haven: Yale University Press, 2.
11. Zarate, Juan. 2013. *Treasury's War: The Unleashing of a New Era of Financial Warfare.* New York: PublicAffairs, 10.
12. *The Banker.* 2021. "Top 1,000 World Banks 2021."
13. World Bank. 2017. "The Global Findex Database 2017." High-income economies include, in alphabetical order ($n = 44$): Australia, Austria, Bahrain, Belgium, Canada, Chile, Cyprus, Czech Republic, Denmark, Estonia, Finland, France, Germany, Greece, Hong Kong, Hungary, Ireland, Israel, Italy, Japan, Korea,

Kuwait, Latvia, Lithuania, Luxembourg, Malta, the Netherlands, New Zealand, Norway, Poland, Portugal, Saudi Arabia, Singapore, Slovak Republic, Slovenia, Spain, Sweden, Switzerland, Taiwan, Trinidad and Tobago, United Arab Emirates, United Kingdom, United States, and Uruguay.

14. This does not mean that there are not high levels of bank account ownership in countries not classified as "high-income": 93 percent of adults in Mongolia, for example, have bank accounts. World Bank 2017.

15. Steil and Litan 2006: 130.

16. DOC 2021; Oatley, Thomas. 2021. "Weaponizing International Financial Interdependence." In Daniel Drezner, Henry Farrell, and Abraham L. Newman, *The Uses and Abuses of Weaponized Interdependence*. Washington, DC: Brookings Institution Press, 115–132, at 117.

17. Caytas, Joanna Diane. 2017. "Weaponizing Finance: US and European Options, Tools, and Policies." *Columbia Journal of European Law* 23 (2): 441–476.

18. See, for example, Mehrling, Perry. 2015. "Elasticity and Discipline in the Global Swap Network." *International Journal of Political Economy* 44: 311–324. For a larger discussion of the Federal Reserve's changing role, see Mehrling, Perry. 2011. *The New Lombard Street: How the Fed Became the Dealer of Last Resort*. Princeton: Princeton University Press.

19. Farrell, Henry, and Abraham L. Newman. 2021. "Weaponized Interdependence: How Global Economic Networks Shape State Coercion." In *The Uses and Abuses of Weaponized Interdependence*, edited by Daniel Drezner, Henry Farrell, and Abraham L. Newman. Washington, DC: Brookings Institution Press, 19–66, at 34.

20. As discussed in Chapters 6 and 7, Great Britain had opportunities to employ a similar strategy during its period as hegemon in the finance domain during the nineteenth and early twentieth century, but did not (with the possible exception of joining in multilateral League of Nations sanctions in the interwar period).

21. Steil and Litan 2006: 149

22. Congressional Research Service. 2009. *North Korean Counterfeiting of U.S. Currency*. Report for Congress. Washington, DC: Congressional Research Service.

23. The Federal Reserve did implement a wire communications system connecting the various Federal Reserve Banks in 1918, however, so Fedwire's origins could be traced back to this development. Bech, Morten L., and Bart Hobijn. 2007. "Technology Diffusion with Central Banking: The Case of Real-Time Gross Settlement." *International Journal of Central Banking* 3 (3): 147–181.

24. Bech and Hobijn 2007; Jeffs, Jennifer A. 2008. "The Politics of Financial Plumbing: Harmonization and Interests in the Construction of the International Payment System." *Review of International Political Economy* 15 (2): 259–288.

25. Jeffs 2008: 259.

26. Farrell and Newman 2021: 34.

27. The ECB is headquartered in Frankfurt, Germany, and its primary purpose—according to its mission statement—is to stabilize the euro as a currency and the European Union market in general. ECB (European Central Bank). 2021. "ECB Mission Statement."

28. SWIFT (Society for Worldwide Interbank Financial Telecommunication). 2021. *SWIFT Oversight*; Zarate 2013.

29. Farrell and Newman 2021.

30. SWIFT 2021.

31. Caytas 2017.

32. Zarate 2013: 50.

33. Oatley 2021: 115.

34. Zarate 2013.
35. FinCEN (Financial Crimes Enforcement Network). 2021a. "311 Special Measures."
36. *Federal Register.* 2002. Vol. 67, No. 24, December 26, 2002. Reuter and Truman provide a working definition of *money laundering*: the "conversion of criminal incomes into assets that cannot be traced back to the underlying crime." Reuter, Peter, and Edwin M. Truman. 2004. *Chasing Dirty Money: The Fight Against Money Laundering.* New York: Columbia University Press.
37. FinCEN 2021a.
38. Oatley 2021.
39. *Washington Post.* 2002. "Text of President Bush's 2002 State of the Union Address." January 29. The US government targeted the third axis of evil country—Iraq—in a more direct manner in 2003.
40. Farrell and Newman 2021.
41. Dainoff, Charles. 2021. *Outlaw Paradise: Why Countries Become Tax Havens.* Lanham MD: Lexington Books.
42. FinCEN 2021a; *Federal Register.* 2005. Vol. 70, No. 79, April 26, 2005.
43. Towne, Robert. 1973. *Chinatown Screenplay, Third Draft.*
44. *Washington Post.* 2014. "Transcript: Putin Says Russia Will Protect the Rights of Russians Abroad." March 18.
45. Oatley 2021: 123.
46. Holland, Steve, and Jeff Mason. 2014. "Update 4: Obama Warns on Crimea, Orders Sanctions over Russian Moves in Ukraine." Reuters, March 6.
47. Mohammed, Arshad, and Bill Trott. 2014. "U.S. Intensifies Sanctions on Russia over Ukraine." Reuters. September 12.
48. Caytas 2017: 456; Christie, Edward. 2015. "Sanctions After Crimea: Have They Worked?" *NATO Review,* May 7; Golubkova, Katya, and Gabriela Baczynska. 2014. "Rouble Fall, Sanctions Hurt Russia's Economy: Medvedev." *Reuters.* December 10.
49. Oatley 2021: 123–124, at 115; Caytas 2017.
50. Farrell and Newman 2021: 51.
51. Oatley 2021; Congressional Research Service. 2021. *U.S. Sanctions on Russia: An Overview.* In Focus, Washington, DC: Congressional Research Service. An aggressive response perhaps aided by another change of administration—one less closely aligned with Russia and its allies—in the United States in 2020.
52. Miller, Chris. 2022. "The Putinomics Playbook Won't Work Forever." *War on the Rocks,* April 25.
53. *Trading Economics.* 2022. "Russian Government Debt to GDP." *Trading Economics* December 5.
54. Hawser, Anita. 2022. "Sberbank Takes De-Swifting in Stride." *Global Finance,* June 2.
55. Miller 2022.
56. Miller 2022; Hirsch, Paddy. 2022. "How Russia Rescued the Ruble." National Public Radio. *Planet Money.* April 5.
57. Hirsch 2022.
58. Hirsch 2022.
59. Oscar, Richard. 2022. "War in Ukraine: A New Paradigm of Sanctions Practice," *Lawfare,* August 1.
60. Miller 2022.
61. Hirsch 2022.
62. Oscar 2022.

63. Oscar 2022.
64. Oscar 2022.
65. Kilcrease, Emily, Jason Bartlett, and Mason Wong 2022. *Sanctions by the Numbers: Economic Measures Against Russia Following Its 2022 Invasion of Ukraine*. Washington DC: Center for a New American Security, June 16.
66. De Luce, Dan. 2022. "Too Big to Sanction? A Large Russian Bank Still Operates Freely Because It Helps Europe Get Russian Gas." *NBC News*, June 18.
67. Wallace, Joe. 2022. "Oil Price Wavers After Russia Cap Kicks In." *Wall Street Journal*, December 5.
68. *The Economist*. 2022. "The West's Proposed Price Cap on Russian Oil Is No Magic Weapon." November 30.
69. Aris, Ben. 2022. "Is Russia's Economy Headed for 'Economic Oblivion,' as a Report from Yale Says?" *BNE Intellinews*, August 8.
70. Oscar 2022.
71. Aris 2022.
72. Aris 2022.
73. Hawser 2022.
74. Blenkinsop, Philip. 2022. "EU Bars 7 Russian Banks from SWIFT, but Spares Those in Energy." Reuters, March 3.
75. Kim, Victoria, Clifford Krauss, and Anton Torianovski. 2022. "Western Move to Choke Russia's Oil Exports Boomerangs, for Now." *New York Times*, June 5.
76. Haynes, Deborah. 2022. "Russia Flew €140m in Cash and Captured Western Weapons to Iran in Return for Deadly Drones, Sources Claim." *Sky News*, November 9.
77. Barnes, Julian E. 2022. "Russia Is Buying North Korean Artillery, According to US Intelligence." *New York Times*, September 5.
78. Miller 2002.
79. *Moscow Times*. 2022. "Government Launches Budget Sequestration After Worst Revenue Collapse in 11 Years." September 15.
80. Hirsch 2022.
81. Korsunskaya, Darya. 2022. "No Catastrophe, but Sanctions on Moscow Are Working, Says Russian Economy Veteran." Reuters, September 20.
82. Tooze, Adam. 2022a. "Chartbook #146: The Russia-Ukraine War at Six Months: Symbolic Anniversary or Economic and Military Turning Point?" *Chartbook*, August 24.
83. Tooze, Adam. 2022b. "Chartbook #163: Warfare Without the State: New Keynesian Shock Therapy for Ukraine's Home Front." *Chartbook*, October 22.
84. Moore, Philip. 2022. "Ukraine Safeguards Relations with International Investors." Official Monetary and Financial Institutions Forum (OMFIF), May 17.
85. Repko, Maria. 2022. "Ukraine's Economy Will Collapse Without More Aid Now." *Foreign Policy*, August 4; DOT. 2022. "Statement by the Group of Creditors of Ukraine." July 20.
86. Google Finance. 2022. "Ukrainian Hryvnia to United States Dollar." December 5; NBU (National Bank of Ukraine). 2022. "NBU Fixes Official UAH/USD Exchange Rate at a New Level and Takes Additional Measures to Balance the FX Market and Support Resilience of Economy During the War." July 21.
87. Walker, Marcus. 2022. "Ukraine Scrapes to Pay Its Soldiers as Western Funds Slow to Arrive." *Wall Street Journal*, August 12.
88. Tooze 2022a: 146.
89. Walker 2022.
90. Walker 2022.

91. Oscar 2022.
92. Stephan, Peter. 2022. "Giving Russian Assets to Ukraine—Freezing Is Not Seizing." *Lawfare*, April 26; Tribe, Lawrence. 2022. "Does American Law Currently Authorize the President to Seize Sovereign Russian Assets?" *Lawfare*, May 23; Anderson, Scott, and Chiméne Keitner. 2022. "The Legal Challenges Presented by Seizing Frozen Russian Assets." *Lawfare*, May 26.
93. Tooze 2022b: 146.
94. Tooze 2022a: 163.
95. Trainer, Jocelyn. 2022. "To Designate or Not? Russia and SST Status." *Lawfare*, November 29.
96. Arti. 2022. "Russia to Lay Down a Legal Framework for National Crypto Exchange." *Analytics Insight*, November 28.
97. Kaushal, Sidharth. 2022. "Can Russia Continue to Fight a Long War?" Royal United Services Institute (RUSI), August 23.
98. White, Olivia, Nicolaus Henke, Elena Kvochko, and Jonathan Woetzel. 2022. "War in Ukraine: Twelve Disruptions Changing the World." McKinsey & Company, May 9.
99. By way of comparison, we estimate that Germany in 1914, when the British government blanched at shutting it out of trade finance, accounted for roughly 9 percent of world trade. Estimates are based on gross domestic product (GDP) and trade share data from the appendix to Klasing, Mariko J., and Petros Milionis. 2014. "Quantifying the Evolution of World Trade, 1870–1949." *Journal of International Economics* 92 (1): 185–197.
100. Oscar 2022.
101. Oatley 2021: 125–126.

10
The Next Fifty Years of Financial Competition

Action goals: By 2023, the digitization of the financial industry should produce a clear transformation; the model of financial services should improve even more, and the product supply and scope of business contact should be wider and more abundant. By 2025, the base of an advanced, reliable, and flexible infrastructure service system should form; the financial industry should realize preliminary digitization and intelligentization, financial inclusiveness and the capability to serve the real economy will notably strengthen; a supervisory system adaptable to financial technology should form, and finance should provide all-around support for the new development pattern.

Improve digital financial infrastructure. Optimize infrastructure layout and facilitate appropriate competition in digital financial services. Promote the interconnection of infrastructure and advance the free flow of factors. Further improve the credit reporting system; accelerate the improvement in key areas of credit processes and credit evaluation models. Upgrade and transform the payment and liquidation system; improve risk prevention and control and operation and maintenance safeguard capabilities. Further improve the comprehensive statistics of the financial industry and accelerate the construction of a basic national financial database. Accelerate the healthy development of the country's financial services industry.

—"Translation: 14th Five-Year Plan for National Informatization," 2021.[1]

As the very existence of this book suggests, governments appear increasingly cognizant of the role that power plays in international finance and vice versa. Leaders in Beijing, Moscow, and Tehran have grown to appreciate the unique advantages that accrue to the United States from hosting the world's reserve currency and have become acutely aware of how the United States has been using that power to pursue its policy objectives and maintain its hegemony. And with this knowledge has come resentment and attempts to slip the bit, with China and Russia working to build their own financial systems independent of the United States. Even ostensible US allies have begun to chafe against US financial power; for example, even after withdrawing from the Joint Comprehensive Plan of Action (JCPOA), the United States has maintained severe financial sanctions against Iran that restrict its ability to conduct foreign trade, actions that run against the stated foreign policy intent of the other parties to the JCPOA.[2]

How will the finance domain develop over the next fifty years? There are two major questions that are part of this. First, will hegemony stay with the United States, will it shift to another power, or will a multipolar financial world develop? Second, how will the finance domain itself change? Will there be another revolution in financial affairs (RFA)? Will the determinants of success in the domain change? In the remainder of this chapter, we lay out some general ideas about the future of US financial hegemony, then develop some specific scenarios under which states could use the finance domain in an innovative way.

There is little doubt that the United States is the hegemon of the current finance domain; the question is whether it can remain so into the future. Certainly, there have been any number of books arguing that China will overtake the United States in the near future, or that the US system will collapse under its own weight, or that the attempt to disengage from the system by the United States itself during the years 2017 to 2020 has accelerated this decline in influence. Given this multiplicity of possibilities, in this chapter we evaluate four scenarios for the next fifty years: (1) the United States remains a financial hegemon; (2) there is a relatively peaceful and orderly transition to another hegemon; (3) a bipolar finance domain develops with equal and competing systems; and (4) a multipolar finance domain develops. We identify the characteristics of each scenario and a rough probability estimate of their occurring.

In the first two scenarios, it is likely that finance will not be a major arena of contestation. Just as hegemony in the maritime commons is a world with a few large navies but few naval battles, hegemony in the finance domain is a world with a few financially dominant states and few financial struggles. If, however, another state—China, for example—can claim hegemony over the finance domain, the result would probably be a "reset" where the global financial system reverts to early Bretton Woods or the gold standard, but now with Chinese characteristics. However, if the finance domain returns to a multipolar world, the result might be some of the more dramatic experiments of the late 1600s and early 1700s as central banking practices in multiple states radically shift in a struggle for hegemony, and possibly new versions of the epic bubbles of the Mississippi and the South Sea Companies.

Our argument regarding the evolution of the finance domain over the next fifty years is necessarily speculative, depending on geostrategic shifts that may result from military conflicts, technological revolutions, and uncertain economic trends. Of course, caution is needed—in 2022 alone, there were numerous developments that shifted reasonable expectations of the future: Russia's invasion of Ukraine, the Biden administration's aggressive controls on semiconductor technology, the collapse of FTX. Overall, we expect that the policy of several major states will affect the structure of the finance domain, including the United States, China, Russia, Japan, and the European Union (EU). With respect to the latter, the financial influence of the EU depends on how long the currency union survives in its present form, and whether the EU itself remains in existence after the defection of the United Kingdom.

However, we do not expect these states to be the only relevant actors in the finance domain. Although the financial changes wrought by the most recent RFA—the emergence of the cyber domain and globalization—have increased the ability of states to surveil and weaponize currency transactions, the rise of the cyber domain has also diffused power away from the center by enabling the development of new forms of currency, thus increasing the options of peripheral actors. These new cryptocurrencies, sometimes designed to avoid problems associated with fiat money but more often constructed with an eye toward avoiding state surveillance or the influence of state power entirely, have the potential to change the relationship between the state and the use of currency by private actors.[3] Perhaps even more unsettling is the development of central bank digital currencies (CBDC) or state-sponsored cryptocurrencies by autocracies like China, either to achieve greater transparency and surveillance of its users, or to undermine the financial advantages enjoyed by the United States in the current finance domain.[4] As we discussed in previous chapters, nonstate actors have played significant roles in the finance domain, particularly before the central bank RFA, but these new developments in currency and payment systems could possibly empower individuals to avoid state detection of, for example, illegal transactions or tax evasion.[5]

How Financial Systems Change, Erode, and Collapse

States cooperate to establish and maintain systems of finance for the same reason they establish any other regime: to accomplish certain policy objectives that they cannot accomplish through unilateral action. These financial systems facilitate the flow and management of capital, and are usually centered around a leading state either by design or through the system's evolution.[6] Leaders of the states within these systems give up some sovereignty to join them and pay the costs of maintaining them because these systems generate benefits for these states that outweigh the costs, and benefits that they could not obtain outside the system due to reputation costs or lack of path dependence. Systems and regimes succeed because they solve the problems they were established to solve, and because the benefits that accrue to their member states are worth the amount of sovereignty the states sacrifice to join them. In addition, George W. Downs, David M. Rocke, and Peter N. Barsoom found that regimes succeed when the regime requires that member states behave in a way these states would have behaved even if the regime had not existed, but also enables these member states to more easily achieve their goals.[7]

In the same way that member state leader behavior can affect a regime's success, however, it can also result in regime failure. For example, Jack Seddon argues that financial system regimes can fail because the architecture of the system is inherently unfair to some member states, which creates an incentive for these states to defect during system crises. Another leadership-driven cause of system failure is poor management by the hegemonic state members of the system, whose unequal treatment of secondary member states can erode confidence in the regime itself and cause it to malfunction.[8] As Charles Dainoff points out, if we start from the assumption that states behave rationally, then their membership in a regime—and cooperation within the strictures of that regime—is contingent on their receiving benefits from membership greater than the costs imposed. At some point, if the regime's managing members—either the states or the decisionmakers representing them—behave in ways that create disincentives for secondary state members to comply with the regime directives, then these states will stop complying. Eventually, if enough of these states stop complying, the regime will collapse.[9] The broader implication of this argument within this book's context is that financial regimes based on domain-altering RFAs can collapse due to hegemonic mismanagement, causing systemic realignment. We argue that this type of mismanagement was partly responsible for the collapse of the Bretton Woods currency system, and emerging threats to US hegemony within the post–Bretton Woods system.

Potential Challengers

China

As of 2022, for the first time since the interwar period there was some ambiguity about who had the world's largest economy, with China the source of this ambiguity.[10] This growth by China represents the first time since the Napoleonic Wars that there has been a real challenge to Anglo-American financial hegemony. One key milestone in this process was the inclusion of Chinese yuan in the basket used by the International Monetary Fund (IMF) to define Special Drawing Rights in 2015.[11] This inclusion by the IMF is a goal China had worked toward for years and is evidence of the substantial increase in the Chinese economy and its international finance infrastructure.[12]

A major component of this effort is China's development of its China International Payment System (CIPS) as a competitor to the Society for Worldwide Interbank Financial Telecommunication (SWIFT) system of international financial transaction messaging. As discussed elsewhere in this book, the United States weaponized the SWIFT system against a number of actors since 2001. In response, the Russian and Chinese governments created alternative systems; the Chinese version, CIPS, allows international financial transactions to be settled in yuan rather than dollars, thereby allowing firms to operate outside the US financial orbit. This, in turn, increases China's sphere of influence and its ability to compete against the United States in the finance domain. Along with the Belt and Road Initiative, the intention is to create an international financial system entirely separate from the one utilized by SWIFT member states, one that China could influence at a level similar to that of the United States. In 2022, responding to sanctions, several Russian banks announced that they were increasing their yuan-denominated service offerings. While CIPS has yet to live up to its lofty ambitions, it continues to develop rapidly and remains a major focus of the Chinese government.[13]

Over the past forty years of growth, China has used a novel version of financial repression, such that there are strict limits to how markets function and how asset prices operate.[14] The Chinese Communist Party (CCP) appears to say "make our financial system liberal, but not just yet," with many cheerful plans over the past decades to liberalize the capital account and let the renminbi move freely that have been only partially realized. Instead, the use of banking and finance as a system for top-down control continues as a vital thread in the Chinese economy. Looking forward, the potential for a liberal liftoff, where markets begin to function as information discovery systems, is certainly possible. However, the government's "visible intervening hands"[15] may choke out the news of threats the system is facing, leading to lost decades of growth.[16] Instead of a Western-style crisis, slow deflation of bank stocks and recession and stagnation are the worst-case scenario.[17]

Chinese engagement in the finance domain also extends to lending. While the latest data show the United States lending to a greater number of developing countries, China may already be tied on that front, and in absolute quantities of lending to low-income countries China surpassed US official lending, IMF lending, private lending, and other sources.[18] This lending is used as a tool to expand Chinese influence: a study from the team of Anna Gelpern, Sebastian Horn, Scott Morris, Brad Parks, and Christoph Trebesch found that Beijing has a standardized approach to lending that sets it apart from other major creditors;[19] that is, China has built-in coercive mechanisms in its loan contracts that enable Beijing to apply a wave of different coercive effects on recalcitrant debtors.[20] Chinese debts have preference over other kinds of debt even when the international community deems it necessary to come to an agreement with a government that has become overindebted, and China's contracts have a variety of cancellation, acceleration, and stabilization clauses that enable China to apply pressure to debtors who run into trouble. In general, the Chinese challenge to US hegemony in the finance domain is significant, but not to the point of contesting for supremacy—yet.

The European Union

In addition to China, the only other region that potentially could lay claim to the overall economic size and sophistication of the United States in the twenty-first century is the European Union and the subset of EU members that are part of the eurozone. Unlike China, the eurozone is committed to the free movement of capital.[21] The EU has also encouraged financial markets to use member country sovereign debt as collateral in an effort to create a competitor to the US treasuries market, which (although not without risks) could increase world demand for euro-denominated assets and increase use of the euro as a reserve currency.[22] Although gross domestic product (GDP) per capita in current US dollars more than doubled in the EU from $16,910 in 2000 to $36,920 in 2008, the 2008 financial crisis seems to have led to conflict and stagnation as fault lines that existed prior to the crisis between citizens and politicians and between Northern and Southern Europe instead of pushing the EU to greater centralization and cohesion to consolidate nearly a decade of steady growth.[23] The result of this widening was an increase in popularity of populist political movements on the left and right in Europe, the most significant of which led to the United Kingdom exiting the EU. The Brexit vote, in addition to being a reflection of the growth of euroskepticism as well as a signal of the growing distrust of financiers and foreigners in general in the United Kingdom, is a sign of further fraying of the fabric of international cooperation knit at Bretton Woods. After Brexit, there has been some effort by the EU to make repairs in the face of continuing populist political gains, but despite GDP per capita remaining close to its 2008 height, the momentum has not yet been significant.[24]

The Further Development of the Finance Domain

The Real Economy

Financial assets are promises to convey real assets at some future date. Thus, the nature of the real economy is a vital backdrop to financial flows and the finance domain.[25] Looking back, we can see how the shift in the real economy has closely affected financial flows and, hence, the finance domain. In the first tax states in Mesopotamia and Egypt, for example, the regularity of agricultural output allowed the state to systematically collect tax revenue. Another example: in the medieval era, the increasing production of manufactured goods—especially those that were high in value and easy to transport—enabled the state creation of effective new fiscal strategies. As economies around the world have developed, agriculture has played a smaller and smaller role and services and manufacturing have expanded. In turn, fiscal advantages have shifted from simple land acquisition (to get greater agricultural produce) to more complex strategies, maintaining a growing economy and increasing complexity, divorced from agriculture.[26] As value added comes more and more from manufacturing and services and less from photosynthesis, financial flows have switched from the centrifugal patterns that dominated most of the past few thousand years to the centripetal patterns of the past few decades.[27]

International financial flows have tended to favor the center over the past few decades, much less taken with the periphery than was the case in the 1900s.[28] The financial flows to imperial possessions that Herbert Feis documents and the expansive lending of the eurocurrency/petrodollar boom of the 1970s have quieted. Low interest rates have led some private sector firms to invest in the developing world, but in what Daniela Gabor terms the "Wall Street Consensus," the role of the public sector is to assume any risks to maximize the attractions of the project.[29] Within this consensus, national security or military goals seem far too risky to get any support. Instead, the major funding sources accessible to the states of the periphery appear to be from a fourth sector: mining and other resource extraction. Notably, some of the most destabilizing regions of the past three decades have been the mineral rich but politically fragile regions of Central Africa and Russia, which have been able to use funds from resource extraction to fund military adventurism.[30] This trend is entirely in keeping with the predictions made by the "resource curse" theoreticians like Michael Ross, who argue that states dependent on natural resource extraction for their economic base are more subject to political instability than states that have more balanced economies.[31] Possibly the world is dividing into: high complexity regions with high incomes and at least some aversion to war; low complexity, resource-rich regions where states may still seek to profit from war; and low complexity, resource-poor regions, where states exist in a state of conflict, fragility, or total collapse.

Nonstate Actors: al-Qaeda and the Islamic State in Iraq and Syria (ISIS)

One unintended consequence of the most recent RFA and the subsequent creation of a finance domain that enables ever faster speeds of capital mobility is the evolution of a variety of creative mechanisms for transferring and hiding funds that allow nonstate actors to avoid scrutiny by law enforcement agencies. In northeastern Nigeria, for example, Boko Haram splinter group the Islamic State West Africa Province (ISWAP) collects what it calls zakat, an obligatory Islamic religious donation, from the farmers in the primarily rural territory it controls. The branding here is key: without the implication of funding used to defend the *umma* against the predations of both the state and non-Muslims created by its title, the zakat would be just another example of armed bandits collecting protection payments from vulnerable citizens. Instead, the payments are a fulfillment of a holy obligation to fight the Salafi jihad and to care for the less fortunate in their community, the latter task being one the state does not perform to any acceptable degree. As detailed in the Quran, it is acceptable for farmers to pay zakat in commodities if they do not have currency, and the ISWAP zakat is no exception: an estimated 80 percent of the proceeds are in the form of livestock, with crops and cash making up the other 20 percent. ISWAP—like other hybrid groups seeking to control territory—then trades these commodities for cash to fund operations and provide social services.[32]

While these groups continue to use the tried and true method of opening accounts in banks in tax havens and states like Dubai that put less emphasis on due diligence procedures for account holders, they have developed newer techniques for obscuring the source and destination of financing such as creating consulting firms headquartered in tax havens like Switzerland—where incorporation laws favor secrecy—that hire real consultants and offer legitimate consulting services while also providing a place to launder money and an excuse to open offices in other tax havens. Another method, which harkens back to Meyer Lansky's original money laundering schemes in the 1930s and 1940s, is for a terrorist financier to transfer money by having a straw man file a civil lawsuit against them, which the financier will then lose and then transfer the "judgment" into the plaintiff's account. This method depends on the relative inability of the court's due diligence procedures to verify the facts of the case, and the financial institutions involved assuming that these procedures are sufficient. There are, however, less complicated methods for transferring and storing funds, including cash deposit boxes and the subject of the next subsection: cryptocurrency.[33]

Future RFAs: Cryptocurrency

The emergence of cryptocurrencies has the potential to upend global finance, especially if those cryptocurrencies receive substantial state support. Central banks worldwide are evaluating options in this area.[34] Russia has created a CBDC, the "digital ruble," to supplement its paper currency. Russia's interest is explicitly strategic, as this quote from the Russian Ministry of Finance makes clear: "Its advantages in the finance department include a reduction in transaction costs and the volume of burden on banks, an increase in cross-border payments, as well as a decrease in dependence on the dollar and exposure to sanctions."[35] That this program was undertaken at the same time that the Central Bank of Russia was calling for a ban on investment in private cryptocurrencies by Russian citizens reinforces the point that the Russian government explicitly viewed the development of digital currency as a tool for competing in the finance domain.

Russia's digital currency project was smaller in scope than the effort by China, whose central bank launched its CBDC the "digital yuan" on a trial basis in 2019. Similar to Russia, China's CBDC program's intention appears to be strategic, although with slightly different objectives. The strategy behind the launch of the digital yuan by the People's Bank of China (PBOC) seems to be of a piece with other Chinese state efforts discussed above to create its own finance domain rather than compete in the current US-dominated one. As China is also moving to restrict cryptocurrency usage domestically, the digital yuan program represents an additional effort to tighten the financial reins on its citizens rather than improve China's competitiveness in the finance domain, with the PBOC offering justification for the program that include an easing of domestic transactions on the one hand, and an improvement of criminal surveillance on the other.[36] The second logic holds a particular relevance for China, as it allows state authorities to monitor—and potentially control—domestic financial transactions on the part of criminals and dissidents.[37] As a report from the Center for New American Security points out, the digital currency project gives the PBOC, and thus the CCP, more control over the activities of firms within its borders, and especially over the powerful financial services and payment companies that have become critical to the functioning of the Chinese economy.[38]

So far, state-backed and -controlled cryptocurrencies are comparative drops in the bucket when compared with the nonstate-backed version. The original purpose of cryptocurrency, after all, is to help individuals evade the notice and authority of the state, not enhance it. This is still cryptocurrencies' primary role in the finance domain. There has been remarkable volatility in cryptocurrency valuations over the early 2020s, but the two most widely used cryptocurrencies—bitcoin and ethereum—had, as of April 10, 2023, market capitalizations of roughly $574 billion and $230 billion, respectively.[39] Despite considerable skepticism about cryptocurrencies from the beginning that seems if anything to have grown more serious, there is also some evidence of legitimate if problematic use cases.[40] The primary threat posed by cryptocurrency to the stability of the finance domain—and by extension the US hegemony of it—is not its use by competitor states to erode US dominance, but in its potential for becoming a tool for transferring illicit funds globally without its users having to resort to jumping through the bureaucratic hoops necessitated by participating in the international financial system. However, the total amount of cryptocurrency in existence limits its use to smaller transfer patterns and states: North Korea has successfully used it as a substantial part of its engagement with the finance domain, but Russia cannot.[41] In this way cryptocurrency is a less sophisticated method tax havens use to evade government scrutiny.

Tax haven states are, however, created within a legal framework; a customer is able to hide assets and conceal financial transfers because these activities are legal and protected by the tax havens and as such are relatively low risk. By contrast, cryptocurrencies operate extralegally by design, with the result being that their users have little to no recourse if, say, they are one of the customers who lost a total of nearly $2.8 billion when the operator of the centralized exchange site Thodex disappeared with client funds in 2021.[42] If a bank president embezzled $2.8 billion from a US bank, not only would US law enforcement be able to track down the embezzler fairly quickly, but the Federal Deposit Insurance Corporation (FDIC) immunizes bank customers against losing their account holdings. These assurances and remedies are—by design—unavailable to the cryptocurrency customer; whether this systemic weakness represents a destabilizing threat as cryptocurrency becomes a more entrenched part of the finance domain, or an incentive for potential cryptocurrency users to return to the safer, more conventional domain provinces and the influence of the United States, or for the US regulatory apparatus to pacify large sections of the cryptocurrency ecosystem remains to be seen. A sign that these issues may be coming to a head is the 2022 collapse of FTX and the prosecution of Sam Bankman-Fried for deceiving his hedge fund clients about the funds he was transferring from the exchange, as well as stealing money from the hedge fund for his own personal use. The significance of the case, however, lies in the implication that the "Wild West" days of nonstate cryptocurrency are numbered.[43]

The interaction of cryptocurrency and public or central banking has some interesting wrinkles. Cryptocurrency values fluctuate too rapidly to be used as a meaningful unit of account or store of value: critical functions of money. Private firms have attempted to fix this by constructing "stablecoins," or cryptocurrency pegged to an existing currency or other object that can be independently valued.[44] As we have seen, however, stable currency that continues to hold par value is almost invariably dependent on a government. Established central banks are actively looking at using digital currency as a way to expand the range of financial services available to their citizens as well as tools of monetary policy available to them.[45]

Another much more toxic option is that a rogue state or criminal organization could set up a primitive central bank—akin to the early public banks in the Mediterranean city-states or the Bank of Amsterdam. If par value of cryptocurrency becomes an important interest of a rogue state or criminal organization with even basic administrative capacity (that is to say, competitive with medieval Barcelona or Genoa), it seems almost certain that it could be achieved. Given the already destabilizing effects of cryptocurrency, the development of par value by an actor antagonistic to world stability would open a new and uncertain chapter.

After Hegemony?

If dollar hegemony ends and the current finance domain collapses, what price will the United States pay? Paul Krugman expresses well-reasoned skepticism that the end of dollar dominance is nigh, then suggests that even the end of dollar dominance might not have the catastrophic effects on the US economy that some suspect. He points out that dollar dominance does not seem to have much of an effect on interest rates on US debt, and that there is little reason to believe that the value of the dollar would crash if it ceased to be the foundational international currency.[46]

But as Henry Farrell and others have pointed out, the defense of the dominance of the dollar has less to do with the prosperity of Americans and American business, and more to do with the weaponization of interdependence.[47] As we discussed in Chapter 9, the dominance of the dollar, combined with advanced digital tools of surveillance and analysis, gives the US government unprecedented insight into the functioning of the international economy.[48] This panopticon access allows the United States to precisely employ sanctions against opponents, monitor tax avoidance and tax evasion, and keep track of the international flow of arms, drugs, and other illicit and semilicit goods. While most other governments are likely to appreciate at least some of these enforcement activities some of the time, there are no doubt specific actions that frustrate them; as we have discussed, a United States that overplays its hand in the global financial system risks the development of alternative systems. Therefore, the relevant question might not concern the economic and financial impact, but the geopolitical one. This position is consistent with the rest of our argument: US political power and influence in the international system is at least partially dependent on its hegemony in the finance domain, and the waning of dollar dominance would at the very least be a harbinger of the decline of US hegemony overall. At its most dire, the decline of dollar dominance and the collapse of the current finance domain would be the warning signal portending a more serious global cataclysm requiring the type of rebuilding effort that installed the United States as financial hegemon in 1945.

Although the integration of the cyber and finance domains has given the United States exceptional coercive power over the past three decades, the ability of great powers to weaponize the international financial system has a long history, as this book shows. The waning of financial power will mostly likely be similar to the dissipation of every other kind of power; the United States will no longer be able to dictate terms at China's twelve-mile limit, nor threaten to render China's financial infrastructure transparent at a glance.

A different and perhaps more important question involves the stability of the global financial system in the wake of US hegemony. A generation of international relations scholars in the United States studied the question of whether the constellation of norms and institutions established by the United States and its allies during the Cold War could persist after US hegemony faded.[49] There is a strong case for doubt as to whether financial institutions are of the same sort as other kinds of international organization, due to the need for careful management by central banks with a degree of independence from their governments. Whether globalization can survive a multipolar financial system remains uncertain, and the question will likely preoccupy bankers and other policymakers over the next few decades.

Thus, we can imagine an extraordinarily complex financial future, in which multiple states and nonstate actors make claims for influence in the finance domain. The United States, with its immense economic power and the sophistication of its financial system, will undoubtedly remain influential, if not dominant. The European Union, assuming that the currency union does not collapse, will have enormous regional influence. It is likewise possible that China will succeed in creating its own Greater East Asia Co-Prosperity Sphere in the coming decades, establishing a separate domain for itself and its client states, further fragmenting the global financial system. It is also possible that increased usage of cryptocurrency will enable nonstate actors to play a more significant role in the financial system, potentially undercutting the power of established currencies and destabilizing the finance domain. It is, however, important to remember that "possible" has a different meaning than "likely." It also is important to consider that if the United States does lose hegemony in the finance domain, it will likely be the result of a chain of events that make worrying about currency exchange rates seem quaint.

Appendix: Scenarios for Future Finance Domain Composition

Below are scenarios based on our analysis of RFAs and the finance domain, with an emphasis on developments in the twentieth and twenty-first centuries. These scenarios could offer useful teaching or discussion tools for thinking about how states and nonstate actors will use the tools available in the finance domain to pursue their national objectives.

Scenarios 1 and 2 assume the international system remains stable and unipolar. In total we believe the probability of the system remaining this way is about 90 percent. The remaining 10 percent is split among scenarios 3, 4, 5, and 6, in which there is a significant change in the polarity of the system.

Scenario 1

The United States retains its hegemony, in part due to any future RFAs reinforcing this hegemony. As a result, the finance domain stays intact and relatively stable. Probability: 75 percent.

Scenario 2

The United States cedes hegemony peacefully to one challenger state, in part due to future RFAs having a significant impact on the international pecking order. Nevertheless, the finance domain stays intact and relatively stable despite the change in hegemon. Probability: 15 percent.

Scenario 2a: If Scenario 2 does occur, the likelihood that China is the challenger state replacing the United States in an intact system is 90 percent.

Scenario 2b: If Scenario 2 does occur, the likelihood that a country that is NOT China is the challenger state replacing the United States in an intact system is 10 percent.

Scenario 3

Rather than being a challenger state as it is traditionally understood in international relations theory, China's plan to carve out a separate domain area succeeds, in part due to strategy and in part due to RFAs. The United States accepts this development peacefully. As a result, the finance domain becomes bipolar with the United States and China as regional powers rather than hegemons and becomes less stable as a whole. Probability: 5 percent.

Scenario 4

The European Union breaks its alliance with the United States and carves out a separate domain area, in part due to RFAs and in part due to policy disagreement. As a result of the European Union becoming a challenger "state"—in this case, a group of states with a single currency functioning as a single unitary actor—the finance domain becomes bipolar with the United States and the European Union as regional powers, with the possibility that the domain becomes tripolar with China if it follows its separation strategy and becomes the third pole. Probability: 1 percent.

Scenario 5

Challenger State X that is not China—for example, the United Kingdom, Russia, Iran, Japan, Nigeria, or Brazil—carves out a separate, regionally based domain area aided by future RFAs. The finance domain then becomes bipolar with US and Challenger State X as regional powers, with the possibility that the domain becomes tripolar with China as the third pole as it follows its separation strategy. Probability: 1 percent.

Scenario 6

A hegemonic war creates a rupture in the global system similar to the one caused by World War II, except this time the United States suffers losses that force it to cede hegemony of the finance domain. Other countries and unitary actors (e.g., the European Union) also suffer serious losses; as a result, no challenger state rises to claim hegemon status. It is also possible that future RFAs create a revamped finance domain that make having a hegemon unnecessary for the preservation of global financial stability. The finance domain becomes multipolar, with anywhere from three to ten regional powers. Probability: 2 percent.

Notes

1. "Translation: 14th Five-Year Plan for National Informatization—Dec. 2021," translated by Rogier Creemers et al., edited by Johanna Costigan and Graham Webster. 2022. Palo Alto: DigiChina Project, Stanford University: 54.
2. China, France, Russia, the United Kingdom, Germany, and the European Union as a single organizational body.
3. This change is not likely to be a significant one until the people in charge of operating the platforms where cryptocurrency is bought and sold are able to protect themselves against theft. These decentralized finance (DeFi) platforms are, by definition, not protected or backed by any government, so account holders who had a claim on any of the $14 billion stolen from DeFi platforms in 2021 have no recourse to government remedies. Sigalos, McKenzie. 2022. "Crypto scammers took a record $14 billion in 2021." *NBC News*. January 6.
4. Federal Reserve. 2022. "Central Bank Digital Currency (CBDC)."
5. Discussed, for example, in Maurer, Bill. 2015. *How Would You Like to Pay? How Technology Is Changing the Future of Money*. Durham: Duke University Press.
6. Gilpin, Robert. 2016. *The Political Economy of International Relations*. Princeton: Princeton University Press.
7. Downs, George W., David M. Rocke, and Peter N. Barsoom. 1996. "Is the Good News About Compliance Good News About Cooperation?" *International Organization* 50 (3): 379–406.
8. Seddon, Jack. 2020. "The Fate of International Monetary Systems: How and Why They Fall Apart." *Perspectives on Politics* 18 (1): 1–19.
9. Dainoff, Charles. 2021. *Outlaw Paradise: Why Countries Become Tax Havens*. Lanham, MD: Lexington Books.

10. Ben Carter, 2014. "Is China's Economy Really the Largest in the World？ *BBC News.* January 16.

11. Special Drawing Rights (SDRs) are a global reserve asset that the IMF awards to its member states. These states can then use them to buy other states' currencies to boost their reserves. The value of SDRs is based on the following currencies (current weighting in parentheses): US dollar (42 percent), euro (31 percent), Chinese yuan (11 percent), Japanese yen (8 percent), and English pound (8 percent). IMF (International Monetary Fund). 2020. "Special Drawing Right (SDR)." March 24.

12. Bradsher, Keith. 2015."China's Renminbi Is Approved by I.M.F. as a Main World Currency." *New York Times,* November 30.

13. Chatterjee, Saikat. 2015. "Exclusive—China's Payments System Scaled Back; Trade Deals Only" *Reuters*, July 13; Reuters. 2022. "Russia's VTB Launches Transfers in Chinese Yuan Bypassing SWIFT." September 6.

14. Song, Zheng, and Wei Xiong. 2018. "Risks in China's Financial System." *Annual Review of Financial Economics* 10: 261–286.

15. Brunnermeier, Markus K., Michael Sockin, and Wei Xiong. 2022. "China's Model of Managing the Financial System." *Review of Economic Studies* 89 (6): 3115–3153.

16. Song and Xiong 2018.

17. Baron, Matthew, Emil Verner, and Wei Xiong. 2021. "Banking Crises Without Panics." *Quarterly Journal of Economics* 136: 51–113.

18. Horn, Sebastian, Carmen M. Reinhart, and Christoph Trebesch. 2021. "China's Overseas Lending." *Journal of International Economics* 133: 13–14, figures 4 and 5.

19. Gelpern, Anna, Sebastian Horn, Scott Morris, Brad Parks, and Christoph Trebesch. 2021. How China Lends: A Rare Look into 100 Debt Contracts with Foreign Governments. Working Paper. Washington DC: Peterson Institute for International Economics.

20. This material appeared in similar form in Farley, Robert. 2021a. "Does China Weaponize Lending?" *The Diplomat*, July 1.

21. Scheinert, Christian. 2022. "Free Movement of Capital." European Union Parliament.

22. It is beyond the scope of this book to fully evaluate the strengths and weaknesses of this effort. For a skeptical evaluation, Gabor, Daniela, and Cornel Ban. 2016. "Banking on Bonds: The New Links Between States and Markets." *Journal of Common Market Studies* 54 (3): 617–635.

23. Krugman, Paul. 2013. "Revenge of the Optimum Currency Area." *NBER Macroeconomics Annual* 27 (1): 439–448. Data from the World Bank https://data.worldbank.org/indicator/NY.GDP.PCAP.CD?locations=EU; Muro, Diego, and Guillem Vidal. 2014. "Mind the Gaps: The Political Consequences of the Great Recession in Europe." *Eurocrisis in the Press Blog.*

24. Eichengreen, Barry. 2018. "Is Renewed EU Optimism Justified?" *Intereconomics* 53 (1): 47–48.

25. Gorton, Gary. 2012. *Misunderstanding Financial Crises: Why We Don't See Them Coming.* Oxford: Oxford University Press.

26. Robinson, James A., and Daron Acemoglu. 2012. *Why Nations Fail: The Origins of Power, Prosperity and Poverty.* London: Profile.

27. Fujita, Masahisa, Paul R. Krugman, and Anthony Venables. 1999. *The Spatial Economy: Cities, Regions, and International Trade.* Cambridge: MIT Press.

28. Tooze, Adam. 2018. *Crashed: How a Decade of Financial Crises Changed the World.* London: Penguin. See also Banerjee, Abhijit V., and Esther Duflo. 2005. "Growth Theory Through the Lens of Development Economics." *Handbook of Economic Growth* 1: 473–552.

29. Gabor, Daniela. 2021. "The Wall Street Consensus." *Development and Change* 52 (3): 429–459.

30. Weinstein, Jeremy M. 2000. "'Africa's Scramble for Africa': Lessons of a Continental War." *World Policy Journal* 17 (2): 11–20.

31. Ross, Michael. L. 2015. "What Have We Learned About the Resource Curse?" *Annual Review of Political Science* 18: 239–259.

32. Thurston, Alex. 2021. "Why Jihadists Are Collecting 'Zakat' in the Sahel." *Political Violence at a Glance,* July 12.

33. Teichmann, Fabian Maximilian. 2019. "Recent Trends in Money Laundering and Terrorism Financing." *Journal of Financial Regulation and Compliance* 27 (1): 2–12; Dainoff 2021.

34. Federal Reserve 2022.

35. Phillips, Tom. 2022. "Russia Launches Digital Ruble Pilot with 12 Banks." *Near Field Communications World*, January 27.

36. Li, Danny. 2021. "China's Digital Yuan Is Aimed at Home, Not Washington," *Foreign Policy,* October 20; Areddy, James T. 2021. "China Creates Its Own Digital Currency, a First for a Major Economy." *Wall Street Journal*, April 5; Tiezzi, Shannon. 2016. "Move over, Bitcoin: China Wants to Issue Its Own Digital Currency." *The Diplomat*, January 22.

37. Karnfelt, Maximilian, and Kai von Carnap. 2020. "China's New Surveillance Currency." *The Diplomat,* December 4.

38. Fanusie, Yaya J., and Emily Jin. 2021. "China's Digital Currency: Adding Financial Data to Digital Authoritarianism." Washington DC: Center for a New American Security

39. Market capitalizations via Catalyst by Coinmarket.com as of April 10, 2023.

40. To pick one example out of thousands of reports, Hairic, Vildana, and Olga Kharif. 2022. "Bitcoin's Status Quo Is Making Some Long-Time Observers Nervous." Bloomberg, December 5; Gorton, Gary B., and Jeffrey Zhang. 2021a. "The Orkney Slew and Central Bank Digital Currencies." *Harvard National Security Journal,* forthcoming.

41. Kilcrease, Emily, Jason Bartlett, and Mason Wong. 2022. "Sanctions by the Numbers: Economic Measures Against Russia Following Its 2022 Invasion of Ukraine." Washington DC: Center for a New American Security, June 16.

42. Greig, Jonathan. 2022. "Report: $2.2 Billion in Cryptocurrency Stolen from DeFi Platforms in 2021ZDNET, January 6.

43. DOJ (Department of Justice). 2022. "FTX Founder Indicted for Fraud, Money Laundering, and Campaign Finance Expenses." Press Release, December 13.

44. An interesting analysis of the link between cryptocurrencies, particularly stablecoins, and the existing financial infrastructure is Kim, Sang Rae. 2022. *How the Cryptocurrency Market Is Connected to the Financial Market.* Working Paper. sangraekim.com.

45. Gorton, Gary B., and Jeffery Zhang. 2021. "Taming Wildcat Stablecoins." Working Paper 3888752. Rochester NY: Social Science Research Network; Gorton 2012.

46. Krugman, Paul. 2013. "Revenge of the Optimum Currency Area." *NBER Macroeconomics Annual* 27 (1): 439–448.

47. Farrell, Henry, and Abraham Newman. 2019. "America's Misuse of Its Financial Infrastructure." *The National Interest,* April 15.

48. Saravalle, Eduardo. 2021. "The Watchful Eye of the US Dollar." *The Alchemist,* May 19.

49. Keohane, Robert. 2005. *After Hegemony: Cooperation and Discord in the World Political Economy.* Princeton: Princeton University Press.

Bibliography

Aaslestad, Katherine. 2014. "Revisiting Napoleon's Continental System: Consequences of Economic Warfare." In *Revisiting Napoleon's Continental System: Local, Regional, and European Experiences,* edited by Katherine Aaslestad and Johan Joor, 1–22. New York: Springer.

Abrahams, Paul Philip. 1968. "The Foreign Expansion of American Finance and Its Relationship to the Foreign Economic Policies of the United States, 1907–1921." *The Business History Review* 42 (2): 177–200.

Aerts, Erik. 2006. "The European Monetary Famine of the Late Middle Ages and the Bank of San Giorgio in Genoa." *Ligurian Society of Homeland History Conference Proceedings,* 27–62.

Ahmed, Mohammed. 2009. "Somali Sea Gangs Lure Investors at Pirate Lair." Reuters, December 1.

Alexander, Keith B. 2007. *Warfighting in Cyberspace.* Washington, DC: National Defense University Institute for National Strategic Studies.

Alstadsaeter, Annette, Niels Johannsen, and Gabriel Zucman. 2018. "Who Owns the Wealth in Tax Havens? Macro Evidence and Implications for Global Inequality." *Journal of Public Economics* 162: 89–100.

Alston, Richard. 1994. "Roman Military Pay from Caesar to Diocletian." *Journal of Roman Studies* 84: 113–123.

Altamura, Carlo Edoardo. 2017. "The Paradox of the 1970s: The Renaissance of International Banking and the Rise of Public Debt." *Journal of Modern European History* 15 (4): 529–553.

Anderson, Scott, and Chiméne Keitner. 2022. "The Legal Challenges Presented by Seizing Frozen Russian Assets." *Lawfare,* May 26.

Aperghis, Gerassimos George. 2004. *The Seleukid Royal Economy: The Finances and Financial Administration of the Seleukid Empire.* Cambridge: Cambridge University Press.

Areddy, James T. 2021. "China Creates Its Own Digital Currency, a First for a Major Economy." *Wall Street Journal,* April 5.

Aris, Ben. 2022. "Is Russia's Economy Headed for 'Economic Oblivion,' as a Report from Yale Says?" *BNE Intellinews,* August 8.

Aristotle. 1920. *Oeconomica.* Translated by Edward Seymour Forster. Oxford: Clarendon Press.

Arnold, Arthur Z. 1996. *Banks, Credit, and Money in Soviet Russia.* New York: Columbia University Press.

Aron, Janine, Ibrahim Elbadawi, and Brian Kahn. 1997. *Determinants of the Real Exchange Rate in South Africa*. Oxford: Centre for the Study of African Economies, Institute of Economics and Statistics, University of Oxford.

Arti. 2022. "Russia to Lay Down a Legal Framework for National Crypto Exchange." *Analytics Insight*, November 28.

Austin, Michael Marting, and Pierre Vidal-Naquet. 1977. *Economic and Social History of Ancient Greece: An Introduction*. Berkeley: University of California Press.

Bajpai, Nirupam. 1994. "India's External Debt: Retrospect and Prospects." *Economic and Political Weekly*, 2232–2245.

Banerjee, Abhijit V., and Esther Duflo. 2005. "Growth Theory Through the Lens of Development Economics." *Handbook of Economic Growth* 1: 473–552.

The Banker. 2021. "Top 1,000 World Banks 2021.".

Baron, Matthew, Emil Verner, and Wei Xiong. 2021. "Banking Crises Without Panics." *Quarterly Journal of Economics* 136: 51–113.

Barnes, Julian E. 2022. "Russia Is Buying North Korean Artillery, According to US Intelligence." *New York Times*, September 5.

Barzel, Yoram, and Edgar Kiser. 2002. "Taxation and Voting Rights in Medieval England and France." *Rationality and Society* 14 (4): 473–507.

Batchelor, Peter, Paul Dunne, and Guy Lamb. 2002. "The Demand for Military Spending in South Africa." *Journal of Peace Research* 39 (3): 339–354.

Bech, Morten L., and Bart Hobijn. 2007. "Technology Diffusion with Central Banking: The Case of Real-Time Gross Settlement." *International Journal of Central Banking* 3 (3): 147–181.

Bell, Stephen. 2013. *The Rise of the People's Bank of China*. Cambridge: Harvard University Press.

Bensch, Stephen P. 2002. *Barcelona and Its Rulers, 1096–1291*. No. 26. Cambridge: Cambridge University Press.

Bernanke, Ben S. 1983. *Non-monetary Effects of the Financial Crisis in the Propagation of the Great Depression*. Cambridge MA: National Bureau of Economic Research (NBER) NBER Working Paper No. 1054.

BIS (Bank for International Settlements). 2019. "Foreign Exchange Turnover in April 2019." September 16.

———. 2021. Press Releases. US Department of Commerce, July 2.

Blackwill, Robert D., and Jennifer M. Harris. 2016. *War by Other Means: Geoeconomics and Statecraft*. Cambridge: Harvard University Press.

Blaisdell, Donald C. 1929. *European Financial Control in the Ottoman Empire*. New York: Columbia University Press.

Blaydes, Lisa, and Christopher Paik. 2016. "The Impact of Holy Land Crusades on State Formation: War Mobilization, Trade Integration, and Political Development in Medieval Europe." *International Organization* 70 (3): 551–586.

Blenkinsop, Phillip. 2022. "EU Bars 7 Banks from SWIFT, but Spares Those in Energy." Reuters, March 3.

Blue, Frederick J. 1987. *Salmon P. Chase: A Life in Politics*. Kent: Kent State University Press.

Boden, Ragna. 2008. "Cold War Economics: Soviet Aid to Indonesia." *Journal of Cold War Studies* 10 (3): 110–128.

Bolt, Jutta, and Jan Luiten van Zanden. 2020. *Maddison Style Estimates of the Evolution of the World Economy: A New 2020 Update*. Gronigen NL: University of Gronigen. Working Paper. Maddison-Project.

Bonney, Richard. 1976. "The Secret Expenses of Richelieu and Mazarin, 1624–1661." *English Historical Review* 91 (361): 825–836.

———. 1981. *The King's Debts: Finance and Politics in France, 1589–1661*. New York: Clarendon Press; Oxford: Oxford University Press.
———, ed. 1999. *The Rise of the Fiscal State in Europe, c.1200–1815*. Oxford: Oxford University Press.
Bordo, Michael. 2007a. "The Bretton Woods International Monetary System: A Historical Overview." In *A Retrospective on the Bretton Woods System: Lessons for International Monetary Reform*, edited by Michael D. Bordo and Barry Eichengreen.. Chicago: University of Chicago Press, 5-108.
———. 2007b. "A Brief History of Central Banks." *Economic Commentary*, December. Cleveland: Federal Reserve Bank of Cleveland.
Bordo, Michael D., and Barrry Eichengreen. 2013. "Bretton Woods and the Great Inflation." In *The Great Inflation: The Rebirth of Modern Central Banking*, edited by Michael D. Bordo and Athanasios Orphanides, 449–498. Chicago: University of Chicago Press.
Bordo, Michael D., and Finn E. Kydland. 1990. *Gold Standard as a Rule*. Series w3367. Cambridge, MA: NBER.
Bordo, Michael D., Eric Monnet, and Alain Naef. 2019. "The Gold Pool (1961–1968) and the Fall of the Bretton Woods System: Lessons for Central Bank Cooperation." *Journal of Economic History* 79 (4): 1027–1059.
Bordo, Michael D., and Hugh Rockoff. 1996. "The Gold Standard as a 'Good Housekeeping Seal of Approval.'" *Journal of Economic History* 56 (2): 389–428.
Bordo, Michael D., and Anna J. Schwartz, eds. 2009. *A Retrospective on the Classical Gold Standard, 1821–1931*. Chicago: University of Chicago Press.
Bordo, Michael D., and Eugene N. White. 1991. "A Tale of Two Currencies: British and French Finance During the Napoleonic Wars." *Journal of Economic History* 51 (2): 303–316.
BP. 2022. "British Petroleum Statistical Review 2022."
Bradsher, Keith. 2015. "China's Renminbi Is Approved by I.M.F. as a Main World Currency." *New York Times*, November 30.
Bramhall, Edith Clementine. 1901. "The Origin of the Temporal Privileges of Crusaders." *American Journal of Theology* 5 (2): 279–292.
Bransbourg, Gilles. 2015. "The Later Roman Empire." In *Fiscal Regimes and the Political Economy of Premodern States*, edited by Andrew Monson and Walter Scheidel, 258–281. Cambridge: Cambridge University Press.
Brecher, Michael. 1977. "India's Devaluation of 1966: Linkage Politics and Crisis Decision-Making." *Review of International Studies* 3 (1): 1–25.
Brewer, John. 2002. *The Sinews of Power: War, Money, and the English State, 1688–1783*. Oxfordshire: Routledge.
Brogan, Pamela. 1992. *The Torturers' Lobby*. Washington, DC: Center for Public Integrity.
Broz, Lawrence J. 1997. *The International Origins of the Federal Reserve System*. Ithaca: Cornell University Press.
Brundage, James A. 1997. "Crusaders and Jurists: The Legal Consequences of Crusader Status." *Publications de l'École Française de Rome* 236 (1): 141–154.
Brunnermeier, Markus K., Michael Sockin, and Wei Xiong. 2022. "China's Model of Managing the Financial System." *Review of Economic Studies* 89 (6): 3115–3153.
Burdekin, Richard C. K., and Forrokh K. Langdana. 1993. "War Finance in the Southern Confederacy, 1861–1865." *Explorations in Ecomic History* 30 (3): 352–376.
Burdekin, Richard C. K., and Marc D. Weidenmier. 2000. "The Option Value of Confederate Currency and Inflation Control, 1861–1865." Unpublished manuscript, Claremont Colleges Working Paper in Economics, July.

Butcher, Kevin. 2015. "Debasement and the Decline of Rome." In *Studies in Ancient Coinage in Honor of Andrew Burnett*, edited by Richard Ashton, Silvia Hurter, and Caroline Petit, 181–205. London: Spink and Son.

Capie, Forrest, Charles Goodhart, and Norbert Schnadt. 1994. "The Development of Central Banking." In *The Future of Central Banking: The Tercentenary Symposium of the Bank of England*, edited by Forrest Capie, Stanley Fischer, Charles Goodhart, and Norbert Schnadt, 1–261. Cambridge: Cambridge University Press.

Cappella Zielinski, Rosella. 2016. *How States Pay for Wars*. Ithaca: Cornell University Press.

Carlos, Ann M., Erin K. Fletcher, Larry Neal, and Kirsten Wandschenider. 2013. "Financing and Refinancing the War of the Spanish Succession, and then Refinancing the South Sea Company." In *Questioning Credible Commitment: Perspectives on the Rise of Financial Capitalism*, edited by D'Maris Coffman, Adrian Leonard, and Larry Neal, 147–168. Cambridge: Cambridge University Press.

Carr, Edward Hallett. 2016. *The Twenty Years' Crisis, 1919–1939*. 2nd ed. Edited by Michael Cox. London: Springer.

Carter, Ben. 2014. "Is China's Economy Really the Largest in the World?" *BBC News*, January 16.

Catterall, Ralph Charles Henry. 1902. *The Second Bank of the United States*. Chicago: University of Chicago Press.

Caytas, Joanna Diane. 2017. "Weaponizing Finance: US and European Options, Tools, and Policies." *Columbia Journal of European Law* 23 (2): 441–476.

Cazel, Fred. 1989. "Financing the Crusades." In *The History of the Crusades*, Vol. 6: *The Impact of the Crusades on Europe*, edited by Harry Hazard and Norman Zacour, 116–149. Madison: University of Wisconsin Press.

Chan, Kenneth S. 2008. "Foreign Trade, Commercial Policies and the Political Economy of the Song and Ming Dynasties of China." *Australian Economic History Review* 48 (1): 68–90.

Chatterjee, Saikat. 2015. "Exclusive—China's Payments System Scaled Back; Trade Deals Only." *Reuters*, July 13.

Christie, Edward. 2015. "Sanctions After Crimea: Have They worked?" *NATO Review*, March 17.

CIA (Central Intelligence Agency). 1975. "The Changing Role of Soviet-Owned Banks in the West."

Cicero, Marcus Tullius. 1913. "The Fifth Philippic." In *The Orations of Marcus Tullius Cicero*, Vol. 4. London: G. Bell and Sons.

Clark, Gregory. 2009. *The Macroeconomic Aggregates for England, 1209–2008*. Working Paper 09-19. Davis: Department of Economics, University of California Davis.

Clarke, Colin P., Kimberly Jackson, Patrick B. Johnston, Eric Robinson, and Howard J. Shatz. 2017. *Financial Futures of the Islamic State of Iraq and the Levant: Findings from a RAND Corporation Workshop*. Santa Monica: RAND.

Cobham, Alex, and Petr Jansky. 2020. *Estimating Illicit Financial Flows: A Critical Guide to the Data, Methodologies, and Findings*. Oxford: Oxford University Press.

Cohen, Benjamin J. 2005. *The Macrofoundation of Monetary Power*. Working Papers 2005/08. San Domenico di Fiesole IT: Robert Schuman Center for Advanced Studies, European University Institute.

Cohen, Eliot A. 1996. "A Revolution in Warfare." *Foreign Affairs* 75: 37–54.

Collet, Stephanie, and Kim Oosterlinck. 2019. "Denouncing Odious Debts." *Journal of Business Ethics* 160 (1): 205–223.

Collier, Paul, and Anke Hoeffler. 2002. "On the Incidence of Civil War in Africa." *Journal of Conflict Resolution* 46 (1): 13–28.
Congressional Research Service. 2009. *North Korean Counterfeiting of U.S. Currency.* Report for Congress. Washington, DC: Congressional Research Service.
———. 2020. *Instances of Use of United States Armed Forces Abroad, 1798–2020.* Report R42738. Washington, DC: Congressional Research Service.
———. 2021. *U.S. Sanctions on Russia: An Overview.* In Focus IF11730. Washington, DC: Congressional Research Service.
Contamine, Philippe. 1986. *War in the Middle Ages.* Translated by Michael Jones. New York: Blackwell.
Cooper, Richard N., Rudiger Dornbusch, and Robert E. Hall. 1982. "The Gold Standard: Historical Facts and Future Prospects." *Brookings Papers on Economic Activity* 1: 1–56.
Cortes, Hernando. 2004. *Five Letters, 1519–1526.* Abingdon: Taylor and Francis.
Cowen, David, and Richard Sylla. 2018. *Alexander Hamilton on Finance, Credit, and Debt.* New York: Columbia University Press.
Creemers, Rogier, Hunter Dorwart, Kevin Neville, and Kendra Schaefer. 2022. *Translation: 14th Five-Year Plan for National Informatization—Dec. 2021.* Edited by Johanna Costigan and Graham Webster. Palo Alto: DigiChina Project, Stanford University.
Cribb, Joe. 1979. "An Historical Survey of the Precious Metal Currencies of China." *Numismatic Chronicle* 19: 185–209.
Curry, Robert L. 1979. "Africa's External Debt Situation." *Journal of Modern African Studies* 17 (1): 15–28.
Dainoff, Charles. 2021. *Outlaw Paradise: Why Countries Become Tax Havens.* Lanham, MD: Lexington Books.
Daley, Jason. 2016. "Archaeologists Uncover Massive Naval Bases of the Ancient Athenians." *Smithsonian Magazine,* June 17.
D'Altroy, Terence N. 2015. "The Inka Empire." In *Fiscal Regimes and the Political Economy of the Premodern States,* edited by Andrew Monson and Walter Scheidel, 253–274. Cambridge: Cambridge University Press.
Daly, Gavin. 2007. "Napoleon and the 'City of Smugglers,' 1810–1814." *The Historical Journal* 50 (2): 333–352.
Dash, Mark. 2012. "'Kipper und Wipper': Rogue Traders, Rogue Princes, Rogue Bishops, and the German Financial Meltdown of 1621–23." *Smithsonian Magazine Blogs,* March 29.
Davis, George K., and Gary M. Pecquet. 1990. "Interest Rates in the Civil War South." *Journal of Economic History* 50 (1): 135–146.
Davis, Lance E., and Stanley L. Engerman. 2006. *Naval Blockades in Peace and War: An Economic History Since 1750.* Cambridge: Cambridge University Press.
Dawson, Frank Griffith. 1990. *The First Latin American Debt Crisis: The City of London and the 1822–25 Loan Bubble.* New Haven: Yale University Press.
de Grauwe, Paul. 1975. "The Development of the Euro-Currency Market." *Finance and Development* 12 (3): 12–17.
Dehing, Pit, and Marjolein t' Hart. 1997. "Linking the Fortunes: Currency and Banking, 1550–1800." In *A Financial History of the Netherlands,* edited by Marjolein t' Hart, Joost Jonker, and Jan Luiten Van Zanden, 38–40. Cambridge: Cambridge University Press.
De Luce, Dan. 2022. "Too Big to Sanction? A Large Russian Bank Still Operates Freely Because It Helps Europe Get Russian Gas." *NBC News,* June 18.

Denmark, Abraham, and James Mulvenon. 2010. *Contested Commons: The Future of American Military Power in a Multipolar World*. Washington, DC: Center for a New American Security (CNAS).

Dent, Julian. 1973. *Crisis in Finance: Crown, Financiers, and Society in Seventeenth-Century France*. New York: St. Martin's Press.

Dessy, Sylvain E., and Desire Vencatachellum. 2007. "Debt Relief and Social Services Expenditure: The African Experience, 1989–2003." *African Development Review* 19 (1): 200–216.

Diaz-Alejandro, Carlos 1985. "Good-Bye Financial Repression, Hello Financial Crash." *Journal of Development Economics* 19 (1–2): 1–24.

Dickson, Peter George Muir. 2017. *The Financial Revolution in England: A Study in the Development of Public Credit, 1688–1756*. Abingdon: Routledge.

Dinan, Desmond. 1994. *Ever Closer Union*. Boulder: Lynne Rienner.

DOJ (US Department of Justice). 2022. "FTX Founder Indicted for Fraud, Money Laundering, and Campaign Finance Expenses." Press Release, December 13.

DOT (US Department of the Treasury). 2021. Press Releases. July 2. https://home.treasury.gov/news/press-releases/jy0260.

———. 2022. "Statement by the Group of Creditors of Ukraine." July 20.

Dowell, Stephen. 1884. *History of Taxation and Taxes in England from the Earliest Times to the Present Day*. London: Longmans, Green.

Downs, George W., David M. Rocke, and Peter N. Barsoom. 1996. "Is the Good News About Compliance Good News About Cooperation?" *International Organization* 50 (3): 379–406.

Drake, Paul W. 1989. *The Money Doctor in the Andes*. Durham: Duke University Press.

Drelichman, Mauricio, and Hans-Joachim Voth. 2016. *Lending to the Borrower from Hell: Debt, Taxes, and Default in the Age of Phillip II*. Princeton: Princeton University Press.

Drezner, Daniel. 2021. "The Uses and Abuses of Weaponized Interdependence." In *The Uses and Abuses of Weaponized Interdependence*, edited by Daniel Drezner, Henry Farrell, and Abraham Newman, 1–18. Washington, DC: Brookings Institution Press.

Dube, Arindrajit, Ethan Kaplan, and Suresh Naidu. 2011. "Coups, Corporations, and Classified Information." *Quarterly Journal of Economics* 126 (3): 1375–1409.

Easterly, William, and Stanley Fischer. 1994. "What We Can Learn from the Soviet Collapse." *Finance and Development* 31 (4): 2–7.

ECB (European Central Bank). 2021. "ECB Mission Statement."

The Economist. 2022. "The West's Proposed Price Cap on Russian Oil Is No Magic Weapon." November 30.

Edling, Max M. 2014. *A Hercules in the Cradle: War, Money, and the American State, 1783–1867*. Chicago: University of Chicago Press.

Eichengreen, Barry. 1987. "Conducting the International Orchestra: Bank of England Under the Classical Gold Standard." *Journal of International Money and Finance* 6 (1): 5–29.

———. 1996. *Golden Fetters: The Gold Standard and the Great Depression, 1919–1939*. Oxford: Oxford University Press.

———. 2011. *Exorbitant Privilege: The Rise and Fall of the Dollar and the Future of the International Monetary System*. Cary: Oxford University Press.

———. 2018. "Is Renewed EU Optimism Justified?" *Intereconomics* 53 (1): 47–48.

Eichengreen, Barry J., and Douglas A. Irwin. 1995. "Trade Blocs, Currency Blocs, and the Reorientation of World Trade in the 1930s." *Journal of International Economics* 38 (1–2): 1–24.

———. 2009. *The Slide to Protectionism: Who Succumbed and Why.* Working Paper 15142. Cambridge MA: NBER.
Eichengreen, Barry, Arnaud Mehl, and Livia Chitu. 2019. "Mars or Mercury? The Geopolitics of International Currency Choice." *Economic Policy* 34 (98): 315–363.
Eichengreen, Barry J., and Richard Portes. 1985. *Debt and Default in the 1930s: Causes and Consequences.* Working Paper 1772. Cambridge MA: NBER.
———. 1990. "The Interwar Debt Crisis and Its Aftermath." *World Bank Research Observer* 5 (1): 69–94.
Eichengreen, Barry J., and Jeffrey Sachs. 1985. "Exchange Rates and Economic Recovery in the 1930s." *Journal of Economic History* 45 (4): 925–946.
Eldem, Edhem. 2005. "Ottoman Financial Integration with Europe: Foreign Loans, the Ottoman Bank, and the Ottoman Public Debt." *European Review* 13 (3): 431–443.
Ellickson, Robert C., and Charles DiA Thorland. 1995. "Ancient Land Law: Mesopotamia, Egypt, Israel." *Chicago-Kent Law Review* 71: 321–358.
EOP (Executive Office of the President). 2021. Executive Order No. 14014. *Federal Register,* February 12.
Epstein, Katherine C. 2014. *Torpedo.* Cambridge: Harvard University Press.
Epstein, Steven. 1996. *Genoa and the Genoese, 958–1528.* Chapel Hill: University of North Carolina Press.
Epstein, Stephan. 2000. *Freedom and Growth: The Rise of States and Markets in Europe, 1300–1750.* London: Routledge.
Ereira, Alan. 2015. *The Invergordon Mutiny: A Narrative History of the Last Great Mutiny in the Royal Navy and How It Forced Britain Off the Gold Standard in 1931.* London: Routledge.
European Union Home Page. 2023. "Principles, Countries, History."
Ezrow, Natasha M., and Erica Frantz. 2013. *Failed States and Institutional Decay: Understanding Instability and Poverty in the Developing World.* New York: Bloomsbury.
Fanusie, Yaya J., and Emily Jin. 2021. "China's Digital Currency: Adding Financial Data to Digital Authoritarianism." Washington, DC: Center for a New American Security.
Farley, Robert M. 2014. *Grounded: The Case for Abolishing the United States Air Force.* Lexington: University Press of Kentucky.
———. 2021a. "Does China Weaponize Lending?" *The Diplomat,* July 1.
———. 2021b. "What Han China's Financial Relations with Rome Can Teach Us Today." *The Diplomat,* May 28.
———. 2021c. "What Does Finance Have to Do with War?" *The Diplomat,* March 31.
Farrell, Henry, and Abraham Newman. 2019. "America's Misuse of Its Financial Infrastructure." *The National Interest,* April 15.
———. 2021. "Weaponized Interdependence: How Global Economic Networks Shape State Coercion." In *The Uses and Abuses of Weaponized Interdependence,* edited by Daniel Drezner, Henry Farrell, and Abraham L. Newman, 19–66. Washington, DC: Brookings Institution Press.
Federal Register. 2002. Vol. 67, No. 24, December 26, 2002.
———. 2005. Vol. 70, No. 79, April 26, 2005.
Federal Reserve. 2022. "Central Bank Digital Currency (CBDC)."
Feis, Herbert. 1930. *Europe, the World's Banker 1870–1914: An Account of European Foreign Investment and the Connection of World Finance with Diplomacy Before the War.* New Haven: Yale University Press.
———. 1940. *Changing Pattern of International Economic Affairs.* New York: Harper & Brothers.

———. 1951. "Keynes in Retrospect." *Foreign Affairs* 29 (4): 564–577.
Feld, Maury D. 1975. "Middle-Class Society and the Rise of Military Professionalism: The Dutch Army, 1589–1609." *Armed Forces and Society* 1 (4): 419–442.
Fernandez, Andres. 2008. "Capital Flows and Business Cycles in Latin America During 1920s and 30s: A Second Look from a Neoclassical Perspective." Working paper. New Brunswick: Rutgers University.
FinCEN (Financial Crimes Enforcement Network). 2021a. "311 Special Measures."
———. 2021b. *USA PATRIOT Act.*
Finley, Moses I. 1982. *Economy and Society in Ancient Greece.* New York: Viking Press
Finnemore, Martha. 2013. *The Purpose of Intervention.* Ithaca: Cornell University Press.
Fisher, Douglas. 1989. "The Price Revolution: A Monetary Interpretation." *Journal of Economic History* 49: 884–902.
Flaherty, Jane. 2009. "The Exhausted Condition of the Treasury on the Eve of the Civil War." *Civil War History* 55 (2): 253–278.
Flandreau, Marc, ed. 2005. *Money Doctors: The Experience of International Financial Advising, 1850–2000.* Vol. 26. London: Routledge.
Flandreau, Marc, and Juan H. Flores. 2012. "The Peaceful Conspiracy: Bond Markets and International Relations During the Pax Britannica." *International Organization* 66 (2): 211–241.
Flandreau, Marc, Norbert Gaillard, and Frank Packer. 2011. "To Err Is Human: Rating Agencies and the Interwar Foreign Government Debt Crisis." *European Review of Economic History* 15 (3): 495–538.
Flandreau, Marc, Juan H. Flores, Norbert Gaillard, Sebastián Nieto-Parra, and Quentin Stoeffler. 2010. "The End of Gatekeeping: Underwriters and the Quality of Sovereign Bond Markets, 1815–2007." NBER International Seminar on Macroeconomics 6 (1): 53–92.
Forder, James. 2003. "'Independence' and the Founding of the Federal Reserve." *Scottish Journal of Political Economy* 50 (3): 297–310.
Frankopan, Peter. 2019. *The New Silk Roads: The Present and Future of the World.* New York: Knopf.
Friedman, Milton, and Anna Jacobson Schwartz. 2008. *A Monetary History of the United States, 1867–1960.* Princeton: Princeton University Press.
Frost, Robert I. 2014. *The Northern Wars: War, State, and Society in Northeastern Europe, 1558–1721.* London: Routledge.
Fujita, Masahisa, Paul R. Krugman, and Anthony Venables. 1999. *The Spatial Economy: Cities, Regions, and International Trade.* Cambridge: MIT Press.
Fynn-Paul, Jeff. 2014. "Military Entrepreneurs in the Crown of Aragon During the Castilian-Aragonese War, 1356–1375." In *War, Entrepreneurs, and the State in Europe and the Mediterranean, 1300–1800,* edited by Jeff Fynn-Paul, 105–124. Leiden: Brill.
Gabor, Daniela. 2021. "The Wall Street Consensus." *Development and Change* 52 (3): 429–459.
Gabor, Daniela, and Cornel Ban. 2016. "Banking on Bonds: The New Links Between States and Markets." *Journal of Common Market Studies* 54 (3): 617–635.
Galli, Marco. 2017. "Beyond Frontiers: Ancient Rome and the Eurasian Trade Networks." *Journal of Eurasian Studies* 8 (1): 3–9.
Garamone, Jim. 2019. "Trump Signs Law Establishing U.S. Space Force." *DOD [United States Department of Defense] News.* December 20.
Garvy, George. 1972. "Banking Under the Tsars and the Soviets." *Journal of Economic History* 32 (4): 869–893.

Gavin, Francis J. 2002. "The Gold Battles Within the Cold War: American Monetary Policy and the Defense of Europe, 1960–1963." *Diplomatic History* 26 (1): 61–94.

———. 2004. *Dollars and Power: The Politics of International Monetary Relations, 1958–1971*. Chapel Hill: University of North Carolina Press.

Gelpern, Anna, Sebastian Horn, Scott Morris, Brad Parks, and Christoph Trebesch. 2021. *How China Lends: A Rare Look into 100 Debt Contracts with Foreign Governments*. Working Paper. Washington DC: Peterson Institute for International Economics.

Gerth, Hans H., and Charles Wright Mills. 1946. *Max Weber*. Oxford: Oxford University Press.

Gienapp, William E. 1992. "Abraham Lincoln and the Border States." *Journal of the Abraham Lincoln Association* 13 (1): 13-46.

Gilpin, Robert. 1981. *War and Change in World Politics*. Cambridge: Cambridge University Press.

———. 2016. *The Political Economy of International Relations*. Princeton: Princeton University Press.

Gilpin, Robert, and Jean M. Gilpin. 2001. *Global Political Economy: Understanding the International Economic Order*. Princeton: Princeton University Press.

Giroux, Gary. 2012. "Financing the American Civil War: Developing New Tax Sources." *Accounting History* 17 (1): 85–107.

Goedhuys, Diederik. 1994. "South African Monetary Policy in the 1980s: Years of Reform and Foreign Financial Aggression." *South African Journal of Economic History* 9 (2): 145–164.

Goff, Brian L., and Mark Toma. 1993. "Optimal Seigniorage, the Gold Standard, and Central Bank Financing." *Journal of Money, Credit, and Banking* 25 (1): 79–95.

Goldberg, Linda S., and Il'dar Karimov. 1991. *Internal Currency Markets and Production in the Soviet Union*. Working Paper w3614. Washington, DC: NBER

Goldman, Marshall I. 1965. "A Balance Sheet of Soviet Foreign Aid." *Foreign Affairs* 43 (2): 349–360.

Goldstone, Jack A. 1991. "Monetary Versus Velocity Interpretations of the 'Price Revolution': A Comment." *Journal of Economic History* 51: 176–181.

Golubkova, Katya, and Gabriela Baczynska. 2014. "Rouble Fall, Sanctions Hurt Russia's Economy: Medvedev." Reuters, December 10.

Google Finance. 2022. "Ukrainian Hryvnia to United States Dollar." December 5.

Gorton, Gary. 2012. *Misunderstanding Financial Crises: Why We Don't See Them Coming*. Oxford: Oxford University Press.

Gorton, Gary B., and Jeffrey Zhang. 2021a. "The Orkney Slew and Central Bank Digital Currencies." *Harvard National Security Journal*, forthcoming.

———. 2021b. "Taming Wildcat Stablecoins." Working Paper 3888752. Rochester NY: Social Science Research Network

Graham, Maj. Matt. 2016. "U.S. Cyber Force: One War Away." *Military Review* 96 (3): 10–18.

Greene, Joshua. 1989. "The External Debt Problem of Sub-Saharan Africa." *IMF Staff Papers* 36 (4): 836–874.

Greene, Joshua, and Mohsin S. Khan. 1990. *African Debt Crisis*. Nairobi: Intiatives.

Gregory, Paul, and Roberrt Stuart. 1994. *Soviet and Post-Soviet Economic Structure and Performance*. New York: HarperCollins.

Gregory, Paul R., and Aleksei Tikhonov. 2000. "Central Planning and Unintended Consequences: Creating the Soviet Financial System, 1930–1939." *Journal of Economic History* 60 (4): 1017–1040.

Greig, Jonathan. 2022. "Report: $2.2 Billion in Cyptocurrency Stolen from DeFi Platforms in 2021." ZDNET, January 6.

Griffith-Jones, S. 1980. "The Growth of Multinational Banking, the Euro-Currency Market and Their Effects on Developing Countries." *Journal of Development Studies* 16 (2): 204–223.

Gulhati, Ravi I. 1972. "India's External Debt." *India Quarterly* 28 (1): 3–11.

Hairic, Vildana, and Olga Kharif. 2022. "Bitcoin's Status Quo Is Making Some Long-Time Observers Nervous." Bloomberg, December 5.

Haldon, John. 2015. "Late Rome, Byzantium, and Early Medieval Western Europe." In *Fiscal Regimes and the Political Economy of Premodern States*, edited by Andrew Monson and Walter Scheidel, 107–127. Cambridge: Cambridge University Press.

Hamilton, Alexander. 1788. *Federalist No. 31*. January 1.

———. 2019. "The Defense of the Funding System." In *Alexander Hamilton on Finance, Credit, and Debt*, edited by Richard Sylla and David J. Cowen, 297–298. New York: Columbia University Press.

Hamilton, Charles D. 2016. *Plutarch's "Life of Agesilaus."* Berlin: DeGruyter.

Hamilton, Earl J. 2013. *American Treasure and the Price Revolution in Spain, 1501–1650*. Cambridge: Harvard University Press.

Hardin, Garrett. 1998. "Extensions of the 'Tragedy of the Commons.'" *Science* 280 (5364): 682–683.

Hawser, Anita. 2022. "Sberbank Takes De-SWIFTing in Stride." *Global Finance*, June 2.

Haynes, Deborah. 2022. "Russia Flew €140m in Cash and Captured Western Weapons to Iran in Return for Deadly Drones, Sources Claim." *Sky News*, November 9.

Heftye, Eric. 2017. "Multi-Domain Confusion: All Domains Are Not Created Equal." Strategy Bridge, May 26.

Helleiner, Eric. 2002. "The Monetary Dimensions of Colonialism: Why Did Imperial Powers Create Currency Blocks?" *Geopolitics* 7 (1): 5–30.

———. 2014. *Forgotten Foundations of Bretton Woods: International Development and the Making of the Postwar Order.* Ithaca: Cornell University Press.

Hendrickson, Joshua R. 2020. "The Riksbank, Emergency Finance, Policy Experimentation, and Sweden's Reversal of Fortune." *Journal of Economic Behavior and Organization* 171: 312–332.

Hensel, Paul R. 1994. "One Thing Leads to Another: Recurrent Militarized Disputes in Latin America, 1816–1986." *Journal of Peace Research* 31 (3): 281–297.

Herodotus. 2008. *The Histories*. Translated by Robin Waterfield. Oxford: Oxford University Press.

Hilton, Stanley E. 1973. "Military Influence on Brazilian Economic Policy, 1930–1945: A Different View." *Hispanic American Historical Review* 53 (1): 71–94.

Hirsch, Paddy. 2022. "How Russia Rescued the Ruble." National Public Radio, April 5.

Hoffman, Frank G., and Michael C. Davies. 2013. "Joint Force 2020 and the Human Domain: Time for a New Conceptual Framework?" *Small Wars Journal*, June 10, 1:30 A.M.

Hoffman, Philip T. 1994. "Early Modern France, 1450–1700." In *Fiscal Crises, Liberty, and Representative Government, 1450–1789*, edited by Philip T. Hoffman and Kathryn Norberg, 172–223. Stanford: Stanford University Press.

Holbik, Karel. 1968. "A Comparison of US and Soviet Foreign Aid, 1961–1965." *Weltwirtschaftliches Archiv* 100 (2): 320–340.

Holland, Steve, and Jeff Mason. 2014. "Update 4: Obama Warns on Crimea, Orders Sanctions over Russian Moves in Ukraine." Reuters, March 6.
Holt, Frank Lee. 2016. *The Treasures of Alexander the Great: How One Man's Wealth Shaped the World.* Oxford: Oxford University Press.
Hoover, Calvin B. 1926. "The Sea Loan in Genoa in the Twelfth Century." *Quarterly Journal of Economics* 40 (3): 372–401.
Horesh, Niv. 2004. "The Transition from Coinage to Paper Money in China: Hallmarks of Statehood in Global Perspective, 8th Century BC to 1935 AD." *Journal of the Institute of Asian Studies* 21 (2): 1–26.
———. 2014. *Chinese Money in Global Context: Historic Junctures Between 600 BCE and 2012.* Palo Alto: Stanford University Press.
Horesh, Niv, and Hyun Jin Kim. 2011. "Why Coins Turned Round the World over? A Critical Analysis of the Origins and Transmission of Ancient Metallic Money." *China Report* 47 (4): 279–302.
Horn, Sebastian, Carmen M. Reinhart, and Christoph Trebesch. 2021. "China's Overseas Lending." *Journal of International Economics* 133: 1–32.
Horowitz, Michael. 2010. *The Diffusion of Military Power: Causes and Consequences for International Politics.* Princeton: Princeton University Press.
Howgego, Christopher. 1992. "The Supply and Use of Money in the Roman World, 200 BC to AD 300." *Journal of Roman Studies* 82: 1–31.
Huff, Gregg. 2007. "Financial Transititon in Pre–World War II Japan and Southeast Asia." *Financial History Review* 14 (2): 149–173.
Huff, Gregg, and Shinobu Majima. 2013. "Financing Japan's World War II Occupation of Southeast Asia." *Journal of Economic History* 73 (4): 937–977.
Hughes, Matthew. 2005. "Logistics and the Chaco War: Bolivia Versus Paraguay, 1932–1925." *Journal of Military History* 69 (2): 411–437.
Ibrahim, Mahmood. 1990. *Merchant Capital and Islam.* Austin: University of Texas Press.
Ikenberry, G. John. 2007. "The Political Origins of Bretton Woods." In *A Retrospective on the Bretton Woods System,* edited by Michael D. Bordo and Barry Eichengreen, 155–198. Chicago: University of Chicago.
———. 2020. *A World Safe for Democracy: Liberal Internationalism and the Crises of Global Order.* New Haven: Yale University Press.
IMF (International Monetary Fund). 2020. "Special Drawing Rights (SDR)." March 24.
Izetzki, Ethan, Carmen M. Reinhart, and Kenneth S. Rogoff. 2017. *Exchange Arrangements Entering the 21st Century: Which Anchor Will Hold?* Cambridge MA: NBER.
James, Harold. 2021. "Weaponized Interdependence and International Monetary Systems." In *The Uses and Abuses of Weaponized Interdependence,* edited by Daniel Drezner, Henry Farrell, and Abraham L. Newman, 101–114. Washington, DC: Brookings Institution Press.
Jansen, Katherine L., Joanna Drell, and Frances Andrews, eds. 2010. *Medieval Italy: Texts in Translation.* Philadelphia: University of Pennsylvania Press.
Jeffs, Jennifer A. 2008. "The Politics of Financial Plumbing: Harmonization and Interests in the Construction of the International Payment System." *Review of International Political Economy* 15 (2): 259–288.
Johnston, Ruth A. 2011. Vol. 1: *Fairs.* In *All Things Medieval: An Encyclopedia of the Medieval World.* Santa Barbara: Greenwood.
Joint Chiefs of Staff. 2000. *Joint Vision 2020.* Washington, DC: US Government Printing Office.
———. 2005. *Capstone Concept for Joint Operations, Version 2.0.* Washington, DC: US Government Printing Office.

Kakinuma, Yohei. 2014. "The Emergence and Spread of Coins in China from the Spring and Autumn Period to the Warring States Period." In *Explaining Monetary and Financial Innovation*, edited by Peter Bernholz and Roland Vaubel, 79–126. Cham: Springer.

Kallianiotis, Ioannis N. 2016. "The Economic History of the Alexander the Great Expedition." *International Journal of Economics and Financial Research* 2 (2): 16–32.

Kaminsky, Graciela L. 2010. "Two Hundred Years of Financial Integration: A New Database with an Example from Latin America." Working Paper 16260. Cambridge MA: NBER, 1-33.

———. 2016. *International Borrowing Cycles: A New Historical Database*. Working Paper w22819. Cambridge MA: NBER.

Kang, Sung Won, and Hugh Rockoff. 2015. "Capitalizing Patriotism: The Liberty Loans of World War I." *Financial History Review* 22 (1): 45–78.

Karaman, K. Kivanic, and Şevket Pamuk. 2010. "Ottoman State Finances in European Perspective, 1500–1914." *Journal of Economic History* 70 (3): 593–629.

Karnfelt, Maximilian, and Kai Von Carnap. 2020. "China's New Surveillance Currency." *The Diplomat*, December 4.

Kaushal, Sidharth. 2022. "Can Russia Continue to Fight a Long War?" Royal United Services Institute (RUSI), August 23.

Kennedy, Hugh. 2015. "The Middle East in Islamic Late Antiquity." In *Fiscal Regimes and the Political Economy of the Premodern State*, edited by Andrew Monson and Walter Scheidel, 290–403. Cambridge: Cambridge University Press.

Keohane, Robert. 1986. *Neorealism and Its Critics*. New York: Columbia University Press.

———. 2005. *After Hegemony: Cooperation and Discord in the World Political Economy*. Princeton: Princeton University Press.

Keynes, John Maynard. 1913. *Indian Currency and Finance*. London: Macmillan.

———. 2018. *The Economic Consequences of the Peace*. London: Routledge.

Kilcrease, Emily, Jason Bartlett, and Mason Wong. 2022. *Sanctions by the Numbers: Economic Measures Against Russia Following Its 2022 Invasion of Ukraine*. Washington DC: Center for a New American Security, June 16.

Kim, Sang Rae. 2022. *How the Cryptocurrency Market Is Connected to the Financial Market*. Working Paper. www.sangraekim.com.

Kim, Victoria, Clifford Krauss, and Anton Torianovski. 2022. "Western Move to Choke Russian Oil Exports Boomerangs, for Now." *New York Times*, June 5.

Kindleberger, Charles. 1986. *The World in Depression, 1929–1939*. Berkeley: University of California Press.

———. 1999. *Essays in History: Financial, Economic, Personal*. Ann Arbor: University of Michigan Press.

Kirshner, Jonathan. 1997. *Currency and Coercion: The Political Economy of International Monetary Power*. Princeton: Princeton University Press.

Kitson, Michael. 1992. "The Move to Autarky: The Political Economy of Nazi Trade Policy." Department of Applied Economics Working Paper 9201. Cambridge: Cambridge University, January.

Klasing, Mariko J., and Petros Milionis. 2014. "Quantifying the Evolution of World Trade, 1870–1949." *Journal of International Economics* 92 (1): 185–197.

Knodell, Jane. 2016. *The Second Bank of the United States: "Central" Banker in an Era of Nation-Building, 1816–1836*. London: Routledge.

Knox, MacGregor, and Williamson Murray. 2001. *The Dynamics of Military Revolution, 1300–2050*. Cambridge: Cambridge University Press.

Kobrin, Stephen J. 1985. "Diffusion as an Explanation of Oil Nationalization: Or the Domino Effect Rides Again." *Journal of Conflict Resolution* 29 (3): 3–32.

Koehler, Benedikt, Mark Duckenfield, and Stefan Altorfer. 2006. *The History of Financial Disasters, 1763–1995*. Vol. 3. Oxfordshire: Taylor and Francis Group.

Korsunskaya, Darya. 2022. "No Catastrophe, but Sanctions on Moscow Are Working, Says Russian Economy Vetern." Reuters, September 20.

Krepinevich, Andrew F. 1994. "Cavalry to Computer: The Pattern of Military Revolutions." *The National Interest* 37: 30–42.

Kroll, John H. 2012. "The Monetary Background of Early Coinage." In *The Oxford Handbook of Greek and Roman Coinage*, edited by William E. Metcalf, 39–52. Oxford: Oxford University Press.

Krugman, Paul. 2013. "Revenge of the Optimum Currency Area." *NBER Macroeconomics Annual* 27 (1): 439–448.

Lacey, James. 2015. *Gold, Blood, and Power: Finance and War Through the Ages*. Carlisle: US Army War College | Strategic Studies Institute.

Lambert, Nicholas. 2012. *Planning Armageddon: British Economic Warfare and the First World War*. Cambridge: Harvard University Press.

Lamont, Thomas. 1930. "The Final Reparations Settlement." *Foreign Affairs* 8 (3): 336–363.

Lane, Frederic C. 1973a. *Venice, a Maritime Republic*. Baltimore: Johns Hopkins University Press.

———. 1973b. "Venetian Bankers, 1496–1533: A Study in the Early Stages of Deposit Banking." *Journal of Political Economy* 45 (2): 187–206.

Laughlin, Laurence James. 1898. *Report of the Monetary Commission of the Indianapolis Convention of Boards of Trade, Chambers of Commerce, Commercial Clubs, and Other Similar Bodies of the United States*. Chicago: University of Chicago Press.

Laves, Walter H. C. 1928. "German Governmental Influence on Foreign Investments, 1871–1915." *Political Science Quarterly* 43 (4): 498–519.

Lenin, Vladimir I. 2010. *Imperialism, the Highest Stage of Capitalism*. London: Penguin.

Levenson, Thomas. 2020. *Money for Nothing: The Scientists, Fraudsters, and Corrupt Politicians Who Reinvented Money, Panicked a Nation, and Made the World Rich*. New York: Random House.

Levy-Leboyer, Maurice. 1977."La Balance des Paiements et L'Exportation des Capitaux Francais." In *La Position Internationale de la France: Aspects Economique et Financiers XIX–XX Siecles*. Paris: Ecole des Haute Etude en Sciences Sociales, 75–142.

Lewis, Mark E. 2015. "Early Imperial China, from the Qin and Han Through Tang." In *Fiscal Regimes and the Political Economy of the Premodern States*, edited by Andrew Monson and Walter Scheidel, 282–307. Cambridge: Cambridge University Press.

Li, Danny. 2021. "China's Digital Yuan Is Aimed at Home. Not Washington." *Foreign Policy*, October 20.

Li, Qiang. 2015. "Roman Coins Discovered in China and Their Research." *Eirene* 51: 279–299.

Li, Yiting. 1995. "Commodity Money Under Private Information." *Journal of Monetary Economics* 36 (3): 573–592.

Libicki, Martin C. 2012. "Cyberspace Is Not a Warfighting Domain." *I/S: A Journal of Law and Policy for the Information Society* 8 (2): 325–340.

Loeb, Vernon, and Thomas Ricks. 2002. "Rumsfeld's Style, Goals Strain Ties in Pentagon; 'Transformation' Effort Spawns Issues of Control." *Washington Post,* October 16.

Lynn, Laurence E., Jr. 2006. *Public Management: Old and New.* New York: Routledge.

Lynn, William F., III. 2010. "Defending a New Domain—The Pentagon's Cyber-strategy." *Foreign Affairs* 89: 97.

Magnusson, Lars. 1994. *Mercantilism.* Abingdon: Taylor and Francis.

Mahan, Alfred Thayer. 1999. "The Influence of Sea Power upon HIstory, 1660–1783." In Vol. 4: *Roots of Strategy,* edited by David Jablonsky. Mechanicsburg, PA: Stockpole Books.

Majd, Mariam. 2018. "The Cost of a SWIFT Kick: Estimating the Cost of Financial Sanctions on Iran." In *The Political Economy of International Finance in an Age of Inequality,* edited by Gerald A. Epstein, 215–235. Cheltenham: Edward Elgar.

Malik, Hassan. 2018. *Bankers and Bolsheviks: International Finance and the Russian Revolution.* Princeton: Princeton University Press.

Maoz, Zeev. 2009. "The Effects of Strategic and Economic Interdependence on International Conflict Across Levels of Analysis." *American Journal of Political Science* 53 (1): 223–240.

Martorelli, Michael A. n.d. "Financing the Civil War." Essential Civil War Curriculum.

Maurer, Bill. 2015. *How Would You Like to Pay? How Technology Is Changing the Future of Money.* Durham: Duke University Press.

McCloskey, Donald N., and J. Richard Zecher. 2005. "How the Gold Standard Worked, 1880–1913." In *Gold Standard in Theory & History,* edited by Barry Eichengreen and Marc Flandreau, 47–60. Abingdon: Routledge.

McGowan, Patrick J. 2003. "African Military Coups D'etat, 1956–2001: Frequency, Trends, and Distribution." *Journal of Modern African Studies* 41 (3): 339–370.

McIntyre, Joan. 1987. "The USSR's Hard Currency Trade and Payments Position." *Gorbachev's Economic Plans* 2: 474–488.

Mehrling, Perry. 2011. *The New Lombard Street: How the Fed Became the Dealer of Last Resort.* Princeton: Princeton University Press.

———. 2015. "Elasticity and Discipline in the Global Swap Network." *International Journal of Political Economy* 44: 311–324.

Meltzer, Allan H. 2021. *Comment on Bretton Woods and the Great Inflation.* Comment c9175. Cambridge MA: NBER.

Metcalf, David Michael. 2001. "Monetary Recession in the Middle Byzantine Period: The Numismatic Evidence." *Numismatic Chronicle 1966–* 161: 111–155.

Michell, H. 1947. "The Iron Money of Sparta." *Phoenix* 1: 42–44.

Mickelson, Karen. 2015. "Greek *polis.*" In *Fiscal Regimes and the Political Economy of Premodern States,* edited by Andrew Monson and Walter Scheidel, 53–77. Cambridge: Cambridge University Press.

Miller, Chris. 2022. "The Putinomics Playbook Won't Work Forever." *War on the Rocks,* April 25.

Milward, Alan S. 1985. "The Reichsmark Bloc and the International Economy." In *Aspects of the Third Reich,* edited by Hannsjoachim W. Koch, 331–359. London: Palgrave.

Mishkin, Frederic. 2014. *The Economics of Money, Banking, and Financial Markets.* 11th ed. London: Pearson.

Mitchell, Brian R. 1988. *British Historical Statistics.* Cambridge: Cambridge University Press.

Mitchener, Kris James, and Marc Weidenmier. 2005. "Empire, Public Goods, and the Roosevelt Corollary." *Journal of Economic History* 65 (3): 658–692.

———. 2008. *Trade and Empire.* Cambridge MA: NBER.

———. 2010. "Supersanctions and Sovereign Debt Repayment." *Journal of International Money and Finance* 29 (1): 19–36.
Mohammed, Arshad, and Bill Trott. 2014. "U.S. Intensifies Sanctions on Russia over Ukraine." Reuters, September 12.
Monson, Andrew, and Walter Scheidel. 2015. "Studying Fiscal Regimes." In *Fiscal Regimes and the Political Economy of Premodern States*, edited by Andrew Monson and Walter Scheidel, 3–27. Cambridge: Cambridge University Press.
Moore, Mick. 2004. "Revenues, State Formation, and the Quality of Governance in Developing Countries." *International Political Science Review* 25 (3): 297–319.
Moore, Philip. 2022. "Ukraine Safeguards Relations with International Investors." Official Monetary and Financial Institutions Forum (OMFIF), May 17.
Morgan, H. Wayne. 1956. "The Origins and Establishment of the First Bank of the United States." *Business History Review* 30 (4): 472–492.
Morgan, T. Clifton, Nevin Bapat, and Yoshiharu Kobayashi. 2014. "Threat and Imposition of Economic Sanctions, 1945–2005: Updating the TIES Dataset." *Conflict Management and Peace Science* 31 (5): 541–558.
Morgenthau, Hans J. 1985. *Politics Among Nations: The Struggle for Power and Peace*. 7th ed.. Edited by Kenneth W. Thompson and W. David Clinton. New York: McGraw Hill.
Mørkholm, Otto. 1991. *Early Hellenistic Coinage from the Accession of Alexander to the Peace of Apamaea (336–188 BC)*. Cambridge: Cambridge University Press.
Morony, Michael G. 2017. "Trade and Exchange: The Sasanian World to Islam." *Late Antiquity and Early Islam, Fifth Workshop: Trade and Exchange in the Late Antique and Early Islamic Near East*, 17–18.
Moscow Times. 2022. "Government Launches Budget Sequestration After Worst Revenue Collapse in 11 Years." September 15.
Mueller, Reinhold C. 1997. *The Venetian Money Market: Banks, Panics, and the Public Debt, 1200–1500*. Baltimore: Johns Hopkins University Press.
Mulder, Nicholas. 2022. *The Economic Weapon*. New Haven: Yale University Press.
Mun, Thomas. 1895. *England's Treasure by Forraign Trade*. London: Macmillan.
Munro, John H. 2001. "The 'New Institutional Economics' and the Changing Fortunes of Fairs in Medieval and Early Modern Europe: The Textile Trades, Warfare, and Transaction Costs." *VSWG: Vierteljahrschrift fur Sozial-und Wirtschaftsgeschichte* 88 (1): 1–47.
———. 2003a. "The Medieval Origins of the Financial Revolution: Usury, Rentes, and Negotiability." *International History Review* 25 (3): 505–562.
———. 2003b. *The Monetary Origins of the "Price Revolution": South German Silver Mining, Merchant Banking, and Venetian Commerce, 1470–1540*. Working Paper. Toronto, Ontario, Canada: Department of Economics, University of Toronto.
———. 2020. *Wool, Cloth, and Gold*. Toronto, Ontario, Canada: University of Toronto Press.
Muro, Diego, and Guillem Vidal. 2014. "Mind the Gaps: The Political Consequences of the Great Recession in Europe." *Euro Crisis in the Press Blog*, June 14.
Murphy, Anne L. 2013. "Financial Markets: The Limits of Economic Regulation in Early Modern England." In *Mercantilism Reimagined: Political Economy in Early Modern Britain and Its Empire*, edited by Philip J. Stern and Carl Wennerlind, 263–281. Oxford: Oxford University Press.
Murray, Williamson. 1997. "Thinking About Revolutions in Military Affairs." Press Release. Public Affairs, Department of Defense, Washington, DC.
Nanto, Dick K. 2008. *North Korean Counterfeiting of Currency*. Washington, DC: Congressional Research Service.

NBU (National Bank of Ukraine). 2022. "NBU Fixes Official UAH/USD Exchange Rate at a New Level and Takes Additional Measures to Balance the FX Market and Support Resilience of Economy During the War." July 21.

Ndikumana, Léonce, and James Boyce. 1998. "Congo's Odious Debt: External Borrowing and Capital Flight in Zaire." *Development and Change* 29 (2): 195–217.

Neal, Larry. 1979. "The Economics and Finance of Bilateral Clearing Agreements: Germany, 1934–8." *Economic History Review* 32 (3): 391–404.

———. 2012. *"I Am Not Master of Events": The Speculations of John Law and Lord Londonderry in the Mississioou and South Sea Bubbles.* New Haven: Yale University Press.

———. 2018. "The Variety of Financial Innovations in European War Finance During the Thirty Years' War (1618–1648)." In *Financial Innovation and Resilience: A Comparative Perspective on the Public Banks of Naples (1462–1808),* edited by Lilia Costabile and Larry Neal, 127–145. London: Palgrave Macmillan.

Nenovsky, Nikolai, and Kalina Dimitrova. 2007. *Exchange Rate Control in Bulgaria in the Interwar Period: History and Theoretical Reflections.* Discussion Paper. Sofia: Bulgarian National Bank.

Nerozzi, Sebastiano. 2009. "Building Up a Multilateral Strategy for the United States: Alvin Hansen, Jacob Viner and the Council on Foreign Relations (1939–45)." In *American Power and Policy,* edited by Martin S. Alexander and William J. Philpott, 24–68. London: Palgrave Macmillan.

———. 2011. "From the Great Depression to Bretton Woods: Jacob Viner and International Monetary Stabilization (1930–1945)." *European Journal of the History of Economic Thought* 18 (1): 55–84.

New York Times. 1972. "Herbert Feis, Historian, Dies; Awarded Pulitzer Prize in '61." March 3.

Nicolet, Claude. 1971. "Les variations des prix et la 'théorie quantitative de la monnaie' à Rome, de Cicéron à Pline l'Ancien." *Annales: Histoire, Sciences Sociales* 26 (6): 1203–1227.

Nimchuk, Cindy L. 2002. "The 'Archers' of Darius: Coinage or Tokens of Royal Esteem?" *Ars Orientalis,* 55–79.

Niskanen, William A. 1971. *Bureaucracy and Representative Government.* Chicago: Aldine-Atherton.

North, Douglass. 1991. "Institutions." *Journal of Economic Perspectives* 5 (1): 97–112.

North, Douglass C., John Joseph Wallis, and Barry Weingast. 2009. *Violence and Social Order: A Conceptual Framework for Interpreting Recorded Human History.* Cambridge: Cambridge University Press.

Nye, Joseph S. 2010. *Cyber Power.* Cambridge: Harvard University Press.

Oatley, Thomas. 2021. "Weaponizing International Financial Interdependence." In *The Uses and Abuses of Weaponized Interdependence,* edited by Daniel Drezner, Henry Farrell, and Abraham L. Newman, 115–132. Washington, DC: Brookings Institution Press.

Oatley, Thomas, and W. Kindred Winecoff, eds. 2014. *Handbook of the International Political Economy of Monetary Relations.* Cheltenham: Edward Elgar.

O'Brien, Patrick. 2006. "The Hanoverian State and the Defeat of the Continental System: A Conversation with Eli Hecksher." In *Eli Hecksher, International Trade, and Economic History,* edited by Ronald Findlay, Rolf G. H. Henriksson, Håkan Lindgren, and Mats Lundahl, 373–406. Cambridge: MIT Press.

Occhino, Filippo, Kim Oosterlinck, and Eugene N. White. 2007. "How Occupied France Financed Its Own Exploitation in World War II." *American Economic Review* 97 (2): 295–299.

———. 2008. "How Much Can a Victor Force the Vanquished to Pay? France Under the Nazi Boot." *Journal of Economic History* 68 (1): 1–45.

Office of the Historian. n.d. *Milestones 1914–1920: Wilson's Fourteen Points.* https://history.state.gov/milestones/1914-1920/fourteen-points.

Oldroyd, David. 1995. "The Role of Accounting in Public Expenditure and Monetary Policy in the First Century AD Roman Empire." *Accounting Historians Journal* 22 (2): 117–129.

Oscar, Richard. 2022. "War in Ukraine: A New Paradigm of Sanctions Practice." *Lawfare*, August 1.

Osokina, Elena. 2021. *Stalin's Quest for Gold: The Torgsin Hard-Currency Shops and Soviet Industrialization.* Ithaca: Cornell University Press.

Palik, Julia, Anne Marie Obermeier, and Siri Aas Rustad. 2022. *Conflict Trends in Africa, 1989–2021.* Working Paper. Oslo: Peace Research Institute Oslo (PRIO).

Palma, Nuno. 2016. *Money and Modernization: Liquidity, Specialization, and Structural Change in Early Modern England.* Program Working Paper 2016/11. Florence: Max Weber Programme, European University Institute.

Palmer, James. 2020. "Oh God, Not the Pelopennesian War Again." *Foreign Policy*, July 28.

Palmer, Michael A. 1988. *Origins of the Maritime Strategy: American Naval Strategy in the First Postwar Decade.* No. 1. Washington DC: US Navy, Naval Historical Center.

Parker, Geoffrey. 1976. "The 'Military Revolution' 1560–1660—a Myth?" *Journal of Modern HIstory* 48 (2): 196–214.

Paybarah, Azi. 2022. "None of Us Should Be Fooled: President Biden's Speech on Russia." *New York Times,* February 22.

Payne, Stanley G. 1973. *A History of Spain and Portugal.* Vol. 1. Madison: University of Wisconsin Press.

Pepys, Samuel. n.d. *Pepys' Diary.* https://www.pepysdiary.com/diary/1667/07/19/.

Perkins, David G. 2017a. "Multi-Domain Battle: The Advent of Twenty-First Century War." *Military Review* 97 (6): 8–17.

———. 2017b. "Multi-Domain Battle: Driving Change to Win in the Future." *Military Review* 97 (4): 6–12.

———. 2017c. "Preparing for the Fight Tonight: Multi-Domain Battle and Field Manual 3-0." *Military Review* 97 (5): 7–12.

Phillips, Tom. 2022. "Russia Launches Digital Ruble Pilot with 12 Banks." Near Field Communications World, January 27.

Piatt, Andrew A. 1901. "Indian Currency Problems of the Last Decade." *Quarterly Journal of Economics* 15 (4): 483–516.

Pieper, Renate. 2012. "Financing and Empire: The Austrian Composite Monarchy, 1650–1848." In *The Rise of Fiscal States: A Global Hiatory,* edited by Bartolome Yun-Casallila, Patrick O'Brien, and Francisco Comin Comin, 111–132. Cambridge: Cambridge University Press.

Piketty, Thomas. 2017. *Capital in the Twenty-First Century.* Translated by Arthur Goldhammer. Cambridge, MA: Belknap Press.

Platt, Desmond Christopher Martin. 1968. *Finance, Trade, and Politics in British Foreign Policy, 1815–1914.* Oxford: Clarendon Press.

Polybius. n.d. "The Histories." University of Chicago.

Posen, Barry R. 2003. "Command of the Commons: The Military Foundation of Hegemony." *International Security* 28 (1): 5–46.

Pryor, John H. 1977. "The Origins of the Commenda Contract." *Speculum* 52 (1): 5–37.
Quinn, Stephen, and William Roberds. 2007. "The Bank of Amsterdam and the Leap to Central Bank Money." *American Economic Review* 97 (2): 263–267.
———. 2014. "How Amsterdam Got Fiat Money." *Journal of Monetary Economics* 66: 1–12.
———. 2019. "A Policy Framework for the Bank of Amsterdam, 1736–1791." *Journal of Economic History* 79 (3): 736–772.
Rankin, David I. 1988. "The Mining Lobby at Athens." *Ancient Society* 19: 189–205.
———. 2003. "The Financing of Maritime Commerce in the Roman Empire, I–II AD." In *Credito e Moneta nel Mondo Romano*, edited by Elio Lo Cascio, 197–229. Bari: Edipuglia.
Rathbone, Dominic. 2007. "Merchant Networks in the Greek World: The Impact of Rome." *Mediterranean HIstorical Review* 22 (2): 309–320.
———. 2019. "Maritime Loans." In *Oxford Classical Dictionary*, edited by Simon Hornblower and Antony Spawforth. Oxford: Oxford University Press.
Rector, Raymond. 2018. "Northern Entrepreneur's Counterfeiting of Confederate Currency and the Impact It Had on Inflation." Undergraduate Honors Thesis, Butler University.
Reinhart, Carmen M., and Jacob Kirkegaard. 2012. "Financial Repression: Then and Now." VoxEU.
Reinhart, Carmen M., and Vincent R. Reinhart. 2009. "Capital Flow Bonanzas: An Encompassing View of the Past and Present." *NBER International Seminar on Macroeconomics* 5 (1): 9–62.
Reinhart, Carmen M., and Kenneth S. Rogoff. 2009. *This Time Is Different: Eight Centuries of Financial Folly.* Princeton: Princeton University Press.
Repko, Maria. 2022. "Ukraine's Economy Will Collapse Without More Aid Now." *Foreign Policy,* August 4.
Reuter, Peter, and Edwin M. Truman. 2004. *Chasing Dirty Money: The Fight Against Money Laundering.* New York: Columbia University Press.
Reuters. 2022. "Russia's VTB Launches Transfers in Chinese Yuan Bypassing SWIFT." September 6.
Rixen, Thomas. 2011. "From Double Tax Avoidance to Tax Competition: Explaining the Institutional Trajectory of International Tax Governance." *Review of International Political Economy* 18 (2): 197–227.
Robbins, Lionel. 1998. *A History of Economic Thought: The LSE Lectures.* Princeton: Princeton Unievrsity Press.
Roberds, William, and Francois R. Velde. 2016. "The Descent of Central Banks (1400–1815)." In *Central Banks at a Crossroads: What Can We Learn from History,* edited by Michael D. Bordo, Øyvind Eltrheim, Marc Flandreau, and Jan F. Qvigstad, 18–61. Cambridge: Cambridge University Press.
Roberts, Priscilla. 1998. "'Quis Custodiet Ipsos Custodes?' The Federal Reserve System's Founding Fathers and Allied Finances in the First World War." *Business History Review* 72 (4): 585–620.
Rockoff, Hugh. 2012. *America's Economic Way of War: War and the Economy from the Spanish-American War to the Persian Gulf War.* Cambridge: Cambridge University Press.
———. 2015. *War and Inflation in the United States from the Revolution to the First Iraq War.* Paper w21221. Washington, DC: NBER.
Rollins, John, and Lianna Sun Wyler. 2013. *Terrorism and Transnational Crime: Foreign Policy Issues for Congress.* Washington, DC: Congressional Research Service, June 11.

Rolnick, Arthur J., François R. Velde, and Warren E. Weber. 1996. "The Debasement Puzzle: An Essay on Medieval Monetary History." *Journal of Economic History* 56 (4): 789–808.

Roosevelt, Franklin D. 1945. "The President's Message to Congress on Bretton Woods." World Bank Group Archives, February 20.

Rosenberg, Emily S. 2004. *Financial Missionaries to the World*. Durham: Duke University Press.

Rosenberg, Matthew, Nicholas Kulish, and Steven Lee Myers. 2015. "Predatory Islamic State Wrings Money From Those It Rules." *New York Times*. November 29.

Rosenblum, Joshua, and Brandon Dupont. 2016. *Impact of the US Civil War on Southern Wealth Holders*. Washington DC: Center for Economic and Policy Research, June 19.

Roseveare, Henry G. 1992. *The Financial Revolution, 1660–1750*. London: Routledge.

Ross, Michael L. 2015. "What Have We Learned About the Resource Curse?" *Annual Review of Political Science* 18: 239–259.

Rothman, Jordan. 2009. "'A Pledge of a Nation': Charting the Economic Aspirations, Political Motivations, and Consequences of Confederate Currency Creation." PhD dissertation, Brandeis University.

Saravalle, Eduardo. 2021. "The Watchful Eye of the US Dollar." *The Alchemist*, May 19.

Sargent, Thomas J. 1997. "Coinage, Debasements, and Gresham's Laws." *Economic Theory* 10 (2): 197–226.

Sargent, Thomas J., and Francois R. Velde. 1995. "Macroeconomic Features of the French Revolution." *Journal of Political Economy* 101 (3): 474–518.

Sarkees, Meredith Reid, and Frank Wayman. 2010. *Resort to War: 1816–2007*. Washington, DC: CQ Press.

Schacht, Hjalmar. 1937. "Germany's Colonial Demands." *Foreign Affairs* 15 (2): 223–234.

Scheidel, Walter. 2008. *The Monetary Systems of the Greeks and Romans: The Divergent Evolution of Coinage in Eastern and Western Eurasia*. Palo Alto: Stanford University Press.

———. 2009a. *A Comparative Perspective on the Determinants of the Scale and Productivity of Maritime Trade in the Roman Mediterranean*. Paper 040902. Princeton: Princeton/Stanford Working Papers in Classics.

———. 2009b. *Rome and China: Comparative Perspectives on Ancient World Empires*. Oxford: Oxford University Press.

———. 2010. "Coin Quality, Coin Quantity, and Coin Value in Early China and the Roman Empire." *American Journal of Numismatics* 22: 93–118.

———. 2015. "The Early Roman Monarchy." In *Fiscal Regimes and the Political Economy of Premodern States,* edited by Andrew Monson and Walter Scheidel, 229–257. Cambridge: Cambridge University Press.

Scheinert, Christian. 2022. "Free Movement of Capital." European Union Parliament.

Schenk, Catherine R. 1998. "The Origins of the Eurodollar Market in London: 1955–1963." *Explorations in Economic History* 35 (2): 221–238.

Schiltz, Michael. 2012. *The Money Doctors from Japan: Finance, Imperialism, and the Building of the Yen Bloc, 1895–1937*. Cambridge: Harvard University Press.

Schumpeter, Joseph. 1991. *The Economics and Sociology of Capitalism*. Princeton: Princeton University Press.

Sebok, Milos. 2011. "President Wilson and the International Origins of the Federal Reserve System—A Reappraisal." *White House Studies* 10 (4): 425–447.

Seddon, Jack. 2021. "The Fate of International Monetary Systems: How and Why They Fall Apart." *Perspectives on Politics* 19(3), 754–772.

Shaikh, Shaan, and Wes Rumbaugh. 2020. *The Air and Missile War in Nagorno-Karabakh: Lessons for the Future of Strike and Defense.* Washington, DC: Center for Strategic and International Studies.

Shearer, David R. 2018. *Industry, State, and Society in Stalin's Russia, 1926–1934.* Ithaca: Cornell University Press.

Sheinin, David. 1999. "The New Dollar Diplomacy in Latin America." *American Studies International* 37 (3): 81–99.

Shelley, Louise I. 2014. *Dirty Entanglements: Corruption, Crime, and Terrorism.* Cambridge: Cambridge University Press.

Shizume, Masato. 2011. "Sustainability of Public Debt: Evidence from Japan Before the Second World War." *Economic History Review* 64 (4): 1113–1143.

Siegel, Katherine Amelia Siobhan. 1996. *Loans and Legitimacy: The Evolution of Soviet-American Relations, 1919–1933.* Lexington: University Press of Kentucky.

Siegfried, Nikolaus A. 2001. "Concepts of Paper Money in Islamic Legal Thought." *Arab Law Quarterly* 16 (4): 319–342.

Silber, William L., and Greg Kaza. 2007. *When Washington Shut Down Wall Street: The Great Financial Crisis of 1914 and the Origins of America's Monetary Supremacy.* Princeton: Princeton University Press.

Simson, Rebecca. 2019. "Africa's Clientelist Budget Policies Revisited: Public Expenditure and Employment in Kenya, Tanzania, and Uganda, 1960–2010." *Economic History Review* 72 (4): 1409–1438.

Singer, J. David, Stuart Bremer, and John Stuckey. 1972. "Capabillity Distribution, Uncertainty, and Major Power War, 1820–1965." In *Peace, War, and Numbers*, edited by Bruce Russett, 19–48. Beverly Hills: Sage.

Skidelsky, Robert. 2000. *John Maynard Keynes: Fighting for Britain, 1937–46.* London: Macmillan.

Smith, Michael E. 2015. "The Aztec Empire." In *Fiscal Regimes and the Political Economy of the Premodern States*, edited by Andrew Monson and Walter Scheidel, 170-198. Cambridge: Cambridge University Press.

Smith, Sydney. 1869. *Wit and Wisdom of the Rev. Sydney Smith.* London: Longmans, Green.

Solce, Natasha. 2008. "The Battlefields of Cyberspace: The Inevitable New Military Branch—The Cyber Force." *Albany Law Journal of Science and Technology* 18 (1): 49–82.

Song, Zheng, and Wei Xiong. 2018. "Risks in China's Financial System." *Annual Review of Financial Economics* 10: 261–286.

Spufford, Peter. 1988. *Money and Its Use in Medieval Europe.* Cambridge: Cambridge University Press.

Stasavage, David. 2011. *States of Credit: Size, Power, and the Development of European Polities.* Princeton: Princeton University Press.

Steil, Benn, and Robert E. Litan. 2006. *Financial Statecraft: The Role of Financial Markets in American Foreign Policy.* New Haven: Yale University Press.

Stephan, Peter. 2022. "Giving Russian Assets to Ukraine—Freezing Is Not Seizing." *Lawfarre,* April 26.

Stergiou, Dimitrios. 2016. "ISIS Political Economy: Financing a Terror State." *Journal of Money Laundering Control* 19 (2): 106–118.

Strange, Susan. 1970. "International Economics and International Relations: A Case of Mutual Neglect." *International Affairs* 46 (2): 304–315.

Sussman, Nathan. 1993. "Debasements, Royal Revenues, and Inflation in France During the Hundred Years' War, 1415–1422." *Journal of Economic History* 53 (1): 44–70.

Sussman, Nathan, and Joseph Zeira. 2003. "Commodity Money Inflation: Theory and Evidence from France in 1350–1436." *Journal of Monetary Economics* 50 (8): 1769–1793.

Sveriges Riksbank. 2021. "Money and Power—The History of Sveriges Riksbank."

SWIFT (Society for Worldwide Interbank Financial Telecommunication). 2021. *SWIFT Oversight.*

Sylla, Richard. 2011. "Financial Foundations: Public Credit, the National Bank, and Securities Markets." In *Founding Choices: American Economic Policy in the 1790s,* edited by Douglas Irwin and Richard Sylla, 59–88. Chicago: University of Chicago Press.

Tan, James. 2015. "The Roman Republic." In *Fiscal Regimes and the Political Economy of Premodern States,* edited by Andrew Monson and Walter Scheidel, 208–228. Csmbridge: Cambridge University Press.

Teichmann, Fabian Maximilian. 2019. "Recent Trends in Money Laundering and Terrorism Financing." *Journal of Financial Regulation and Compliance* 27 (1): 2–12.

Temin, Peter. 2004. "Financial Intermediation in the Early Roman Empire." *Journal of Economic History* 64: 705–733.

———. 2012. *The Roman Market Economy.* Princeton: Princeton University Press.

't Hart, Marjolein C. 1989. "Cities and Statemaking in the Dutch Republic, 1580–1680." *Theory and Society* 18 (5): 663–687.

———. 1993. *The Making of a Bourgeois State: War, Politics, and Finance During the Dutch Revolt.* Manchester: Manchester University Press.

Thompson, Iain A. A. 2020. *The Military Revolution and the Trajectory of Spain: War, State, and Society, 1500–1700.* Trowbridge: Paragon.

Thompson, John A. 2002. *Woodrow Wilson.* London: Taylor and Francis Group.

Thornton, Mary K., and Robert L. Thornton. 1990. "The Financial Crisis of AD 33: A Keynesian Depression?" *Journal of Economic History* 50 (3): 655–662.

Thucydides. 2009. *The History of the Pelopennesian War.* Translated by Martin Hammond. Oxford: Oxford University Press.

Thurston, Alex. 2021. "Why Jihadists Are Collecting 'Zakat' in the Sahel." *Political Violence at a Glance,* July 12.

Tiezzi, Shannon. 2016. "Move over, Bitcoin: China Wants to Issue Its Own Digital Currency." *The Diplomat.,* January 22.

Tilly, Charles. 1990. *Coercion, Capital, and European States, AD 990–1990.* Oxford: Basil Blackwell.

Toll, Ian W. 2008. *Six Frigates: The Epic History of the Founding of the US Navy.* New York: Norton.

Tomz, Michael. 2007. *Reputation and International Cooperation: Sovereign Debt Across Three Centuries.* Princeton: Princeton University Press.

Tooze, Adam. 2007. *The Wages of Destruction: The Making and Breaking of the Nazi Economy.* New York: Viking Penguin.

———. 2015. *The Deluge: The Great War, America, and the Remaking of the Global Order, 1916–1931.* New York: Penguin Group.

———. 2018. *Crashed: How a Decade of Financial Crises Changed the World.* London: Penguin.

———. 2022a. "Chartbook #146: The Russia-Ukraine War at Six Months: Symbolic Anniversary or Economic and Military Turning Point?" *Chartbook,* August 24.

———. 2022b. "Chartbook #163: Warfare Without the State: New Keynesian Shock Therapy for Ukraine's Home Front." *Chartbook,* October 22.
Tooze, Adam, and Martin Ivanov. 2011. "Disciplining the 'Black Sheep of the Balkans': Financial Supervision and Sovereignty in Bulgaria, 1902–38." *Economic History Review* 64 (1): 30–51.
Torr, Cecil. 1905. "Triremes." *Classical Review* 19 (9): 466–466.
Towne, Robert. 1973. *Chinatown Screenplay, Third Draft.* Arizona State University Public Site.
Tracy, James D. 1985. *A Financial Revolution in the Habsburg Netherlands: Renten and Rentiniers in the Country of Holland, 1515–1565.* Berkeley: University of California Press.
———. 2002. *Emperor Charles V, Impresario of War: Campaign Strategy, International Finance, and Domestic Politics.* Cambridge: Cambridge University Press.
Trading Economics. 2022. "Russian Government Debt to GDP." December 5.
Trainer, Jocelyn. 2022. "The Legal Challenges Presented by Seizing Frozen Russian Assets." *Lawfare,* May 26.
Tribe, Lawrence. 2022. "Does American Law Currently Authorize the President to Seize Sovereign Russian Assets?" *Lawfare,* May 23.
Tyerman, Christopher. 2007. *God's War: A New History of the Crusades.* London: Penguin UK.
UCL (University College London). 2021. *The Bentham Project.*
Udovitch, Abraham L. 1962. "At the Origins of the Western Commenda: Islam, Israel, Byzantium?" *Speculum* 37 (2): 198–207.
———. 1967. "Credit as a Means of Investment in Medieval Islamic Trade." *Journal of the American Oriental Society* 87 (3): 260–264.
———. 1975. "Reflections on the Institutions of Credits and Banking in the Medieval Islamic Near East." *Studia Islamica* 87 (3): 5–21.
UN. 2021. "Myanmar: From Political Crisis, to 'Multi-Dimensional Catastrophe'—Bachelet." *UN News,* July 6.
US Army Headquarters. 2018. "The Army in Multi-Domain Operations: 2028." Initial Coordination Draft v0.6h, August 7.
US Army War College. 2017. "Theory of War and Strategy Course Directive."
US Space Force. 2021. "US Space Force."
Usher, Abbott Payson. 1943. *The Early History of Deposit Banking in Mediterranean Europe.* Vol. 1. Cambridge: Harvard University Press.
USJFD (US Joint Force Development). 2018. "Strategy." Joint Doctrine Note.
Van Doosselaere, Quentin. 2009. *Commercial Agreements and Social Dynamics in Medieval Genoa.* Cambridge: Cambridge University Press.
Velde, Francois, and David R. Weir. 1992. "The Financial Market and Government Debt Policy in France, 1746–1793." *Journal of Economic History* 52 (1): 1–39.
Viner, Jacob. 1928. "Political Aspects of International Finance." *Journal of Business of the University of Chicago* 1 (2): 141–173.
———. 1929. "International Finance and Balance of Power Diplomacy, 1880–1914." *Southwestern Political and Social Science Quarterly* 9 (4): 407–451.
———. 1944. "The Economic Problem." In *New Perspectives on Peace,* edited by George B. De Huszar, 13–45. Chicago: University of Chicago Press.
———. 1947. "International Finance in the Postwar World." *Journal of Political Economy* 55 (2): 97–107.
Von Glahn, Richard. 1996a. *Fountain of Fortune: Money and Monetary Policy in China, 1000–1700.* Berkeley: University of California Press.
———. 1996b. "Myth and Reality of China's Seventeenth-Century Monetary Crisis." *Journal of Economic History* 56 (2): 429–454.

———. 2004. "Revisiting the Song Monetary Revolution: A Review Essay." *International Journal of Asian Studies* 1 (1): 159–178.

———. 2010. "Monies of Account and Monetary Transition in China, Twelfth to Fourteenth Centuries." *Journal of the Economic and Social History of the Orient* 53 (3): 463–505.

———. 2016. *An Economic History of China: From Antiquity to the Nineteenth Century.* Cambridge: Cambridge University Press.

Wakefield, Andre. 2014. "Cameralism: A German Alternative to Mercantilism." In *Mercantilism Reimagined: Political Economy in Early-Modern Britain and Its Empire,* edited by Andre Wakefield, 134–150. Oxford: Oxford University Press.

Walker, Marcus. 2022. "Ukraine Scrapes to Pay Its Soldiers as Western Funds Slow to Arrive." *Wall Street Journal,* August 12.

Wallace, Joe. 2022. "Oil Price Wavers After Russia Cap Kicks in." *Wall Street Journal,* December 5.

Wallis, John J., and Barry R. Weingast. 2005. *Equilibrium Impotences: Why the States and Not the American National Government Financed Economic Development in the Antebellum Era.* Series w 11397. Cambridge, MA: NBER.

Walter, Carl E. 1985. "Dual Leadership and the 1956 Credit Reforms of the People's Bank of China." *China Quarterly* 101: 277–290.

———. 2010. Interviewed by Ben Stone for the Asia Society's *China Boom Project.* August 10.

Walter, Carl, and Fraser Howie. 2012. *Red Capitalism: The Fragile Foundatioin of China's Extraordinary Rise.* Hoboken: Wiley.

Walters, Raymond, Jr. 1945. "The Origins of the Second Bank of the United States." *Journal of Political Economy* 53 (2): 115–131.

Waltz, Kenneth. 2010. *Theory of International Politics.* Long Grove, IL: Waveland Press.

Warburton, David A. 1997. *State and Economy in Ancient Egypt: Fiscal Vocabulary of the New Kingdom.* Vol. 151. Friebourg: University Press; Gottingen: Vandenhoeck and Ruprecht.

Washington Post. 2002. "Text of President Bush's 2002 State of the Union Address." January 29.

———. 2014. "Transcript: Putin Says Russia Will Protect the Rights of Russians Abroad." March 18.

Wassink, Alfred. 1991. "Inflation and Financial Policy Under the Roman Empire to the Price Edict of 301 AD." *Historia: Zeitschrift fur Alte Geschichte* 40 (4): 465–493.

Weidenmier, Marc D. 1999. "Bogus Money Matters: Sam Upham and His Confederate Counterfeiting Business." *Business and Economic History* 28 (2): 313–324.

———. 2000. "The Market for Confederate Cotton Bonds." *Explorations in Economic History* 37 (1): 76–97.

———. 2005. "Gunboats, Reputation, and Sovereign Repayment: Lessons from the Southern Confederacy." *Journal of International Economics* 66 (2): 407–422.

Weinstein, Jeremy M. 2000. "'Africa's Scramble for Africa': Lessons of a Continental War." *World Policy Journal* 17 (2): 11–20.

Wetterberg, Gunnar, and Patrick Hort. 2009. *Money and Power: From Stockholms Banco 1656 to Sveriges Riksbank Today.* Stockholm: Sveriges Riksbank.

Whalley, Philip. 2009. "The Invergordon Mutiny and the National Economic Crisis of 1931: A Media and Parliamentary Perspective." *Journal for Maritime Research* 11 (1): 1–23.

Wheeler, James Scott. 1999. *The Making of a World Power: War and the Military Revolution in Seventeenth-Century England.* Stroud: Sutton.

White, Eugene N. 1989. "Was There a Solution to the Ancien Regime's Financial Dilemma?" *Journal of Economic History* 49 (3): 545–568.

———. 1995. "The French Revolution and the Politics of Government Finance, 1770–1815." *Journal of Economic History* 55 (2): 227–255.

———. 1999. *Making the French Pay: The Costs and Consequences of the Napoleonic Reparations.* Working Paper 6876. Cambridge MA: NBER.

———. 2001a. "France and the Failure to Modernize Macroeconomic Institutions." In *Transferring Wealth and Power from the Old to the New World: Monetary and Fiscal Institutions in the Seventeenth Through the Nineteenth Centuries,* edited by Michael D. Bordo and Roberto Condés-Conte, 59–99. Cambridge: Cambridge University Press.

———. 2001b. "Making the French Pay: The Costs and Consequences of the Napoleonic Reparations." *European Review of Economic History* 5 (3): 337–365.

———. 2004. "From Privatized to Government-Administered Tax Collection: Tax Farming in Eighteenth-Century France." *Economic History Review* 57 (4): 636–663.

White, Olivia, Nicolaus Henke, Elena Kvochko, and Jonathan Woetzel. 2022. "War in Ukraine: Twelve Disruptions Changing the World." McKinsey & Company, May 9.

Whitlock, John. 1695. *Some Observations upon the Bank of England.* London: Printed for John Dunton at the Raven in the Poultry, near Cornhill.

Williams, Geoffrey. 2020. "Lending Money to People Across the Water": The British Joint Banking Acts of 1826 and 1833, and the Panic of 1837. Working Paper. Lexington: Transylvania University.

Wolfe, Martin. 1972. *The Fiscal System of Renaissance France.* New Haven: Yale University Press.

World Bank. 2017. "The Global Findex Database 2017."

Wyman, Patrick. 2021. *The Verge: Reformation, Renaissance, and Forty Years that Shook the World.* New York: Hachette Book Group.

Xenophon. 1998. *Anabasis.* Cambridge: Harvard University Press.

Xiao, Qing. 1984. *Zhong-guo gu-dai huo-bi shi.* Beijing: Ren-min chu-ban-she.

Zarate, Juan C. 2013. *Treasury's War: The Unleashing of a New Era of Financial Warfare.* New York: PublicAffairs.

Zimmerman, Hubert. 2002. *Money and Security: Troops, Monetary Policy, and West Germany's Relations with the United States and Britain, 1950–1971.* Cambridge: Cambridge University Press.

Ziskind, Jonathan R. 1974. "Sea Loans at Ugarit." *Journal of the American Oriental Society* 94 (1): 54–62.

Index

ABLV Bank, 171
Achaemenid Empire, 43–44, 48, 53. *See* Persia
Achilles' heel, 90
Admiralty (UK), 132
Afghanistan, 152
Africa, 25, 40, 80, 111, 114, 150, 156–158: British colonial possessions in, 114; debt forgiveness, 156, 158; decolonization, 156; looting of, 157; slave trade with South America and the United Kingdom, 80
African debtor states, 156
African states, 156
agoge, 46
agriculture 13, 70, 79, 90, 108, 191; dry land, 70
aircraft, 5, 8, 32; fighter, 5; invention of, 8
aircraft carriers, 8
air force, 4, 8, 16(n27), 32; United States, 8, 16(n27)
airpower, 8, 32–33; financial demands of, 33; institutions of, 32
al-Qaeda, 30(table), 169, 171, 191; and 9/11, 169; as nonstate actor, 171
Albania, 151
Alexander the Great, 48–49, 52–53; conquest of Achaemenid/Persian Empire, 48, 53; financial debt to troops, 48
Allied: powers, 144–145; victors, 144; aka Allies, 145
Alstadsaeter, Annette, on tax avoidance and evasion, 170
America: Pre-Columbian, 40; empires, pre-Columbian, 68

Americans, 101, 125, 128–130, 148–149, 151, 195; *See* United States (US)
American bank failures, Federal Reserve intervention in, 122;
American: economists, support for John Maynard Keynes, 148;
American Civil War, 94, 106–109, 128
American Economic Association, 148
American strategic class, 43
American textbook, 151
Americas, 64, 69, 129, 132; conquest of, 64; European conquerors of, 69; political instability in, 132; political structure of, 69; Pre-Columbian, 40, 64, 68–69
Anatolia, 63
Anglo-American, 123
Anglo-American banking spree, 129
Anglo-American financial hegemony, Chinese challenge to, 188
Angola, 154, 156–157
An Lushan Rebellion, 70
anti-federalism, 108
Antony, 3
Antwerp stock exchange, 85
Appalachia, 40
Arab: armies/forces, 62–63; empire, 63; Middle East, 64
Arabian Peninsula, 62
Arabian polity, 63
arbitrage, 146, 150
Archidamus, King of Sparta, 46–47
Argentina, 110, 112(table), 130–131, 157; backer of Paraguay in Chaco war, 131; nationalized oil company, 157; participation in Triple Alliance War, 110

Aristotle, 48
Armenia, 33
armed forces, 153, 155; South Africa, 155
armed services, 4
armies, 4, 21–22, 33, 60, 74, 93, 96, 103
arms, 46, 59, 162(n56), 195
arms embargoes, Russia, 172
arms purchases, Africa, 157
arms race, 131
army, 6, 86, 93, 101, 107, 135; Dutch Republic, 86; imaginary American, 101; Sparta, 6; US, 107
Articles of Confederation (US), 93
Asia, 25, 50, 111
Asia Minor, 34, 41
Asian continent, 72
Asia Society, 161(n46)
Aswan Dam, 151
atomic bomb, 90
atomic bombs, 134
Athens, 44–45, 48, 53, 60; coins, 48; Greek city-state, 44; Hellenic, 45, 60; liturgies, 45–46; mercenaries, 45; taxation and tribute schemes, 44–45
Augustus, Emperor of Rome, 49, 51
Aung Lin Dwe, 180(n7)
Aung Mar Mint, 180(n7)
Aung Naing Oo, 180(n7)
Australia, 114, 130, 172, 180(n13)
austerity, 130, 134, 152, 156, 158; financial, 152, 177; measures, 130, 156; programs, 134, 158
Austin, Michael M., on Sparta, 46
Austria, 13–14, 82(table), 83, 87, 103, 111, 112(table), 116, 125, 161(n42), 180(n13); expansion of voting franchise, 125; German investment in, 111; investment in Bulgaria, 116; monarchy, 87; overthrow of autocratic government, 13–14, 125
Austria-Hungary, 111, 112(table), 114; Austro-Hungarian Empire, 130; dual monarchy; French ban on investment in, 114; French investment in, 114; successor states to, 130
autarkic states, 7
autarky/autarchy, 121–122, 136
authoritarian states, 49
"axis of evil," 170, 182(n39)
Aye Nu Sein, 180(n7)
Aye Than Than, 180(n7)
Azerbaijan, 33
Aztec Empire, 69, 151; city-states in, 69

Bachelet, Michelle, United Nations High Commissioner for Human Rights, 164
Bahrain, 180(n13)
balance of power, 3, 10, 29
balance of trade, 84
Balkan Wars, 116
Balkans, 110
Balkan States, 111, 112(table), 116
ballistic missile, 8, 175
Banca d'Italia, 168
Banco della Piazza, 67, 80
"bancor," 147
bandits, 192
bank account, 166, 181(n14)
bank accounts, 41, 163, 181(n14)
bankers: American, 129; investment, 129
Bank for International Settlements (BIS), 166
banking and corporate secrecy, 170, 192
Bank of Amsterdam, 87, 194
Bank of Canada, 168
Bank of England, 1, 2, 67, 68, 80, 86, 87, 98(n32), 102, 117(n2), 168
Bank of Japan, 168
Bank of St. George (Casa di San Giorgo), 67
Bankman-Fried, Sam, 194
bank money, 87
"bank runs," 117(n7), 146, 149
banks: American, 127; "money center," 127, 139(n31); public deposit, 86; Russia, post-Soviet, 172–174, 189; Banque Commerciale pour l'Europe du Nord (BCEN or Eurobank), 152
Banque de France, 168
Banque Royale, 87, 89
Banyar Aung Moe, 180
Barings Bank, 103
Barcelona, 57, 66–67, 80, 195; as proto-state, 80; medieval, 66
Barsoom, Peter, on regime theory, 188
barter, 32–33, 47, 151; Sparta, 47; USSR, 33, 151
Basel, Switzerland, 67
basic factor endowments: energy, 10; labor, 10; land, 10; resources, 10
Basra, Iraq, 63
Battle of Agnadello, 67
"beggar-thy-neighbor," 137
Beijing, 185, 189–190
Belgium, 110, 153, 161(n40), 180(n13); secession from Holland, 110
Belt and Road Initiative (PRC), 189
Bentham, Jeremy, on panopticons, 27
Biafra, 6
Biden, Joe, president 163; administration, 187; Executive Order (EO) 14014, 163
Bikini Atoll, 90

Index

bilateral agreements, 146
bipolarity: finance domain, 14, 186, 197–198; international system, 145
bitcoin, 193
Black, Manafort, Stone, and Kelly, 154
blockade, 6, 102, 108–109, 118(n30), 122, 124; by British Royal Navy of Germany, 6; by France of United Kingdom, 102; by US Navy of Confederacy, 108, 118(n30)
Blunt, John, 88
Board of Ordnance (UK), 88
Boko Haram, 192
Bolivia: involvement in Chaco War, 131–132; loan negotiations, 129
bonds, 2, 103, 110, 129; English, 24; European, 108; French, 24; junk, 110 "seven-thirty" US Treasury bonds, 107; US bonds, 107–109, 118(n30); Venetian bonds, 67; war bonds, 129
Bond Street, 101
Bonney, Richard, 19, 99(n46) and Joseph Schumpeter, 19
Bordo, Michael, 23–24, 106, 146, 148, 159(n9); on Bretton Woods, 146, 148; on European tax systems, 24; on the gold standard, 159(n9)
Borniss, Jacob, on bullion, 85
bottomry loan, 30(table), 45. *See* sea loan
Boxing Day, 169
Boyce, James, on capital flight in Africa, 157
brassage, 65
Brazil, 106, 110, 112(table), 130–132, 154, 161(n44), 198; BRICS member country 154, 161(n44); conflict with Paraguay, 132; involvement in Triple Alliance War, 110
Brazil, Russia, India, China, and South Africa (BRICS), 154, 161(n44)
Bretton Woods, 9, 14, 30(table), 144, 146–150, 159(n1), 186, 190; agreement, 150; conference, 147; currency system collapse, 143, 188; fixed exchange system, 153; gold standard, 158; Institutions, 14, 148, 155, 158; monetary system, 144
Bretton Woods international financial system, 27, 144; as benevolent financial hegemony, 144; survival of, 158
Bretton Woods RFA, 14, 143–153; components, 158
Bretton Woods system, 12, 104, 133, 144–148, 150, 188; 1972 collapse of, 104; design of, 146; end of, 150; launch of, 148; new, 147; post-, 188

Brexit, 190
British, the, 93, 102, 121, 123, 128–129; drowning the US, 93
British: cabinet, 146; civil service, 146; colony (imaginary) in Central America, 106; colonies in India and West Africa, 123; concerns regarding the devil, 8; country banking, 117(n1); devaluation, 121; difficulties in paying naval personnel, 122; dominance, 102; British financial centrality, 117(n1); forces in Crimea, 115; GDP, 119(n44); history, 58; influence in Europe, 102; investors, 115; merchants, 26; prewar approach to fiscal policy, 128; public, 89; sailors, 117(fn7); sanctions of Russia, 174; semimercantilism, 111; wealth, 102; yields, 24. *See also* United Kingdom of Great Britain (UK).
British government, 26, 88–89, 110–111, 114, 121, 132, 184(n99); blanching, 184(n99); debt, 89; policy approach to hegemony, 110. *See also* United Kingdom of Great Britain (UK).
British Petroleum, 157. *See also* "seven sisters."
British sterling bloc, 132
Broadway, 101
bronze: coinage, 40, 48, 52, 72–73; mining, 72
Broz, Lawrence J., on central banks, 126
Brussels, Belgium, 168
bubble, 89, 186
bubonic plague, 63
Bucha, Ukraine, 174
Buenos Aires, Argentina, 106
Bulgaria, 116
bullion, 22, 48, 52, 65, 84–85, 108; American, 108; Chinese, 22, 52; French, 65; Persian, 48
"bullionism," 84
Bureau of Industry and Security (BIS), 164, 180(n4)
Bureaucratic RFA, 14, 123, 134, 137
Burgundy, 65
Bush, George W., President, 169–170
businesses, American, 127
buying power, 65
Byzantine Empire, 57, 60, 62–63, 73; in the Eastern Mediterranean, 57; fall of, 62–63; coinage in, 73
Byzantium, 22, 48; imperial overland transport, 22

Caesar, 101
Cambridge, 146

Index

cameralism, 83, 85
Canada, 36(n24), 114, 129, 180(n13)
capital accounts, 158
capital controls, 147, 150, 173, 176
capital flight, 157, 173
capitalism, 145, 148, 150–151, 157; managed, 145
capital markets, 175
capital mobility, 192
caravans, 62
Carolingian descendents of Western Roman Empire, 63
Carr, Edward Hallett, 9; *Twenty Years Crisis, The*, 9
Carthage, 47, 53
Catalonia city-states, 81
cattle, 21, 43
Cayman Islands, 170
Caytas, Joanna Diane on SWIFT, 168
Center for a New American Security (CNAS), 24, 193
Central Africa, 191
Central America, 106
Central Asia, 63
central bank, 2, 24–25, 64, 80, 86–87, 89, 94, 95(figure), 96, 126–128, 153, 166–168, 173, 176, 194, 196: currency swap lines network, 166; public bank as precursor, 64; United Kingdom, 24; US, 95, 126–128; USSR, 136
central bank digital currencies (CBDC), 187, 192–193; China, People's Republic of, 187, 193; Russia, 192
Central Bank of Russia, 193
Central Bank/Public Banking RFA, 13, 64–68, 187
central banking, 13, 22, 80, 83, 86, 92, 126, 128, 147, 186, 194
central banks, 4, 29, 30(table), 34, 42, 67, 80, 86–87, 96, 126, 128, 130, 136, 167–168, 192, 194, 196; creators of SWIFT, 168; G-10 members, 168; in Europe, 29, 80, 87, 136; in US, 126, 128; RTGS users, 167. *See also* central bank; Group of 10 (G-10); Society for Worldwide Interbank Financial Telecommunication (SWIFT); real-time gross settlement (RTGS) system.
Central Europe, 60, 64, 130; mining techniques in, 64
Central European currency bloc, 132
Central Intelligence Agency (CIA), 160(n29)
Central Powers, 124
Chaco War, 131; Bolivia, 131; Paraguay, 131
Chad, 157

challenger state, 197–198
Chamber of Deputies (France), 114
chambre de justice (France), 92
Charles V, Holy Roman Emperor, 22
Chase Manhattan Bank loans to South Africa, 156
Chase, Salmon P., Treasury Secretary, 107
chemical weapon, 173
Chiang Kai-shek, 135
Chile, 106, 180(n13)
China, dynastic/premodern, 3, 13, 22, 30(table), 40, 43, 51–52, 69–73, 74; census, 69; coinage, 22, 40, 51–52, 73; financial statecraft, 70; Imperial Period, 22, 51–52; paper money in, 13, 51, 72–73; Period of Disunion, 69; Spring and Autumn Period, 3; Tang-Song Transition, 70
China International Payment System (CIPS), 189
China, modern/prerevolutionary, 110–111, 114–115, 130, 134–135; British investment in, 110–111, 114, 135; civil war against Communists, 135; defense industry, 134; dollar reserves, 135; German investment in, 115; Nationalist, 135; rivalry with Imperial Japan, 134–135
China, People's Republic of, 5, 22, 37(n48), 154–155, 161(n47), 177, 178(table), 179, 186–187, 188–190, 193, 196–198, 198(n2); BRICS member, 154; centrally planned economy, 154; client states of, 196; domestic financial transactions, 193; economic growth of, 188; financial infrastructure, 196; financial repression, 189; military buildup, 5; national financial database, 185; rising power, 155; state-owned financial enterprises, 155; strategic lending, 155, 189; twelve-mile limit, 196; use of corvee' labor, 37(n48)
Chinatown, 171
Chinese aristocrats, 70
Chinese Communist Party (CCP), 134–135, 154, 189, 193
Chinese states, 73, 80
Chinggisid Empire, 72. *See also* Mongolia.
Chit Naing, 180(n7)
choke point effect, 27–28
Chongqing, 135
chreokoinōnia (or *chreokoinonia*) contract, 60
Cicero, 3, 39, 85, 166; Fifth Philippic of, 3
cigarettes, 40–41

Index

city-states, 2, 23, 40, 44–45, 47–48, 60, 64–67, 69, 80–81, 85–86, 96, 194
civil wars, 90–91, 134–135, 144
City of London, 103, 114, 146. *See* London
Claus, Santa, 147
Clausewitzian, 47
clientelist, 33, 44, 60
clientelistic community structure, 5
cocaine, 21
coal, 153
coinage, 25, 41–46, 48, 50–51, 53, 69, 71, 73, 77(n57), 86; debasement 42, 50, 64, 84
Coinage RFA, 13, 40–51, 53
coins, 2, 13, 20–22, 24–25, 30(table), 34, 41, 54(n5), 54(n7), 63, 64–65, 70–71, 73, 77(n57), 78(n59), 84, 86–87, 97(n13), 194, 200(n44). *See* Coinage RFA
Colbert, Jean Baptiste, French minister of finance and minster of the navy, 85;
Colbertism, 85
Cold War, 9, 11, 14, 30(table), 145, 150, 152, 154–158, 196; developing world and, 154–158; financial environment of, 9; great power competition in, 150; regimes of, 11
collective security, 145
Colombia, 106, 132; involvement in conflict with Peru, 132
colonial currencies, 122–123, 134
colonialism, 122
colonial powers, 10
Colonial Stocks Act of 1900 (US), 114
colonization, 134
Columbus, Christopher, 30(table), 74. See also Ferdinand, King of Spain; Isabella, Queen of Spain
Combined Bomber Offensive, 6
comitatenses, 58
command economy, 151
commenda contract, 60, 62, 64
commendator, 60
commodity: currency, 70; markets, 157; money, 41, 69
commons, 3, 24. *See* financial commons
Composite Index of National Capability (CINC), 5, 15(n13)
complex states, 44
Confederate States of America/Confederacy, The, 94, 108–109, 118(n30); bond issues, 108, 118(n30); European representative of, 118(n30); financial problems, 108; paper currency, 108; transportation networks, 109

conflict, 4, 8, 24, 28, 52, 70, 73, 103, 110, 148, 151, 190–191; character and conduct of, 28; spaces of, 8; use of defensive financial operations in, 70
conflicts, 1, 53, 102–103, 128, 187; financing of, 102; European, 128
Confucianism, 72–73
Congo, 157
Congress of Vienna of 1814–1815, 30(table), 101, 115
Constantinople, 7, 62
Contamine, Phillipe, on war in the Middle Ages, 59
"Contested Commons: The Future of American Military Power in a Multipolar World," 24
continental powers, 111
Continental System, 6, 102
financial warfare, 102
constructivism, 9, 11
consulting firms, 192
Cooke, Jay, 107
Union fundraiser, 107
copper, 40, 72, 87; coinage, 87; mines, 72
Cordova, Gonzalo, President of Ecuador, 131
Correlates of War, 5
correspondent accounts, 169
Cortés, Hernando, 79
corvée labor, 13, 20, 32
as tax payment in premodern era, 13
forced labor by peasants, 20
cotton, 108, 118(n30)
Council for Mutual Economic Assistance (COMECON), 151
Council on Foreign Relations, 148
Council of State, 87; *See* Doubleth, Philips
Court of the Exchequer, 58
counterfeiting, 6, 109, 167
counterfeit pharmaceuticals, 22
country devaluation, 132
coup, 28, 163–164, 180(n4)
crash, 89, 195
South Sea Company, 89
credit: in Confederate States of America, 108; in Japan, 134; in Roman Empire, 49, 51; in United States, 101, 136
crime syndicates, 31, 168
Crimea, 115, 171; British forces in, 115; Russian invasion of, 171
crops, 21, 39, 70, 192
cross-border lending, 129
Crown Treasury, 114
Crusader/s, 60–62; access to credit, 61 collaboration with local Christians, 60; land mortgaging, 61; motivation, 61;

stabilizing in their absence, 62; targeting of Christians, 61; temporal privileges granted, 61; territorial gains, 61
Crusades, 34, 60–62, 74, 106; expense of, 34; impact, 62; knights, 60; mercenaries, 60
cryptocurrency, 177, 187, 192–195, 196, 198n3, 200(n44); nonstate, 194; state-backed, 192–193; state-controlled, 193; state-sponsored, 187; "Wild West," 194
Cuba, 151
currency blocs, 133
currency controls, 130, 146
currency crisis, 146, 165(table)
currency devaluations, 122, 146, 150
currency exchange, 122, 133, 146, 153, 196
currency markets, 159(n9), 173
currency pegs, 150
currency smuggling, 135
currency speculation, 146
currency union, 165(table), 187, 196
currency valuation, 147
currency zone, 153
cursus clabularis/platys dromos, 22, 36(n16)
cursus velox/oxys dromos, 22, 36(n16)
cyberspace, 8
cyberspace commons, 24
Cyprus, 180(n13)
Cyrus the Younger, King of Persia, 48
Czechoslovakia/Czech Republic, 131, 180(n13); supported Bolivia in Chaco War, 131

Dainoff, Charles, 170, 188; on tax havens, 170
Dark Ages, The 64
Davis, Jefferson, 108
Daw Nilar, 180(n7)
Dawes Plan, 125
De Cavour, Camillo, prime minister of Sardinia, 110
De Male, Louis, Count, 64 Flemish coin debasement, 64
De Nederlandsche Bank, 168
De Quintanilla, Alonso, 74
De Santangel, Luis, 74
debt, 7, 19, 21, 43, 57, 70, 80, 86–87, 125, 127, 129–131, 146, 165(table); Africa, 156; British, 24; China, People's Republic of, 190; Confederate States of America/Confederacy, The, 108; Crusader, 61; France, Ancien Regime, 89; France, post-Napoleonic, 24, 103, 139(n19); Genoa, Republic of, 57, 66;
Germany, 133; Japan, 134; long-term, 86; long-term securitized, 21; private, 86; Russia, Czarist, 115; Russia, post-Soviet, 163, 173–174; securitized, 26; South Africa, 156; United States, 92, 94, 95(figure), 96, 195. *See also* sovereign debt
debt markets, 32
decentralized finance (DeFi) platforms, 198(n3)
deferred net settlement (DNS) system, 167
deflation, 118(n13)
Delian League, 45; alliance of city-states, 45; silver mines, 45
demesne (properties), 58–59
democracy, 109, 131, 148, 157, 164
Deng Xiaoping, 154, 161(n49)
deniers, 65
Denmark, 180(n13)
Dent, Julius, on French financiers, 91
Department of Commerce, (US), 128, 164
Department of Defense, (US), 5
Department of Homeland Security, (US), 169
Department of Justice, (US), 4
Department of State/State Department, (US), 128–131, 146, 171
Department of the Treasury, (US), 4, 163, 169–170
dependent states, 151
deposit accounts, 105
depression, 14, 131, 149. *See* Great Depression
Deutsche Bundesbank, 168
détente, 152
devaluation, 87, 132–133, 137, 138(n6), 159(n7)
developed states, 4
developing world, 154, 191
Di Rustico, Caffaro, "The Genoese Capture of Almería," 57
digital: currency, 193–194; financial infrastructure, 185; financial services, 185
Digital RFA, 14, 158, 163–180, 187
"digital ruble," 192
"digital yuan," 193
diplomatic, informational, military, and economic (DIME), (US), 165
diplomatic power, 47
Diocletian, Emperor of Rome, 50
dollar, 4, 27, 31, 41, 105, 126, 147, 149–150, 153, 160(n22), 160(n27), 160(n35), 166, 176–177, 190, 193; dominance/hegemony, 153, 195; gold value of, 147; "greenbacks," 109;

political power of, 153; importance of, 4, 27; valuation, 149–150
dollar diplomacy, 128, 130, 157
dollarization, 165(table)
dollars, 41, 111, 131, 149, 157, 166, 170, 173, 189–190, 193, 199(n11)
domain, 2–4, 5–7, 8, 10, 16, 19, 20, 24, 28, 29–34, 43–44, 46, 50, 53, 59, 68–69, 71, 93, 96, 102, 107, 121, 150, 152, 171, 186–188, 194–198; air, 2, 8, 10, 29, 32; cyber, 3, 8, 29, 31, 187, 195; interactions between, 7–8; land, 2, 8, 10, 33, 93, 107; military definition of, 2; maritime/naval/sea, 2, 8, 10, 16(n24), 31–32, 53, 93, 102, 107; space, 3, 16(n27); terrestrial, 150. *See* finance domain
domains, 2–3, 5–8, 10, 24, 28–29, 31–32, 34, 46, 93, 96, 171, 195
domain state, 19–20, 46, 59, 68–69. *See* Schumpeter, Joseph
domain states, 19, 44
Doomsday Book, 58
Doria, Ansaldo, 57
double gros, 65
Doubleth, Philips, receiver-general of the Dutch Republic, 86–87; sons, 87
Dowell, Stephen, on England under Roman rule, 58
Downs, George W. on regime theory, 188
drachma, 45
drachmae, 45
Dreyfus affair, 116. *See* France; Jews
Drezner, Dan, on weaponized interdependence, 27
drugs, 23, 195
Dubai, 192
ducats, 79

East Asia, 51, 59, 63
East Asian history, 12
Eastern Europe, 61
East India Company, 84, 88
Eastern Mediterranean, 3, 43, 48, 57, 59–60
Eastern Roman Empire, 50, 62
economic development, 20, 73, 151, 159(n5)
economic power, 9, 47, 50, 144, 196
economic statecraft, 4, 6, 165, 180(n10)
economic warfare, 6
Ecuador, 131–132; involvement in war with Peru, 132; July Revolution, 131; junta, 131; legislature, 131
Egypt, 13, 43, 49–50, 63, 113(table), 114, 191; Arab conquest of, 63; censuses, 43; first tax state, 191; New Kingdom, 43; Old Kingdom, 43; Roman client state, 49–50; UK intervention in, 114
Eichengreen, Barry, on adherence to the gold standard, 159(n9)
Eighty Years' War, 85
Eisenhower, Dwight D., President, 32; administration, 149; "military-industrial complex," 32
eisphora, 45
elites, 6, 62, 126, 163
El Salvador, 129
emerging market states, 167
"empty battlefield," 28. *See also* trench warfare
English economy in 1700s, 26
Enlightenment, The, 123
Entity List (US), 164
Epstein, Stephen, on taxation in Genoa, 66
Eritrea, 157
Estonia, 180(n13)
ethereum, 193
Ethiopia, 157
Eurasia, 13, 42, 50, 52, 58, 63, 73; coinage, 42, 52; fiscal impact of Roman Empire, 50; long-distance trade across, 63; premodern cultural and economic exchange in, 52; taxation system in, 13
Eugene III, Pope, granting of secular privileges to Crusaders, 61
euro, 153, 181(n27), 190; currency competitor for dollar, 153
eurocurrency, 30(table), 150, 156–158, 160(n29), 191, 199(n11)
eurodollar, 150, 152
Europe 1–3, 10, 13, 19, 23, 25, 34, 42, 50–51, 60–62, 64, 66–67, 69, 73–74, 79, 80–81, 86, 89–90, 92, 102–104, 106, 108, 111–114, 118(n30), 124–125, 128, 130–131, 132–133, 137, 149, 152–154, 167, 173, 175, 190; comparison with dynastic China, 73; competitive landscape of, 90; connections to Asia, 50; economies of early modern, 10; financial institutions in, 69; first financial revolution of, 67; first paper currency, 89; inflation in, 64; medieval, 64, 84; public debt in, 13, 23, 66; state-building in, 66; territorial states in, 80; transformation from domain state to tax state, 59
European aristocrats, prejudice against trade and finance of, 114
European Central Bank (ECB), 153, 168, 181(n27)
European Common Market, 133
European countries, 79, 80, 83, 108

232 Index

European states, 7, 11, 20, 23, 29, 81, 82(table), 103, 125, 137, 152–153; and Bretton Woods, 152–153; and China, 73; debt financing methods, 103; expansion of franchise in, 125; large-scale borrowing by, 23; medieval, 73
European fiscal-military state, 29
European politics, 13, 115, 122, 125
European Union (EU), 153, 167, 172–174, 178, 181(n27), 187, 190, 196–198; financial influence, 187; market, 181(n27); member country sovereign debt, 190; member states, 153; sanctions campaign by, 172. *See also* Schuman Declaration of 1950
euroskepticism, 190
eurozone, 153, 190
Exchange Alley, 88. *See* London
exchange bank, 15(n5)
exchange controls, 30(table), 133, 137
"exchange of notes," 129
exchange rates, 14, 144–146, 147–148, 150, 158, 196; fixed, 144, 148, 150; flexible, 150, 158; floating, 146, 148; parities, 147; stable, 145; valuations, 147
exotic animal species, 22
exports, 33, 63, 73, 109, 134–135, 139(n19), 152, 173, 175–176, 178; energy, 173, 175–176; oil and gas, 152; silver, 135
export controls, 172, 175
export restrictions, 164
extortion, 19, 21
Extremadura, 74

face value, 41–42, 54(n7), 71–72, 109
fairs, 64, 76(n22); of medieval Western Europe, 64. *See* souk
farmers, 126, 143, 192
Farrell, Henry, 166, 168, 195; on network theory and international finance, 166
Federal Deposit Insurance Corporation (FDIC)(US), 194
Federal Reserve Act of 1913 (US), 126–127
Federal Reserve (US), 4, 122, 126–128, 149, 166, 168, 181(n18), 181(n23); governors, 127
Fedwire system (US), 167
feiqian ("flying cash"), 70
Feis, Herbert, 110–111, 114, 147–148, 155, 191; *Europe, the World's Banker 1870–1914*, 148; on national security vs. prosperity, 110
Ferdinand, King of Spain, 74. *See* Christopher Columbus; Isabella, Queen of Spain

Fertile Crescent, 43
feudalism, 20, 29, 33, 51, 58–59
fiat money, 187
finance domain, 2–7, 8, 9, 11–14, 19–38, 40, 42, 44, 48, 50–51, 53, 58, 60–61, 64, 71–74, 79–80, 83, 86, 88–89, 92–94, 96, 102–103, 106–107, 110, 114, 116, 122–125, 129, 132, 137, 143–144, 146–147, 150–152, 154–155, 158, 165–167, 171–172, 176, 180, 181(n20), 186–187, 189, 190–195, 196, 197, 198. *See also* domain
financial assets, 2, 25, 190
financial capacity, 47
financial centers, 103, 139(n20)
financial commons, 3, 6, 14, 24–27, 28, 31, 44, 51, 59–60, 73, 80–81, 103, 147, 150, 152, 156, 165, 167, 177, 179; Eurasia, 73; Europe, 80; global, 103, 167; Hellenic Greece, 44; Mediterranean, 60; Roman Empire, 51; Russia, 177
financial conflict, 177
Financial Crimes Enforcement Network (FinCEN), 169
financial crises, 80, 158, 166; of 2008, 166, 190
financial flows, 3, 14, 21, 26, 63, 67, 73, 122, 132, 169, 190–191; international, 3, 191
financial instruments, 20, 25, 80
financial institutions, 9–11, 13, 25, 31, 47, 52, 60, 86, 96, 192, 196
financial markets, 7, 134, 190
financial messaging and payment systems, 167
financial networks, 28, 50; Roman Empire, 50
financial panic, 23, 176
financial policy, 3, 9; effects of war on, 3
financial power, 9, 11, 12, 27, 47, 61, 114, 164, 177, 186, 196
financial revolution, 67
financial sanctions, 28, 103, 165(table), 167, 171, 173, 177–179, 186
financial statecraft, 4, 6, 40, 70, 149, 164, 165–170, 171
financial system, 11, 25, 124, 144, 187–188, 196; American/in United States/US, 28, 94, 117(n1), 126, 129, 164, 166, 168, 196; British, 102, 132; cryptocurrency in, 196; in China, People's Republic of, 154, 189; in Mediterranean, 58; in Roman Republic, 49–50; in Seleucid, 48; regimes, 188; Russian, post-Soviet, 175–177; Russian,

Soviet, 135, 143; Spartan, 47; Triple Entente–dominated, 9. *See also* Bretton Woods financial system; global financial system; international financial system; multipolar financial system; world financial system
financial systems, 3, 10, 23, 186
financial technologies, 42, 58, 185
Financial Times, 166; *The Banker*, 166
financial tools, 3, 28, 39–40, 68, 74, 80, 177–178
financial transfers, 194
Finland, 180(n13)
Finley, Moses, on sea loans, 45
Finnemore, Martha, *The Purpose of Intervention*, 12
First Bank of the United States, 94–95, 126
First Crusade (1096), 61
fisc/*fiscus*, 20
fiscal-military state, 20, 29, 51, 68
fiscal sociology, 20
fiscal state, 20–24, 27, 63
"five-twenty" bond series (US), 107
fixed exchange system, 150
fixed parities, 147, 149
Flandreau, Marc, on nineteenth century financiers, 110
Flores, Juan, on nineteenth century financiers, 110
foederati (non-Roman allied forces), 58
foreign aid, 149, 151, 154, 165(table)
foreign direct investment, 170
foreign exchange, 160(n29), 166, 168, 173; earnings, 173; operations, 160(n29); reserves, 166; trading, 166; transaction systems, 168
foreign policy, 27, 110, 129, 155, 164–168, 172, 179, 180(n10), 186
foreign wars, 1, 95(figure)
Fourth Crusade, 61
fracking, 172
France, Ancien Régime, 24, 58–59, 64–65, 67, 80–81, 82(table), 83, 88, 89–90, 90–92; alliance with Spain in War of Spanish Succession, 88; coinage debasement, 65; forced loans, 90–91; king, 59, 62, 65, 81, 90–92; king's officers, 59; knights, 58; minting, 65, 89; nobility reluctance to pay tax, 81; Norman conquest of England, 58–59; novel financial contracts, 89; takeover of Republic of Genoa, 67; tax farming, 89–91; tax revenue, 59, 81, 83, 90
France, Napoleonic/Revolutionary, 6, 87, 92, 102–103, 123, 188; collapse, 102; general embargo against Britain, 102; law enforcement, 123; Napoleon as emperor of France, 102–103; reparations, 103, 139(n19); Revolution, 90, 92; use of bimetallic standard, 104; war with United States, 92
France, post-Napoleonic, 30(table), 36(n24), 102–104, 110–111, 112(table), 114, 116, 121, 125, 129, 132–134, 139(n19), 146–147, 153, 161(n40), 180(n13), 198(n2); alliance with Bulgaria, 116; as "colonial empire," 121; bailout of Russia, 115; ban on loans to Germany, 114; "financial pacifism," 114; financial policy, 104, 114; financial sanctions, 103; G7 membership, 36(n24); German occupation of, 133; gold standard bloc, 132; gold surplus, 146; occupation of Ruhr, 125; post–Dreyfus Affair, 116; Russian bond issue in, 116; Schuman Declaration of 1950 signatory, 153; war reparations, 103
Franco-German War, 104
Franco-Prussian War, 111, 114
francs, 103
Frankfurt, Germany, 181(n27)
Frankopan, Peter, on trade between Europe and Asia, 50
free riding, 24
Friedman, Milton, on government intervention in currency markets, 159(n9)
Fronde (France), 91
FTX, 187, 194. *See* Bankman-Fried, Sam
Fuerzas Armadas Revolucionarias de Colombia (FARC), 21; as Latin American VNSA, 21
Fugger, house of, 22
full employment policies, 146

gabelle (salt tax), 81
Gabor, Daniela, on the "Wall Street Consensus," 191
gains from trade, 50
Gallatin, Albert, US Secretary of the Treasury, 94–95
galleys, 57, 66
Gandhi, Indira, 155
gas, 152, 173
Gazprom, 172
Gazprombank, 172, 174
Gazprom Neft, 172
Gelpern, Anna, on Chinese lending, 189
Genghis Khan, 72. *See* Chingissid Empire
Genoa, Republic of, 57, 66–67, 74, 195; Doge of, 67; fiscal system, 66; knights,

234   Index

57; popular revolt, 66; rivalry with Venice, 67; supplier of Crusades, 74; trade in debt securities, 66. *See* Italian city-states
Genoese, 57, 67, 74; impact of War of Chioggia, 67; merchant network in Seville, 74; swords of, 57
Germany, ancient to Weimar, 6, 9, 12–14, 26, 58, 81, 83, 83(table), 84–85, 97(n13), 102, 104, 110–111, 112–113(table), 114–116, 117(n1), 119(n44), 121–122, 124–125, 129–130, 133, 139(n19), 139(n24), 147, 184(n99); adoption of gold standard, 104; debasement, 84; extension of franchise, 125; financial policy strategy, 114; investment in Austria Hungary, 111; investment in Russia, 115; overseas investments of, 110–111, 112–113(table); overthrow of autocratic government, 12–13; overthrow of Romans, 58; reparations, 122, 124–125, 133, 139(n19); rivalry with Britain and France, 102; Weimar government, 133; Wilhelmine, 114
Germany, Nazi, 6, 121, 123–124, 132–134; attempt to stay on gold standard, 133; fetters, 132; industrial capacity, 6; trade bloc, 133
Germany, postwar and unification, 30(table), 36(n24), 149, 153, 161(n40), 170, 180(n13), 198(n1); G7 membership, 36; Schuman Declaration of 1950 signatory, 153, 161(n40)
Gilpin, Robert, on international political economy, 11
Giufre the Hairy, Count of Barcelona, 66
global financial framework, 167
global financial hegemony, 14
global financial network, 166
global financial stability, 198
global financial system, 27, 143, 147, 158, 164, 166, 186, 195–196; centrality of dollar in, 166
global interbank payment system network, 167
globalization, 167, 187, 196
global money supply, 146
global network, 27
global nuclear annihilation, 144
global trade flows, 179
global trade system, 145
God, 57
gold, 1, 4, 6, 26, 40–41, 44, 52, 64, 79, 103–106, 108–109, 121, 124, 127, 136, 146, 148–149, 152, 156

gold-backed currency, 103
gold-based money, 105
gold deficit, 146
gold deposits, 106
gold drain, 26, 121
gold exchange standard, 123, 146
gold exploration, 105
gold force, 4
gold prices, 122
gold reserves, 105, 127
gold standard, 11, 13–14, 23, 30(table), 41, 101–120, 122–123, 126, 128–130, 132–133, 137, 144–146, 149, 158, 159(n9), 186; and international borrowing, 104–106; as basis for new financial system, 158; as British-centered, 14, 144; attempt to return to, 122; classical, 11, 13, 41, 137, 144, 146; creation of, 103; development of, 13, 102; establishment of, 13, 106; expansion of, 104; inflation and deflation during, 118(n13); leaving, 137; maintenance and development, 103; overall performance (1700–1980), 105; success and spread of, 101; UK abandonment of, 23, 103, 122, 132, 149; US abandonment of, 145; US elite desire for, 126; US maintenance of, 128
Gold Standard Act of 1900 (US), 126
Gold Standard RFA, 96, 101, 102–106, 116
gold stocks, 104–105, 149
gold surplus, 146
"Good Housekeeping Seal of Approval," 106
"good neighbors," 128. *See* United States
Gorton, Gary, on the National Bank Acts, 109
Gosbank, 136
government debt, 80, 86, 89, 91
grain, 21, 43, 49, 152
Grand Alliance, 88; Habsburgs, 88; Holy Roman Empire, 88; Netherlands/Dutch Republic, 88; United Kingdom, 88; War of Spanish Succession, 88
Great Depression, 103, 122, 130–132, 137, 146. *See* depression
Great Inflation, 149
Great Northern War, 88
great-power competition, 144, 150
great powers, 23, 30(table), 43, 94, 102–104, 115, 132, 144–145, 148, 150, 152, 196
Greater East Asia Co-Prosperity Sphere, 134, 196; China, People's Republic of, 196; Imperial Japan, 134
Greater Mediterranean, 43

Index

Greco-Persian War, 43–44. *See* Herodotus
Greece, 39, 44, 46–47, 80, 106, 161(n40), 180(n13); city-states, 47–48
gross domestic product (GDP), 26, 81, 83(table), 94–95, 104(figure), 105–106, 111, 112(table), 117(n9), 119(n44), 147, 184(n99), 190
gross national income (GNI), 162(n51)
Group of 7 (G7), 23, 36(n24), 166
Group of 10 (G-10), 168
Group of 20 (G-20), 170
Guatemala, 129
guifang ("counting houses"), 70
Guinea, 151
guinea, 101

Habsburgs, 85–88, 97(n20); House of Habsburg, 86; as monarchs, 87; Holy Roman Empire, 88; raising money on credit, 85; removal from power, 97(n20)
Haiti, 130
Hamburg, Germany, 67
Hamilton, Alexander, 19, 93–95; "Defense of the Funding System," 93; *Federalist no. 31*, 93; on credit, 93; tariff and taxation system, 95
Haradheere, Somalia, 31
hard currency, 33, 134, 136, 152, 154–155, 175; imports, 152
hard money, 126
Harley, Robert, Chancellor of the Exchequer (UK), 88
Harvard University, 148
Han Dynasty: 22, 50–52, 69
Haute Finance, 110
heavy horse debtors, 101
Heckscher, Eli, on mercantilism, 84
hedge fund, 194
Heftye, Eric, 5
hegemonic aspirations, 44–48; Athens, 44–46; Sparta, 46–48
hegemonic mismanagement, 188
hegemonic role, 122, 150
hegemonic stability, 11
hegemonic status, 27
hegemonic war, 198
hegemon, 14, 49, 110, 137, 158, 181(n20), 186, 195, 197–198; Alexander the Great, 49; United Kingdom, 110, 181(n20); United States, 14, 158, 186, 195
hegemons, 9, 116, 197
hegemon-in-training, 125
hegemony, 3, 5, 10–12, 14, 44, 47, 50, 53, 69, 102, 125–126, 128, 143–144, 150, 166–167, 185–186, 188, 190, 193, 195–198; British, 102; nature of, 3; Roman, 47, 50; Spartan, 53. *See also* hegemony, US
hegemony, US: 5, 11–12, 14, 125–126, 143–144, 150, 158, 166–167, 185–186, 188, 190, 193, 195–197
helots, 46
Henry VIII, King of the United Kingdom, 64
heretics, 60
Herodotus of Halicarnassus, 3, 21, 39, 43–44; *The Histories*, 3
"high-income economies," 166, 180–181(n13), 181(n14)
hijacking, 31
His Majesty's Ships, 132; *Hood*, 132; *Nelson*, 132; *Rodney*, 132; *Valiant*, 132. *See* Invergordon Mutiny; Royal Navy of Great Britain
Hitler, Adolf, 122
Hlaing Bwar Aung, 180(n7)
Hobbes, Thomas, 84
Hoffman, Philip, on France, 90–91
Holland, States of 67, 85, 110. *See also* Netherlands
Hollow Sword Blades Company, 88
Holy Land, 60
Holy Roman Empire, 85, 88; Central European countries under Habsburg control, 88
Homoioi, 46
Hong Kong, 180(n13)
Hongwu, Emperor, Ming Dynasty, 72
Hope and Co., 103
Horn of Africa, 31
Horn, Sebastian, on Chinese lending, 189
House of Rothschild, 101, 110
Horowitz, Michael, 12
Howie, Frazier, on China, 154–155
Huai River, 71
huizi notes, 77(n50)
human rights, 152, 163–164, 173
Hungary, 115, 125, 180(n13)
hyperinflation, 42, 50, 72, 125, 133

Iberia, 49, 63; caliphate in, 63; Roman conquest of, 49
Iberian maravedis, 74
Iberian Peninsula, Crusades in, 61
Ikenberry, John, 144, 146; on the "liberal international order," 144
ilaf contract, 62
illicit trade, 173
Imperial Japanese Army, 135
imports, 26, 102, 152
Incas/Incan Empire, 20, 68–69, 151; development level, 68–69

incorporation laws, 192
India, 40, 48, 50, 114, 123, 130, 154–155, 161(n44), 177; BRICS membership, 154, 161(n44); British colonial administrators in, 123; debt load, 130; debt service ratio, 155; external debt, 155; loans strategy, 155; monetary system, 123; rupee devaluation, 155; third way during Cold War, 155; trade with British, 114; trade with Roman Empire, 50; western India as part of Seleucid, 48
Indianapolis Monetary Commission, 127
Indian nations, 94. *See* United States
Indonesia, 151
Indo-Pakistani War, 155
inflation, 14, 21, 42, 48, 64, 71, 74, 77(n50), 92, 108, 118(n13), 126, 130–131, 134–137, 145, 147, 150, 153, 175, 178–179
infrastructure, 20, 130, 135, 157–158, 176, 185, 189, 196, 200(n44)
Innocent III, Pope, 61
Inquisition, The, 61
institutional debt instruments, 80, 86–87
interest rates, 45, 49, 91, 98(n39), 173, 175–176, 191, 195
"International Clearing Union," 147
international community, 156–157, 169–170, 172, 190
international cooperation, 11–12, 23, 124, 145, 148, 158, 190
international cooperative network, 144
international currency, 147, 195; dollar as, 195
international energy markets, 174
international finance, 5, 8–9, 16(n26), 110, 128, 150, 185, 189
international financial system, 9, 11, 27–28, 81, 103, 106, 150, 166, 168–170, 179, 189, 194, 196
international financial transactions, 174, 189; in yuan, 189
international lending, 106, 150, 156
international markets, 7, 33, 131
International Monetary Fund (IMF), 146, 156, 158, 170, 177, 188
International Narcotics Strategy Control Report (INSCR), published by US Department of State, 171
international political economy (IPE), 9, 11
international power, 5
international relations, 8–9, 11–12, 17(n30), 125, 196–197; foundational texts, 8–9; theory, 197
international sovereign debt market, 106
international sovereign lending, 156

international system, 2–3, 5–6, 10–11, 13, 26–27, 29, 33, 52, 124, 128, 137, 145, 148, 166, 180, 195, 197; anarchic, 10; as network, 27; stability of, 5, 124
international trade, 7, 13, 26, 127, 135, 148–149, 166
interstate conflict, 110
interstate rivalry, 14
interwar period, 13, 125, 130, 135, 138(n12), 145–146, 148, 159(n9), 181(n20), 188
intrastate armed conflict, Africa, 157
Invergordon Mutiny, 23, 103, 117(n7), 132, 146. *See* His Majesty's Ships; Royal Navy of Great Britain
IOUs, 21, 24, 133
Iran, 7, 169–172, 175, 178–179, 186, 198; access to international financial markets, 7; nuclear programs, 169–170; relative weakness, 172; Section 311 of the USA Patriot Act, 169; US financial sanctions against, 186. *See* Persia
Iranian, 50, 170; as Parthian, 50
Iraq, 34, 63, 182(n39)
Iraqi, 21
Ireland, 180(n13)
Isabella, Queen of Spain, 74. *See* Christopher Columbus; Ferdinand, King of Spain
Islamic caliphate, 63
Islamic State in Iraq and Syria (ISIS), 21, 34, 191–192
Islamic State West Africa Province (ISWAP), 192
Islamic world, 60
isolationism, 147
'*isqa* (or *isqua*) contract, 60
Israel, 180(n13)
Italian city-states, 23, 60, 62, 64, 66, 74, 81; forced loans, 23; princes, 66
Italy, 36(n24), 49, 63, 65–66, 81, 83, 110, 112(table), 115, 125, 131, 134, 153, 161(n40), 180(n13); borrowing by, 134; European Union (EU) membership, 161(n40); G7 membership, 36(n24); loans to, 110, 115; medieval, 65; Schuman Declaration of 1950 signatory, 153; support of Paraguay in Chaco War, 131
Ivanov, Martin, on Bulgaria, 116

James I, King of the Britons, 84; Privy Council of, 84
Japan: 30(table), 36(n24), 94, 115, 123–124, 134–135, 141(n66), 158, 172–174, 180(n13), 187, 198; default on public

debt, 134; economic boom, 134; Empire, 134–135; G7 membership, 36n24; merchant marine, 134; occupation of China, 135; pre-Meiji, 94; regional fiat currencies, 135; sanctions of Russia, 174; semiautarkic, 134; wartime boom, 141(n66)
Jefferson, Thomas, President, 94
Jeffs, Jennifer, on the RTGS system, 167
Jerusalem, 62–63
Jewish traders, 60
Jews, 61, 115; European, 61, pogroms against, 115, Russian, 115. *See also* Dreyfus Affair; Inquisition, The; Germany, Nazi
jiaochou, 72
jiaozi credit bill, 71
Jin Dynasty, 69
Johannsen, Niels, on tax avoidance and evasion, 170
Johnson, Lyndon B., President, 149; administration, 149
Joint Comprehensive Plan of Action (JCPOA) (US), 186
Joint Chiefs of Staff (US), 5; "Capstone Concept for Joint Operations" 5
Joint Vision 2020 (US), 5
Jurchen Jin, 70–73; conquering and sacking of Northern Song, 71
Justwan, Florian, 97(n13)

Kantian, 109
Karl X Gustav, King of Sweden, 1, 2, 84
Kautilya, 39
Kemmerer, Edwin, 123, 130–131; American money doctor, 123
Kennedy, John F., President, 149; on what scared him, 149
Keohane, Robert, *After Hegemony*, 11
Keynes, John Maynard, 124, 146–148
Keynesian, 148
Khang Moe Myint, 180(n7)
Khitan, 70
kidnapping, 21, 31
King Royal Technologies, Ltd., 180n4
Kipper-und Wipper-zeit, 84–85, 97(n13)
Kitson, Michael, on Nazi Germany, 133
Knight, Frank, 147; Chicago School, 147
Korea, 123, 134, 174, 180(n13); South Korea, 174
Krepinevich, Andrew, on revolutions in military affairs (RMAs), 28
Krugman, Paul, on dollar dominance, 195
Kublai Khan, 72. *See* Mongolia; Yuan Dynasty
Kufa, Iraq, 63
Kuhn Loeb, 115
Kuwait, 181(n13)
Kyiv, Ukraine, 178
Kyu Kyu Hla, 180(n7)

Laconia, 39, 47
laissez faire, 157
Lambert, Nicholas, 26
land: 5, 8, 19–20, 29, 39, 62, 79, 81, 191; acquisition, 191; as resource, 19; competition, 8; imperial, 20; markets, 62; ownership, 5; royal, 81; state ownership of, 20
landowners, taxation of, 71
land power, 8, 10, 29, 33–34
Lansky, Meyer, 192
Lao, 70
large states, 90
Latin America, 21, 111, 112(table), 128–129, 130–132, 150, 157–158; and the US, 130–132; debt crisis of, 157–158; eurocurrency finance in, 150; mouths, 129; sovereign debt issue, 131; states in, 157; US loans to, 128–129; violent nonstate actors in, 21
Latvia, 2, 161(n42), 171, 181(n13); as Russian tax haven, 171; "jurisdiction of primary concern," 171
Law, John, 89–90; Scottish, 89. *See* France, Ancien Régime
League of Nations, the, 124–125, 139(n21), 145, 181(n20); US Senate opposing US membership in, 125
lending, 32, 61, 91, 128–131, 149, 157, 191
Leopold I, King of Belgium, 110
Levant, 3, 51, 60–62, 63, 73–74
Levy-Leboyer, Maurice, on nineteenth century competition, 111
liberalism, 9, 11
licai ("regulating wealth"), 71
Liechtenstein, 170
liquid assets, 4, 6–7, 20, 22, 24–25, 80, 84–85, 90
Litan, Robert E., on financial statecraft, 165
Lithuania, 161(n42), 181(n13), as part of Poland-Lithuania, 1, 82(table)
livre, 65, 92
loan: 2, 9, 13, 15(n5), 45–46, 48, 61, 74, 81, 91, 103, 107–108, 156–157; bank, 15(n5); contracts, 13; defaults, 157; forced, 81; repayment, 156; strategic, 9
London, 4, 9, 106, 129, 145, 157, 168. *See* City of London
London Stock Exchange, 132
long nineteenth century, 9

Louis the Stammerer, King of Aragon, 66–67
Louis XVII, King of France, 90
Louis XVIII, King of France, 90
Lukoil, 172
Luxembourg, 153, 181(n13); Schuman Declaration of 1950 signatory, 153
Lycurgus, 39
Lydian Kingdom, 41, 44; Achaemenid conquest of, 44; coinage, 44; western Turkey, 41

Macedon Kingdom, absorption by Roman Republic, 49
Macedonia, 44, 48; conquest of Achaemenid/Persian Empire, 44, 48; financing techniques, 48; Greek city-states controlled by, 48; minting in, 48. *See* Alexander the Great
Machiavelli, Niccolo, 67, 85
Mahan, Alfred Thayer, on maritime spaces, 24
Magnusson, Lars, on mercantilism, 84
major European power, 132, 151
major European powers, 128
major powers, 123, 144, 151
major war, 133
major Western powers, 123
Malaysia Airlines flight 17, 172
Mali, 151
Malta, 181(n13)
Manchuria, 71. *See* Jurchen Jin
Maoz, Zeev, on interdependence, 27
Marcus Aurelius, 64
maritime trade, 13, 45, 53, 79; long-distance, 53. *See also* trade
mark, 113(table), 115, 133
mark bloc, 133
market: 14, 48, 57, 63, 72, 85, 134, 143, 145, 148, 151, 157, 163, 167, 178, 189; economies, 151; economy, 72; forces, 14, 145; value, 77(n50), 117(n9)
marobotini, 57
Marshall Plan, 149
Maung Maung Kya, 180n7
Maximum (France), 123
McAdoo, William Gibbs, US treasury secretary, 121
McDonald, Ramsay, Prime Minister, 132
McGregor, Gregor, 106. *See* Poyais
Mecca, 62
Mediterranean, 3, 13, 25–26, 40, 43–51, 52, 57–60, 62–63, 66–67, 73, 194; ancient, 43; city-states, 40, 66, 194; contracts in, 60; Eastern, 3, 43, 48, 57, 59–60; Greater, 43; Islamic conquests in, 57; 63; Roman hegemony of, 47, 50, 62; Sparta, 47; strategic competition in, 43; tax systems in, 51; Western, 60
Medvedev, Dmitry, President, 172. *See* Russia, Post-Soviet
Mehrling, Perry, on central bank networks, 166
Melos, as domain state, 44. *See* Peloponnesian War
Mencius, 72
Mercantile Era, 30(table)
mercantilism, 13, 79, 81, 83–85, 96, 166; British school of, 83; form of protectionism, 81; theories of, 83–84, 96
mercantilist revolution, 74
Mercantilist RFA, 13, 29, 67, 79–96
mercantilists, 26. *See* Mun, Thomas
mercantilist thought, 83
mercenaries, 42, 44–45, 48, 60, 74
merchant banks, 127
Merovingian, descendents of Western Roman Empire, 63
Mesopotamia, 13, 43, 63, 191; Arab conquest, 63; coins in, 43; private debt in, 43; tax state, 191; use of taxation, 13
metoikoin, 44
Mexican-American War, 128
Mexico, 94, 112(table), 131
Middle Ages, 26, 64, 66
Middle East, 13, 21, 34, 60–62, 64; Crusades in, 34, 61–62; empires of, 13; governments in, 21; Islamic proto-states in, 60; souks, 64; taxation in, 13
Midlands Bank, 160(n29)
Milan, 67. *See* Italian city-states
militarized interstate disputes (MIDs), 131–132; military, informational, diplomatic, financial, intelligence, economic, law, and development (MIDFIELD) (US), 165
military power, 4–5, 9, 34, 43, 47, 50, 52–53, 62, 69, 74, 96, 114, 137
military-technical revolution, 28
military technology, 151, 164, 175
Milward, Alan, on Nazi Germany, 133
Min Aung Hlang, 180(fn7)
Ming Dynasty, 72–73; Mongolian in character, 72
Ministry of Finance (MOF) (PRC), 154
Ministry of Finance (Russia), 192–193
mint, 41–42
mint master, 65
minting coins, 21, 41
missile, 7, 33
missionary, 128

Mississippi, 186
Mobutu Sese Seko, 157
Moe Mint Tyun, 180(n7)
Moe Myint Tun, 180(n7)
monasteries, 74, 81
monetarist criticism of Keynes, 147
monetarists, 159(n9)
monetary demand, 105, 118(n12)
money, 2–4, 6–7, 11, 19–20, 22, 25–26, 34, 39–44, 46, 48, 51–53, 57–58, 61, 65–66, 69–71, 73–74, 80, 84–85, 87–88, 90–92, 95, 101–102, 105, 107, 109, 115–116, 118(n12), 125–127, 147, 157–158, 163, 165–166, 170, 176, 178, 187, 192, 194; commodity, 41, 69; fiat, 187
money doctors, 130
money laundering, 169, 182(n36), 192
money-of-account, 64
money supply, 26, 41, 49, 70, 105, 108, 146, 149, 159(n9)
Mongolia, 71–72, 181(n14); paper money, 72. *See* Chingissid Empire
monopoly, 70, 81, 134
Morgan, J. P., loans to British, 121
Morgenthau, Hans, *Politics Among Nations*, 9
Morris, Scott, on Chinese lending, 189
Morris, Robert, 94
Moscow, 152, 163, 171, 173, 175, 177–178, 185; Kremlin, the 163, 175
Mount Washington Hotel, 159. *See* Bretton Woods
Mozambique, 157
Mulder, Nicholas, on the League of Nations, 125
Multibanka, 171
multi-domain battle, 8
multilateral diplomatic and financial institutions, 145
multilateral organizations, 148
multipolarity: finance domain, 198; financial commons, 14, 186, 196; financial system, 196; international system, 145
Mun, Thomas, 26, 84; *England's Treasure by Forraign Trade or the Ballance of Our Forraign Trade Is the Rule of Our Treasure*, 84. *See also* mercantilism
Munro, John, 64–65; on European debasement, 64
Muslim Empire, 63
Muteczuma, 79
Myanmar, 28, 163–164, 169, 180(n2), 180(n4); coup, 28; formerly Burma, 180(n2); junta, 163–164, 180(n7); US response to coup, 163–164, 169, 180(n4)
Myanmar Economic Holdings Limited, 180(n4)
Myanmar Mining Copper Ltd., 180(n4)
Myanmar Yang Tse Copper Ltd., 180(n4)
Mya Tun Oo, 180(n7)
Myint Kyaing, 180(n7)

Nagorno-Karabakh, 33
Namibia, 156
Naples, 67. *See* Italian city-states
Napoleon Bonaparte, 6, 87, 92, 102–103, 123; and Continental System, 6, 102; emperor of France, 102; invasions of Spain and Russia, 103
Napoleonic Wars, 23–24, 101–103, 188
Narodnaya Volya (The Peoples' Will), 106
National Bank Acts of 1863–1864, 107, 109
National Bank of Belgium (NBB), 168
National Bank of Ukraine (NBU), 176–177
National City Bank, 127
national debt instruments, 88
national power, 22, 44
national security, 3–4, 6, 8, 13, 23–24, 79, 83, 90, 93–94, 110, 122, 126–127, 144, 164–165, 191
national security policy, American, 94
National Union for the Total Independence of Angola (UNITA), 154. *See* Savimbi, Jonas
nationalized oil companies, 157
natural resources, 23
Nauru, 169
naval/maritime commons, 7, 186
navy, 4, 6, 8, 23, 46–47, 66, 85, 88, 111, 117(n7), 132; Barcelona, 66; France, 85; Sparta, 46–47
Navy Board (UK), 88
Ndikumana, Léonce, on capital flight from Africa, 157
Near East, 43
negotiable debt, 6
Neo-Assyrian Empire, 43; tribute collection, 43; use of corvee' labor, 43
neoliberal institutionalism, 11
neorealist theory and texts, 10
Nerve der Dinge (nerve of things), 85. *See also* Borniss, Jacob
Netherlands, 67, 81, 82(table), 83, 85–86, 87–88, 94, 97(n20), 103, 110, 153, 161(n40), 181(n13); coinage debasement, 87; Council of State, 87; Dutch Republic, 81, 85–88, 94; Dutch states, 85; financial innovations, 86;

independence from Spain, 87; member of Grand Alliance in the War of Spanish Succession, 88; Pragmatic Sanction of 1549, 97(n20); raising money on credit, 85; Schuman Declaration of 1950 signatory, 153, 161(n40); States of Holland, 85; under Habsburg control, 85
Netherlands East Indies, 130
network, 20, 27–28, 59, 130, 166, 168; central bank currency swap lines, 166
network theory, 166
neutral states, 26
Newman, Abraham, 166, 168; on network theory and international finance, 166
New Economic Policy (NEP) (USSR), 136
New Plan (Germany, Nazi), 123
Newton, Sir Isaac, Master of the Royal Mint, 103
New World, 68, 110, 116
New York City, 126–127, 129, 154, 157, 168
New York Stock Exchange, 26, 121
New York Times, 21, 163
New Zealand, 114, 181(n13)
Nicholas II, Czar 116
Nigeria, 6, 192, 198; currency conversion of, 6; northeastern, 192
Nixon, Richard M., President, 149
nongovernmental organizations (NGOs), 174
non-interest-bearing notes, 108
nonstate actors, 21–22, 31, 33–34, 60, 158, 165(table), 168, 171, 187, 191–192, 196; violent nonstate actors (VNSAs), 21–22, 158, 168
nonviolent dispute resolution, 124, 145
North Africa, 63
North American history, 12
North Atlantic Treaty Organization (NATO), 145, 151
North Korea, 167, 169, 171–173, 175, 178–179, 194
Northcote-Treveleyan reforms, 123
Northern and Southern Europe, 190
Northern Song, 71; collapse, 71; sacking of Kaifeng, 71. *See* China, dynastic/premodern
Northern Wei, 70
Northwest Europe, 26, 74
Norway, 181(n13)
nuclear: deterrence, 144; missile silos, 5; weapons, 149
Nuremburg, 67
Nurkse, Ragnar, on currency devaluation, 146

Oatley, Thomas, on weaponizing financial interdependence, 168, 179

Office of Foreign Assets Control (OFAC), 163–164, 169
Ogarkov, Marshal Nikolai, on the "military-technical revolution," 28
Ohn Mar Myint, 180(n7)
oil, 152, 157, 172–174, 177
oil embargo of 1973, 150
oligarchs, 171, 174
Olynthians, 48
Order of St. John of Jerusalem, 106
Ordonnances de Comptant, 92
Oregon, 101
Organization of Petroleum Exporting Countries (OPEC), 14, 145
organized crime syndicates, 168
"Orient, the," 114
Ortiz, Luz, 84
Oscar, Richard, on sanctions against Russia, 179
Ottoman Empire, 7, 82(table), 111, 116; European states of, 7
Ottone de Bonovillano, 57
overseas investments, 111, 112(table), 130
overseas lending, 129

pagans, 60
Pakistan, 155
Palmstruch, Johan, 2, 87
Pan-Africa, 156–157; Western lending to, 156–157
pan-European, 26
panopticon, 27–28, 195; effect, 27–28. *See* choke point
Papal States, 67
Pa Pa Chit Khaing, 180(n7)
paper currency, 13, 30(table), 34, 41, 71–73, 89, 192
paper money, 15(n5), 51, 70–71, 73–74
par value, 25, 41, 54(n5), 89, 109, 194–195
Paraguay, 94, 131–132; involvement in Chaco War, 131–132
pariah state, 156, 169, 171; North Korea/Iran, 169, 171; South Africa, 156
Paribas Bank loans to Bulgaria, 116
Paris, 87, 118(n30), 124, 152
Parks, Brad, on Chinese lending, 189
Parthian Empire, 50, 52, 62. *See* Persia
path dependence, 188
Pax Britannica (1815–1914), 13, 30(table), 96, 109–116, 147. *See* gold standard
"Pax Mongolica," 72
payments systems, 24, 96, 167
Peloponnesian War, 3, 6, 22, 44–48, 53
Peloponnesian War, The, 3. *See* Thucydides
pence, 65
Pendleton Act, 123

Pennsylvania, 101, 107
People's Bank of China (PBOC), 154, 193
Pepys, Samuel, on "the devil shits Dutchmen," 81
permanent armed bureaucracies, 96
Pericles, 45
Perioikoi, 46
Persia: 3, 34, 39, 43–44, 47–48, 52–53, 62–63, 110, 114; "archer" coins, 34, 44; Empire, 48, 52; financial practice, 15; financial resources, 48; hiring of Greek mercenaries, 48; participation in Peloponnesian War, 48; systems of finance, 3. *See* Achaemenid Empire
Peru, 112(table), 132; conflict with Colombia, 132; conflict with Ecuador, 132
pesos, 79
petrodollars, 150, 191
Philadelphia Inquirer, 107
Philadelphia, Pennsylvania, 107
Philip IV, King of France, 64
Philip VI, King of France, 81
Philippines, The, 123, 130
photosynthesis, 191
Phyo Arkar Aung, 180(n7)
pirates, 31, 34; Somali, 31
"pirate stock exchange," 31. *See* Haradheere, Somalia
pirate vessels, 31
Pisani, Alvise, 67
Platt, D.C.M., on nineteenth century competition, 111
pogroms, 115. *See* Jews; Russia
Poincare, Raymond, Prime Minister of France, 114
Poland, 1, 82(table), 115, 125, 181(n13); as part of Poland-Lithuania, 1, 82(table); as western Russian territory, 115
political power, 9, 50, 83, 153, 195
polities: 13, 40, 63, 73, 90, 125–126; ancient world, 40; Arabian, 63; early Islamic, 13; France, Ancien Regime, 90; German, 125; Western Europe, 13; Western Europe and the Levant, 73
Polybius, 39, 43, 47, 53; *The Histories*, 39
Ponzi scheme, 89
Pope, The, 34, 61; financing the Crusades, 34
populist political movements, 190
Portugal, 83(table), 112(table), 161(n40), 181(n13)
Posen, Barry, on command of the commons, 24
pound, 4, 57, 65, 85, 88–89, 113(table), 131–132, 199(n11); British pounds, 131

power, 3, 10–11, 19–20, 27, 32–34, 39, 42–44, 47, 49–53, 62, 67, 70, 85–86, 92–93, 97(n20), 102, 110, 115, 122, 124–125, 136, 147, 151, 154, 156, 165–166, 169, 177, 185–187, 196; American, 9; concept of, 11; European, 115; instruments of, 165; power politics, 9, 115; role of, 11
Poyais, 106
Pre-Columbian Americas, state consolidation in, 68–69
premodern: armies, 33; era, 3; history, 7; states, 7, 20–21; times, 34, 52; world, 12
"primary money laundering concerns," 169
Princeton University, 130, 148; Institute for Advanced Studies, 148
printing money, 176
private bank loans to Confederacy, 108
private sector, 191
protectionism, 81
"proto-central banks," 86
proto-states, 58, 60, 68, 80–81; Americas, 58; European, 80–81; Islamic, 60; New World, 68
proxy wars, 157, 179
Prussia: 82(table), 83, 103, 106, 123; civil service, 123; member of Sixth Coalition in Napoleonic Wars, 103. *See* Germany
public bank: 2, 26, 30(table), 64, 66–67, 68(figure), 87, 194
public debt 13, 23, 64–68, 80, 87, 134
public debtholders, 88
public goods, 126, 168
public money, 95
public-private partnership, 80
public-private structure, 89
public relations, 107, 154
public sector, 131–132, 191
Punic Wars, 47
Putin, Vladimir, President, 163, 171, 174, 178

Qatar, use of corvee' labor, 37(n48)
Qin Dynasty/Empire, 21, 30(table), 51–53; Chinese states in, 52; coin use, 53
qirād (*quirad*) contract, 60
Quran, 192

ratings agencies, 129
rationalism, 123
raw materials, 6, 33, 121, 133, 154
real assets, 190
real economy, 185, 190–191
realism, 9–11
real-time gross settlement (RTGS) system, 167

real-time messaging, 30(table), 174
recession, 157–158, 172, 189
Red Cross, 110
refugees, 176
Reichsbank, 115, 133
regional powers, 44, 197–198
regional trade system, 51
regime theory, 188
relative state power, 2–3
renminbi, 189
rentes sur l'hotel de ville, 87
rentes system, 85
reserve loss, 133
"reset," 186
"resource curse," 191
resource extraction, 133, 191
retail investors, 129
revisionist powers, 9
Revolutions in Financial Affairs (RFAs), 3–4, 7, 12–14, 22, 28–30, 31, 34, 40–51, 53, 58, 60, 64–68, 71, 73–74, 79–96, 101, 102–106, 116, 122–123, 134, 143, 144–153, 158, 163–180, 186–188, 191, 192–195, 196–198. *See* Bretton Woods RFA; Bureaucratic RFA; Central Bank/Public Banking RFA; Digital RFA; Gold Standard RFA; Mercantilist RFA
Revolutions in Military Affairs (RMAs), 3, 28–29, 31–32, 58; cavalry, 58; naval, 31–32
rice, 70
Richmond, Virginia, 107
Riga, Latvia, 171
Robbins, Lionel, on fusty relics, 122
Roberts, Michael, 29
Rocke, David M., on regime theory, 188
Rockoff, Hugh, 106, 150; on "Good Housekeeping Seal of Approval," 106
rogue state: 158, 179, 194–195
Roman Catholic Church, 34, 57, 60–62, 74; control of credit, 74; financial power, 61; financial strategies, 60; funding of Crusades, 34; indulgences, sale of, 61, 74; regional dominance, 57
Roman Empire, 13, 20, 22, 30(table), 42, 47, 49–51, 53, 60, 62; coinage debasement in, 42, 50; collapse of, 53; conquest of Africa and Iberia, 49; corruption in, 50; corvee' labor and taxes, 20; dominant power in the Mediterranean, 62; financial environment, 50; financial networks, 50; Imperium, 53; legions, 58, 101; maintenance of troop positions, 53; military expansion, 51; minting authorities, 77(n57); payments to troops in coins, 22; senators, 49; survival in east, 62; tax farming, 49; trade with China, 50–51
Roman Republic/Principate, 49–51, 74; mercenaries, 74; mining, 50; tribute collection (by *tribunii*), 49
Rome, 13, 22, 47, 50–51, 53, 58, 60; defense of, 58; fall of, 13, 53, 58; overland transport system, 22; use of navy, 53
Roosevelt Corollary to the Monroe Doctrine, 128
Roosevelt, Franklin D., President, 143–145, 148; administration, 145, 148
Rosenberg, Emily, on American financial stability, 129
Rosneft, 172
Ross, Michael, on the "resource curse," 191
Rosselkhoz, 172
Royal Africa Company (UK), 88
Royal Navy of Great Britain, 4, 6, 23, 88, 111, 117(fn7), 132; battleships, 132; sailors, 23, 117(n), 132 *See also* Invergordon Mutiny
ruble, 151, 172–173, 175
Rumsfeld, Donald, US secretary of defense, 29
rupee, 123, 155; British control of, 123
Russia, Czarist 82(table), 83, 103, 106, 111, 112(table), 115–116, 121, 134, 161(n44); bond issues, 106, 116; British loans to, 115; czar, 106, 136; financial problems, 115; foreign lending to, 106; franc reserves, 115; French investment in, 111, 115; German loans to, 115; German doubts about, 115; member of Sixth Coalition in Napoleonic Wars, 103; Order of St. John of Jerusalem headquarters, 106; pogroms, 115
Russia, as USSR/Soviet Union, 14, 33–34, 115, 125, 135–137, 143–145, 150–152, 153–156, 158, 160(n29), 171, 176; acquisition of technology, 33; aggression, 145; and decolonization, 156; as pole of bipolar system, 145; as primary adversary of US, 143; banks in Europe, 152; client states of, 151; collapse, 144, 155, 158; Communist Party, 135–136; dollar assets, 152; easing of tensions with Europe, 153; expansion of voting franchise, 125; financial austerity, 152; financial and trade limitations of, 152; foreign trade volume of, 151; global financial pressure, 144; gold, 136; gold-

producing nation, 152; hard currency trade of, 152; influence in Latin America, 158; international financial relations, 136; loans from the West, 135–136, 151; loans to India, 155; nuclear deterrence strategy, 144; overthrow of autocratic government, 14; possible client of Midlands bank, 160(n29); similarity to Incas and Aztecs, 151; spending cuts, 176; support for Angola, 154; tight money policy, 136; trade patterns of, 151–152; use of Latvia as tax haven, 171

Russia, Post-Soviet, 14, 154, 161(n44), 163–164, 167, 171–179, 182(n51), 186–187, 189, 191–194, 198, 198(n2); armies, 115; as possible challenger state to US hegemony, 198; as possible "State Sponsor of Terror," 177; as sanctions target, 172; BRICS membership, 154, 161(n44); cost of sanctions, 172; cryptocurrency ban, 193; currency protection, 173–174; financial capacity, 175; financial institutions, 163; impact of financial sanctions on, 174–176, 177–179; imports and exports, 178; leverage of energy supply, 173–174; national cryptocurrency exchange, 177; paper currency, 192; preparing to invade Ukraine, 173; recession, 172; reparations, 177; resource extraction, 191; state-backed cryptocurrency, 192, 194; stock market, 175

Russian banks sanctioned, 172

Russian/Bolshevik Revolution, 135–136, 152; property confiscated during, 136

Russian invasion of Ukraine, 14, 163–164, 167, 171–179, 187

Russo-German relations, 115

Russo-Japanese War (1905), 106, 115

"safe assets," 107
Saladin, 62
Salafi jihad, 192
salt, 48, 70, 81
Samoa, 170
sanctions: 6, 30(table), 31, 122, 125, 137, 158, 163, 165(table), 169–170, 171–179, 180(n4), 186, 189, 193, 195; campaign, 171–172, 176; economic, 173, 178; multilateral, 30(table); package, 172, 175, 179; program, 171; regime, 170, 172–173, 175, 178–179; smart, 158; targeted, 31; trade, 165(table), 178

San Salvador, El Salvador, 129
Saracen, 57
Sassanid Empire, 62–63. *See* Persia
Saudi Arabia, 37(n48), 181(n13); use of corvee' labor, 37(n48)
Savimbi, Jonas, 154
Saw Daniel, 180(n7)
Sberbank, 172, 174
Schacht, Hjalmar, Nazi reichminister of economics, 121, 123, 133
Schiff, Jacob, 115
Schuman Declaration of 1950, 153
Schumpeter, Joseph, 19; "domain states," 19; *The Crisis of the Tax State*, 19
scirgerefa (sheriff), 58
scutage (knight's fee), 59
sea loan, 45–46, 74; Athens, 45–46; debt contract, 45; Genoa, 74; Rome, 46. *See* bottomry loan
seapower, 8, 10, 29, 31, 69, 74, 114
Second Bank of the United States, 95–96, 126
Second Crusade, 61
Second Northern War, 1
Second Treaty of Paris (1815), 103
Section 311 of USA PATRIOT Act, 167, 169, 171
secular power, 57
Seddon, Jack, on regime theory, 188
seigniorage, 25, 42, 48, 50, 65, 134; in Athens, 48; in the Roman Empire, 50
Seleucid Kingdom: 48–49; absorption by Roman Republic, 49; coinage, 48
self-dealing, 90
semiconductor technology, 187
semistate actors, 60
September 11, 2001, 169
Service for Transfer of Financial Messages (SPFS), 172–173, 175, 186, 189; Russian alternative to SWIFT, 172–173, 186, 189
"seven sisters," 157; British Petroleum, 157; Chevron, 157; Exxon, 157; Gulf, 157; Mobil, 157; Royal Dutch Shell, 157; Texaco, 157
Seville, Spain, Genoese merchants in, 74
"shadow banking system," 150
Sharpeville massacre, 156
shilling, 65
short-term liabilities, 105
Shwe Ye Phu Aung, 180(n7)
signals intelligence (SIGINT), 14
silver, 40–42, 48, 52, 64, 77(n57), 77(n59), 79, 81, 82(table), 104, 124, 126, 135; as unit of account, 104; coinage, 40–42, 48, 52, 77(n57); importation by China,

77(n59); mines in Athens, 45, 48; price collapse, 104; supply, 64, 81
silver standard, 124, 126
sinews of power, 85
"sinews of war, infinite money," 3, 7
Singapore, 181(n13)
Sino-Indian War, 155
Sixth Coalition, 103
slaves, 88
slave labor, 6
slave trade, 80
Slovak Republic, 181(n13). *See* Czechoslovakia/Czech Republic
Slovenia, 181(n13)
Smith, Adam, 9, 84, 110
Smith, Rev. Sydney, 101
snowplows, 151
societas contract, 30(table), 60
Society for Worldwide Interbank Financial Telecommunication (SWIFT), 14, 27–28, 167–168, 169–170, 172–175, 189; as sanctioning tool, 169–170, 172, 174, 189; Chinese alternative to, 189; member states, 189; Russian alternative to, 173, 175
Soe Win, 180(n7)
Sofia, Bulgaria, 116
soft money, 126
soft power, 151–152
solliciteurs-militair, 86
Somalia, 31, 34
Song Dynasty, 71–72, 74; commercial and financial sophistication, 71; New Policies, 71; paper money, 71, 74
South Africa, 114, 154, 155–156, 161(n44); apartheid, 156; arms manufacturing, 156; BRICS membership, 154, 161(n44); British trade with, 114; formation of, 155
South America, 69, 80, 88, 115, 131; militarized interstate disputes in, 131; Spanish conquest, 69; state building in, 131; western, 69
South Sea Bubble, 80
South Sea Company, 80, 88–89, 186; aka "the Governor and Company of Merchants of Great Britain Trading to the South Seas and other parts of America and for encouraging the Fishery," 88
Southern and Eastern Europe, 125
Southern Song Dynasty, 71–73; defeat by Mongols, 71; financial sophistication, 71
sovereign debt: 20–21, 23, 25, 30(table), 33, 47, 106, 129, 131, 139(n20), 150,

163, 190; evaluating risks, 139(n20); Latin American, 131; privatization, 150; USSR, 33; Wall Street, 129
sovereigns, 59, 65
sovereign states, 19, 26; in Middle Ages, 26
sovereignty, 5, 116, 172, 187–188; Bulgaria, 116; Ukraine, 172
sovereign wealth, 31
Spain: 66, 69, 74, 81, 82(table), 83–84, 86–88, 92, 103, 112(table), 161(n40), 181(n13); advantage from conquests of the Americas, 81; kings of Aragón-Catalonia, 66; navy, 66; specie in, 84
Sparta: 6, 20, 44–45, 46–49, 53; armies, 47; coinage, 46; emergency loans and tributes, 46; finances, 53; fiscal structure in, 47; hegemony, 53; kings, 3, 46–47; military, 46; similar to domain state in structure, 46; slavery in, 6, 46
Special Drawing Rights (SDRs), 188, 199(n11)
Specially Designated Nationals List (SDN List)(US), 28, 164, 169, 180
specie, 24, 42, 79
speculators, 108, 114, 150
stabilization fund, 135, 147
"stablecoins," 194, 200(n44)
Stalin, Joseph, 136
standing army, American suspicion of, 93
Stasavage, David, on Italian city-states, 23, 66–67
state: 2–13, 15(n13), 16(n24), 19–29, 30(table), 31–34, 35(n9), 36(n24), 39–44, 46, 48–53, 54(n7), 54(n18), 58–60, 62–69, 71–74, 79–83, 83(table), 84–90, 92–93, 96, 103, 105–110, 115, 122, 124, 130–131, 137, 143–144, 146–147, 149, 151, 154–155, 157–158, 163, 165–168, 170–174, 178, 178(table), 179, 180(n10), 186–189, 191–194, 196–197, 199(n11); characteristics, 7; choice, 9–10; coercion, 59; competition, 2; domains, 50; detection, 187; financial centers, 146; fragility, 23; interests, 4; intervention, 158; investment, 32, 49; military financing, 80; military spending, 88; modern, 9, 34, 35(n9), 85, 171; propaganda, 44; security, 80; surveillance, 187. *See also* state actors; state behavior; state capacity; state power
state actors, 31, 33–34, 106, 171
state behavior, 7, 11, 13, 24, 81, 152–153, 179
state capacity, 4–5, 9, 29, 31, 33–34, 40, 62, 69, 74, 107, 109, 122, 126, 137, 147,

155; English, 62; of Confederacy, 109; of India, 155; of United States, 107, 126
statelike entities, 39
state power, 2–4, 9, 15(n13), 22, 52, 84, 165, 187; external, 84; instruments of, 165; nature of, 15(n13); relative, 2–3
State Sponsor of Terror designation (US), 177
States of Holland, 85. *See* Netherlands
steel, 15(n13), 31, 153
Steil, Benn, on financial statecraft, 165
Stockholm International Peace Research Institute (SIPRI), 162(n56)
Stockholms Banco, 2, 87
strategic interaction, 5, 24, 26
strategic interdependence, 165
strategic power, 23
strong states, 6
sub-Saharan Africa, 157
substate actors, 13
substate regions, 103
suicides, 89
Sun Tzu, 39
super-colonialism, 122
"supernotes," North Korean counterfeiting of, 167
superpowers, 152–155
surface-to-air missile, 172
Surgutneftegas, 172
Sveriges Riksbank, 2, 86, 87, 168
Sweden: 1–2, 26, 80, 83(table), 86, 168, 181(n13); armed forces, 1; army, 2; Board of Trade, 2; central bank, 80; currency devaluation, 1; minting coins, 1; land sale, 1
Swedish Deluge, 1
Swedish Empire, 1
Swiss National Bank, 168
Switzerland, 6, 181(n13), 192
Sylla, Richard, on colonial United States, 94
Syria, 34, 173
systemic interdependence, 26

Table of Change (Taula de Canvi), 66, 80
taille (land tax), 81
tallage (war fee), 59
Taiwan, 123, 134, 181(n13)
talents, 45
Tang Dynasty, 70
Tangut, 70
targeted financial sanctions, 28
tariff, 21, 165(table)
tariff barriers, 84
tariff disputes, Russia and Germany, 115
tax avoidance, 170, 195

tax collection, 1, 20, 70, 85; China, 70; Netherlands, 85; Sweden, 1
tax evasion, 170, 187, 195
tax farming: 20, 49, 89, 91; France, 89, 91; Roman Empire, 49
tax havens, 170–171, 179, 192, 194
tax in kind, 108–109, 133; Confederacy, 108–109; German, 133
tax states: 19–20, 59, 68, 143, 191
Tehran, Iran, 185
terms of trade, 133, 151
terrorist financier, 192
terrorism financing, 14
terrorist financing networks, 169
terrorist group, 21
terrorist groups, 168
territorial integrity, 172
territorial sovereignty, 172
territorial states, 30(table), 64–67, 74, 80, 85, 87
Than Than Nwe, 180(n7)
t' Hart, Margolein C., on European debt, 80
Theit Thinzar Ye, 180(n7)
Thet Thet Aung, 180(n7)
Thet Thet Khine, 180(n7)
Thirty Years' War, 1, 87, 91
Thodex, 194
Thucydides, 3, 22, 39, 43, 45–46, 52; influence of, 43; *Peloponnesian War, The*, 3
Tiberius, Emperor of Rome, 49
Tilly, Charles, on borrowing, 23
Timotheus, 48
Tin Aung San, 180(n7)
Tissaphernes, 47
tobacco tax, 116
token currencies, 123
Tomz, Michael, on borrowing, 23
Tooze, Adam, on Bulgaria, 116
Torgsin stores, 136
Torre, Oberto, 57
total war, 122, 137, 144
tractator/socius portat, 60
tractors, 151
Tracy, James, on the Habsburg Netherlands, 85
trade, 6–7, 13–14, 22, 24–26, 31, 33, 40–44, 50, 52–53, 58–61, 63–64, 66, 70, 72–73, 79, 83–84, 88–90, 102–103, 105, 108, 111, 114, 122, 127–128, 133–135, 137, 143, 146–149, 151–153, 163, 165(table), 166, 173, 178–179, 184(n99), 186, 192; blocs, 132–133; contracts between China and Rome, 51; East Asian, 89; external, 72–73; financing, 111; foreign, 186; free, 146–147; imbalances, 125;

interdependence, 102; interregional, 64, 135; long-distance, 31, 42, 52–53, 63, 73; long-range, 22; Mediterranean, 58, 63; network, 124; networks, 63; paper, 127; Roman, 46. *See also* global trade; international trade; maritime trade; trade flows; world trade

trade flows, 14, 21–22, 26, 73, 80, 86, 102, 122, 132–133, 145, 147, 152, 179; limitations on, 80

traders, 48, 52, 60; Chinese, 52; Jewish, 60

"tragedy of the commons," 24

traite, 65

travel bans, 172

Treaty of Amiens, 102

Treaty of Versailles, 124–125, 128, 146

Trebesch, Christoph, on Chinese lending, 189

"trench warfare," 28

tresoriers de l'Epargne (savings treasurers), 99(n44)

tribute: 19–20, 39–40; from conquered territories, 20; in ancient Mediterranean, 40; state, 19–20

Trinidad and Tobago, 181(n13)

trireme, 45, 58; Athenian, 45; Roman, 58

Triple Alliance War, 110

Triple Entente, 9

tripolarity, 197–198

"Trustee Securities," 114

Turkey, 41, 110–111, 112(table), 114–115; "Sick Man of Europe," 111

umma, 192

unbacked currency, 134

unilateral actors, 137

ukase (Czarist edict), 115

Ukraine, 14, 163–164, 167, 169, 171–173, 176–177, 178, 187; as sovereign territorial unit, 178; currency peg to dollar, 176; debt service payments, 176; designated by US as "money laundering concern," 169; economic weakness of, 176; financial aid to, 177–178; financial countermeasures by, 176; Russian invasions of, 14, 163–164, 167, 171–173, 176, 187

United Arab Emirates (UAE), 181(n13)

United Kingdom of Great Britain (UK), 6, 9, 14, 21, 23–24, 26, 30(table), 36(n24), 58–59, 62, 65, 81, 83–84, 88, 90, 94, 101–103, 106, 110–111, 112(table), 114–115, 117(n7), 119(n41), 121–122, 125–132, 134–135, 137, 138(n6), 139(n24), 144–146, 150, 155, 157, 161(n40), 168, 172–174, 181(n13), 181(n20), 187, 190, 198, 198(n2); and South Sea Company, 88–89; approach to financial matters, 111; as England, 21, 26, 58–59, 62, 65, 81, 83–84, 101; as English Crown, 81; as Great Britain/Britain, 6, 9, 24, 26, 58, 88, 90, 94, 102–103, 110–111, 112(table), 114–115, 117(n7), 121, 125, 139(n24), 150, 181(n20); as Kingdom of Great Britain, 88; as great power, 23; as hegemon, 102, 110; as member of Grand Alliance, 88; as member of Sixth Coalition, 103; classical gold standard, 14; colonies, 102; cross-border lending, 129; damage done by Invergordon Mutiny, 117(n7), 132; economic school of mercantilism, 83; embargo of Germany, 26, 121, 184(n99); financial competitor to France, Germany, and Italy, 83; forced off gold standard, 103; former hegemon, 137; G7 membership, 36(n24); government, 110–111, 114, 121, 132, 184(n99); government debt to Board of Ordnance, 88; imperial client territories, 129; influence in Europe, 102; involvement in World War I, 26; loans to Russia, 115; Norman conquest of, 58; overseas investments of, 111; revenue sources, 21; rivals of, 102; school of mercantilism, 83; taxes under Roman rule, 58; Tory government, 132; victory in Napoleonic Wars, 24; Whitehall, 114

United Nations (UN), 143, 145, 148, 153, 155–156, 170; arms embargo of South Africa, 156; Deng Xiaoping visit, 155; UN Security Council, 170

United States (US), 2, 4–5, 7–9, 11–12, 14, 26–28, 30(table), 31, 36(n24), 41, 79, 92–96, 101, 107, 109, 111, 121–122, 125, 126–132, 135–136, 138(n6), 143–147, 149–158, 164–168, 169–170, 171–174, 176–179, 181(n13), 182(n51),185–187, 189–190, 194–198; 2016 presidential election, 172; access to choke point, 167–170, 179; access to panopticon, 167–170, 179, 195; and Latin America, 130–132; anti-money laundering law, 168; arms embargo of Russia, 172; as baby Hercules, 92; as central node in global financial network, 166; as former UK colony, 111; as global financial power, 27; as the world's banker, 149; balance of payments deficit, 149; capital account, 149; Constitution, 93; current account,

149; customs and tariffs revenue, 107; executive branch, 149, 169; "Federalist financial revolution," 94; finance domain operations, 92; financial crisis, 126; financial diplomacy, 130; financial hegemon, 14, 158, 186, 195; financial hegemony, 167, 186; financial institutions, 27; financial networks, 14; financial power, 27, 164, 177, 186, 196; financial proxy war, 179; financial revolution, 94; gold force, 4; gold reserves, 149; gold stock, 149, 160(n22); international financial policy, 128; lending, 149, 189; loans to Germany, 125; marine corps, 8; monetary gold stock, 149, 160(n22); paper currency, 107; rejection of mercantilism, 166; Revolutionary War debt, 95; South, the, 108–109, 118(n30); state capacity, 107; states of, 106; strategic loans to Latin America, 128–129; tools of financial statecraft, 164; treasuries market, 190; use of financial messaging systems, 168; use of weaponized interdependence, 166 American wars, 95(table); War of 1812 debt, 92, 96; weapons, 149. *See also* United States Congress; United States government; United States Navy.
United States Congress, 93, 95–96, 107, 125–126, 143, 154; Senate, 95, 125
United States government, 28, 31, 94, 107–109, 127–129, 149–150, 158, 164, 166, 167, 169–170, 180(n2), 182, 195
United States Navy, 4, 8, 93, 107–108
unit of account, 41–42, 65, 78(n59), 87, 103–104, 194
University of Cincinnati, 148
unmanned aerial vehicles (UAVs), 33, 175; aka drones, 33, 175
urban markets, 85
Uruguay, 181(n13)
US Army, 8
US Joint Doctrine Note 1–18, 165
US Space Force, 8, 16(n27)

VEF Banka, 171
velocity of money, 64, 105, 118(n11)
Venezuela, 157, 173
Venice, Republic of, 67. *See* Italian city-states
Vickers, 131
Vienna City Bank, 87
Vietnam War, 150, 158; US involvement, 150, 158
Vidal-Naquet, Pierre, on Sparta, 46

Viner, Jacob, 110, 147–148, 155; Chicago School, 148; on turn of the century competition, 110
Vnesheconombank, 172
von Bismarck, Otto, German Chancellor, 115
von Schmoller, Gustav, on mercantilism, 84
VTB, 172

Wall Street, 115, 129–131; lending, 131
"Wall Street Consensus," 191
Walter, Carl, on China, 154–155, 161(n46), 161(n47)
Waltz, Kenneth, *Theory of International Politics*, 9
Wanbao Mining, 180(n4)
Wang Anshi, 71
war: 1–4, 6–7, 10, 13–14, 19–20, 26, 29, 33, 39, 42–43, 46–49, 52, 57–60, 63–64, 66, 86–87, 90–94, 98(n37), 99(n61), 101–103, 107–110, 116, 121–128, 131, 133–135, 137, 143–145, 148, 150–153, 155, 157, 166, 171–173, 175–179, 191, 198. *See also* warfare
war chest, France, 90
war effort, 46, 107, 109, 134, 177–179; Confederate, 109; Imperial Japan, 134; Northern (US), 107; Ukraine, 177–179
warfare, 6, 13, 29, 40, 44, 77(n50), 79; modern warfare, 6, 8, 13, 29, 127; financing of, 13; nature of, 29; technologies of, 6
warfighting, 4, 108; expenditures, 108
war finance, 2, 42, 66, 127–128
warlike power, 101
war machines, 64
warmaking, 2, 7, 19, 67; ability, 2; entities, 7, 19; state, 7
War of 1812, 92, 94–96; financial demands of, 95
War of Chioggia, 67
War of Independence/ Revolutionary War, 92, 94, 95
War of Spanish Succession, 88–90
warplanes, 32–33
Warring States Period, 3, 51
Warsaw Pact, 151
Warship: 5, 23, 32–33, 42, 45
wars of finance, 2
Washington, DC, 4, 107, 126, 145, 154, 157, 173
WASP, 121
weak states, 6
weaponized interdependence, 27, 124, 166
weapons proliferation, 173
Weber, Max, on bureaucracy, 123

Welser, house of, 22
Weltanschauungen, 9
West Africa, British colonial finance in, 123
West African, trade with France, 89
Western and Central Europe, 60
Western bloc, 145
Western, 136, 174–175, 178; credit markets, 178; financial campaign, 174–175; powers, 136
Western Europe: 13, 34 57–60, 64, 73–74, 158; armies in, 74; collapse of trade, 73; fairs, 64; financial crises in, 158; fragmentation of power and authority in, 57; monarchs, 34; new polities in, 73; post-Roman, 58–60
Western Hemisphere, 129
Western Pacific, 5
Western Roman Empire, 13, 50–51, 57–58, 62–63, 73; collapse, 13, 51, 57–58, 62, 73; descendants of, 63; Roman taxation system prior to collapse, 58
West Germany, signatory of Schuman Declaration of 1950, 153. *See also* Germany
West, the, 69, 135–136, 152, 163, 173
wheat, 70
whiskey, 40–41
White, Eugene, 20, 23, 90, 92, 98(n37), 124; on France, 90; on German reparations, 124; on tax farming, 20; on the United Kingdom tax system, 23
White, Harry Dexter, 147, 159(n12); senior US Treasury official, 147; Soviet spy, 159(n12)
Wilson, Woodrow, President, 124–125, 127, 139(n21), 145; "Fourteen Points," 139(n21)
Wolfe, Martin, on "inside credit," 91
World Bank, 130, 146, 148, 155–156, 166; Global Findex, 166
world economy, 104–105, 122, 149–150, 179

world financial history, 28, 174
world financial system, 105
world market, 151, 178(table)
world money supply, 149
world trade, 102, 122, 132, 178–179, 184(n99)
world war, 14
World War I, 6, 9, 13, 26, 28, 30(table), 103, 110, 114, 116, 121, 124–126, 128–129, 134–135, 137, 139(n24), 145; British involvement in, 26; Japanese involvement in, 134
World War II, 6, 11, 14, 27, 30(table), 110, 121, 124–125, 133–134, 137, 143–145, 152, 155, 198; devastation of, 137; end of, 30(table), 152; US involvement in, 110
Wu, Emperor, Han Dynasty, 22
wuzhu coins, 70

Xenophon, 3

yachts, 174
Yangtze River, 80
Ye Win Oo, 180(n7)
Yellow River, 80
yen, 199(n11)
yuan, 135, 188–189
Yuan Xie, 71
Yuan Dynasty, 71–73. *See* Mongolia

zakat, 192
Zarakol, Ayse, on Mongolia, 72
Zarate, Juan C., on banks and the international system, 166
Zeeland, 85
Zelensky, Volodymyr, 177
Zhong-tong chao, 72
Zimbabwe, 157
Zucman, Gabriel, on tax avoidance and evasion, 170

About the Book

"The sinews of war," posited Cicero, "are infinite money." Can the same be said of security? Tackling this thought-provoking question, the authors of *Waging War with Gold* show how states across the centuries have weaponized the global finance domain—a constellation of economic, legal, and monetary relations—in order to exert influence and pursue national interests.

Charles A. Dainoff is assistant professor of political science at the University of Idaho. **Robert M. Farley** is senior lecturer in the Patterson School of Diplomacy and International Commerce at the University of Kentucky. **Geoffrey F. Williams** is associate professor of economics at Transylvania University.